JC328.6 .S7 2003

0134107N.71788

The stat
violenc
200

MW01474362

The State, Identity and Violence

Political disintegration in the post-Cold War world

Edited by R. Brian Ferguson

LONDON AND NEW YORK

First published 2003
by Routledge
11 New Fetter Lane, London EC4P 4EE

Simultaneously published in the USA and Canada
by Routledge
29 West 35th Street, New York, NY 10001

Routledge is an imprint of the Taylor & Francis Group

© 2003 Selection and editorial matter, R. Brian Ferguson; individual chapters the contributors

Typeset in Baskerville by Taylor & Francis Books Ltd
Printed and bound in Great Britain by Antony Rowe Ltd, Chippenham, Wiltshire

All rights reserved. No part of this book may be reprinted or reproduced or utilised in any form or by any electronic, mechanical, or other means, now known or hereafter invented, including photocopying and recording, or in any information storage or retrieval system, without permission in writing from the publishers.

British Library Cataloguing in Publication Data
A catalogue record for this book is available from the British Library

Library of Congress Cataloging in Publication Data
A catalog record for this book has been requested

ISBN 0–415–27412–5

Contents

Notes on contributors vii

Introduction: violent conflict and control of the state 1
R. BRIAN FERGUSON

PART I
Commentaries 59

1 **Comments on state, identity and violence** 61
ERIC R. WOLF

2 **Forces of reaction and changes of scale in the world system of states** 68
JOSEPH A. TAINTER

3 **The state concept and a world of polities under perpetual siege** 89
YALE H. FERGUSON

4 **Tribalism, ethnicity and the state** 96
DAVID MAYBURY-LEWIS

5 **Culture, violence and ethnic nationalism: weighing alternative strategies of explanation and media representation** 102
KAY WARREN

PART II
Cases 115

6 **Civil war in Peru: culture and violence in historical perspective** 117
LINDA J. SELIGMANN

7 "Religious" violence in India: Ayodhya and the Hindu right   149
JOHANNA M. LESSINGER

8 The specter of superfluity: genesis of schism in the dismantling of Yugoslavia   177
BETTE DENICH

9 From the margins to the center: the Macedonian controversy in contemporary Greece   199
ANASTASIA KARAKASIDOU

10 Liberia: civil war and the "collapse" of the settler state   217
DIANA DEG. BROWN

11 Angola and the fragmentation of the post-colonial African state   243
HELIO BELIK

12 A Cold War story: the barbarization of Chad (1966–91)   261
S.P. REYNA

13 The Cold War and chaos in Somalia: a view from the ground   285
CATHERINE BESTEMAN

14 Conflicts versus contracts: political flows and blockages in Papua New Guinea   300
ANDREW STRATHERN AND PAMELA J. STEWART

Index   318

Contributors

The late **Helio Belik** was formerly of the City University of New York Graduate Program.

Catherine Besteman is Associate Professor of Anthropology at Colby College.

Diana DeG. Brown is Associate Professor of Anthropology at Bard College.

Bette Denich is Research Fellow at the Department of Anthropology, University of Boston.

R. Brian Ferguson is a cultural anthropologist at Rutgers University-Newark.

Yale H. Ferguson is Professor of Political Science at Rutgers University.

Anastasia Karakasidou is Assistant Professor of Anthropology at Wellesley College.

Johanna M. Lessinger is Research Associate in the Department of Anthropology, Barnard College.

David Maybury-Lewis is Professor of Anthropology at Harvard University.

S.P. Reyna is Professor of Anthropology at the University of New Hampshire and a Fellow at the Max Planck Institute for Social Anthropology.

Linda J. Seligmann is Professor of Anthropology at George Mason University.

Pamela J. Stewart is Research Associate in the Department of Anthropology, University of Pittsburgh.

Andrew Strathern is Andrew W. Mellon Professor in the Department of Anthropology, University of Pittsburgh.

Joseph A. Tainter is Director of the Cultural Heritage Research Project at the Rocky Mountain Research Station, New Mexico.

Kay Warren is Professor of Anthropology at Harvard University.

The late **Eric R. Wolf** was Professor Emeritus at Lehman College.

Introduction
Violent conflict and control of the state

R. Brian Ferguson

No one expected it. In 1988, the Cold War died. The main frame of global political orientation disintegrated, and talk turned to how to spend "the peace dividend." Yes, there were a few lingering "hot spots" around the world that needed to be "tidied up," but the United Nations (UN) was taking care of that (Loomis 1993: 125). Like any moment in time, you had to be there. In the late 1980s and early 1990s, however, strange and especially brutal conflicts erupted in Eastern Europe, Central Asia, Africa and elsewhere. The linkage of "nation" and "state," long unquestioned as the irreducible unit of global politics, suddenly seemed very questionable indeed. In some places, the future existence of a state, at least as we *thought* we knew it, was in doubt. Optimism gave way to bleak scenarios of collapse and carnage fed by nothing more than cultural difference. The term "civil war" seemed inadequate for mass violence carried out by irregular forces, deliberately targeting civilians. New labels were coined: "wars of the third kind" (Holsti 1996), "non-trinitarian wars" (non-Clausewitzian) (Van Creveld 1991), or simply, "new wars" (Kaldor 1999). Not the end of history that one scholar had predicted (Fukuyama 1992), to many it looked more like the end of civilization, "the coming anarchy" (Kaplan 1994). What was happening to the world? This book was started during that time.[1]

In retrospect, the situation was less extreme than it seemed. Bloody intra-state wars, often involving cultural divides, had in fact been increasing for decades, especially since the 1960s (Gantzel 1997). There was indeed a sharp surge with the end of the Cold War, peaking in 1992. Perception of this violence was amplified in its contrast to the suddenly deflated great power rivalry, and if local bases of "low intensity conflicts" had been overlooked while subsumed to the East/West rivalry, they became very apparent in its absence. But the number of ongoing internal wars quickly fell back to the long-term trend line, and by 1995 was around the level of 1988 (Gurr 2000: 30–34; Wallensteen and Sollenberg 1997: 339). Some scholars have found grounds for optimism about further reductions in the future (Byman and Van Evera 1998: 45), while others point out the great number of potential eruptions still stewing out there (Aklaev n.d.; Gurr and Marshall 2000). In 1998 and 1999, the number of major internal armed conflicts surged back up to the 1992–93 level, primarily due to new fighting in Africa (SIPRI 2001). No one expects such conflicts to disappear in the near future.

Many of these conflicts hit anthropologists like a train, engulfing field situations which at the start of their research had been peaceful. That too was not new – it had happened in the 1980s, especially in South and Central America. As discussed in this volume by Warren, those earlier situations gave rise to an analytical framework focused on government repression and popular resistance. But the newer violence was different, commonly pitting one broad category of people against another, rather than targeting politically active opponents to the status quo. Although the contrast between struggle along lines of identity versus those of ideology can be drawn too starkly (e.g. Kaufmann 1996), ignoring overlaps and obscuring origins, in general terms the difference is quite real (Van den Berghe 1990: 13), and this challenges us to develop new paths toward understanding.

Over the past fifteen years, anthropologists have produced a substantial literature on violence within states, including monographs (Brown and Fernandez 1991; Daniel 1996; Feldman 1991; Kapferer 1988; Lan 1985; Markakis 1990; Richards 1996; Tambiah 1992, 1996; Taussig 1987; Taylor 1997) and edited collections (Carmack 1988; *Cultural Survival Quarterly* 1994; Das 1990; Fukui and Markakis 1994a; Halpern and Kideckel 2000; Kleinman, Das and Lock 1997; Nordstrom and Martin 1992; Nordstrom and Robben 1995; Rich 1999; Riches 1986; Robben and Suarez-Orozco 2000; Sluka 2000a; Turton 1997a; Villalon and Huxtable 1998; Warren 1993a; Young 1993a; and see Nagengast 1994). Most of this work reflected new theoretical interests quite independent of the established anthropology of war (see Ferguson 1984, 1999; Haas 1990; Otterbein 1973; Reyna and Downs 1994; Simons 1999; Van der Dennen 1995). Although a wide variety of theoretical perspectives are employed in these works, prominent among them are efforts to understand violence through explication of local systems of meaning. In several, actual physical violence, bloodletting, is looked at as only one part of a range of conflicts, along with more routine injuries of structural and/or symbolic violence.

The cases collected here complement but do not duplicate that perspective. This volume aims to develop a new anthropological approach, one that emphasizes the anthropological premise of *holism*. Our approach to political violence integrates structures, processes and beliefs ranging from the world system to the grass roots, from the most global trends in political economy to the most local subsistence and symbolism. In the cases discussed here, the late 1980s and 1990s saw a fundamental challenge to existing states which went far beyond routine politics, and which in one form or another played out along lines of contrasting identities. Born during what seemed like a global political meltdown, the goal of this collective effort is to develop a new anthropological framework for understanding internal political struggles *in extremis*. It provides a guide to the big picture, and how the parts fit together for all those future situations where a state implodes into identity-linked violence.

In Peru, Linda Seligmann shows how the Maoist Shining Path emerged out of rural social and political contradictions, and tried to mobilize Quechua peasants against urban, mestizo rule to create a radical communist regime. Johanna

Lessinger portrays the fundamentalist Hindu challenge to the secular charter of India, and its orchestrated "mob" violence against Muslims and other targets before and after its capture of government. Bette Denich discusses the historical moment when Yugoslavia came apart, setting the stage for ethno-nationalists to use terror and war in attempts to carve out new "pure" states. Anastasia Karakasidou focuses on what happened when "the Former Yugoslav Republic of Macedonia" tried to cultivate a new national identity, and thus provoked intense opposition from Greeks who perceived yet another threat to their painfully constructed sense of nationhood. Liberia, the oldest republic in Africa, was torn apart by irregular armies which, as Diana Brown describes, took on ethnic identifications. Similar "ethnicized" wars occurred in the post-colonial states of Angola and Chad (discussed by Helio Belik and Stephen Reyna respectively), leading to chronic territorial fragmentation that obstructed central rule. In Somalia, Catherine Besteman considers escalating warlord violence which draws on an existing structure of clans to destroy any semblance of central government. In the culturally diverse highlands of Papua New Guinea, Andrew Strathern and Pamela Stewart discuss how a central government that never had administrative control is attempting to use popular reaction against rampant criminal violence as a unifying national quest.

Arranged in this order, these studies illustrate a rough progression from situations where the future existence of the state seems secure (if politically contested), through ones where states are fragmenting into smaller states, to areas where the sovereignty of a national government is in serious doubt. Other cases could certainly fit in this collection. Studies of Cambodia, Afghanistan and Tajikistan were sought, but proved impossible to include. Time has brought new candidates – the Democratic Republic of the Congo, Indonesia, Kosovo. Any additional cases would bring in a different mix of factors and processes, but even a complete compilation of crises would only raise the issue of situations where conflict was not so extreme. The goal of this work is not to exhaust all possibilities. Indeed, one might say that a problem of current research in political science is the proliferation of an unwieldy number of categories and factors applicable to different situations (see Ayoob 1998: 46; Brown 1997; Van Evera 1997: 128–130).[2] Our collective goal, rather, has been simply to gain a better understanding of recent struggles by comparison of several cases, to identify factors in common within the variation, and thus to get a handle on the mind-boggling particularities of specific situations. The objective was not to create an encyclopedia, but rather to help develop a general framework that could be applied, always with caution and modification, to other and future contests.

A few themes were identified in advance as particular concerns, and are discussed in the five commentaries following this introduction. Eric Wolf gives us a brief history of the "nation-state," and considers the special problems of being peripheral in today's global capitalist economy. Joseph Tainter makes us examine our preconceptions and prejudices about complexity and collapse. Yale Ferguson, a political scientist, cautions us about the use of "the state" as a category in fact and theory. David Maybury-Lewis examines issues of states as they relate to the rights and well-being of indigenous peoples. Kay Warren emphasizes the need to understand local struggles in terms of the distinctive cultures of the participants. In this Introduction, I will present one view of the conclusions supported by all these discussions and cases, a preliminary map of the interrelationships between global connections, control of the state, nationalist programs, ethnicity and culture, "ethnic violence," and identity politics. Before closing, the Rwandan genocide is considered as a unified application of the synthesized findings. The opinions stated are not necessarily shared by other authors in this volume.

Global connections

The signal importance of outside connections for generating and shaping local violence among "tribal" people has recently received much attention in the anthropology of war (Blick 1988; Ferguson 1990, 1995a; Ferguson and Whitehead 2000a). On a parallel track, world system theorists have explored external factors aggravating warfare in the global periphery (Boswell and Dixon 1990; Chase-Dunn and Hall 1993; Nagel and Whorton 1992; Schmidt 1990; White 1990). The authors in this volume were asked to consider how recent global processes were affecting the local violence they encountered.

Discussion may begin with the global system of states, its historical rise and its restructuring after World War II, as described by Wolf. The United Nations became the gatekeeper for international recognition, and protector of the norm that the state was the only legitimate basis of sovereignty, as discussed by Maybury-Lewis. As far as established powers, great and small, were concerned, all land area and much of the sea was under at least the nominal authority of some state (Herbst 1997: 375–378; Holsti 1996: 73–79; Taylor 1995). As often noted, the breakup of old empires often led to newly created states, with no prior political coherence. Writing about the weak political integration of post-colonial countries, especially in Africa, Herbst (1990; 1992; and see Ayoob 1995: 173; Southall 1974) notes that one of their most important supports was the tacit agreement of both superpowers that existing boundaries should be upheld. Should internal controls weaken, one superpower was always ready to move in where the other's client faltered, preventing collapse in a way highlighted by Tainter. But with the geostrategic rivalry ended, there was a sharp retraction of political and material support to that end.

The post-Cold War era began in 1988 with the collapse of the communist system which preceded the break up of the USSR.[3] It had two primary dimensions: the disintegration of the Soviet Union, and the end of Cold War polarization and superpower support and control over client states. The crumbling of Soviet central control opened the door to new kinds of politics within its former borders, contests that went beyond normal jockeying for power to the more rare and critical issues of defining new polities, creating new boundaries and new rules for playing the political game (Rubin and Snyder 1998). Violence in Tajikistan and Chechnya illustrate one kind of outcome. But it must be remembered that most areas of the former Soviet Union went non-violently, if chaotically, to new forms of governance. Most crises occurred in two areas, Central Asia and the Trans-Caucasus regions, where political elites clung to more authoritarian political and economic structures (see Motyl 1997).

The breakup of Yugoslavia parallels the fall of the Soviet Union, and probably would not have occurred if the USSR had remained unified – it had been both a perceived threat holding Yugoslavia together, and capable of intervening if it fell apart. Such an enabling of disintegration happened on a more global level as well, as weak client states lost their powerful patrons. This was most apparent in Africa. As one indicator of this, combined military assistance from the US and the USSR to African governments, which ran at $3,287 million per year from 1980 to 1988, dropped to $332 million per year from 1992 to 1994, leaving many African national armies in disrepair (Byman and Van Evera 1998: 38; Herbst 1997: 377). But again, most of Eastern Europe and many African states have not experienced an upsurge in internal violence since 1988, and in Central America and other Cold War hot-spots the effect has been just the opposite.

At another level, the end of the Cold War has had varying implications for domestic politics in many countries. As described by Seligmann in relation to Peru, it upset political alliances along the anti-communist fault line, which actually gave Sendero more room to maneuver. In India, on the other hand, Lessinger describes anti-communism as alive and well, in fundamentalist Hindu form. In other chapters the issue is not discussed directly, but around the world it has been observed that the collapse of communism and its opposition has encouraged ethnic identification as a fallback ideology in power politics (Brubaker and Laitin 1998: 2). In sum, the "decompression effect," as international relations theorists call it, has been a critical factor encouraging violent conflict in some areas but not others (Acharya 1998: 169–180; Ayoob 1998: 32) – in this volume, in the former Yugoslavia, Greece/Macedonia, Liberia and Somalia. The fall of the Soviet Union and end of the Cold War are essential facts for understanding the surge of violence around 1992, but they do not explain where, when and why war broke out, and where it did not.

In many cases, the later history of the Cold War itself is an important consideration for understanding violence. While "realist" strategic thinkers (see Y. Ferguson, in this volume) lament the lost stability of a bipolar world order, it was bipolar disorder in much of the less-developed world (Acharya 1998: 165–171). Many of the wars that have torn apart states are continuations of struggles initially supported by the US or USSR, as in the cases of Angola, Chad and Somalia, discussed in this volume. The Cold War poured lethal weapons into many regions (Hartung 1994). In Uganda in 1995, an AK 47 cost as much as a chicken (Byman and Van Evera 1998: 39). The huge amounts of small arms (responsible for 90 per cent of recent casualties) circulating in both legal and black markets makes any concept of arms control very difficult (Cooper 1999)[4] – aggravated at the time of this writing by US opposition to UN efforts at small-arms limitations (Crossette 2001).

Less dramatic, less well-studied, but probably more important than any "decompression effect" are global economic trends. The new possibilities of political disintegration came on top of what for much of the less developed world was the "lost decade" of the 1980s, the global capitalist weakening that set in after the 1970s oil crisis, and falling prices for primary products (Herbst 1997: 376). Globally, the connection between major national economic setbacks and mass violence is so strong that Brown (1997: 20–23) concludes that the former is a necessary condition for the latter. Conversely, there are few cases where violence erupts in a booming economy. Indonesia is a classic illustration. Except for the long running struggle in East Timor, Indonesia was calm while it remained a World Bank success story. But when predatory international currency speculation combined with a corrupt and inefficient government to create a major crisis in standards of living, several latent social cleavages suddenly turned violent (Estrade 1998; Langhorne 2001: 32–33).

Peru and India, as discussed in this volume, experienced deepening ties to the world economy, yet their exports were so marginalized that growth was little or none. As IMF restrictions tightened, much of the population experienced increasing immiseration and uncertainty, directly setting the stage for violence. The "superfluity" of Yugoslavia's economy was masked by loans of petrodollars, but this just made the eventual decline even sharper. Greece constructed the Macedonian threat contemporaneously with a series of economic setbacks, but let it fade as economic benefits from regional trade grew. African countries faced with desperately weak markets for their desperately few exports had little basis for developing national economies or tax bases. Access to government has been, in some places, one of the very few arenas for tapping into wealth (Nyang'oro and Shaw 1998; and see Southall 1974: 157–159).

In this context, three other aspects of the current global economy come to the fore. First is aid. The poorer the country, the more reliant on aid it tends to be. In Liberia, the Doe regime was utterly dependent on US government support, and fell when that was cut off. Somalia illustrates broader problems associated with humanitarian assistance, from governments or non-governmental organizations (NGOs) (de Waal and Omaar 1993). Warlords' guns diverted its flow, which was then used to feed irregular soldiers and otherwise pay supporters. At the same time, those in local power abdicated responsibility for basic governmental services, leaving the job to NGOs. In these and other ways, humanitarian assistance and NGO presence have come to be major factors in the course of local conflicts, and not always for the better (Anderson 1999; Shearer 2000).

Second is the extra-official way products now enter international trade. This is not just a matter of free trade, but its militarization. As detailed studies in Berdal and Malone (2000) show, this must be recognized as an aspect of contemporary globalization that directly encourages internal wars and other violence.[5] Increasingly multi-national corporations protect their enclaves with corporate mercenaries (Reno 1997), or through agreements with warlords. This includes legal acquisitions of petroleum, woods, etc., but also precious contraband such as "blood diamonds" in Liberia, as discussed in this volume, and of course, drugs, as in Peru. In the past decade, several African countries have become transhipment points in the Asian–Euro–American drug trade, providing major support for local warlords (Segell 1999).

The disruptive impact of this trade is amplified by a third trend. The transnationalization of capital and workers weakened the economic power of governments, as discussed by Wolf. Latitude of government economic policy is even more sharply curtailed by conditions imposed by the IMF, three little letters which appear repeatedly in this book. Thus governments are often not able to respond to pressing needs or provide the patronage that brings internal support, while extra-governmental and often illegal operations, not recognized or constrained by the IMF, are increasing their wealth and power (Reno 1995; Richards 1996).

Other global processes affect recent domestic conflicts. The expanded role of the UN intervention in conflicts is obvious, but fraught with the potential to make conflicts worse (Thakur 1994). In a larger sense, the UN's avowed role as defender of state sovereignty – "[T]he U.N. seeks to preserve the nation-state as the very foundation of international life" (Boutros-Ghali 1993) – as discussed by Maybury-Lewis, is increasingly problematic (Thakur and Newman 2000). The expanding role of NGOs, beyond providing aid (see Fisher 1997), is a major part of what some see as the key development of contemporary globalization: the growth of horizontal cross-national connections, and the erosion of hierarchical national systems of control (Langhorne 2001: 10–35; Ury 1999: 92–98). Of special significance here are diasporas. Those who have moved away from their homeland can play a crucial role in developing a sense of national identity, and in various ways may increase agitation for independent national homelands (Appadurai in Gledhill 2000: 161–163). International religions, of course, may also play such a role, as Lessinger's discussions of India illustrate well. Also of signal importance is intensifying global communications. Concerning war in Sierra Leone, Richards (1996: xvii) makes a strong case that violence is shaped by and plays to "the media flows and cultural hybridizations that make up globalized modernity."

Finally, below the level of global process but linked to it is the increasing significance of regional developments in affecting internal challenges to states. This takes several forms. In parts of Africa, and in Chad and Liberia specifically, the old Francophone–Anglophone fault line has been re-energized with direct implications for military support (although France now sees its interests challenged more by the US than the UK) (Schraeder 1997). That same western African region sees increased influence of regional powers, Libya and Nigeria. Regional security arrangements are becoming more active and interventionist (Acharya 1998: 182–188; Talbot 2000), but can further complicate hostilities, as Brown discusses in relation to ECOMOG in Liberia (and see Schnabel and Thakur 2000 on NATO in Kosovo). Around the world, domestic political violence becomes a regional issue, through cross-border refugees, insurgencies, transborder trade, and arms networks (Duffield 2000; Premdas 1991: 10–13), giving rise to what are being called "bad neighborhoods" (Kaldor 1999: 107–109).

Regional connections to national conflicts are dramatically illustrated in south Asia. The collapse of the USSR and its withdrawal from Afghanistan led not only to internal war there, but also to "blowback" (a CIA term applied to its former pupils) training of Islamic fighters for new central Asian states and elsewhere around the world. There was a surge of arms and fighters to Pakistan which spilled over into Kashmir, the course of which struggle will affect India's stance in dealing with its many other identity-linked conflicts, not to mention its nuclear face-off with Pakistan. Currently, Pakistan, Saudi Arabia, Russia, and central Asian states are very actively involved in prolonging the civil war in Afghanistan (Ganguly 1997: 203, 227; Human Rights Watch 2001; Rubin et al. 2001; Weiner 1994). "Internal violence" often does not stay that way.

Global connections are unmistakably significant, but the specific character and salience of external ties for understanding recent violence within states varies greatly. Generally, external connections shape local conflicts indirectly, working through domestic agents, institutions, interests, processes and collectivities, which themselves are products of earlier colonial processes (see Jenkins and Shock 1992: 180–181; Southall 1974: 160). This has led some to argue that recent violent conflict should be seen as internally, rather than externally, generated (Ayoob 1995: 189; 1998: 48; Holsti 1996: 128–140). Without disagreeing that it is local actors who make the violence, I believe that this should not be seen as an either/or question. Many aspects of the political game have been shaped by global connections. These may be foregrounded by those on the inside, who with substantial justification can blame current situations on a history of outside meddling. If agencies of the more developed world hope to ameliorate violent struggle in less developed regions, it is important to keep these interactions in the conceptual foreground. They are factors that the outside world can affect to shape the future. And at present, they seem to be dangerously misunderstood in important circles.[6]

The state

This volume is distinguished by an explicit focus on the state. But the state itself is a problematic concept. Wolf recounts that forms of states differ radically over a long history of state-building projects. Y. Ferguson cautions about the danger of reification, learned the hard way in political science and international relations theory. "The state" is not a unitary thing. It has no interests, it does not act. States are made up of a variety of individuals and institutions, which may have competing or even contradictory concerns. Ferguson sees the problems inherent in this concept as so great that theory might be better off without it. Wolf also appreciates those dangers, but sees value in conceptualizing states as multidimensional political arenas, with important tasks including management of the conflicts generated by capital accumulation, and construction of hegemonic national cultures (see also Anderson 1991; Evans et al. 1986; Giddens 1985; Hobsbawm 1994; Mann 1988; Tilly 1975).

At least some of the dispute about the meaning and utility of "the state" is semantic, a product of ambiguous phrasing and connotations inferred from past associations with different schools of thought. Abrams (1988: 69–72), following Miliband, recognizes a "state system" made up of all the institutions and personnel of political and executive control – what I would call government – but distinguishes this set of powerful structuring agencies from the fiction of an interested, acting entity called "the state." Yet that fiction keeps creeping into and distorting analyses, so better to dispense with "the state" and use more precise descriptive terminology. Skocpol (1985: 3, 9), in contrast, sees the term "government" bringing along functionalist notions of a neutral space where different interests work out their disagreements. The state, for her, is a "weighty actor" made up of "organizationally coherent collectivities of state officials," which structures relationships both between civil society and public authority and within civil society itself. Thus it is most important to "bring the state back in" to comparative and historical analysis. It is hard to see much substantive disagreement between these seemingly opposed positions. As another example, in this volume, Tainter and Y. Ferguson start off very differently in conceptualizing the state, but end up not that far apart as they progress through discussions of current trends.

Anthropology has its own history of this debate. In the preface to *African Political Systems*, Radcliffe-Brown (1940: xxiii) concluded "The State ... does not exist in the phenomenal world; it is a fiction of the philosophers." In *The Evolution of Political Society*, Fried (1967: 227–229) took issue with similar conclusions, and described "a state" as *a kind of society*, where governmental institutions of coercion maintain a stratified social order. Major anthropological theorists on political evolution have continued to see states in this way (Carneiro 1970: 28; Haas 1982: 76, 172; Harris 1995: 151). Government, a set of institutions superordinate over ties of kinship, maintains – by force, if necessary – a social system where order goes from the top down and extraction from the bottom up. Unlike developed governmental institutions among, for example, the Cheyenne (Hoebel 1978) or the Iroquois (Morgan 1972), governments of states *rule*. Although this supports the validity of "the state," in contrast to Abrams, it dovetails with his most important insight (1988: 75–76): what is very real about "the state" is the myth of its independent existence. Belief in the state is acceptance of being ruled. The *idea* of the state legitimates the compulsory control of a population by a political elite.

Missing from the discussion up to this point has been the idea that states are territorially bounded, with a capital that at least theoretically exerts sovereign rule up to those borders (Buzan 1991: 90–96; Ruggie 1993). Even as internal political systems collapse, borders by and large remain acknowledged, if not respected, by neighbors. The world is divided into territorial "countries," a meaning of "state" that is accepted even by Y. Ferguson. International political culture demands it. This is hardly a trivial meaning. The bounded character of states makes them "containers," enabling a government to concentrate its allocative and authoritative resources, thus increasing its administrative power (Giddens 1985: 13) – even if those resources have recently been undercut by globalization (see Wolf, this volume; Comaroff 1995). Within state boundaries, that power is applied in a spatially structured way by spatially constituted administrative organizations (Rubenstein 2001; Taylor 1994; Vandergeest and Peluso 1995). It is the boundedness of a state that makes government such a "weighty actor," and social geography within those bounds structures how that weight is thrown around. Seen this way, "government" loses any functionalist tint of neutrality. Governments develop policies which affect the course of lived history within their borders. Peru's agrarian reform, seen as critical by Seligmann, though reflecting broader international trends, was particular to Peru.

It is the fact that so much violence is happening within the borders of states that has caused so much consternation among policy makers, who are far more accustomed to dealing with good old-fashioned international war. Conceptualization of the state is a critical factor in efforts to develop new policy. "Realist" international relations theory is premised on an unexamined idea of the state as the indivisible unit of politics (see Y. Ferguson, in this volume; Ferguson and Mansbach 1991). From this premise, recent problems of internal violence are the result of "weak states" (see Migdal 1988) or "state collapse" (see Zartman 1995a), and the solution is international support to build up these states (Holsti 1996; Zartman 1995a). Ayoob (1995, 1998; and see Buzan 1998) criticizes standard realism for neglecting the problematic character of Third World states, comparing their current status to an "earlier stage" of state construction such as that described by Tilly (1975) for fifteenth–seventeenth-century medieval Western Europe. But Ayoob's "subaltern realism" reiterates that state weakness is the problem, and its strengthening the solution.

Anthropologists, on the other hand, are much less likely to envision "the state as the security guarantor for a populated territory" (Zartman 1995b: 5). In their sharing of the lived experience of peoples around the world, it is the local authorities who are often the source of violence and *in*security for the population (Nagengast 1994: 114–116; Sluka 2000b: 1–6; Van den Berghe 1990: 3–4; and see other citations on page 2 of this chapter). The state as a system of compulsion and exploitation is nakedly evident. As Rummel (1997a, b) has quantified, "death by government" has been several times more likely than death by war in this century. Too often "the greatest threat to most of the people in the Third World comes not from internal war, but from their own leaders" (David 1998: 93).

Nor are anthropologists likely to be persuaded that wars within Third World states can be understood as an early stage in a unilinear scheme of state evolution. The economic and political structures forged in violent struggle are reacting to very contemporary global inputs previously discussed, and promise more war without leading to increasing integration (Berdal and Malone 2000; Rich 1999; Kaldor 1999: 90–111) Elites associated with government may avow global norms about state sovereignty, as Ayoob (1995: 71–77) stresses, but that is because such norms support their own control and interests, and it is pursuit of those interests which commonly takes precedence over considerations of state building (David 1998: 87–90; Herbst 1997: 393).

The idea that it is state weakness or collapse that is the cause of fighting ignores the fact that it is government itself which is the object of struggle. The institutions and instruments of government, though not unitary, are pinnacles of the structural landscape, magnetized nodes of wealth and power. This is especially true in post-colonial states, as summarized by Villalon (1998: 11–14; and see Fukui and Markakis 1994b: 8–9) for Africa but with application beyond that continent. Even if "weak" compared to some others, these governments are often "overdeveloped" or "swollen" in terms of employment, they play a critical role in domestic reallocation of available resources, and they claim the major benefits of mineral and other resource extraction. Sometimes, the struggle involves a widespread movement of people who want the government off their backs. Other times, it involves a range of actors who use force to wall off government authority so they can pursue their own profit through violence and patronage – warlords (Rich 1999). Commonly, the goal is to keep or gain control of government. As Reyna notes for Chad in this volume, internal wars "have involved officials, ex-officials, and would-be officials killing each other … for control over the state." Discussions which stress the weakness of governments as the cause of internal violence, with the policy implication that external powers should do more to prop them up, ignore the fact that in most cases the government is what the fighting is all about. The more resources and power channeled through it, the more valuable a prize it becomes.

Reno (1998, 2000) has developed the concept of the "shadow state," a version of patrimonial rule attuned to current global political economy. The shadow state is a network of elite power and patronage that exists alongside the official government institutions. Those at its pinnacle exploit the facade of government, but personally "call the shots" and appropriate as much wealth as they can by tapping foreign aid and enclave-based production of valued commodities. The beneficiaries of this system, Reno argues, have a vested interest in promoting insecurity (hence the need for patrons) and a war economy (smuggling, arms trade, etc.), and are against diversion of resources to public goods. Old-style capital accumulation via exploitation of peasant production is too limited, and would require counter-profitable expenditures on security. As Reno points out, such systems are unlikely to create peace or develop functioning institutions of government. Brown discusses this concept as it applies to Liberia, and raises the question of what violence transpires when the established shadow network and official government are separated by an usurper.

Always and forever, there is competition over who controls government, or parts thereof, and what the government controls. But this volume focuses on struggle that goes well beyond normal politics (see Bailey 1969), and which lays siege to constituting elements of a state. One type of siege challenges basic premises of government, such that the old state persists, but under a radically different regime. A second type challenges the territorial bounding of a state, more by partition than conquest, but rule by *some* central government is not in doubt. In the third type, there is real doubt whether *any* centrally dominating government will establish any semblance of control over its official borders in the future. The case studies reflect these categories and this order.

Peru's war since the mid-1980s superficially resembles the insurgencies common in Latin America since the 1960s, fueled by oppressive conditions endured by much of the population. But the nature of the challenge to the state and the government response has been unique, perhaps even postmodern. The Maoist strategy of people's war was transferred to the Andes, carried on while international communism collapsed, funded by drug money, and finally put on the defensive not by a fascist general, but by a "politically neutral" technocrat. What was at stake in this struggle was not the future existence of Peru – Sendero was defined by its borders – but rather the basic character of the Peruvian state, which the rebels promised (or threatened) to utterly transform.

India faces multiple challenges, including international boundary conflicts and insurgencies along regional, tribal and other lines which could lead to some boundary changes. But the challenge described by Lessinger comes from a movement which is adamant about preserving current territorial integrity. Hindu fundamentalists aimed to (and did) succeed the Congress Party which had ruled since independence with a commitment to secularism. Secular government had not delivered the goods for many people, and its increasing debility was such that it was incapable even of attempting force against orchestrated mobs. The Hindutva combine's goal is a state which supports their vision of Hindu culture as the basis of society.

Yugoslavia, paralleling processes in the Soviet Union, also had a party identified with government, which also failed as a provider, but with a suddenness that created a new opening for those already in power. Here men, often previously Communists, framed a governmental crisis in terms of ethnonationalism – to carve up the old state territory. The breakup of Yugoslavia was followed by serial warfare to create new, "pure" states. The state is dead; long live the state.

Greece is one of the strongest states discussed in this book. Its imagined adversary, which became officially known as the Former Yugoslav Republic of Macedonia, is most fragile, virtually forced into statehood by the course of events in Yugoslavia and seeking to consolidate its position via historical self-definition. ("FYROM" illustrates Tainter's point that states are unlikely to collapse completely when other states are in the neighborhood.) But the construction of contemporary Greece, against several other possibilities, is too recent even to let potential alternatives go unchallenged. Taking all the above cases together, we see that different constructions of historicized identity can be used to overthrow, divide, reinforce or generate states, as will be discussed later. But in all cases, the future existence of *some* central government dominating within defined borders seems assured.

Liberia is one of the oldest of the contemporary states of Africa. For a century and a half, the USA supported a patrimonial, repressive government. US aid papered over existing cleavages and tensions, even after the fall of the Americo-Liberians. But when the superpowers lost interest, and regional powers became more active and divisive, the center could not hold, and violent struggle broke out over who would rule. Still, as Brown observes, there is no move for division or secession. All participants in the conflicts accept the existence of a Liberian state, and expect it to solidify again in the future.

The future of states is more ambiguous in other parts of Africa. Post-colonial states in Africa were weak to begin with, created by pronouncement along arbitrary colonial borders, and lacking both evolved instruments and experience in government (see Wolf, in this volume). Angola exemplifies this fragility – given no preparation at all for self-government, torn apart by wars since its inception, at no time has it constituted a single state at peace. Much of that fighting directly involved one of the hottest superpower confrontations of the late Cold War. But unlike other former superpower hot spots (e.g., Nicaragua), the Angolan war kept going when the Cold War ended. The continuing turmoil reflects both the weakness of the central government in anarchic Luanda, lacking even a functioning currency, and the wealth to be had by whoever could control the regions into which Angola had fragmented.

The brief history of independent Chad is another tale of woe. State breakdown in Chad is not so much territorial fragmentation as it is an oscillation of governmental expansion and collapse. A relatively fixed political center which represents the only avenue for rising above subsistence labor periodically gains control over its nominal territory, but never truly consolidates this position. Taxes go unpaid, roads crumble. Soon a regime is falling back before shifting coalitions, powered by internal and external interests, which develop "autarkic institutions of violence." This has happened five times.

Somalia was not a typical post-colonial creation. Seizure of power by the "scientific socialist," Siyad Barre, profoundly altered the character of the state. First with Soviet and then US support, this government set out to forcibly remake society in its desired image. The state was more a predator than servant to most Somalis. Local resistance grew just as superpower interest and support lapsed, and the Somali state blew away. It is hard to imagine any central government reestablishing control over diverse locally grounded powers, and in fact a major region has declared its independence. According to Besteman, Somalia today may be one of the "most stateless places on earth."

Highland Papua New Guinea might be characterized as one of the "last stateless places on earth." Government control, as measured by the prohibition of local warfare, arrived within living memory, and proved fragile, crumbling as Australian authority receded. Government since then has been a constant negotiation with local tribes, with the latter often setting the terms. "Tribal violence" returned, but in forms that changed with the highlands' changing connections to electoral politics, government, and the world beyond (see Strathern 2000). High levels of violent crime and brigandage in the highlands testify to the effective absence of government authority, yet some of the offenders seem politically well-connected. Violent crime itself has become an issue upon which government and local peoples can try to negotiate some new form of contract.

The cases collected here illustrate the great variation which exists across challenges to states. The cumulative effect of these and other internal crises and carnages created, in the early 1990s, the fear that some general political sea-change was underway. But there was something else that made the violence of the early 1990s so frightening. In stark contrast to the cool calculus of national interests invoked by realist descendants of Clausewitz to explain modern warfare, these wars seem *driven* by apparently irrational personal attachments, primal loyalties and conflicting identities (see Van Creveld 1991). They were a challenge to the very idea of the modern nation-state, which for decades had been so fixed in our political firmament that we could blithely overlook the blatant problem of that hyphenated construction. Today those two meanings of "nation" are butting heads. Struggling contenders within one country advance radically different ideas of what the nation is or should be.

Nationalist visions

The word "nationalism" first appeared in 1774 (Hechter 2000: 5). It is a modern, Western invention, which like so many others has swept over the world. Many meanings have been ascribed to this malleable term, often tied to the political agendas of specific practitioners or analysts (Anderson 1991; Gellner 1997; Hechter 2000; Hobsbawm 1994; Rossel 1997; Smith 1983; Van Evera 1997; Young 1993b). The core idea, however, is that a bounded sovereign country should be associated with a "nation," an identifiable people, contrastable to other peoples. "[A] broad consensus does exist in the scholarly literature that ... nationalism consists of political activities that aim to make the boundaries of the nation – a culturally distinctive collectivity aspiring to self-governance – coterminous with those of the state" (Hechter 2000: 7). Comaroff and Stern (1995: 4) add a second very important meaning: "the authoritative claim of a nation-state to expressions of common sentiment and exclusive commitment, of loyal attachment and joint responsibility, on the part of its citizens." The *sine qua non* of nationalism is a defined territory. You cannot be a nationalist without it (Hechter 2000: 13–14; Smith 1983: xiii, xxxv). Thus, territory assumes symbolic value beyond the material worth of what it contains. Recognized boundaries so provide an analytic bridge from nationalist movements through states to the global system.

Nationalists take the existence of a state for granted, it is a premise of their program. The idea of "the state" legitimates the fact of rule, nationalism legitimates who controls the state, for whom, and to what general ends – even if it means killing those who do not fit in. To the degree that a nationalist vision confers *legitimacy* on a movement or government, it reduces, but does not eliminate, the need for punishments or rewards to secure compliance. A successful nationalist program increases the security and power of a regime.

Nationalist visions are collective, employing unifying tropes such as "family," "community," "folk," or "the people," yet nationalist visions typically privilege some social categories over others. They are supposed to encompass all people within state borders, but often are associated with one region, such as the coast and not the interior as described in this volume by Belik. They make a claim for unification of city and country which would have seemed absurd in earlier epochs (Eriksen 1993: 102), but typically find most advocates in cities, especially capitals. National identity is said to transcend class, but it is typically supported by the intelligentsia (Smith 1983: xxii). Political elites often identity *their* culture with *national* culture (Van den Berghe 1990: 8). Particular nationalisms may be identified with one generation, as seen in Africa with the passing of the leaders of nationalist movements whose personal charisma had been a foundation of regime stability (Villalon 1998: 12). Nationalism often is forwarded as a defense of traditional womanhood, but commonly results in the suppression of women's movements and freedoms (Enloe 1989; Sapiro 1993: 42–45). Generally, particular nationalist visions are likely to benefit the core group which propounds them, and to be well received by those larger numbers who can anticipate personal benefit (Hechter 2000: 30, 123–124).

Given such contradictions, it is not surprising that advocates of new nationalisms may proselytize them with an enthusiasm suggestive of millennial movements, well-known for their capacity to unify disparate groups. Indeed, in some cases, nationalist and religious missions are one (Lessinger, in this volume; and see Mahmood 1996: 20). But as Smith (1983: xxiv–xxix) concludes, usually this is "a matter of stylistic affinity, of a common fervor and rhetoric, not of doctrine or organization." Nationalism comes not from a prophet, but from calculating political entrepreneurs; not from revelation but from self-serving interpretations of established knowledge. And it does not spread purely because of its appeal, but is imposed through violence and political control of education, publications, and other media. In a more general sense, however, nationalism *can* be seen as being like a religion (Kapferer 1988), as a set of beliefs, symbols, and rituals which draws on local political culture to, in Geertz's (1979: 79) words, "establish powerful, pervasive and long-lasting moods and motivations" that impel action – for instance, the hierarchy of Sri Lankan nationalism versus the egalitarianism of Australian nationalism.

The very term "nation-state" can be seen as an expression of faith. The concept derives from a France–England model of national unity, which Y. Ferguson and Maybury-Lewis remind us has precious few exemplars in the real world (see Buzan 1991: 72–77). Recent events have focused attention on two fundamentally different meanings of "nation": an "imagined community" which comes together through unifying civic institutions within a state, *e pluribus unum*; or some collectivity recognized as culturally distinctive in its own right. This distinction has been glossed as "civic" or "assimilationist" nationalism, versus "particularisitic" or "ethnic" nationalism (Brown 1997: 8–9; Hechter 2000: 6; Tambiah 1996: 11–12; cf. Comaroff 1995: 262–267). Until recently, these two meanings of "nation" could be elided, if not in the present, at least as an inexorable future development.

For decades, both socialist and capitalist powers propounded different versions of the trinity of economic development, sociocultural modernization, and a mildly patriotic nationalism. Elites and scholars the world over, even non-aligned ones, espoused the faith that rising prosperity would wear away "pre-modern" social institutions and identifications in favor of a secular individualism. Enlightened self-interest and participation in the spreading, beneficial institutions of civil society (see Comaroff and Comaroff 1999) and the state would foster new allegiances to governments which effectively mediated relations with the world outside, to the benefit of all. There was "a religion of modernization" (Smith 1983: xxviii, 41–64). Instead, the opposite happened. Modernization and the increasing power of governments created more to fight over, and the need for regional bases of mobilization. Commentators from very different perspectives agree that, contrary to expectations, the modern state and nationalism have generated or intensified, rather than diminished, ethnic identification (Geertz 1963: 120; Guidieri et al. 1988: 8; Horowitz 1985: 5; Smith 1981: 18–20; Stack 1986: 6; Tambiah 1988: 3, 1996: 12–18).

These sub-national identifications can be tolerable while the modernization paradigm is backed with increasing or at least anticipated prosperity. In some places, the dream came true, at least for some people, at least for a while. Several East Asian countries stood out in this way until recently, whereas they now illustrate how quickly economic decline can lead to identity-linked violence. But for many, prosperity never happened at all. Worse, economic reversals threatened even the status quo. Aspirations were raised, then dashed. Assaults on the purveyors of modern nationalism have been mounted by segments of society which were stranded while others prospered. The cases in this volume well illustrate permutations on nationalist visions.

In Peru, the Velasco reforms were formulated by urban intellectuals to bring the rural population more actively into national society, with education a key instrument. Rural folk responded with enthusiasm for education, but found it wanting. They found the nationalist vision meant progress for some but not others, dividing the countryside into winners and losers. Much of the rural middle class, including teachers, saw their aspirations first lifted and then blocked. These failures opened the door for Sendero's revolt. In the struggle that ensued, rural peoples, besieged at times by both Sendero and the government, managed to hammer together their own civic institutions and networks, with strong ties to the towns and cities. It is this more cohesive civil society that is being targeted by new nationalist visions from politicians wearing Inka symbols. The political future remains most uncertain, with increased rural integration creating new and not entirely untroubling potentials.

The national idea of India remains firm, though challenged by numerous local movements. But which nationalism will triumph? The Congress Party which had ruled since independence was firmly committed to development and a secular, modernized country. But its impact over decades had been highly uneven. The Hindu nationalists assembled a cross-caste coalition of the left-behind. Ideological opposition to Westernization was tied to a promise of economic relief. Now Hindu nationalists have gained control of government. Their loose network allows anti-Islamic and other violence to continue while government disclaims responsibility. But the BJP's ideology limits its potential political base, and global economic realities force them to follow paths trodden by their predecessors. All these tensions stretch forward into the future, for a governing party which found that detonation of a nuclear bomb was a great unifying national symbol.

Yugoslavia was until recently a model of modernizing, integrating nationalism, with its geographic integrity accepted on faith up until the moment it fell apart. With all that has happened since, it seems surprising that Milosevic began as a technocrat, an economic reformer. But with the sudden, dramatic failure of development, official transcripts of nation and progress crumbled, and hidden ones burst forth. Politicians seeking survival hit on ethnonationalist themes as a fallback, reinforced by rapidly polarizing views in different regions. European recognition of initial claims to national independence triggered a cascade of mobilizations, dramatically illustrating that acceding to new ethnic boundaries may only set off new warfare.

The history of Greece provides an insight into the long difficult process and the human costs of construction of national identity. It shows the role of commerce, church, and state, in not only fending off competitors, but in stifling local alternatives. Historians are very much a part of this process. In Greece, it worked. But when the economic prosperity which had encouraged assimilation stumbled, "slavo-macedonians" found a minority approach linked to FYROM appealing. The reaction was strong and delved deep into the grass roots, with Greek identity proclaimed from t-shirt to bumper sticker. Macedonia itself is another story, and its rocky road to national identity is at present the stuff of newspaper headlines.

Liberia takes us into all the problems of nationalism built on Africa's colonial past. Its national elite is "civilized" – English-speaking, literate and Christian. As its patrimonial government gradually extended rule away from the coast, it fixed the cultural variation it encountered into tribes, and developed an enclave economy which did not unify the country. The 1970s efforts at modern, de-tribalized nation-building held sway primarily in the capital. Doe's coup came from the tribal areas, and once in power he and his opponents effectively used these cleavages to divide and rule. Yet the war did not destroy the intersubjective sense of Liberians that Liberians they were, above their own more particular identities. Ironically, the fact that so many became cross-border refugees reinforced their Liberian identity even more.

Angolan nationalism is even more problematic. Divided into tribes by colonialism, given independence with no preparation, unified only by past anti-colonialism, coping with fragmentation from territory through ideology, it grapples with what is "genuine Angolidade." When elections produced thirteen political parties, there were thirteen views on the subject. While Savimbi and the UNITA rebels espouse an assertively African version (Heywood 1998), Belik shows us some of the gyrations in the capital, the plumbing of history and myth, the funding of national authors, the use of ambiguous and double-edged symbols – such as a Russian tank on a pedestal, or the sinking "Angolan Tower of Pisa" – and above all, the claim that the authentic Angolan must be a Christian.

In Chad, nationalism is again at center stage. As in Angola, there have been strenuous efforts from the center to develop a national identity. Tombalbaye's vision was first based on modernization, then Islam, then "Tchaditude." The sequential opponents from the hinterlands also pressed nationalist visions for the "grande famile tchadienne," as their justifications to govern. But analyzing events in sequence shows that the nationalist visions are ex post facto rationalizations of quests for power already begun.

Somali nationalism was championed by "scientific socialist" Siyad, who invaded Ethiopia in an irredentist campaign to unify Somalis. Internally, his drive to modernize the nation meant an attack on "tribalism" by literally outlawing clans, even as he covertly used their old structures to solidify support and weaken enemies. Rapacious predation on societal resources by Siyad and those who followed in his wake devastated civil society, setting the stage for warlordism which seemed unneedful of unifying visions. Now we see efforts to reconstruct a workable social order from the ground up, but what nation may emerge from this is very much open to question.

Papua New Guinea is both similar to and different from Somalia. In its great diversity there had been no national narrative, but local clan loyalties remained strong. Given the weakness of government (lacking the categorical support of key players in the Cold War), no direct suppression of clan activities was possible. But roads have been joining areas together, and new wants and possibilities (and perhaps not yet enough failures) have stirred aspirations for progress. Integrating factors such as Christianity and Tok Pisin, the *lingua franca*, are being used creatively and symbolically in careful negotiations between local groups and with government to create a more civil society, less rent by violence. If a meaningful PNG nationalism emerges, it will be through transactions such as these.

In these cases and others, there is no argument against modernization, development, education, or democracy. Problems associated with modernization or political openings tend to be associated with abrupt changes from older systems, and/or the *failure* to deliver what was promised. In the long run, however, they offer the surest safeguards against internal violence (Brown and de Jonge Oudraat 1997; Kaldor 1999; Rummel 1997c). It is true that new democracy and press freedom may be used to whip up hatreds (Premdas 1991: 14–15; Snyder and Ballentine 1997), but not in most transitions to democracy (Acharya 1998: 175–176). Developed democracy provides the best, though not foolproof, protections against internal state terror (Sluka 2000a: 7) and interstate war, as two democracies rarely if ever go to war against each other (the "democratic peace") (Russett 1990). Moreover, for some time there has been increasing global consensus that democratic elections are the only valid basis of legitimate governance (Gottlieb 1993: 20–24).

But failure of development and democracy bring ideological vacuums. For those passed over by the dream of modernization, there was both a loss of faith in the brightly constructed future, and a need for some other vision to replace it. That brings us to ethnicity.

Ethnicity and culture

As Eriksen notes (1993: 100), despite "the remarkable congruence between theories of nationalism and anthropological theory of ethnicity ... the two bodies of theory have largely developed independently of each other" (cf. Smith 1981, 1983). Within academia, and anthropology in particular, ethnicity has become a virtual industry (Alonso 1994; Ausenda 1997; Cohen 1978; Gonzalez and

McCommon 1989; Hall *et al.* 1996; Vincent 1990; Williams 1989). There are serious differences in the way that terms are used. In the sub-Saharan Africa literature (e.g. Vail 1989), for instance, "tribe" is commonly used for what I would call "ethnie." As I use the terms, "ethnie" refers to a people who are perceived by themselves or others as being *culturally* distinctive – who are seen as having a distinctive way of life – whether or not they have any political organization as a group (see Eriksen 1993: 10–12). A tribe, in contrast, is a *polity* – a political organization uniting different local groups (see Ferguson 1997; Fried 1975; Haas 1990: 172; Southall 1970). Ethnies may encompass one, many, or no tribes; tribes may amalgamate people from more than one ethnie – a variable relationship not unlike that of nation and state. A related term is clan, one division in a wider and multifaceted system of social organization, based on constructed descent, which can act as a basis for political cohesion at different, more-or-less inclusive levels of organization. If one fairly broad level of clan organization regularly acts as a political unit, this may be called a tribe.

Theoretically, from the work of the past thirty years there has emerged a widely accepted synthesis – with plenty of argument remaining, of course – of three basic views of ethnicity (Gurr 1993: 3–5; Smith 1983: xxviii–xxxii; Tambiah 1996: 21; Turton 1997b: 6–14; Young 1993b: 23–25): (1) ethnies are socially constructed, their defining characteristics and boundaries a product of dialectical interactions with others ("constructionist"); (2) ethnic identity is used instrumentally, to obtain political and material advantages in competitive or conflicted situations ("instrumentalist"); and (3) ethnic identity can be a powerful psychological factor strongly affecting perceptions and actions in political struggles, beyond instrumental advantage ("primordialist").

The term primordialist has two meanings, which must be clarified. As often applied to recent conflicts, it is a shorthand way of saying "ancient loyalties and animosities," the idea that current fights are continuations of a grudge match going back centuries (e.g., Kaplan 1993; or a *New York Times* headline about Indonesia, from 24 March 1999: "Ancient hatreds, new battles"). The other meaning, as originally proposed by Geertz (1963: 109; and see Stack 1986), refers to ascribed identities with a powerful emotional hold. The operative word is not "ancient," but "givens." It is the original meaning which can be synthesized with constructionist and instrumentalist approaches to ethnicity. What I will refer to as the "ancient animosity" perspective contradicts them – ethnicity is *not* constructed but ancient, the conflict is *not* about political and economic interest but about identity before all else. Although the ancient animosity lives on in popular discussions, it has been widely considered and uniformly rejected (Ayoob 1998: 48; Brown 1997: 3–4; Comaroff 1995: 247–248; Hamburg *et al.* 1999), as it is in this volume.[7]

In this current synthesis, ethnic identification is anything but natural. Ethnies are not timeless, unchanging social groups – although it is important to note that their boundedness, fixity at birth, and salience varies greatly from situation to situation (Bell-Fialkoff 1996: 80). They are inherently relational, the product of historically fluctuating "dialogues" with people who are not of that ethnie –

either horizontally layered and ranked, or unranked parallel divisions, or some combination of both (Horowitz 1985: 21–24). To be sure, cultural variation is entirely real, but sharp breaks between cultures are far more the exception than the norm, and more often than not internal differentiation within ethnies provides the raw material for additional or other divisions. (In a sense, the situation is quite similar to that of "race."[8]) That is, until ethnic identity is used for political mobilization. Crystallization of ethnic boundaries is promoted "from above" by state agents and agencies and "from below" by local representatives and brokers. In their interaction, ethnic identity becomes crucial, a categorical filter strongly affecting a person's life circumstances and chances. Recognized identities, as Wolf, Seligmann and Brown each discuss in this volume, are labels and gateways for interacting with power centers. In atmospheres of political competition, salient ethnicities come, go, and are transformed with astonishing swiftness, however fixed and ancient they may seem at any one point. Examples of instrumental ethnogenesis are legion (Ferguson and Whitehead 2000; Fukui and Markakis 1994a; Hill 1996; Vail 1989).

The impermanent, contingent, relational character of ethnicity in no way diminishes the significance of local culture, although local culture is itself continually being transformed by connection to larger global processes, and by violence itself. As emphasized in the contributions to this volume from Warren, Seligmann, Denich, Brown, Strathern and Stewart, local culture provides distinct phenomenologies, different ways of perceiving and reacting to events (and see Nordstrom and Martin 1992; Warren 1993a). Local culture is a system of meaning, providing the cognitive material essential for political definition, communication and mobilization. The very existence of a collective identity is expressed and bounded by adherence to commonly held symbols (Bell-Fialkoff 1996: 80–89; Linke 1999). The symbol of a group is a passage to the self. Collective identity is integrated with individual identity (a point stressed by new social movement theory, drawing on established understandings from social psychology (Larana *et al.* 1994; Morris and McClurg Mueller 1992)).

Critical symbols are dense, multi-layered, and ambiguous (Ortner 1973; Turner 1967), and symbols linked to group identity can mean many things to different people. By their nature, they are suited to ongoing reinterpretation by leaders, even though they may be experienced as "unconditional, inescapable, and timeless" (Turton 1997b: 21). It has become axiomatic that ethnic leaders manipulate critical symbols to fashion a self-serving vision of "us." But while the autocratic, manipulative, top-down generation of these bloody visions should never fade from sight, it is not enough, as Warren reminds us. It may be comforting to conclude that it is a few bad men, rather than "the people," who are to blame for the carnage, but along with coercion there is undeniably a passionate, deadly commitment to the cause by many of those carrying out the orders. It is important to understand how promulgated messages resonate with lived experience to truly motivate killing and atrocity. Local belief systems must be understood in order to understand how individual persons take a message and act on it, make sense of it, live with it, resist it, and recover from it, as

Hinton (1998a, b) details regarding the Cambodian genocide. Here is where it is important to get down to local cultural texts and tropes.

One criticism from outside anthropology of "culturalist" approaches to "ethnic violence" is that they cannot predict or explain when and why it actually occurs.[9] But the eminent historian of war Jeremy Black (1998a) has concluded that *in general*, "cultural suppositions about the use of force" are critical in determining when bellicosity is rational, "why some disputes lead to war and others do not." Ideas *about* violence are crucial to the way it is acted out, who it is acted out by, and who it is directed against. Violence is among other things a performance, a ritual, a symbol, a communication in itself, deeply related to one's sense of self and other (Ferguson and Whitehead 2000b: xxi–xxviii; Kapferer 1988; Mahmood 1996: 15–16; Tambiah 1996: 309–311; Taussig 1987). It is "a unified language of material signification, circulating between and formative of antagonistic blocs" (Feldman 1991: 1). This should be self-evident with regard to suicide bombers of various persuasions, or mass rape as occurred in Bosnia (Enloe 1998; Rejali 1998; Stiglmayer 1994). Without understanding the roles of culture, torture, mutilation and other atrocities – elements which undeniably shape the course of violence and the possibilities of reconciliation – the study of ethnic violence will remain just a mind-numbing glimpse into the heart of darkness.[10]

The sense of its past is also an important part of any culture. In situations where peoples have long shared close contact and become quite similar, a belief in different histories may be the biggest distinguishing feature between them (see Horowitz 1985: 52). Popular history is the ultimate symbol of collective identity. It is the becoming, "how we came to be who we are." Other symbols are enfolded within a version of the past, gaining their power from perceived historical association with the group. Along with political leaders themselves, idea workers in education and the media play a crucial role, emphasizing, ignoring, and recasting events in the past. They shape and disseminate highly partisan constructions, usable in political struggle, particularly (in this volume) in the cases of India, Yugoslavia and Greece. To any historian not engorged with partisan passion, these narratives may seem transparently inadequate – mytho-histories – but they are not made up of whole cloth.

Constructed, manipulated histories must be true enough to the known past, and responsive enough to present anxieties, to be believable, to become compelling to those involved in struggle. As with all symbols, power comes not from objective reality, but from this shared belief. Cries to "our history" then evoke strong if variable images for each person. They may be especially powerful for the young, still in the throws of identity formation, and particularly to socially superfluous young men, who otherwise find themselves adrift, unwanted and disrespected. Not knowing any better, they may rally when those who *do* know, those with *power*, tell them of their historic mission, which also allows otherwise unattainable gratifications. It is the internalization of these mytho-histories by combatants themselves that has led so many outside commentators to accept the explanation of ancient loyalties and animosities.

Beyond "ethnic violence"

Having discussed the meaning and importance of ethnicity and culture in political struggle, it is now imperative to critique the idea that contemporary violence can be explained as "ethnic conflict." While many eminent students of the subject use the word "ethnic" to apply to almost any group imagined to have a common origin (e.g. Horowitz 1985: 53; Maybury-Lewis, in this volume), in my opinion, indiscriminate application of that label to conflict situations impedes our understanding. "The very phrase 'ethnic conflict' misguides us. It has become a shorthand way to speak about any and all violent confrontations between groups of people living in the same country" (Bowen 1996: 3; and see Brubaker and Laiton 1998: 4–5). As Gantzel (1997: 123, 136–138) notes, it is analogous to the concept "proxy wars," which muddied our understanding of collective violence in previous decades. In his survey of internal wars from 1945 to 1992, very few began in ethnic confrontations (the Rwandan genocide is one), though many took on ethnic dimensions as they progressed. Moreover, the great majority of ethnically oriented conflicts within nations have not led to violence (Licklider 1998: 126). A related idea, that cultural difference itself gives rise to violent conflict, although it does receive credence in high-policy circles (Huntington 1993), is contradicted by so many ethnographic examples of symbiotic coexistence that it is hard to see how anyone could assert it. There is no necessary connection between actual cultural diversity and violent conflict. Heterogenous peoples get along well, and nearly identical peoples can be riven by factional strife (Bowen 1996: 10–12).

Even careful scholars tend to apply the label "ethnic conflict" more widely than is strictly warranted. Eriksen (1993: 2) writes that "most" of the thirty-five major armed conflicts in the world in 1991 "could plausibly be described as ethnic conflicts," including violence in Northern Ireland. In a massive current study of state failures initiated at the request of Vice-President Gore and Secretary of State Allbright, "ethnic wars" are one of four categories of intra-state violence, accounting for fifty-nine of 233 instances between 1954 and 1996, including "violent contention among clan-based warlords" in Somalia (Gurr *et al.* n.d.: 3–5). Gurr and his colleagues certainly understand the variable, complicated, and changing nature of identifications, which elsewhere (Gurr 1993) are more accurately referred to as "communal groups" or minorities. Perhaps Gurr *et al.* fall back to "ethnic" in frustration over the mismatch between our limited vocabulary and an extremely complicated reality, a problem with which this author is very sympathetic. People "know what ethnic conflict means." But our inadequate language may be seriously misleading.

"Ethnic" is a multivocalic *symbol*, meaning different things to different people, and expressing and eliciting strong reactions. This makes it perfect for political discourse in arenas where policy is made. Lately, "ethnic" has taken on negative tones, like the old "tribalism" with which it is often interchanged.[11] It conjures up the idea of "ancient loyalties and animosities". The image that violent conflict bubbles up from the people themselves once central restraining power has weakened is persuasive. It epitomizes the Hobbesian myth-charter justifying coercive government, and acts as a magnet for widely disseminated pop-science speculations about an evolved instinct of "in-group amity, out-group enmity" (Fukuyama 1998: 33; Shaw and Wong 1987).[12] The label can be a way of objectifying and delegitimizing others, an excuse for washing one's hands of the matter. Casual or even studied application of "ethnic conflict" may actually close minds and make it more difficult to understand what is really going on. We need to rethink "ethnic conflict."

As Y. Ferguson reminds us in this volume, there are a great many bases of political identity formation, and the analytic task is to understand why certain ones become salient at a particular moment (see also Bell-Fialkoff 1996: 74–106). The cases presented here suggest a set of variables which in different combinations structure struggles along identity lines. These include cultural difference or ethnicity, but also distinctions based on geographic region, rural versus urban living, class or caste position, race, language, religion, tribe, clan, generation, and gender. Not all or even most are involved in any given case, at least as described in these chapters, but some combination of several is evident always. This section discusses such compound identities as portrayed in the chapters to come.

In Peru, speakers of Quechua languages vary considerably in culture, and historically they have lacked a sense of common identity, but the Quechua became an ethnie – at least in the eyes of *mestizos* – through a common history of oppression. Since it has been *mestizos* who have done the oppressing, this can also be seen as a racial divide. Since those being squeezed have tended to be peasants and agricultural laborers, Quechua identity has a major class and rural character – indeed the insurgents' strategy was to strangle the cities. Sendero Luminoso arose among a frustrated rural middle class, with special appeal to those women who were additionally constrained by conventional gender relations. It saw itself as a vanguard leading Quechua, and had some success in recruiting the economically dispossessed; but eventually it created even more indigenous opposition by its racism, its violation of rural norms of consensus and equality, and its terror. Through this conflict, the state-encouraged, extremely un-indigenous rural civil defense structure, by bringing together local leaders and fostering common approaches to common problems, may have contributed to the development of a new pan-Quechua sense of ethnic identity.

In India, we see similar elements combined in very different ways. "Hindutva," or Hindu-ness is an ideological system which converts political issues into religious ones. It is not so much matters of faith that are at issue, but rather a competing vision of culture. Hindu fundamentalism is arrayed against a government which has enshrined secular administration. The religious call emanates from the cities. Its source is high caste/class Hindus left behind by modernization and threatened by claims of women and those of low caste. But the new divinely ordered world they envision appeals to many – high and low, rural and urban – who justly feel victimized by "progress." Poor young men with no future are especially attracted to this alternative, and provide much of the muscle used against the movement's enemies. Hindutva also appeals to Hindus in diaspora, cultivating an international identity and support network. Muslims are Hindutva's prime scapegoats (despite centuries of coexistence and mutual influence), but religious animosity is also very serviceable against Christians, regional separatists, leftists, and any other political opponents.

Understanding the breakdown of Yugoslavia begins with exploring the standard Leninist pattern of local administrations linked to local ethnic majorities (see Aklaev 1992; Barfield 1994; Rudensky 1992). When regional economic disparities between the north-west and the south-east developed through government policies, this took on a distinct, though officially suppressed, ethnic character. When Communism suddenly lost legitimacy and living standards crashed, political and intellectual elites quickly tapped these suppressed critiques, constructing ethnonationalist histories complete with scapegoats. Strictly controlled media conjured up new "realities," with each crystallizing group portraying itself as the righteous victims of perfidious others. A deliberate policy of "ethnic cleansing" hardened the boundaries, as "Muslim" went from a religious preference to an ethnohistorical divide. Again, young men with little hope provided the shock troops (see Enloe 1998). However recently these oppositional identities were constructed, atrocities, many by deliberate policy, gave them an emotional immediacy that fueled further hostilities.

In Greece, we see the historical heritage of an earlier empire, the Ottoman, which used religion as its basis of administrative divisions, over a variegated cultural tapestry. With the breakup of the Ottoman empire, an earlier wave of nationalism spread out from cities into the more Slavic countryside, both offered and imposed by Church, government and school. Slavs became Greek. This case also illustrates the relevance of anthropological efforts to provide more accurate constructions of culture and history. Karakasidou's term "slavo-macedonians" in itself challenges Greek claims to the heritage of Philip and Alexander, so much so that one publisher dropped her book for fear of violence against their employees. At the time of this writing, Macedonia also illustrates the internal political differences among Serb and Albanian peoples, and the polarizing effect of calculated violence.

Liberia has a very different but equally complex history of mixed and shifting identities. A convoluted historical process installed former US slaves in government, who in typical colonial fashion imposed cultural and political divides on the natives. The Americo-Liberians were distinctive in terms of language, culture, religion and racial characteristics. They were identified with the state from its creation, and used their position to subjugate others. Ethnic and/or tribal identities were forged in the city, then transferred to the countryside and institutionalized in political districts that channeled access to resources, law and power. After the fall of the Americo-Liberians, the Doe government – though officially pluralist – played the ethnic game, entrenching oppositions. When politics turned into war, contenders adroitly used the regional ethnic terrain to their advantage. Ethnicity thus configured the war, just as war radically altered the meaning of ethnicity. But as Brown emphasizes to great effect, the application of ethnic labels, often erroneously, by those waging war must not be mistaken for self-perception primarily in ethnic terms, versus terms of clan, village, economic position, etc. When the fighting died down, so did the salience of ethnic labels. Here again, gender and even generation appear in twisted form – as Brown related at the conference which gave rise to this book – with boy soldiers who rape old women because "that's what men do."

Angola's seemingly endless war is structured by the ethnic and racial division (of "mulatto") imposed and played upon by the Portuguese. From the anti-colonial struggle into the Cold War superpower maneuverings, three military movements emerged, each associated with geographic regions with substantial economic autonomy and dominant ethnic identities. In each, elite elements of local ethnies developed their own identities and ideologies for war. Two interior-based movements challenged the ruling MPLA, which they saw as promoting a mixture of Portuguese and Umbanda as the Angolan national culture. The appeal of the more persistent rebels, UNITA, was both racist and anti-urban, against the stereotyped mulatto elite of the capital Luanda, thus generating more middle-class support for the MPLA. Problematic populations became "others" to be blamed, such as the Luandans returning from Zaire with French accents, while suspected criminals were brutally killed by dwellers of shanty towns unreachable by law.

Chad offers variations on the same themes. In the repeated cycle of region-based rebellions against the political center, local elites used local cultural themes in mobilizing local followers. However Reyna demonstrates, first, that these conflicts cannot, in any analytical sense, be seen as "tribal," as they did not involve existing tribes, or disputes between tribes, or use tribal institutions. Nor can they be understood as "ethnic," since they did not arise out of "primordial" loyalties, or privilege as a class some particular ethnic group(s). What Reyna sees involved here are factions seeking wealth and power through government, backed by various outside powers for their own geostrategic interests.

If cultural differences were the source of violent conflict, Somalia should have enjoyed peace, being entirely Islamic and ethnically more uniform than any other country in Africa. But if the violence cannot be ethnic, is it "tribal," or clan-based? Siyad outlawed tribal (clan) institutions, thus destroying their normal functioning and internal authority. Yet he continued to rely on men from clans closest to himself, thus intensifying rivalries. The region-based rivals who brought him down of course reflected the major clans of their areas. While a northern region seceded with little notice, the main game was in the south. There, urban elites intensified their predation on rural groups, relying especially on an African "racial" division at the occupational bottom of southern clans. In this situation, warlords rose by mobilizing marginal young men, set loose from clan constraints, whose guns earned them both food and power over their seniors. In a sense, this is a *negation* of clan-based conflict.

Papua New Guinea illustrates the non-correspondence of cultural differences and conflict from the opposite direction. Extreme diversity – 700 languages for three and a half million people – actually impedes development of regional movements.[13] Of two kinds of conflict discussed in relation to Papua New

Guinea, one actually does involve clan issues and institutions, most notably the sanction of violence for failure to live up to clan obligations, but with very new elements and inequalities mixed in. New economic disparities between individuals and regions result in efforts to extract wealth through compensation payments. Backing candidates for island elections entails new animosities and costs. (At our meetings, Strathern described a practice of enemies demanding opponents' *votes* as homicide compensation.) The other kind of violence is criminal, associated with "raskals," usually young men who operate outside clan institutions, but are often connected with businessmen or politicians. In both these and other kinds of violence, such as that involving assault sorcery or elections, women are often the victims.

Although the authors in this volume were given no checklist of topics to cover, generalizations still emerge. All the conflicts described in this volume have a strong spatial dimension involving some combination of geographic region and position in the rural–urban continuum. Nationalist and other identities, along with critical governmental decisions, emanate from central cities, especially capitals (see Herbst 1997: 376, 385) to meet counter-nationalisms and identifications that dwell in or emerge from the hinterlands. Location situates people in relation to ecology, resources, production regimes and markets, and places them in the hierarchy of controls that flow from cities to towns to villages and countryside. Where people live in most cases determines how they make a living, how well they live, and how they relate to whatever is being contested.

Interests are further specified by broad social divisions. Social class, especially middle-class status, shapes political allegiance in several cases. Other major categories are elites associated with the state, food producers (versus everyone else), and a "lumpen" element of those with little prospect of permanent employment who are easily recruited for violence.[14] Caste and "race" outline important categories with class correlations, at the same time bringing in major markers of social identity. More generally, throughout the cases there is a rough division between those benefiting and those suffering from the status quo, and this in part reflects people's connections to those in power. Political elites and those who seek to replace them typically attempt to create a coalition of supporters that crosses class lines.

Gender, generation, and age are primary identities which strongly shape one's lived experience, interests and perceptions. Armies and women's movements around the world are only the most visible expressions of these ordering principles. Educated women of rural Peru, raised a little only to be obstructed and repressed, gave strength to Sendero Luminoso. Elsewhere, women are special targets of violence, and polarized violence unsurprisingly will overwhelm agendas of women's rights (see Warren 2000: 228–229). More commonly, poor young men, powerless and sometimes disparaged by both women and elders, have been those more easily turned to violence. This has emerged as one of the great commonalities of recent conflicts – young men without prospects, isolated from regular politics, are regularly recruited and launched by the powerful when there is dirty work to be done (Abdullah 1998; Enloe 1998; Tambiah 1996: 17).

As Collier (2000: 94), an economist, points out, the success of a rebellion depends in part on the cost of attracting recruits, and uneducated, young men with no other income opportunities, come cheap.[15]

Religion and language are very well-suited to mass organization. Flexible and able to encompass people who differ in many other ways, both provide a basic aspect of personal identity which can hook up with structuring parameters of interests. Like ethnicity, a recognized common language is not a given, as exemplified by the ideological breakup of Serbo-Croatian into four putatively distinct languages in the 1990s (Hudson 2000). Religion, and sometimes language, can be an imposition of urban centers on hinterlands. Language, and sometimes religion, can be regional, and thus integral to ethnic identity. Ethnic identity itself typically crystallizes in urban interactions, and then in one way or another is applied to restructure the country (see Enloe 1980). This social and symbolic geography is only partially aligned with, and sometimes in opposition to, grounded social reality. This creates a big potential for all sorts of problems – if someone is looking to pick a fight. Where routine interaction with the land, the neighbors or the state has given rise to bounded clans or tribes, these confer an immediate political identity, and a ready-made though highly malleable basis for organization, as do no doubt a host of more modern local social structures which are less likely to receive anthropological notice.[16]

It is important not to reify any of the analytical categories used in this discussion. They morph into each other, as clan becomes tribe, as religion becomes ethnic identification becomes anyone in a region, etc. Endless combinations come and go, all with endless variations in their social construction by active political agents, each with distinctive implications for political action. It is also important to think about how these categories apply to individual persons. Ethnic identity, however important it may be in a given situation, is only one dimension. Individuals as described in this volume have multi-dimensional, compound social identities. A person is not just a member of a particular ethnicity, but an individual of specific gender, age, residence, occupation, religion, etc.

Each dimension of a person's position in society can affect their practical interests, the way they interpret the world around them, and the symbols they respond to, as well-described in relation to Afghanistan by Canfield (1986, 1988).[17] In many cases, what is interest and what is self-identity may become a purely academic distinction. Interest and identity are not separable, but fused, and any issue can take on identity overtones. When identity is involved, issues will always be about more than interests, since one's sense of self opens the door to passions beyond material concerns. A successful pitch for mobilization will play to existing material needs, and threaten tangible punishment for recalcitrance, but it is much more compelling if it becomes a matter of identity. The identities involved, however, are anything but simple and uniform.

A growing political force will not be constructed upon ethnicity or any other single factor. It will bring together an initially amorphous and shifting constellation of compound identities and interests. Far from resuscitating some ancient social collectivity with ancient animosities – however much those symbols may be invoked – the coalition which goes into political combat is itself *new*, and responding directly to issues of here and now. How can we refer to such a thing? If "ethnic" is misleading, is any other term more accurate? None that I know. Thus I would suggest coining a new term: "identerest." An *identerest group* is an ad hoc amalgamation of different kinds of people who, in a given historical and political situation, come together to pursue common material and symbolic gain. An *identerest conflict* is one in which at least one such group targets what it perceives as another such group said to pose a collective threat.

This term and idea calls attention to another fact repeatedly shown in this volume, that collective violence is a *process*, with a developmental history. Political entrepreneurs who seek to create a following will construct a message that appeals to the interests and identities of different kinds of people, and appeals to each person in different but congruent ways. Those who hear the call are likely to respond differently, according to how well the message plays to their total, compound sense of self and self-interest, and what potential for action is associated with who they are. Some will support from the sidelines, some will rush to the core, some will reject the message. As Warren emphasizes, we must not lose sight of counter-narratives, which may provide a crucial means for resistance, for communicating across conflicted boundaries, and for re-establishing peace.

The critical role of political leaders or "ethnic entrepreneurs" seeking to maximize their own wealth and power has been recognized in many studies of internal political violence and war (see, for example, Carnegie Commission 1997; David 1998: 87; Kahl 1998).[18] Even when social collisions are driven by mass demands and fears rather than instigated from the top down, leaders secure their elevated position through progressively more confrontational "ethnic outbidding" (Kaufman 1997: 176–177). This is a dialectical process. As Warren, Seligmann, and the "identerest" concept highlight, self-interest is culturally and situationally constructed. Political leaders catalyze, but are also products of, prevailing ideas about others (Lake and Rothchild 1997: 109–111). "The challenge for elites is therefore to define the interest of the collective in a way that coincides with their own power interests" (Gagnon 1997: 137). A key conclusion of the Carnegie Commission was that since political leaders are so critical in fomenting strife, "the methods and insights of psychiatry and of cognitive, clinical, and social psychology must be brought to bear" to understand that role (Hamburg *et al.* 1999: 7). But presumably such individuals have always been with us. If we want to understand how their psychology is translated into collective violence, it is most important to understand how their messages fit with local culture and conditions.

Forging an identerest coalition is phase one. Abstractly at least, three other phases can be identified. Phase two is creation of an internal "security dilemma." As realists try to adapt their theory to recent events, a key bridge has been to posit that in "weak states," the security dilemma at the heart of their theories of international "anarchy" exists within a state – that is, since the state cannot guarantee security, one group has good reason to fear another, and that is where conflict begins (Lake and Rothchild 1997; Posen 1993), a perspective which dovetails with influential earlier theories of ethnic conflict (Horowitz 1985: 179–180). But such fear is hardly automatic or universal (nor are ethnic groups equivalent to states (Brubaker and Laitin 1998: 12)), and promotion of such fear is one of the best documented roles for ethnic entrepreneurs (Kaufman 1997: 167–170). Still, where lived experience, current conditions and relentless propaganda lead people at the grass roots to conclude that old authorities will not protect them, and that others who have victimized them in the past may be doing it again soon, there will be a strong tendency to fall back into local networks – of kinship, clientage, neighborhood, faction, sect, etc. – and get ready to fight (Denich, in this volume; Simons 1997: 82–85).

Phase three is polarization. This social dynamic has been well studied (Gagnon 1997: 137–140; Lake and Rothchild 1997: 109–112), as has the process of psychological projection which demonizes others (Robben and Suarez Orozco 2000: 30). Some of the emotional power may be *because* new enemies were previously so close, activating themes of treachery and betrayal (Appadurai 1996: 154–155). The most critical and clear phase shift is to actual violence (Brubaker and Laitin 1998: 3–4). Nothing is a better indicator of carnage to come than the sudden appearance of small organized groups of violent men (Posen 1993: 33). Once one side begins to kill others because of some categorical identity, when atrocities stain a social distinction in blood, then that single dimension – be it ethnicity, religion or whatever – becomes the overriding identity. As Ignatieff (1997: 38) described in relation to Croatia, once the killing began, all the variations and nuances of local co-existence were swept away, leaving participants themselves to wonder at how, in such a short time, one became "only a Serb."

Violence hardens sides, undercuts middle ground, poisons reconciliation (Kaufmann 1996: 63, 1997: 268–273). Yet realists such as Kaufmann may overstate the universality and permanence of such effects, for even where much blood has been spilled, in places such as Sarajevo (Halpern and Kideckel 2000: 14) or the center of Sikh nationalism (Mahmood 1996: 2), and through the pages of this book and the daily newspaper, we find those who struggle against further violence and continuing polarization.

Summary and an application: Rwanda

The substantive conclusions of this introduction can be summarized as follows. An international system has required and supported the universality of territorially defined states. The end of the Cold War, after many years of Cold War aggravations and weapons proliferation, sharply curtailed external supports to central governments, and in some cases encouraged aggressive challengers. Global economic processes play an even more central role, including over a decade of increasing economic immiseration of populations linked to changing commodity markets, the rising importance of humanitarian aid capable of diversion or control, new forms of transnational trade that skirt established channels, and regulation of local government activities by international financial organizations. Together these forces have undermined the control of many governments.

States are bounded units with political centers, and government administration is socially and spatially biased. Within this total context, it is local political actors (not external forces) who create actual violent conflicts, seeking to alter who controls a government, who a government controls, and/or how a government rules. Thus internal violence is not just a matter of the weakness of government; rather the government itself is the prize that is being contested. Often, a parallel network of the political elite controls and uses the official institutions of a government for its own power and profit, and they may actually promote instability, war, and government dysfunctionality. Conflicts over control of government play out in three main ways: radically altering or replacing the social base of those who rule and the premises of government; tearing apart old states into new domains with different geographic centers of rule; or retracting the rule of a center away from peripheral areas.

Those who would rule develop a nationalist ideology for control of a territory and state, which justifies themselves and hopefully persuades others to join in their project, although its appeal will vary according to the characteristics and circumstances of different people in their arena. In recent years nationalist visions followed a creed of modernization and development which commanded respect only as long as it delivered the goods, or seemed likely to in the future – a creed which has lost its following in many places. Modernizing nationalism, like any other, was spatially and socially rigged to favor or harm different kinds of people, and it inevitably generated counter-ideologies, whose strength grew as development failed.

Spatially structured inequalities are often keyed into local populations with distinctive cultures, or ethnies. Local cultural identities are not fixed but socially and historically constructed. They are manipulated for political advantage, and yet local culture and identity are very important to the way people perceive themselves, their situations and their interests. Ideas about violence affect its usage, and its usage is itself an expressive, communicative act that redefines a conflict situation. Ideas of historical origins are also critical in providing lessons and symbols that can be used to define collective identity, and to variably construct understandings of current circumstances and options.

But cultural difference or ethnicity is only one of several important aspects of identity. Others include region and rural/urban location, political-economic position, religion, language, caste, race, tribe, clan, gender and age. Variable mixes of such features will produce variable responses to any calls for mobilization. As identity and interest are often fused, or can be made that way in conflict situations, I suggest that the groups and conflicts which involve them be called by the neologism "identerest," rather than labeling them all "ethnic." Identerest conflicts have four distinguishable opening phases, although these will overlap in practice: (1) formation of a core identerest group; (2) creation of mutual fears or a "security dilemma"; (3) polarization and projection of negative attributes; and (4) calculated violence. From that point, full scale war may ensue, although there is also the possibility of countervailing constructions halting the escalation.

To illustrate how this summary perspective can be applied, I will consider the Rwandan genocide, frequently cited as the epitome of ethnic violence, and a case not otherwise discussed in this volume. In April 1994, thousands of Hutu went out to deliberately slaughter Tutsi. Around 800,000 Tutsi died, in an orgy of violence that stunned the world. But the closer one looks, the less Rwanda seems to illustrate ancient loyalties and animosities, and the more it seems a product of the forces and processes discussed in this Introduction. This overview does not offer any new information. It is based on the thorough research already undertaken, by de Waal (1994), Gourevitch (1998), Hintjens (1999), Lemarchand (1994), Longman (1998), Mamdani (2001), McNulty (1999a), Percival and Homer-Dixon (1995), Prunier (1995, 1997), Taylor (1999), and Turton (1997b). (Direct citations will be provided only for the most focused discussions of particular topics, or specific points not frequently reported.) My goal here is to illustrate the feasibility and utility of approaching mass political violence as a layered problem, with contributing factors running from the most global to the most local, and from subsistence to symbol.

Factors external to Rwanda set the stage for genocide. Before the colonial era, autonomous political developments created a centralized state which saw the Tutsi superordinate over Hutu. German then Belgian administrations and the Catholic Church, however, rigidified this formerly fluid distinction, increasing Tutsi exploitation of Hutu, and fixed it as *racial*, with profound consequences. As the global wave of decolonization approached in the 1950s, radical tendencies within the ruling Tutsi minority prompted both colonial and Church administrators to shift support to Hutu, who overthrew the Tutsi elite in a social revolution in 1959–1961, with independence following in 1962. After that, the east/west divide of the Cold War had little impact on this non-strategic area, but the French moved into the vacuum left by departing Belgians to bolster their Francophone sphere in central Africa. In the 1970s, Rwanda became a showcase of externally supported modernization, development and democracy, the "little Switzerland of Africa." In 1986, however, plunging prices for its main export coffee began the downward slide. Lost income meant soaring international debt, leading in 1990 to an IMF/World Bank structural adjustment program that severely curtailed government spending on welfare and services. Famine in southern Rwanda and rising death rates without major government response aggravated social tensions.

At this point, regional politics moved center stage. In the violence that accompanied the revolution of 1959, hundreds of thousands of Tutsi fled to neighboring Uganda and elsewhere. In the 1980s, they helped overthrow a Ugandan government that was trying to push them back out. In 1990, the Ugandan regime they had helped to install turned against them, giving impetus to a military invasion of Rwanda in late 1990 by the Tutsi-dominated Rwanda Patriotic Front (RPF). Localized slaughters of Rwandan Tutsi began at this time. The RPF received support from Tutsi in diaspora in Africa, Europe and North

America. Meanwhile, the French government began a massive increase in military support for the governmental Rwandan Patriotic Army (RPA), which grew from 5,200 in 1990 to 35,000 in 1993. The French also trained an elite Presidential guard, which in turn trained many of the lead killers in the genocide (see McNulty 1999a). Regional tensions were vastly exacerbated in 1993 when Tutsi officers in the Burundi army led a coup, killing a popularly elected Hutu president, along with an estimated 50,000 Hutu. International pressure forced them back to their barracks, but without further punishment. Burundi developments precipitated fighting between Hutu and Tutsi in the neighboring North Kivu area of Zaire (Prunier 1997).

In this volatile, violent context, intense pressure by the UN, the Organization of African States, Rwanda's main financial donors, and NGOs combined with RPF military advances to force President Habyarimana to the bargaining table in Arusha. Plans for a coalition government were signed, with a cease-fire in August 1993. Continuing pressure kept Habyarimana to the timetable, with the transitional government due to be installed on 8 April 1994. A Structural Adjustment Program payment of $30 million was conditional on political progress, and set to expire on 23 April (Hintjens 1999: 258, 262). According to de Waal (1994: 4), up to this point Rwanda "was a model for a transition to democracy and the peaceful resolution of armed conflict," with international supervisors inattentive to the extremist factionalism that was building against Habyarimana within his own government. On 6 April, President Habyarimana and the President of Burundi were killed when a ground-launched missile destroyed their plane as it returned to Kigali. The genocide began immediately.

At this point, international response was notable for its absence. After debacles in Somalia and Angola, no one was willing to intervene. The humanitarian price was not *just* the death of 800,000 people in Rwanda. The genocide, and the RPF's subsequent defeat of the Rwandan army, set the stage for a drawn-out series of violent clashes throughout the Great Lakes region, involving Rwanda, the former Zaire, Burundi, Tanzania and Uganda, in what is being called "Africa's First World War." These distinct but interrelated conflicts are being driven by grabs for valuable resources, especially in the Democratic Republic of the Congo, by high government and military officials, using national armies crossing borders, creating or cooperating with local warlords and criminal networks (see "Panel of Experts" 2001; McNulty 1999b; Prunier 1997; Weinstein 2000).

Rwandan developments illustrate the centrality of the state. First, as a country, all of the regional influences just noted were shaped by international borders, as membranes affecting the flow of people, ideas and violence. Policies originating in the different capitals are key pieces in the regional mix. Of critical importance is Uganda, which in many ways shaped the RPF invasion (see Mamdani 2001). The Habyarimana government had kept those Rwandan Tutsi refugees from coming back across the border since 1973, claiming that densely populated Rwanda (see Percival and Homer-Dixon 1995) simply had no more land to support them (McNulty 1999a: 87). Within the geopolitical container of Rwanda's borders, administrative policies were decidedly skewed. Habyarimana's coup in 1973, following a time of economic stagnation, replaced regime domination by southern Hutu with northern Hutu, and power and benefits were redirected accordingly.

The genocide provides a glaring counter-example to the idea that state weakness is the cause of violence (Hintjens 1999; Longman 1998). Even in pre-colonial times, the Rwandan polity had been extraordinarily centralized and controlling. This had been fostered by external patrons during its golden years of development, with chains of command that reached down to individual households. The *interahamwe*, the local militia groups which did much of the killing in the genocide, began as state-controlled rural self-help groups which were internationally praised as essential to Rwanda's development. "[I]f anything, the state became so powerful and efficient that it crushed and overwhelmed Rwandan society completely" (Hintjens 1999: 245, 268). The actual genocide, all observers agree, was meticulously planned over a long period, with detailed procedures and death lists, and carried out through centralized directives.

What was the core issue? Control of government, with the ruling clique about to lose it to an internationally supervised, inclusive coalition. Although Rwanda had long had a reputation for government efficiency and comparatively little overt corruption, connection to the government was the most important key to success. "President Habyarimana held absolute power and ... political and economic advancement were largely dependent on proximity to the President and his coterie" (Taylor 1999: 108), i.e. to those of the northern clans that were his power base. Until the crash in coffee prices, however, prosperity was sufficiently general that many could do well, even Tutsi, if they did so quietly. From 1990, with war and structural adjustment, conditions led to the development of what Reno would call a shadow state. "[S]omething new was emerging ... a militarization of Rwandan state expenditure and growing corruption among the political elite." Humanitarian aid was diverted, drug trafficking and money laundering were linked to high places.

> The regime's determination to remain in power gradually led to the defensive creation of a "state within a state," centered on control of paramilitary youth organizations, which operated in tandem with the army and other state institutions at national, district and municipal levels. As the paid militias of young men grew, fewer and fewer Rwandan people benefited from the protection and patronage of the Rwandan state.
>
> (Hintjens 1999: 257, 261)

As opposition from the RPF, Rwandan Tutsi, poor and southern Hutu, and international agencies increased, this northern elite saw its association with the state imperiled. Habyarimana, forced to compromise and looking out for his own political future, became part of the threat. It was this shadow state that planned the genocide, an effort to crush any and all domestic opposition.

Nationalist visions have been key ideological tools throughout recent Rwandan history, and all revolve around "the Hamitic hypothesis" (Mamdani 2001; Taylor 1999). Positioning in relation to its various elements has been a clear indicator of political affiliation through the years. This tale of Rwandan history was fabricated by Church authorities, anthropologists and other scholars. Simply, it holds that Rwanda was originally inhabited by forest-dwelling pygmies, called Twa (who now make up less than 2 per cent of the population). Then came Bantu farmers, the Hutu, as part of a great migration from western Africa. Finally, cattle-raising Tutsi came from the north to conquer the lands. The Tutsi were alleged to be racially superior "Hamitic" people, with "Aryan blood," thus explaining their development of indigenous states, and justifying Euopean and Catholic reliance on them to rule.

An emergent Hutu elite with broad peasant support, who expelled Tutsi from positions of authority in 1959–1961, accepted the idea that the Tutsi were racially alien invaders, though of course rejecting their superiority. Their leaders stressed the coercion and exploitation experienced under recent Tutsi dominance, and cross-border attacks by refugee Tutsi reinforced fears and led to internal attacks by Hutu against Tutsi. The revolution itself was seen as the embodiment of democratic rule. It brought opportunity and dignity for the Hutu, and it became a central icon of Hutu nationalism. After the 1973 coup, Habyarimana, attentive to external patrons, redefined the distinction between Hutu and Tutsi from racial to ethnic, and officially advocated the latter's greater inclusion in national life as a minority in a plural society. Yet this vision excluded the hundreds of thousands of Tutsi who had fled Rwanda for Uganda, who were still seen as threats, and were refered to as "insects."

As Mamdani (2001) emphasizes, Habyarimana did not eliminate the Hutu/Tutsi divide in political institutions, thus creating conditions for its social reproduction. The idea of the Tutsi as an alien race threatening to the Hutu remained as a partially repressed text, with intellectual advocates ready to bring it forth when Habyarimana found it expedient. With the RPF invasion, radio and other media blasted this message in the most inflammatory ways, so that anyone who was not solidly with Hutu (i.e., the current government) was linked to invaders, who wished to overturn the effects of 1959, and reinstate Tutsi rule. The Tutsi with the RPF – and since they won the civil war, the current government – have claimed on the other hand that the Hamitic hypothesis is completely wrong, that Tutsi, Hutu and Twa have always been one people, and that is and should be the basis of the Rwandan nation. "RPF leaders complain that the ethnic labels Hutu and Tutsi are some sort of 'mistake'. They popularize this by harking back to the mythical origins of a unified Rwandese people unsullied by colonialism" (de Waal 1994: 3). Their highest value is "justice," rather than democracy, which is seen as limited while the majority Hutu tend to be inveterate tribalists.

Ethnicity in Rwanda well illustrates the three elements of the current scholarly synthesis on the subject. Certainly, major categories are historically and socially constructed. Although in Rwanda the Hamitic hypothesis is fiercely argued in all its details, the weight of evidence does indicate that Tutsi moved into this area from around the fifteenth century, from somewhere around the Horn. Most probably they arrived as pastoral migrants, not conquerors. While it may be justified to speak of them as having been an ethnie, the same cannot be said for Hutu, who originated out of culturally diversified and distinctive local populations. Tutsi and Hutu developed as political identities of super- and subordination. These categories were fluid and permeable, with Hutu becoming Tutsi and vice versa. Moreover, Tutsi and Hutu were vertically linked and mutually dependent, so violence was not between the two, but rather between geographically separated polities of Hutu and Tutsi combined. The colonial apparatus rigidified and racialized the two categories, and broke down local patron–client hierarchies so that two national strata emerged. Identity cards were issued to fix placements, a rule of patrilineal inheritance of racial status imposed, and in some cases categorically ambiguous persons were pigeon-holed on the basis of how many cattle they owned (though the widely reported "fact" that anyone with more then ten head of cattle was categorized Tutsi apparently was applied only in some instances, see Mamdani 2001: 98–99).

Still, in terms of language and life-style, Tutsi and Hutu became one. "[T]he predecessors of today's Hutu and Tutsi indeed created a single cultural community, the community of Kinyarwanda speakers, through centuries of cohabitation, intermarriage, and cultural exchange" (Mamdani 2001: 74). In the countryside the average Hutu and Tutsi are economically indistinguishable. Although Hutu and Tutsi are physically distinctive, there is such overlap and blending that the genocidal killers had to rely on identity cards and pointing fingers to know who to kill. Yet before the build-up to genocide, "there was little evidence of overt hostility from Bahutu towards their Batutsi neighbors and relatives" (Hintjens 1999: 248). During his fieldwork in 1983–85, Taylor (1999: 86, 108) found that "ethnicity seemed to be receding as a political issue," and that "Rwanda was more divided by class and region than by ethnicity."

The political manipulation of the historically constructed Hutu/Tutsi divide which led to genocide was transparent, and it was effective.

> [S]ixty years of colonial and Tutsi rule, and thirty-five years of Hutu supremacy [have] created distinct and mutually opposed Hutu and Tutsi identities, which for all the hesitations of social scientists, are identifiably "ethnic" … [I]t is impossible to interpret recent events without recourse to tribal labels, and they are the labels used by the people themselves. Above all, people kill each other because of them.
>
> (de Waal 1994: 3)

But we should hesitate to apply "ethnic" to two groups which are culturally identical, and the two categories certainly do not correspond to tribes, much less races. Powerful as they are as markers of identity, they are, as Mamdani (2001) cogently argues, essentially *political* identities, shaped by a long history of differential incorporation into a variety of stratified systems, carried along by malleable retellings of distinctive histories. To call what happened ethnic, tribal, or racial violence inevitably suggests "ancient hatreds" or irrational xenophobia, and obscures the fact that the genocide was, by all accounts, deliberate *political* violence. Yet "political violence" fails to convey the identity-linked passions involved. In my view, "identerest violence" is more accurate and adequate than either alternative.

That does not diminish the importance of culture. It is Mamdani who stresses that the Rwandan genocide, in contrast to that of the Nazis, was done by hand, in the neighborhood, face to face, with many thousands of Hutu actively participating. "[T]he main agents of the genocide were the ordinary peasants themselves" (Prunier 1995: 47). Discussion of this disturbing fact must begin by repeating that the killing was centrally planned and directed. Furthermore, all agree that there was a major element of coercion – those Hutu who refused to join in killing were often killed themselves – and great numbers of Hutu fled rather than being drawn into the carnage. But those who were initially forced to kill, and many who were not forced but volunteered, often became quite enthusiastic in their tasks. As one killer later put it: "I am ashamed, but what would you have done if you had been in my place? Either you took part in the massacre or else you were massacred yourself. So I took weapons *and I defended the members of my tribe against the Tutsi*" (Prunier 1995: 247). As this quotation indicates, one motivation was fear, fear created by media overflowing with Tutsi plots and atrocities. Some have also stressed that Rwandans have been long conditioned to obey orders – yet there were plenty who resisted authority.

Mamdani emphasizes two aspects of political ideology introduced by colonialists, and never purged from Rwandan culture. Unlike in other "ethnic" oppositions in Africa, Tutsi had been framed as both racially distinctive and foreign – much like the Europeans they once abetted. This contributed to a greater moral gulf, a justification for "victims to become killers." It helps explain why this violence, in stark contrast to other violence in Africa, was a deliberate effort to exterminate an entire category of people. Taylor (1999) emphasizes other aspects of Rwandan culture, connected to images of the world and the body, and flows and blockages. He points out that killing was far from simple slaughter. It regularly involved rape, torture, mutilation, degradation, all inscribing messages on Tutsi bodies in ways soon recognized as "thematic," even "formulaic." In his view, Hutu hate propaganda played into indigenous themes about "menacing 'blocking beings'" such as sorcerers, and applied itself to all Tutsi. Perpetrators of atrocity were then, in their minds, acting out "a massive ritual of purification" (Taylor 1999: 101). Furthermore, this ritual was highly gendered. Tutsi women were not spared, but specially targeted, even by their Hutu husbands. The politics of desire was long active in Rwanda, with many Hutu men finding Tutsi women especially attractive and seductive. As the hate built up, this came to be seen as a Tutsi strategy of racial pollution, that had to be eliminated at the root. Even beyond the Hutu/Tutsi divide, in modernizing sectors of Rwanda, women were making strides, even surpassing men. The killing of successful women, even Hutu women, was thus part of reasserting patrimony.

Despite the overwhelming importance of the Hutu/Tutsi divide – however one characterizes it – it is still a poor indicator of who killed who. It was not only Tutsi who were killed. Recall that there was a substantial Hutu opposition to the government, and the leaders of this opposition were among the first victims of the death lists. The shock troops were the organized militias, who had been trained for this purpose, and other military associated with those who killed Habyarimana – himself the head Hutu. When more arms were needed, rootless young men of the cities were enlisted, liquored up, and given the even more intoxicating power of life and death over those who had once been their "betters." Teachers, students, doctors, even the well-dressed were murdered. Killing methodically spread to the towns and country, following well-laid plans. But still, it was not simply Hutu against Tutsi. In the countryside, there were economic differences, "the people whose children had to walk barefoot to school killed the people who could buy shoes for theirs" (Prunier 1995: 250). Looting was often a motive. And it was especially Hutu from the north who excelled in killing, spreading the plague southward, often including southern Hutu politicians.

Lastly, the case of Rwanda illustrates the phases of identity-linked violence, although since this was a centralized plan, there was much temporal overlap (see Hintjens 1999: 262–267; McNulty 1999a: 93–95; Prunier 1995: 226–255; Taylor 1999: 6–26). The identerest coalition was led by elite members of northern clans, associated with government, the army and commerce. They were aided by intellectuals, whose rabid message was relentlessly disseminated by radio and other media. The call was to all Hutu, although those opposing the current clique were not welcome, and those not benefiting from it were not enthusiastic. It relied on disciplined militia, and poor people who saw an opportunity against the rich. Key to the success of this program was the creation of a "security dilemma," by repeatedly uncovered "proofs" that domestic Tutsi were conspiring with invaders from Uganda to reverse the 1959 revolution, and secure their position by exterminating as many Hutu as they could ("the Bahima conspiracy"). Polarization proceeded apace, with moderates killed by death squads (called "Network Zero"). Projection of fears was equally clear, with many Hutu accepting tales that the invading RPF were demonic cannibals. Finally, the violence, which had begun with the RPF invasion, was already so prevalent before the actual genocide began, that many Tutsi seemed passively resigned to their slaughter when it finally arrived (see Gourevitch 1998).

Prunier (1995: 228) asks "did the plotters actually think they could carry it off?" He and McNulty (1999a: 96) think they did, and they almost succeeded. But – even disregarding the manifest inhumanity – there is reason to question whether deciding to engage in the genocide of a major segment of the population, which was supported by a disciplined invading army that had been halted only by a negotiated cease-fire, in the face of international powers ready to apply isolating sanctions (if not actually intervene), can be called "rational." Was it more rational than trying to use the official and unofficial powers they still controlled to maneuver themselves into an acceptable, if diminished, position in the new system? I doubt a simple "yes" is possible. Rather, this may be a case of leaders believing in their own self-justifying propaganda, and caught up in the fears and hatreds that they themselves have created. If so, they would not be unusual. I argue elsewhere (Ferguson 1999: 407, 2001: 105–106), that it is one of the most depressing constants of war, that those who initiate killing believe in the moral correctness of what they do.

The Rwandan genocide shows the hollowness of an "ancient loyalties and animosities" approach. It illustrates the need to get beyond the label "ethnic conflict." That catch-all term is applied to situations where cultural difference is not critical or even present, and even in the most salient examples, such as Rwanda, it proves to be a misleading guide to the development of violence. We need to develop a more complex but more realistic understanding of how a system of identities is brought into and shapes violent struggle. To do that, we need a perspective that can encompass everything from global economic trends to local cultural symbols.

Implications of and for anthropology

As noted at the start of this introduction, anthropologists' close encounter with intra-state violence in the 1970s and 1980s challenged practitioners to find new forms of analysis, and ethically, to find new ways to politically respond to the suffering they observed. Analytically, the focus turned to systems of meaning and overlapping fields of power. Ethically, the main response was that anthropologists could bear witness, expose and write against terror that usually originated within the government/elite social matrix, and was directed downward against opponents (Robben and Suarez-Orozco 2000: 12; Sluka 2000b: 11–13, 30; Starn 1997: 236–237; Warren 2000: 229–231). Dealing with the politics of the Reagan and Thatcher era, the idea of working with people in power to lessen violence seemed a contradiction in terms. Similarly, as writers coming from the more traditional anthropology of war tried to grapple with the Cold War (Foster and Rubenstein 1986; Rubinstein and Foster 1988; Turner and Pitt 1989), I cautioned about directing our efforts to policy centers, which would use only what furthered already established goals. Rather, I argued, anthropologists *generally* should engage with protest politics – while seriously considering on an *individual* basis opportunities for input into policy (Ferguson 1988a, 1989: 154–159).

Times change. Many who were most committed to stopping superpower involvement in "proxy wars" are now calling for more aggressive involvement of various organizations – the US, NATO, the UN, NGOs – to prevent, stop or recover from local political violence. But understanding of the causes of such struggles is limited, and we are currently in a real conceptual dilemma as to how they will be approached. Realism – an extremely powerful current in policy circles – has formulated a new, state-centered paradigm for intra-state violence, as described in pieces throughout this Introduction. The problem is weak states, which cause ethnic groups to react to each other the way states do in international "anarchy," and the solution is to build up strong state centers. Some realists acknowledge this will be difficult to do while adhering to values of human rights (Ayoob 1998: 49; Zartman 1995b: 269–271) – more than difficult I would say, and how would it be done?

Others provide clear, if frightening, policy guidelines, such as Kaufmann (1996, 1997). His formula for intervening in and successfully resolving "ethnic civil wars" is to choose one side to support (on what grounds is not specified), draw a separation line between areas with different ethnic majorities, occupy the territory inside the separation line, and then "exchange populations." "Once the conquest is complete, all enemy ethnics in custody must be moved across the separation line. At the same time, all friendly ethnics who wish to immigrate from beyond that line – or more likely, are expelled by the opposing side – must be resettled" (1996: 95–97). Then there are even more frightening prospects and solutions being forcefully advocated: a "west against the rest" policy of fomenting divisions within rival "civilizations" (especially "Confucian" and Islamic) (Huntington 1993: 49); rapid and overwhelming use of military force against any localized threat (Van Creveld 1991: 198); or a bunker mentality of walling out the impending anarchy (Kaplan 1994).

It is well worth noting that of the contributors to this volume, the most explicit call for anthropologists to involve themselves in policy issues comes from an international relations theorist, Yale Ferguson. I agree with him (though not because of clan loyalty). Certainly, there will continue to be a great many situations around the world where anthropologists will be called on to write against the state oppression of local peoples, as Maybury-Lewis has encouraged us all to do. But it is also our responsibility to help develop new, alternative ways of seeing and dealing with the terrible violence so commonly breaking out between different groups over control and direction of a state. What can anthropologists contribute?

We can apply our understanding of culture and ethnicity in relation to conflict. It is common to read non-anthropologists speaking of these as fixed and bounded. Culture and ethnic divisions are inherently fluid – contested, selected, always an interpretation. They exist in versions and variations, like jazz, as Jean Jackson has suggested about culture. As Maybury-Lewis challenges us, anthropology can and should make it clear to students, other scholars, policy makers, and anyone else we can reach, that cultural differences and identities are not by nature exclusive, although they certainly can be made that way.

Our position must be nuanced. Static, divisive views of culture are used as weapons in some of the conflicts described in this book. But people who seek just redress for real grievances also appeal to local meanings and identities to mobilize support. Struggles for redress are inherently conflictive, and conflict encourages boundary formation. Some sort of us/them division is built into the process. But this can be done in different ways, with radically different consequences. Political and military mobilization can be much easier and more excitable when there is a clear-cut, personal enemy, a scapegoat. That is where ethnic entrepreneurs using ideas of primordial animosities come in – conjuring up demonic cultural others that need to be vanquished. That is where the real danger lies today, and where basic anthropological premises can be applied. We could actively promote the idea of a world community which respects not only human rights, but also cultural difference. Reaction to any claim of a self-identified people for international recognition or hearing could be linked explicitly to a commitment to respect cultural difference. One people's rights end where another people's nose begins.

The "identerest" concept could also be brought into policy consideration. Because of the disparate bases of support for identerest groups, alternative group formations may be possible. If one political faction seeks to mobilize experienced hardship and perceived disrespect by targeting a constructed enemy other, different leaders may be able to build a competing movement by bringing together a different constellation of identities in a more constructive, cooperative path toward redress. For outside powers, perhaps the most productive path to a peaceful world order may be to identify, encourage, and if need be to protect internal political movements which understand and address local needs and values in a non-violent way. (When the history of the Kosovo war is written, one of the sad lessons from it will be how little was done to support such domestic movements (Demjaha 2000: 33–34).) Alternatively, efforts to reconstruct a more civil society *after* collective violence could be more effective if shaped by better understanding of what kinds of people were in the hard core, and what kinds were drawn in later, and so might be more easily "peeled off."

We could also expand our role as "cross-cultural translators." Anthropologists do this already when they show how people involved in violence see the world around them. But typically, our readers have been other academics or college students. One can imagine another route, where two anthropologists working together seek to represent the views of opposing groups, so each can better understand the other's perceptions, emotions and fears. This would be more productive if informed by basic concepts of conflict resolution, as in Ury (1999) or Hopmann (n.d.). It could be done before violence occurs, preferably, or afterwards. Those who advocate separation as a solution for ethnic violence do so because they believe reconciliation after such bloodshed is impossible. But as Warren observes, the twentieth century demonstrates that "antagonists are rarely immutably at war with each other," however firmly that opposition is constructed at a given moment. South Africa, Guatemala and Argentina have created commissions to establish "truth and reconciliation" among those formerly at war (although these bodies also demonstrate the difficulties in reaching either goal) (Avruch and Vejarano 2001; Warren 2000: 232–233). Such bodies could in the future include anthropologists seeking to present opposed cultural interpretations in a way that might foster better mutual understanding.

Another fundamental concept of anthropology is holism, which in one sense means that societies should be approached as complex integrated systems. In the anthropology of war, however, there has been a longstanding divide between those who seek explanation in the material bases of social life, or in the symbols and understandings of local culture. In my view, both of these positions have now advanced, separately, to the point where real synthesis is possible – as I argue regarding Yanomami warfare (Ferguson 2001). Both the need for and the possibility of such synthesis are even more apparent in recent identity-linked violence. As the summary which began the previous section indicates, understanding such conflict entails looking at all aspects of a sociocultural system, from the most elevated values, to the most practical exigencies of making a living. This volume does not exhaust what needs to be brought in. It does not address the entire issue of ecology in relation to violence, which has achieved policy prominence under the title of "environmental security" (Homer-Dixon 1999; Homer-Dixon and Blitt 1998).[19] Also in the tradition of holism, understanding requires attention to factors operating from the most global to the most local levels, and the interactions between them.

Anthropological holism can offer an alternative to simple and inaccurate mono-causal explanations, situating the reality of communal violence along these two dimensions of symbol to subsistence and local to global. Developing a framework of interrelated, important factors, such as those outlined in this Introduction, and applying it to any given case would be laborious. But it would, I believe, offer a clearer, more accurate understanding of how violent conflict actually comes about, as illustrated by the Rwandan horror. It seems more practically illuminating for real situations than statistical approaches seeking to identify common denominators of violence. And for its complex, multi-factorial nature, it offers more levers and pathways to derail locomotives of destruction.

Anthropology can join in transdisciplinary study and reconceptualization of "the state," about which our own and others' theory is much less sophisticated than it is on ethnicity. The lessons from political science about reifying the state, as emphasized by Y. Ferguson, fit well with the cases presented here, which highlight the extreme variation in both the institutional systems and national control of states. However, focus on "the state" is still in order, since it is control of governments-within-borders that is usually the objective of contestants in violent struggles, and the concept of "shadow state" offers new ways to approach the issue. As previously noted, the realist prescription for recent turmoil is to build up central authority. But it is primarily the more authoritarian governments of the former USSR that have experienced the greatest internal violence in recent years (Aklaev n.d.; Motyl 1997), and it has been the heavy handed policy of Indian governments which has generated the protracted rebellion in Kashmir (Ganguly 1997: 230).[20]

As noted at the start of this introduction, anthropologists have first handknowledge of what suffering under a dominating government can bring. We need to make that point, loud and clear, in relation to the future of "weak" or "collapsing" states. The report of the Carnegie Commission on Preventing Deadly Conflict concludes (1997: chapter 4) that ultimately "structural prevention" requires sustainable development, respect for human rights, non-violent dispute resolution, real democracy, and social justice (see also Brown and de Jonge Oudraat 1997). This is what anthropological and other peace researchers refer to as "positive peace," and the conditions which Carnegie identifies as contributing to deadly conflict are "structural violence" (Sponsel 1994). If history is any guide, structural violence will not be diminished by hasty external support for central governments.

Anthropologists could join those already questioning the premise that "the state" is the fundamental, necessary unit for local peace and the international order (David 1998: 95; Holsti 1996: 203). The universal rule of states is a recent wrinkle on this planet. States and non-state political systems have been intimately connected since the beginning of European expansion, and indeed since the beginning of states (Ferguson and Whitehead 2000a; Wolf 1982). Not only can there be co-existence and cooperation between different kinds of polities, but given the terrible costs associated with the rule of and fights over some postcolonial governments, we should at least consider the possibility that in some places, returning governance to non-centralized, locally grounded and autonomously developed political structures might work better. One point that merits particular consideration is the pernicious effects of territorial boundaries. This is one iron linkage between the current international system, the state, nationalism and many types of communal violence. If globalism is transcending state boundaries in many ways, they are still fundamental constitutive elements of processes of intra-state violence. Greater recognition of authority based on allegiances of *people*, rather than territorial control – as was the case through much of humankind's past[21] – might be one step away from violence, and fully consistent with the increasing horizontal networks of globalism.

Buzan (1998: 218–219) has considered this "radical" stance, of possibly moving beyond the "transplanted European state system," and rejects it. "[T]he radicals have no obvious template. They can try to look back or try to look forward, but the view is seriously hazy in both directions. It is far from clear how useful it is to dig in the arcadian mine of the social and political constructions that existed before the European imposition." Well then – look at the present. For decades – and even more so now – "failed states" have been respected in international fora without any ability to deliver to their people any of the services and securities associated with government. The international community's exclusive focus on state governments prohibits establishing moderating relationships with other political entities or sub-state peoples, and may actually criminalize them. It imposes major limitations for approaching political violence as a regional problem (see Herbst 1997). At the same time, the world today is full of political structures which have a "special status," already outside the narrow framework of what a state should be. Puerto Rico, the Free Associated State (as it is titled in Spanish) has been one for more than half a century (see Ferguson 1988b); Kosovo has just become another. And European countries, of course, are sloughing off one vital characteristic of statehood after another.

It is not a question of reverting to the political structures of an earlier epoch – if this were even possible. As regards the future, there are ideas already out there which seem more clear than the idea of somehow strengthening states without violating human rights, as seen in Kaldor's (1999) or Falk's (1995, 2000) calls for global institutions to check violence and abuse, or Gottlieb's (1993) "states plus nations" proposal to recognize new political forms, varieties of boundaries, and layers of sovereignty. International relations theorist Wendt (1999: 371–377) invokes cultural anthropology when he shows how the international system is based on a set of common assumptions. To ignore that culture is to support the status quo, when what is called for now – he says – is a "design orientation."

One can take this too far. Anthropology teaches us that new political forms are not likely to follow any preconceived plan – they will evolve in practice, as they have throughout human history. Yet planning can make a real difference to the directions taken, if it goes with the flow. "Real realism" would try to envision humane possibilities by looking at the *realities* of global developments, state systems, nationalist agendas, and ethnic and other identity-linked conflicts, to identify multiple points where calculated action can encourage peaceful process. As Villalon (1998: 6–7) suggests regarding contemporary Africa, we might think of our time in terms of the evolutionary theory of punctuated equilibria, where what emerges over the next few years will structure political process for decades to come. Thus it is especially important now to gain some perspective, and to try to keep an open mind.

True collapse is unlikely, as Tainter points out. Channels of communication and transportation will be maintained somehow at some level, and functions such as the issue of passports will still be performed somewhere, because people need these things. Accommodations will be reached. *People* will build needed structures, if allowed to. But all that can be done without a capital exercising real control over its claimed territory. If in the future, developed industrial nations – themselves transforming into new kinds and levels of structures – are required to deal with a welter of different types of polities, that is no reason to panic. We have been there before.

Notes

1 Most of these cases were discussed at a session of the 1993 Meetings of the American Anthropological Society in Washington, DC. They were elaborated, compared, and discussed at a workshop titled "The State Under Siege" in April 1994 – during the very days of the slaughter in Rwanda – at the New York Academy of Sciences and the Research Institute for the Study of Man. The workshop was funded by the Wenner-Gren Foundation. John Schoeberlein-Engel presented a paper on Tajikistan at both gatherings, which could not be included here due to his other commitments. Anastasia Karakasidou was not in the AAA session, but joined us in New York. A version of this Introduction was presented and discussed in February 1999 at a meeting of the Working Group on Political Violence, War, and Peace in the Contemporary World, at the Center for Global Change and Governance at Rutgers-Newark. I wish to thank everyone involved in all those sessions for ideas that have been incorporated into this Introduction, and also give special thanks to Anna Skinner, my research assistant during the penultimate revision.
2 For instance, in his survey of recent Russian literature, Aklaev (n.d.) describes three different types of classification of ethnic conflict, with a total of eighteen categories between them.
3 The reason for this collapse will be debated by generations of scholars. To my knowledge, the only anthropological theory on it has been offered by Marvin Harris (1992), who attributes it to a political economy that impeded and degraded the performance of its own infrastructure. Or as Marx might have put it in terms of his own theory of

revolution, the system fell because relations of production had become fetters on the means of production.

4 It should be noted that Cooper (1999) concludes that it is not the presence of weapons itself that leads to violence. In calm situations, they can be present without being used. Cooper also discusses some of the ethical and policy quandaries in arms supply, such as cases where one side is clearly being victimized by better-armed opponents.

5 An interesting turn in recent research has been that economists, who long ago abandoned the study of war (as opposed to studying military spending) (Goodwin n.d.), are now at the cutting edge of explaining how current trends in globalization are responsible for new wars and instability within less-developed countries (e.g. Berdal and Malone 2000; Collier 2000; Duffield 2000). Contrary to current ideas that environmental scarcities are generating conflict (Homer-Dixon 1999; Homer Dixon and Blitt 1998), in this view it is precisely an *abundance* of internationally sought resources that fuels protracted violence (de Soysa 2000). These arguments dovetail closely with the concept of a "shadow state," as described later in this Introduction.

6 For instance, an ongoing research project, requested from and funded by the highest US governmental levels, finds closure to outside trade to be one of the best predictors of state failure, thus invalidating dependency analyses. "Trade openness was measured as the total value of imports plus exports as a percentage of a country's GDP" (Gurr *et al.* n.d.: 8, 26). Twenty years ago, a low value of external trade might indeed have reflected a government's import-substitution and other economic policies, but by the late 1980s it was far more likely a result of crashing export markets and international supervision and restriction of government spending. Other more internal explanatory variables in this study – concerning "partial democracies" and the significance of massive urbanization, seem similarly misunderstood.

7 One can actually pinpoint the shift away from "ancient hatreds" to "manipulative leaders" in the Clinton administration. From the *New York Times*: "Balkan Ghosts" (editorial), 7 March 1999, WK14; "Historians Note Flaws in President's Speech," 26 March 1999, A12; "Clinton Blames Milosevic, Not Fate, for Bloodshed," 14 May 1999, A12; "Coming to Terms With Kosovo's 'Old' Hatreds" (column), 12 June 1999, A14.

8 Many anthropologists are striving to provide relevant findings about race to their classes and other publics. Tightly analogous points could be made about ethnies, such as: there is no "pure" ethnie, within-ethnie variation exceeds between-ethnie variation, ethnic boundaries perceived to be intrinsic are historically constructed and malleable, ethnies can be redefined at higher and lower levels of inclusiveness, and the on-the-ground reality of ethnic difference is usually some form of gradient or cline rather than a sharp break.

9 Culturalist accounts "tend to explain too much and to overpredict violence. They cannot explain why violence occurs only at particular times and places, and why, even at such times and places, only some persons participate in it. Cultural contextualizations of ethnic violence, however vivid, are not themselves explanations of it" (Brubaker and Laitin 1998: 17).

10 This should not be understood as exempting our own culture. Certainly, air drops of napalm are as much of a cultural product, and arguably as savage, as deliberate torture and mutilation. Indeed, one security scholar has concluded that the "American way of war," once initiated, is *more* ruthless and destructive than that of even other Western states (Mead 1999/2000).

11 Just as "tribal" has very different connotations in Africa and North America, "ethnic conflict" has different meanings in different places. The "ethnic conflict" that people currently worry about is mainly of the Old World. In Latin America, struggles involving ethnicity typically involve non-violent resistance of indigenous peoples to

Violent conflict and control of the state 45

the oppressive hegemony of state structures (Guidieri *et al.* 1988; Urban and Sherzer 1991; Warren 1993a).
12 A good example of this is Vanhanen (1999: 187–189), who writes that "ethnic groups may be national, tribal, racial, religious, linguistic, cultural, or communal groups" and castes. The crucial characteristic of all these, he claims, is that "members are genetically more closely related to each other than to the members of other groups," thus they all "can be perceived as extended kin groups." All group conflict is thus a culturally universal expression of pan-human strategy to maximize reproductive success.
13 Collier and Hoeffler (1998) find that very high ethnic diversity is correlated with a low likelihood of conflict between groups. The highest likelihood is when a population is sorted into just two polarized groups.
14 It is often observed that class analysis has been left behind by the "ethnic resurgence." Interesting observations on this are offered by Coughlan and Samarasinghe (1991). They note two alternative views of ethnicity and economics: a straightforward Marxist approach which focuses on class, development, and markets; and a resource competition model which looks to differential political incorporation and the role of the state. They conclude that either version of rational choice theory, but especially the former, cannot stand against the manifest importance of culture, religion, and manipulated ideologies. However, in many cases it is still very clear that ethnic conflict is related in more complex ways to some form of ethnic stratification or economic discrimination. Aklaev's (n.d.: 15) review of recent Russian literature also shows that while ethnic divisions, fears, and symbols strongly affect recent conflicts, basic economic grievances underlying them show up repeatedly in survey research.
15 Because of a recent spate of popular biologistic writings about an evolved young male syndrome of using violence to enhance life and reproductive chances (e.g., Wilson and Daly 1985), it should be noted that all these are cases where social processes have created large numbers of socially superfluous young men, something which has no analogue in any theorists' rendering of the evolutionary environments of the human species. For that and other reasons (Ferguson 2001: 108–109; work in progress), this should not be mistaken as any kind of "evolved response."
16 Local social structures (networks, etc.) which can contribute to political mobilization have received a great deal of attention in "new social movement" theory, but these have had little investigation with regard to the kinds of violent struggle described here (Jenkins and Schock 1992: 179; McAdam *et al.* 1996: 21–26). Although there is clearly room for cross-disciplinary communication, that large sociological literature is oriented toward more diffuse, largely non-violent and non-authoritarian movements, built from the ground up in the most developed societies.
17 This does not imply, however, the high degree of individuation associated with the multiple roles of people in modern societies, where each person may have a unique mix of significant social identities (see Simons 1997). In less complex societies, identities may be compound but still primarily collective – e.g., all the mature women of "x" clan of "y" tribe of "z" region.
18 The primary role of leaders' self-interest is one of the features that may seem to distinguish new forms of violence from traditional wars, which were supposedly waged in the interests of a state. But military historians have shown that a more refined sense of political self-interest has been key in shaping decisions for war by statesmen throughout history (Black 1998b).
19 Joseph Tainter and I organized a conference on "Environmental Dimensions of Cultural Conflicts" (Ferguson 1995b), the results of which will hopefully appear in a future volume.

20 Even fully within the realist paradigm, caution should be taken from recent experience in Africa. The Clinton administration provided increased military support to seemingly stable and responsible states, and several of these have used their militaries in war with their neighbors. "[T]wo years later, Clinton's trip can be seen not as a series of visits with a new generation of forward-looking African leaders but rather as stops in the governing capitals of Africa's new warmongers" (Weinstein 2000: 10). Also, Collier and Hoeffler (n.d.) present a preliminary analysis of data which indicate government military expenditures prompted by internal threats led to "neighborhood arms races" among low income countries, becoming "a regional public bad." "[A]n initial exogenous increase in military expenditure by one country is more than doubled in both the originating country and its neighbors," without having a statistically measurable impact on the risk of internal violent conflict in either. It seems a very real possibility that a policy to stabilize weak states by rebuilding and professionalizing their military would contribute significantly to a resurgence of "old style" inter-state wars.

21 It might be disputed that diminishing the importance of territorial boundaries goes against "human nature." Sociobiology's founder E.O. Wilson (1999: 185), for instance, claims that "*territorial expansion and defense* by tribes and their modern equivalents the nation states is a cultural universal" (emphasis in original). Quite typically, this claim is made without any effort here or elsewhere to provide empirical substantiation. In fact, this is an excellent example of sociobiology's penchant for projecting contemporary patterns on to human nature. In the anthropology of war, it is rather unusual to find any indication of territorial expansion or defense as an important factor in war. This is not hard to discover. Van Creveld (1991: 152) is quite aware of it. Concern with territorial borders, though not unknown in simpler societies, is more characteristic of state-level societies, and not even all of them (Ferguson 1999: 392–393, 417–418).

References

Abdullah, Ibrahim (1998) "Bush Path to Destruction: The Origin and Character of the Revolutionary United Front/Sierra Leone." *The Journal of Modern African Studies* 36: 203–235.

Abrams, Philip (1988) "Note on the Difficulty of Studying the State." *Journal of Historical Sociology* 1: 58–89.

Acharya, Amitav (1998) "Beyond Anarchy: Third World Instability and International Order after the Cold War." In *International Relations Theory and the Third World*, Stephanie G. Neuman (ed.), pp. 159–211. New York: St. Martin's Press.

Aklaev, Airat (1992) "War and Social Stress and their Effects on the Nationalities in the U.S.S.R." In Giorgio Ausenda (ed.), *Effects of War on Society*. Republic of San Marino: Center for Interdisciplinary Research on Social Stress, pp. 194–210.

—— (n.d.) "Causes and Prevention of Ethnic Conflict: An Overview of Post-Soviet Russian-Language Literature." Report prepared for the Carnegie Commission on Preventing Deadly Conflict, Carnegie Corporation of New York. http://www.ccpdc.org/pubs.aklaev/4.htm

Alonso, Ana Maria (1994) "The Politics of Space, Time and Substance: State Formation, Nationalism, and Ethnicity." *Annual Review of Anthropology* 23: 379–405.

Anderson, Benedict (1991) *Imagined Communities*. London: Verso.

Anderson, Mary B. (1999) *Do No Harm: How Aid Can Support Peace – Or War*. Boulder: Lynne Rienner.

Appadurai, Arjun (1996) *Modernity at Large: Cultural Dimensions of Globalization*. Minneapolis: University of Minnesota.

Ausenda, Giorgio (1997) "Postscript: Current Issues in the Study of Ethnicity, Ethnic Conflict and Humanitarian Intervention, and Questions for Future Research." In David Turton (ed.), *War and Ethnicity: Global Connections and Local Violence*. Republic of San Marino: Center for Interdisciplinary Research on Social Stress/University of Rochester Press, pp. 217–251.

Avruch, Kevin and Beatriz Vejarano (2001) "Truth and Reconciliation Commissions: A Review Essay and Annotated Bibliography." *Social Justice: Anthropology, Peace, and Human Rights* 2: 47–108.

Ayoob, Mohammed (1995) *The Third World Security Predicament: State Making, Regional Conflict, and the International System*. Boulder: Lynne Rienner.

—— (1998) "Subaltern Realism: International Relations Theory Meets the Third World." In Stephanie G. Neuman (ed.), *International Relations Theory and the Third World*. New York: St. Martin's Press, pp. 31–54.

Bailey, F.G. (1969) *Stratagems and Spoils: A Social Anthropology of Politics*. New York: Basil Blackwell.

Barfield, Thomas (1994) "Prospects for Plural Societies in Central Asia." *Cultural Survival* Summer/Fall: 48–51.

Bell-Fialkoff, Andrew (1996) *Ethnic Cleansing*. New York: St. Martins Press.

Berdal, Mats and David M. Malone (eds) (2000) *Greed and Grievance: Economic Agendas in Civil Wars*. Boulder: Lynne Rienner.

Black, Jeremy (1998a) "Why Wars Happen." *History Review* 31. http://web5.infotrac-college.com/wadsworth

—— (1998b) *Why Wars Happen*. New York: New York University Press.

Blick, Jeffrey (1988) "Genocidal Warfare in Tribal Societies as a Result of European-Induced Culture Conflict." *Man* 23: 654–670.

Boswell, Terry and William Dixon (1990) "Dependency and Rebellion: A Cross-National Analysis." *American Sociological Review* 55: 450–459.

Boutros-Ghali, Boutros (1993) "Don't Make the U.N.'s Hard Job Harder." *The New York Times*, 20 August, A29.

Bowen, John R. (1996) "The Myth of Global Ethnic Conflict." *Journal of Democracy* 7(4): 3–14.

Brown, Michael E. (1997) "The Causes of Internal Conflict." In Michael E. Brown, Owen R. Cote, Jr., Sean M. Lynn-Jones and Steven Miller (eds), *Nationalism and Ethnic Conflict*. Cambridge, MA: MIT Press, pp. 3–25.

Brown, Michael E. and Chantal de Jonge Oudraat (1997) "Internal Conflict and International Action: An Overview." In Michael E. Brown, Owen R. Cote, Jr., Sean M. Lynn-Jones and Steven Miller (eds), *Nationalism and Ethnic Conflict*. Cambridge, MA: MIT Press, pp. 235–264.

Brown, Michael F. and Eduardo Fernandez (1991) *War of Shadows: The Struggle for Utopia in the Peruvian Amazon*. Berkeley: University of California Press.

Brubaker, Roger and David D. Laitin (1998) "Ethnic and Nationalist Violence." *Annual Review of Sociology* 24: 423–453. http://web5.infotrac-college.com/wadsworth

Buzan, Barry (1991) *People, States and Fear: An Agenda for International Security Studies in the Post-Cold War Era*, second edition. Boulder: Lynne Rienner.

—— (1998) "Conclusions: System versus Units in Theorizing about the Third World." In Stephanie G. Neuman (ed.), *International Relations Theory and the Third World*. New York: St. Martin's Press, pp. 213–234.

Byman, Daniel and Stephen Van Evera (1998) "Why They Fight: Hypotheses on the Causes of Contemporary Deadly Conflict." *Security Studies* 7: 1–50.

Canfield, Robert L. (1986) "Ethnic, Regional, and Sectarian Alignments in Afghanistan." In A. Banuazizi and M. Weiner (eds), *The State, Religion, and Ethnic Politics: Afghanistan, Iran, and Pakistan.* Syracuse: Syracuse University Press, pp. 75–103.

—— (1988) "Afghanistan's Social Identities in Crisis." In J.-P. Digard (ed.), *Le Fait Ethnique en Iran et en Afghanistan.* Paris: Editions du CNRS, pp. 185–199.

Carmack, Robert M. (ed.) (1988) *Harvest of Violence: The Maya Indians and the Guatemalan Crisis.* Norman: University of Oklahoma Press.

Carnegie Commission on Preventing Deadly Violence (1997) *Preventing Deadly Conflict.* New York: Carnegie Corporation. http://www.ccpdc.org/pubs

Carneiro, Robert (1970) "A Theory of the Origin of the State." *Science* 169: 733–738.

Chase-Dunn, Christopher and Thomas Hall (1993) "Comparing World-Systems: Concepts and Working Hypotheses." *Social Forces* 71: 851–886.

Cohen, Ronald (1978) "Ethnicity: Problem and Focus in Anthropology." *Annual Review of Anthropology* 7: 379–403.

Collier, Paul (2000) "Doing Well out of War: An Economic Perspective." In Mats Berdal and David M. Malone (eds), *Greed and Grievance: Economic Agendas in Civil Wars.* Boulder: Lynne Rienner, pp. 91–111.

Collier, Paul and Anke Hoeffler (1998) "On Economic Causes of Civil War." *Oxford Economic Papers* 50: 563–574. http://web5.infotrac-college.com/wadsworth

—— (n.d.) "Regional Military Spillovers." Paper presented at the Center for Global Change and Governance, Rutgers University, Newark, April 2001.

Comaroff, John L. (1995) "Ethnicity, Nationalism and the Politics of Difference in an Age of Revolution." In John L. Comaroff and Paul C. Stern (eds), *Perspectives on Nationalism and War.* Luxembourg: Gordon & Breach, pp. 243–276.

Comaroff, John L. and Jean Comaroff (eds) (1999) *Civil Society and the Political Imagination in Africa.* Chicago: University of Chicago Press.

Comaroff, John L. and Paul C. Stern (eds) (1995) *Perspectives on Nationalism and War.* Luxembourg: Gordon & Breach.

Cooper, Neil (1999) "The Arms Trade and Militarized Actors in Internal Conflict." In Paul B. Rich (ed.), *Warlords in International Relations.* New York: St. Martin's Press, pp. 17–37.

Coughlan, Reed and S.W.R. de A. Samarasinghe (1991) "Introduction – Economic Dimensions of Ethnic Conflict: Theory and Evidence." In S.W.R. de A. Samarasinghe and Reed Coughlan (eds), *Economic Dimensions of Ethnic Conflict.* New York: St. Martin's Press, pp. 1–15.

Crossette, Barbara (2001) "Effort by U.N. to Cut Traffic in Arms Meets a U.S. Rebuff." *The New York Times* 10 July, A8.

Cultural Survival Quarterly (1994) "Ethnic Conflict: The New World Order?" Summer/Fall issue.

Daniel, E. Valentine (1996) *Charred Lullabies: Chapters in an Anthropography of Violence.* Princeton: Princeton University Press.

Das, Veena (ed.) (1990) *Mirrors of Violence: Communities, Riots and Survivors in South Asia.* New York: Oxford University press.

David, Steven R. (1998) "The Primacy of Internal War." In Stephanie G. Newman (ed.), *International Relations Theory and the Third World.* New York: St. Martin's Press, pp. 77–101.

Demjaha, Agon (2000) "The Kosovo Conflict: A Perspective from Inside." In Albrecht Schnabel and Ramesh Thakur (eds), *Kosovo and the Challenge of Humanitarian Intervention: Selective Indignation, Collective Action, and International Citizenship.* New York: The United Nations University Press, pp. 44–63.

de Soysa, Indra (2000) "The Resource Curse: Are Civil Wars Driven by Rapacity or Paucity?" In Mats Berdal and David M. Malone (eds), *Greed and Grievance: Economic Agendas in Civil Wars*. Boulder: Lynne Rienner, pp. 113–135.

de Waal, Alex (1994) "The Genocidal State: Hutu Extremism and the Origins of the 'Final Solution' in Rwanda." *The Times Literary Supplement* 1 July, 3–4.

de Waal, Alex and Rakiya Omaar (1993) "Somalia: Adding 'Humanitarian Intervention' to the U.S. Arsenal." *Covert Action* 44: 4–11, 53–54.

Duffield, Mark (2000) "Globalization, Transborder Trade, and War Economies." In Mats Berdal and David M. Malone (ed.), *Greed and Grievance: Economic Agendas in Civil Wars*. Boulder: Lynne Rienner, pp. 69–89.

Enloe, Cynthia (1980) *Ethnic Soldiers: State Security in Divided Societies*. Athens: University of Georgia Press.

—— (1989) *Bananas, Beaches, and Bases: Making Feminist Sense of International Politics*. London: Pandora.

—— (1998) "All the Men Are in the Militias, All the Women Are Victims: The Politics of Masculinity and Femininity in Nationalist Wars." In Lois Ann Lorentzen and Jennifer Turpin (eds), *The Women and War Reader*. New York: New York University Press, pp. 50–62.

Eriksen, Thomas Hylland (1993) *Ethnicity and Nationalism: Anthropological Perspectives*. Boulder: Pluto Press.

Estrade, Bernard (1998) "Fragmenting Indonesia: A Nation's Survival in Doubt." *World Policy Journal* 15: 78–85. http://web5.infotrac-college.com/wadsworth

Evans, Peter B., Dietrich Rueschemeyer and Theda Skocpol (eds) (1986) *Bringing the State Back In*. Cambridge: Cambridge University Press.

Falk, Richard A. (1995) *On Humane Governance: Toward a New Global Politics*. Philadelphia: Pennsylvania State Press.

—— (2000) *Human Rights Horizons: The Pursuit of Justice in a Globalizing World*. New York: Routledge.

Feldman, Allen (1991) *Formations of Violence: The Narrative of the Body and Political Terror in Northern Ireland*. Chicago: University of Chicago Press.

Ferguson, R. Brian (ed.) (1984) *Warfare, Culture, and Environment*. Orlando: Academic Press.

—— (1988a) "How Can Anthropologists Promote Peace?" *Anthropology Today* 4(3): 1–3.

—— (1988b) *Class Transformations in Puerto Rico*. Doctoral dissertation, Columbia University, Department of Anthropology.

—— (1989) "Anthropology and War: Theory, Politics, Ethics." In David Pitt and Paul Turner (eds), *The Anthropology of War and Peace: Perspectives on the Nuclear Age*. South Hadley, MA: Bergin and Garvey, pp. 141–159.

—— (1990) "Blood of the Leviathan: Western Contact and Warfare in Amazonia." *American Ethnologist* 17: 237–257.

—— (1995a) *Yanomami Warfare: A Political History*. Santa Fe: School of American Research Press.

—— (1995b) "(Mis)Understanding Resource Scarcity and Cultural Difference in Contemporary Conflicts." *Anthropology Newsletter* November: 37.

—— (1997) "Tribe, Tribal Organization." In Thomas Barfield (ed.), *Blackwell Dictionary of Anthropology*. Oxford: Blackwell, pp. 475–476.

—— (1999) "A Paradigm for the Study of War and Society." In Kurt Raaflaub and Nathan Rosenstein (eds), *War and Society in the Ancient and Medieval Worlds*. Cambridge: Center for Hellenic Studies and Harvard University Press, pp. 409–458.

—— (2001) "Materialist, Cultural, and Biological Theories on Why Yanomami Make War." *Anthropological Theory* 1: 99–116.

Ferguson, R. Brian and Neil L. Whitehead (eds) (2000a) *War in the Tribal Zone: Expanding States and Indigenous Warfare*, second printing, Santa Fe: School of American Research Press.

—— (2000b) "Preface to the Second Printing." In R. Brian Ferguson and Neil L. Whitehead (eds), *War in the Tribal Zone: Expanding States and Indigenous Warfare*, second printing. Santa Fe: School of American Research Press, pp. xi–xxxv.

Ferguson, Yale H. and Richard W. Mansbach (1991) "Between Celebration and Despair: Constructive Suggestions for Future International Theory." *International Studies Quarterly* 35: 363–386.

Fisher, William (1997) "Doing Good? The Politics and Anti-Politics of NGO Practices." *Annual Review of Anthropology* 26: 439–464.

Foster, Mary LeCron and Robert Rubenstein (ed.) (1986) *Peace and War: Cross-Cultural Perspectives*. New Brunswick: Transaction.

Fried, Morton (1967) *The Evolution of Political Society: An Essay in Political Anthropology*. New York: Random House.

—— (1975) *The Notion of Tribe*. Menlo Park, CA: Cummings Publishing.

Fukui, Katsuyoshi and John Markakis (eds) (1994a) *Ethnicity and Conflict in the Horn of Africa*. Athens: Ohio University Press.

—— (1994b) "Introduction." In Katsuyoshi Fukui and John Markakis (eds), *Ethnicity and Conflict in the Horn of Africa*. Athens: Ohio University Press, pp. 1–11.

Fukuyama, Francis (1992) *The End of History and the Last Man*. New York: The Free Press.

—— (1998) "Women and the Evolution of World Politics." *Foreign Affairs* September/October: 24–40.

Gagnon, V.P., Jr. (1997) "Ethnic Nationalism and International Conflict: The Case of Serbia." In Michael E. Brown, Owen R. Cote, Jr., Sean M. Lynn-Jones and Steven E. Miller (eds), *Nationalism and Ethnic Conflict*. Cambridge, MA: MIT Press, pp. 132–168.

Ganguly, Sumit (1997) "Explaining the Kashmir Insurgency: Political Mobilization and Institutional Decay." In Michael E. Brown, Owen R. Cote, Jr., Sean M. Lynn-Jones and Steven E. Miller (eds), *Nationalism and Ethnic Conflict*. Cambridge, MA: MIT Press, pp. 200–231.

Gantzel, Klaus Jurgen (1997) "War in the Post-World War II World: Some Empirical Trends and a Theoretical Approach." In David Turton (ed.), *War and Ethnicity: Global Connections and Local Violence*. Republic of San Marino: Center for Interdisciplinary Research on Social Stress/University of Rochester Press, pp.123–144.

Geertz, Clifford (1963) "The Integrative Revolution: Primordial Sentiments and Civil Politics in the New States." In Clifford Geertz (ed.), *Old Societies and New States: The Quest for Modernity in Asia and Africa*. London: The Free Press, pp. 107–157.

—— (1979) "Religion as a Cultural System." In William A. Lessa and Evon Z. Vogt (eds), *Reader in Comparative Religion: An Anthropological Approach*. New York: Harper and Row, pp. 79–89.

Gellner, Ernest (1997) *Nationalism*. New York: New York University Press.

Giddens, Anthony (1985) *The Nation-State and Violence: Volume Two of a Contemporary Critique of Historical Materialism*. Berkeley: University of California Press.

Gledhill, John (2000) *Power and Its Disguises: Anthropological Perspectives on Politics*. Sterling, VA: Pluto Press.

Gonzalez, Nancie and Carollyn McCommon (eds) (1989) *Conflict, Migration, and the Expression of Ethnicity*. Boulder: Westview Press.

Goodwin, Crauford (n.d.) "Economics and the Study of War." Paper presented at "The Study of War Summary Conference," Triangle Institute for Security Studies, Wheaton, IL, June 1997.

Gottlieb, Gidon (1993) *Nation against State: A New Approach to Ethnic Conflicts and the Decline of Sovereignty*. New York: Council on Foreign Relations Press.

Gourevitch, Philip (1998) *We Wish to Inform You that Tomorrow We Will be Killed with Our Families: Stories from Rwanda*. New York: Farrar, Straus and Giroux.

Guidieri, Remo, Francesco Pellizzi and Stanley J. Tambiah (eds) (1988) *Ethnicities and Nations: Processes of Interethnic Relations in Latin America, Southeast Asia, and the Pacific*. Austin: University of Texas Press for Rothko Chapel.

Gurr, Ted Robert (1993) *Minorities at Risk: A Global View of Ethnopolitical Conflicts*. Washington: US Institute of Peace Press.

—— (2000) *Peoples versus States: Minorities at Risk in the New Century*. Washington: United States Institute of Peace Press.

Gurr, Ted Robert, Daniel C. Esty, Jack A. Goldstone, Barbara Harff, Pamela T. Surko and Alan N. Unger (n.d.) "The State Failure Project: New Approaches, New Findings." Chapter prepared for Michael Stohl (ed.), *Failed States*, Cambridge: Cambridge University Press, in press.

Gurr, Ted Robert and Monty G. Marshall (2000) "Assessing Risks of Future Ethnic Wars." In Ted Robert Gurr, *Peoples versus States: Minorities at Risk in the New Century*. Washington: United States Institute of Peace Press, pp. 223–260.

Haas, Jonathan (1982) *The Evolution of the Prehistoric State*. New York: Columbia University Press.

—— (ed.) (1990) *The Anthropology of War*. Cambridge: Cambridge University Press.

Hall, Thomas, Christopher Bartalos, Elizabeth Mannebach and Thomas Perkowitz (1996) "Varieties of Ethnic Conflict in Global Perspectives: A Review Essay." *Social Science Quarterly* 77: 445–452.

Halpern, Joel M. and David A. Kideckel (eds) (2000) *Neighbors at War: Anthropological Perspectives on Yugoslav Ethnicity, Culture, and History*. University Park, PA: Pennsylvania State University Press.

Hamburg, David A., Alexander George and Karen Ballentine (1999) "Preventing Deadly Conflict: The Critical role of Leadership." *Archives of General Psychiatry* 56: 971–976.

Harris, Marvin (1992) "Distinguished Lecture: Anthropology and the Theoretical and Paradigmatic Significance of the Collapse of Soviet and East European Communism." *American Anthropologist* 94(2): 295–305.

—— (1995) *Cultural Anthropology*, fourth edition. New York: Harper Collins.

Hartung, William D. (1994) *And Weapons For All*. New York: Harper Collins.

Hechter, Michael (2000) *Containing Nationalism*. Oxford: Oxford University Press.

Herbst, Jeffrey (1990) "War and the State in Africa." *International Security* 14(4): 117–139.

—— (1992) "The Potential for Conflict in Africa." *Africa Insight* 22(2): 105–109.

—— (1997) "Responding to State Failure in Africa." In Michael E. Brown, Owen R. Cote, Jr., Sean M. Lynn-Jones and Steven E. Miller (eds), *Nationalism and Ethnic Conflict*. Cambridge, MA: MIT Press, pp. 374–398.

Heywood, Linda M. (1998) "Towards an Understanding of Modern Political Ideology in Africa: The Case of the Ovimbundu of Angola." *Journal of Modern African Studies* 36: 139–167.

Hill, Jonathan (ed.) (1996) *History, Power, and Identity: Ethnogenesis in the Americas, 1492–1992*. Iowa City: University of Iowa Press.

Hintjens, Helen M. (1999) "Explaining the 1994 Genocide in Rwanda." *The Journal of Modern African Studies* 37: 241–286.

Hinton, Alexander Laban (1998a) "Why Did You Kill? The Cambodian Genocide and the Dark Side of Face and Honor." *The Journal of Asian Studies* 57: 93–122.

—— (1998b) "A Head for an Eye: Revenge in the Cambodian Genocide." *American Ethnologist* 25: 352–377.

Hobsbawm, E.J. (1994) *Nations and Nationalism Since 1780*. Cambridge: Cambridge University Press.

Hoebel, E. Adamson (1978) *The Cheyennes: Indians of the Great Plains*, second edition. New York: Holt, Rinehart and Winston.

Holsti, K.J. (1996) *The State, War, and the State of War*. New York: Cambridge University Press.

Homer-Dixon, Thomas (1999) *Environment, Scarcity, and Violence*. Princeton: Princeton University Press.

Homer-Dixon, Thomas and Jessica Blitt (1998) *Ecoviolence: Links Among Environment, Population, and Security*. Oxford: Rowman and Littlefield.

Hopmann, P. Terrence (n.d.) "Disintegrating States." Carnegie Commission for the Prevention of Deadly Violence, the Carnegie Foundation, New York. http://www.ccpdc.org/pubs/zart/ch6.htm

Horowitz, Donald (1985) *Ethnic Groups in Conflict*. Berkeley: University of California Press.

Hudson, Robert (2000) "Identity and Exclusion through Language Politics: The Croatian Example." In Robert Hudson and Fred Reno (eds), *Politics of Identity: Migrants and Minorities in Multicultural States*. New York: St. Martin's Press, pp. 243–264.

Human Rights Watch (2001) "Afghanistan: Crisis of Impunity: The Role of Pakistan, Russia, and Iran in Fueling the Civil War." 13(3).

Huntington, Samuel P. (1993) "The Clash of Civilizations?" *Foreign Affairs* Summer: 22–49.

Ignatieff, Michael (1997) *The Warrior's Honor: Ethnic War and the Modern Conscience*. New York: Henry Holt and Company.

Jenkins, J. Craig and Kurt Schock (1992) "Global Structures and Political Processes in the Study of Domestic Political Conflict." *Annual Review of Sociology* 18: 161–185.

Kahl, Colin (1998) "Population Growth, Environmental Degradation, and State-Sponsored Violence." *International Security* 23(2): 80–119.

Kaldor, Mary (1999) *New and Old Wars: Organized Violence in a Global Era*. Cambridge: Polity Press.

Kapferer, Bruce (1988) *Legends of People, Myths of State: Violence, Intolerance, and Political Culture in Sri Lanka and Australia*. Washington: Smithsonian Institution Press.

Kaplan, Robert D. (1993) *Balkan Ghosts: A Journey Through History*. New York: St. Martins Press.

—— (1994) "The Coming Anarchy." *Atlantic Monthly* February: 44–76.

Kaufman, Stuart (1997) "Spiraling to Ethnic War: Elites, Masses, and Moscow in Moldava's Civil War." In Michael E. Brown, Owen R. Cote, Jr., Sean M. Lynn-Jones and Steven E. Miller (eds), *Nationalism and Ethnic Conflict*. Cambridge, MA: MIT Press, pp. 169–199.

Kaufmann, Chaim (1996) "Intervention in Ethnic and Ideological Civil Wars: Why One Can Be Done and the Other Can't." *Security Studies* 6(1): 62–100.

—— (1997) "Possible and Impossible Solutions to Ethnic Civil Wars." In Michael E. Brown, Owen R. Cote, Jr., Sean M. Lynn-Jones and Steven E. Miller (eds), *Nationalism and Ethnic Conflict*. Cambridge, MA: MIT Press, pp. 265–304.

Kleinman, Arthur, Veena Das and Margaret Lock (eds) (1997) *Social Suffering*. Berkeley: University of California Press.

Lake, David and Donald Rothchild (1997) "Containing Fear: The Origins and Management of Ethnic Conflict." In Michael E. Brown, Owen R. Cote, Jr., Sean M. Lynn-Jones and Steven E. Miller (eds), *Nationalism and Ethnic Conflict*. Cambridge, MA: MIT Press, pp. 132–168.

Lan, David (1985) *Guns and Rain: Guerrillas and Spirit Mediums in Zimbabwe*. Berkeley: University of California Press.

Langhorne, Richard (2001) *The Coming of Globalization: Its Evolution and Contemporary Consequences*. New York: Palgrave.

Larana, Enrique, Hank Johnston and Joseph R. Gusfield, eds. (1994) *New Social Movements: From Ideology to Identity*. Philadelphia: Temple University Press.

Lemarchand, Rene (1994) *Burundi: Ethnocide as Discourse and Practice*. Cambridge: Cambridge University Press.

Licklider, Roy (1998) "Early Returns: Results of the First Wave of Statistical Studies of Civil War Termination." *Civil Wars* 1: 121–132.

Linke, Uli (1999) *Blood and Nation: The European Aesthetics of Race*. Philadelphia: University of Pennsylvania Press.

Longman, Timothy (1998) "Rwanda: Chaos from Above." In Leonardo A. Villalon and Phillip A. Huxtable (eds), *The African State at a Critical Juncture: Between Disintegration and Reconfiguration*. Boulder: Lynne Rienner, pp. 75–91.

Loomis, Don G. (1993) "Prospects for UN Peacekeeping." *Global Affairs* Winter: 125–140.

McAdam, Doug, Sidney Tarrow and Charles Tilly (1996) "To Map Contentious Politics." *Mobilization: An International Journal* 1: 17–34.

McNulty, Mel (1999a) "The Militarization of Ethnicity and the Emergence of Warlordism in Rwanda, 1990–94." In Paul B. Rich (ed.), *Warlords in International Relations*. New York: St. Martin's Press, pp. 81–102.

—— (1999b) "The Collapse of Zaire: Implosion, Revolution or External Sabotage?" *The Journal of Modern African Studies* 37: 53–82.

Mahmood, Cynthia Keppley (1996) *Fighting for Faith and Nation: Dialogues with Sikh Militants*. Philadelphia: University of Pennsylvania Press.

Mamdani, Mahmood (2001) *When Victims become Killers: Colonialism, Nativism, and the Genocide in Rwanda*. Princeton: Princeton University Press.

Mann, Michael (1988) *States, War and Capitalism: Studies in Political Sociology*. New York: Basil Blackwell.

Markakis, John (1990) *National and Class Conflict in the Horn of Africa*. Athens: Ohio University Press.

Mead, Walter Russell (1999/2000) "The Jacksonian Tradition." *The National Interest* 58: 5–30.

Migdal, Joel S. (1988) *Strong Societies and Weak States: State-Society Relations and State Capabilities in the Third World*. Princeton: Princeton University Press.

Morgan, Lewis Henry (1972) *League of the Iroquois*. Secaucus, NJ: The Citadel Press.

Morris, Aldon, D. and Carol McClurg Mueller (eds) (1992) *Frontiers in Social Movement Theory*. New Haven: Yale University Press.

Motyl, Alexander J. (1997) "Institutional Legacies and Reform Trajectories." In Adrian Kratnycky, Alexander Motyl and Boris Shor (eds), *Nations in Transit 1997: Civil Society, Democracy and Markets in East Central Europe and the Newly Independent States*. New Brunswick, NJ: Transaction Publishers, pp. 17–21.

Nagel, Joanne and Brad Whorton (1992) "Ethnic Conflict and the World System: International Competition in Iraq (1961–1991) and Angola (1974–1991)." *Journal of Political and Military Sociology* 20: 1–35.

Nagengast, Carole (1994) "Violence, Terror, and the Crisis of the State." *Annual Review of Anthropology* 23: 109–136.

Nordstrom, Carolyn and JoAnn Martin (eds) (1992) *The Paths to Domination, Resistance, and Terror*. Berkeley, CA: University of California Press.

Nordstrom, Carolyn and Antonius C.G.M. Robben (eds) (1995) *Fieldwork under Fire: Contemporary Studies of Violence and Survival*. Berkeley, CA: University of California Press.

Nyang'oro, Julius E. and Timothy M. Shaw (1998) "The African State in the Global Economic Context." In Leonardo A. Villalon and Phillip A. Huxtable (eds), *The African State at a Critical Juncture: Between Disintegration and Reconfiguration*. Boulder: Lynne Rienner, pp. 27–42.

Ortner, Sherry (1973) "On Key Symbols." *American Anthropologist* 75: 1138–1346.

Otterbein, Keith (1973) "The Anthropology of War." In John Honigmann (ed.), *Handbook of Social and Cultural Anthropology*. Chicago: Rand McNally College Publishing, pp. 923–958.

"Panel of Experts" (2001) "Report of the Panel of Experts on the Illegal Exploitation of Natural Resources and Other Forms of Wealth of the Democratic Republic of the Congo." New York: The United Nations. http://www.un.org/News/dh/latest/drcongo.htm

Percival, Valerie and Thomas Homer-Dixon (1995) "Environmental Scarcity and Violent Conflict: The Case of Rwanda." Washington: Program on Science and International Security, American Association for the Advancement of Science.

Posen, Barry R. (1993) "The Security Dilemma and Ethnic Conflict." *Survival* 35(1): 27–47.

Premdas, Ralph R. (1991) "The Internationalization of Ethnic Conflict: Some Theoretical Explorations." In K.M. de Silva and R.J. May (eds), *Internationalization of Ethnic Conflict*. New York: St. Martin's Press, pp. 10–25.

Prunier, Gerard (1995) *The Rwanda Crisis: History of a Genocide*. New York: Columbia University Press.

—— (1997) "The Great Lakes Crisis." *Current History* 96 (May): 193–199.

Radcliffe-Brown, A.R. (1940) "Preface", In M. Fortes and E.E. Evans-Pritchard (eds), *African Political Systems*. London: Oxford University Press, pp. xi–xxiii.

Rejali, Darius M. (1998) "After Feminist Analyses of Bosnian Violence." In Lois Ann Lorentzen and Jennifer Turpin (eds), *The Women and War Reader*. New York: New York University Press, pp. 26–32.

Reno, William (1995) *Corruption and State Politics in Sierra Leone*. New York: Cambridge University Press.

—— (1997) "Privatizing War in Sierra Leone." *Current History* 96 (May): 227–230.

—— (1998) *Warlord Politics and African States*. Boulder: Lynne Rienner.

—— (2000) "Shadow States and the Political Economy of Civil Wars." In Mats Berdal and David M. Malone (eds), *Greed and Grievance: Economic Agendas in Civil Wars*, pp. 43–68.

Reyna, S.P. and R.E. Downs (eds) (1994) *Studying War: Anthropological Perspectives*. Langhorne, PA: Gordon & Breach.

Rich, Paul B. (ed.) (1999) *Warlords in International Relations*. New York: St. Martin's Press.

Richards, Paul (1996) *Fighting for the Rain Forest: War, Youth, and Resources in Sierra Leone*. Portsmouth, NH: Heinemann.

Riches, David (ed.) (1986) *The Anthropology of Violence*. New York: Basil Blackwell.

Robben, Antonius C.G.M and Marcelo M. Suarez-Orozco (eds) (2000) *Cultures under Siege: Collective Violence and Trauma*. Cambridge: Cambridge University Press.

Rossel, Jakob (1997) "Nationalism and Ethnicity: Ethnic Nationalism and the Regulation of Ethnic Conflict." In David Turton (ed.), *War and Ethnicity: Global Connections and Local Violence*. Republic of San Marino: Center for Interdisciplinary Research on Social Stress/University of Rochester Press, pp. 145–162.

Rubenstein, Steven (2001) "Colonialism, the Shuar Federation, and the Ecuadorian State." *Environment and Planning D: Society and Space* 19: 263–293.

Rubin, Barnett R., Ashraf Ghani, William Maley, Ahmed Rashid and Olivier Roy (2001) "Afghanistan: Reconstruction and Peace-building in a Regional Framework." KOFF Peacebuilding Reports 1/2001. Bern: Center for Peacebuilding/Swiss Peace Foundation.

Rubin, Barnett R. and Jack Snyder (eds) (1998) *Post-Soviet Political Order: Conflict and State Building*. New York: Routledge.

Rubinstein, Robert A. and Mary LeCron Foster (eds) (1988) *The Social Dynamics of Peace and Conflict: Culture in International Security*. Boulder: Westview Press.

Rudensky, Nikolai (1992) "War as a Factor of Ethnic Conflict and Stability in the U.S.S.R.." In Giorgio Ausenda (ed.), *Effects of War on Society*. Republic of San Marino: Center for Interdisciplinary Research on Social Stress, pp. 181–192.

Ruggie, John Gerard (1993) "Territoriality and Beyond: Problematizing Modernity in International Relations." *International Organization* 47: 139–174.

Rummel, Rudolph J. (1997a) *Death by Government*. New Brunswick: Transaction.

—— (1997b) *Statistics of Democide: Genocide and Mass Murder since 1900*. Charlottesville, VA: Center for National Security, School of Law, University of Virginia.

—— (1997c) *Power Kills: Democracy as a Method of Nonviolence*. New Brunswick: Transaction.

Russett, Bruce (1990) *Controlling the Sword: The Democratic Governance of National Security*. Cambridge: Harvard University Press.

Sapiro, Virginia (1993) "Engendering Cultural Differences." In Crawford Young (ed.), *The Rising Tide of Cultural Pluralism: The Nation-State at Bay?* Madison: University of Wisconsin Press, pp. 36–54.

Schmidt, Sabine (1990) "Conflict and Violence at the Local Level: A World-System Perspective." *Zeitschrift für Ethnologie* 115: 3–22.

Schnabel, Albrecht and Ramesh Thakur (eds) (2000) *Kosovo and the Challenge of Humanitarian Intervention: Selective Indignation, Collective Action, and International Citizenship*. New York: The United Nations Press.

Schraeder, Peter J. (1997) "France and the Great Game in Africa." *Current History* 96 (May): 206–211.

Segell, Glen (1999) "Warlordism and Drug Trafficking: From Southeast Asia to Sub-Saharan Africa." In Paul Rich (ed.), *Warlords in International Relations*. New York: St. Martin's Press, pp. 38–51.

Shaw, R. Paul and Yuwa Wong (1987) "Ethnic Mobilization and the Seeds of Warfare: An Evolutionary Perspective." *International Studies Quarterly* 31: 5–31.

Shearer, David (2000) "Aiding or Abetting? Humanitarian Aid and Its Economic Role in Civil War." In Mats Berdal and David M. Malone (eds), *Greed and Grievance: Economic Agendas in Civil Wars*. Boulder: Lynne Rienner, pp. 189–204.

Simons, Anna (1997) "Democratization and Ethnic Conflict: The Kin Connection." *Nations and Nationalism* 3: 273–289.

—— (1999) "War: Back to the Future." *Annual Review of Anthropology* 8: 73–108.

SIPRI (2001) "Major Armed Conflicts." Stockholm International Peace Research Institute. http://projects.sipri.se/conflictstudy/MajorArmedConflicts.html and http://www.pcr.uu.se/data.htm

Skocpol, Theda (1985) "Bringing the State Back In: Strategies of Analysis in Current Research." In Peter B. Evans, Dietrich Rueschemeyer and Theda Skocpol (eds), *Bringing the State Back In*. Cambridge: Cambridge University Press, pp. 3–37.

Sluka, Jeffrey A. (ed.) (2000a) *Death Squad: The Anthropology of State Terror*. Philadelphia: University of Pennsylvania Press.

—— (2000b) "Introduction: State Terror and Anthropology." In Jeffrey Sluka (ed.), *Death Squad: The Anthropology of State Terror*, pp. 1–45. Philadelphia: University of Pennsylvania Press.

Smith, Anthony D. (1981) *The Ethnic Revival*. Cambridge: Cambridge University Press.

—— (1983) *Theories of Nationalism*. New York: Holmes and Meier Publishers.

Snyder, Jack and Karen Ballentine (1997) "Nationalism and the Marketplace of Ideas." In Michael E. Brown, Owen R. Cote, Jr., Sean M. Lynn-Jones and Steven E. Miller (eds), *Nationalism and Ethnic Conflict*. Cambridge: MIT Press, pp. 61–96.

Southall, Aidan (1970) "The Illusion of Tribe." *Journal of Asian and African Studies* 5: 28–50.

—— (1974) "State Formation in Africa." *Annual Review of Anthropology* 3: 153–165.

Sponsel, Leslie E. (1994) "The Mutual Relevance of Anthropology and Peace Studies." In Leslie E. Sponsel and Thomas Gregor (eds), *The Anthropology of Peace and Nonviolence*. Boulder: Lynne Rienner, pp. 1–36.

Stack, John F., Jr. (1986) "Ethnic Mobilization in World Politics: The Primordial Perspective." In John F. Stack (ed.), *The Primordial Challenge: Ethnicity in the Contemporary World*. New York: Greenwood Press, pp. 1–11.

Starn, Orin (1997) "Villagers at Arms: War and Counterrevolution in Peru's Andes." In Richard G. Fox and Orin Starn (eds), *Between Resistance and Revolution: Cultural Politics and Social Protest*. New Brunswick, NJ: Rutgers University Press, pp. 223–249.

Stiglmayer, Alexandra (ed.) (1994) *Mass Rape: The War against Women in Bosnia-Herzegovina*. Lincoln, NB: University of Nebraska Press.

Strathern, Andrew (2000) "Let the Bow Go Down." In R. Brian Ferguson and Neil L. Whitehead (eds), *War in the Tribal Zone: Expanding States and Indigenous Warfare*, second printing. Santa Fe: School of American Research Press, pp. 229–250.

Talbot, Strobe (2000) "The Crisis in Africa: Local War and Regional Peace." *World Policy Journal* 17. http://web5.infotrac-college.com/wadsworth

Tambiah, Stanley (1988) "Foreword." In Remo Guidieri, Francesco Pellizzi and Stanley J. Tambiah (eds), *Ethnicities and Nations: Processes of Interethnic Relations in Latin America, Southeast Asia, and the Pacific*. Austin: University of Texas Press, for Rothko Chapel, pp. 1–6.

—— (1992) *Buddhism Betrayed: Religion, Politics, and Violence in Sri Lanka*. Chicago: Chicago University Press.

—— (1996) *Leveling Crowds: Ethnonationalist Conflicts and Collective Violence in South Asia*. Berkeley: University of California Press.

Taussig, Michael (1987) *Shamanism, Colonialism, and the Wild Man: A Study in Terror and Healing*. Chicago: University of Chicago Press.

Taylor, Christopher C. (1999) *Sacrifice as Terror: The Rwandan Genocide of 1994*. New York: Oxford.

Taylor, Diana (1997) *Disappearing Acts: Spectacles of Gender and Nationalism in Argentina's "Dirty War"*. Durham, NC: Duke University Press.

Taylor, Peter J. (1994) "The State as Container: Territoriality in the Modern World-System." *Progress in Human Geography* 18: 151–162.

—— (1995) "Beyond Containers: Internationality, Interstateness, Interterritoriality." *Progress in Human Geography* 19: 1–15.
Thakur, Ramesh (1994) "From Peacekeeping to Peace Enforcement: The UN Operation in Somalia." *The Journal of Modern African Studies* 32: 387–410.
Thakur, Ramesh and Edward Newman (eds) (2000) *New Millennium, New Perspectives: The United Nations, Security, and Governance*. New York: The United Nations University Press.
Tilly, Charles (ed.) (1975) *The Formation of National States in Western Europe*. Princeton: Princeton University Press.
Turner, Paul R. and David Pitt (1989) *The Anthropology of War and Peace: Perspectives on the Nuclear Age*. Granby, MA: Bergin and Garvey.
Turner, Victor (1967) *The Forest of Symbols*. Ithaca: Cornell University Press.
Turton, David (ed.) (1997a) *War and Ethnicity: Global Connections and Local Violence*. Republic of San Marino: Center for Interdisciplinary Research on Social Stress/University of Rochester Press.
—— (1997b) "Introduction: War and Ethnicity." In David Turton (ed.), *War and Ethnicity: Global Connections and Local Violence*. Republic of San Marino: Center for Interdisciplinary Research on Social Stress/University of Rochester Press, pp.1–45.
Urban, Greg and Joel Sherzer (eds) (1991) *Nation States and Indians in Latin America*. Austin: University of Austin Press.
Ury, William (1999) *Getting to Peace: Transforming Conflict at Home, at Work, and in the World*. New York: Viking.
Vail, Leroy (ed.) (1989) *The Creation of Tribalism in Southern Africa*. Berkeley: University of California Press.
Van Creveld, Martin (1991) *The Transformation of War*. New York: The Free Press.
Van den Berghe, Pierre L. (ed.) (1990) *State Violence and Ethnicity*. Niwot, CO: University Press of Colorado.
Van der Dennen, Johan M.G. (1995) *The Origin of War* (2 volumes). Groningen, Netherlands: Origin Press.
Vandergeest, Peter and Nancy Lee Peluso (1995) "Territorialization and State Power in Thailand." *Theory and Society* 24: 385–426.
Van Evera, Stephen (1994) "Hypotheses on Nationalism and War." *International Security* 18(4): 26–60.
—— (1997) "Hypotheses on Nationalism and War." In Michael E. Brown, Owen R. Cote, Jr., Sean M. Lynn-Jones and Steven Miller (eds), *Nationalism and Ethnic Conflict*. Cambridge, MA: MIT Press, pp. 235–264.
Vanhanen, Tatu (1999) "Ethnic Conflicts and Ethnic Nepotism." In Johan M.G. van der Dennen, David Smillie and Daniel R. Wilson (eds), *The Darwinian Heritage and Sociobiology*. Westport, CT: Praeger, pp. 187–199.
Villalón, Leonardo A. (1998) "The African State at the End of the Twentieth Century: Parameters of the Critical Juncture." In Leonardo A. Villalón and Phillip A. Huxtable (eds), *The African State at a Critical Juncture: Between Disintegration and Reconfiguration*. Boulder: Lynne Rienner, pp. 3–25.
Villalón, Leonardo A. and Phillip A. Huxtable (eds) (1998) *The African State at a Critical Juncture: Between Disintegration and Reconfiguration*. Boulder: Lynne Rienner.
Vincent, Joan (1990) *Anthropology and Politics: Visions, Traditions, and Trends*. Tucson: University of Arizona Press.
Wallensteen, Peter and Margareta Sollenberg (1997) "Armed Conflicts, Conflict Termination and Peace Agreements, 1989–96." *Journal of Peace Research* 34: 339–358.

Warren, Kay (ed.) (1993a) *The Violence Within: Cultural and Political Opposition in Divided Nations*. Boulder: Westview Press.

—— (1993b) "Introduction: Revealing Conflicts Across Cultures and Disciplines." In Kay Warren (ed.), *The Violence Within: Cultural and Political Opposition in Divided Nations*. Boulder: Westview Press, pp. 1–23.

—— (2000) "Conclusion: Death Squads and Wider Complicities: Dilemmas for the Anthropology of Violence." In Jeffrey A. Sluka (ed.), *Death Squad: The Anthropology of State Terror*. Philadelphia: University of Pennsylvania Press, pp. 226–247.

Weiner, Tim (1994) "Blowback from the Afghan Battlefield." *The New York Times Magazine*, 13 March, 52–55.

Weinstein, Jeremy M. (2000) "Africa's 'Scramble for Africa': Lessons of a Continental War." *World Policy Journal* 17. http://web5.infotrac-college.com/wadsworth

Wendt, Alexander (1999) *Social Theory of International Politics*. Cambridge: Cambridge University Press.

White, Douglas R. (1990) "World-System and Regional Linkages as Causally Implicated in Local Level Conflicts at the Ethnographic Horizon." *Zeitschrift fur Ethnologie* 15: 111–137.

Williams, Brackette F. (1989) "A CLASS ACT: Anthropology and the Race to Nation Across Ethnic Terrain." *Annual Review of Anthropology* 18: 401–444.

Wilson, Edward O. (1999) *Consilience: The Unity of Knowledge*. New York: Vintage.

Wilson, Margo and Martin Daly (1985) "Competitiveness, Risk-Taking and Violence: The Young Male Syndrome." *Ethology and Sociobiology* 6: 59–73.

Wolf, Eric (1982) *Europe and the People without History*. Berkeley: University of California Press.

Young, Crawford (ed.) (1993a) *The Rising Tide of Cultural Pluralism: The Nation-State at Bay?* Madison: University of Wisconsin Press.

—— (1993b) "The Dialectics of Cultural Pluralism: Concept and Reality." In Crawford Young (ed.), *The Rising Tide of Cultural Pluralism: The Nation-State at Bay?* Madison: University of Wisconsin Press, pp. 3–35.

Zartman, I. William (ed.) (1995a) *Collapsed States: The Disintegration and Restoration of Legitimate Authority*. Boulder: Lynne Rienner.

—— (1995b) "Introduction: Posing the Problem of State Collapse." In I. William Zartman (ed.), *Collapsed States: The Disintegration and Restoration of Legitimate Authority*. Boulder: Lynne Rienner, pp. 1–11.

Part I
Commentaries

1 Comments on state, identity and violence

Eric R. Wolf

If we are to speak of "state, identity and violence," it may behove us to say more clearly how we think about the state and what kind of state we are talking about. A first and perhaps obvious point to raise is that state-making and state unmaking have gone on for a long time, and states have assumed many structural forms. This has some serious implications. I believe that Marx and Engels were essentially correct in trying to understand the state as an instrument of class rule over the accumulation process. But I also think that the variability of state forms and functions has much to do with how this is actually accomplished. States have varied in size from statelets to empires; in their reliance on strategic resources; in the degree and manner of their incorporation, integration and centralization; in their modes of administration; in the ways they have used to gain compliance and legitimacy.

A second point is that states not only come in many forms, but they also change form over time. Contrary to impressions, they are rarely rock-solid; they are organized into domains and levels internally, as well as in their dealings with their external sociocultural environments. They may present facades of seamless architecture, but they are better thought of as multidimensional arenas in which different groups compete for resources by using all kinds of means – technological, organizational, ideological – to occupy strategic nodes in the distribution of power. These nodes are always contested.

Moreover, state governance, under whatever dominant mode of production, always involves politics as well as structure: conflicts over who is to run the state, conflicts over strategies, and conflicts over how to deal with unforeseen challenges from both within and without the society. If we are to understand these conflicts we must move from the abstract understanding of the state as an instrument of class rule to a more concrete analysis of who rules whom and how. Classes manifest themselves in relation to one another, but they rarely, if ever, *act* as total entities. Both classes that rule and classes that are ruled are usually made up of arrays of historically differentiated and variable sub-entities. States are not run by unitary ruling classes but by coalitions or alliances of class splinters and segments. It will not do to confuse the logic or *telos* of state rule in the accumulation process with its actual management. The classes that are the primary beneficiaries of the accumulation process are not identical to the administrative, political, legal, military and public-relations managers of the multidimensional state apparatus. We must also not forget that both the protagonists of capital and the managers of the state machinery of coercion and consensus often mismanage the state as well as manage it.

The object of our attention here, moreover, is not just any kind of state but specifically the nation-state and the world-wide system made up of such states. In that connection we should remind ourselves that this "sovereign, territorial nation-state is very young" (Mann 1993: 116). It was preceded by centralizing states with absolutist pretensions, which nevertheless left the management of large reaches of society to long-established corporate bodies; did little to expand the economic and legal infrastructure; eschewed the establishment of citizen armies, preferring to hire mercenaries as needed; and – crucially – placed severe limitations on the social and psychological mobilization of the people at large. The main duty of the citizenry was, as Heine put it, "to keep quiet" – "Ruhe is die erste Bürgerpflicht."

In trying to understand how the earlier lumbering absolutisms came to be replaced by this emphatically more dynamic kind of entity, it is usual to ascribe that dynamism to the advent of capitalism pure and simple. This hypothesis is persuasive; what escapes us still, however, is the precise nature of this relationship, its "how" as well as its structural "why." There is no systematic theoretical discourse on the relation between nation and capital in Marx and Engels (see Poulantzas 1973: 19–20). They seem to have merely adopted Hegel's view that each successive epoch in the forward march of humanity would be spearheaded by some exemplary nations – the non-exemplary peoples were the ones "without history." When the Bolsheviks seized power in Russia in 1917, they took it quite for granted that their Soviet Union would be a federation of nation-states, each associated with a nationality dominant over minorities within its territory.

Immanuel Wallerstein, who has pioneered the concept of a capitalist world-system associated with a political system of nation-states, avers that the nation-state was "more efficient." This is likely, but just what made the nation-state so much more efficient than the clumsy empires it replaced? It is becoming increasingly clear that its special advantages lay in its ability to commit the resources of capitalistically organized economies to the creation of large, standing armies (see Tilly 1990: 6, 58). If capital was indeed its mother, the god of war was its genitor. If the state is under siege in the present, both its paternity and maternity are in question.

Let me outline briefly the salient features of the nation-state. First, it produced a much more effective war machine than its predecessors, by drawing its soldiery from "the people" under unified military command. Second, it entered into partnerships with capital to equip these new armies. Third, it recognized the need for political and economic strategies that would aid the accumulation process, including the expansion of industry, the growth and intensification of transport, and the development of a reliable financial and legal infrastructure. Fourth, it undertook the management of the social conflicts engendered in the processes of accumulation. This management produced many of the important institutions that channel, articulate, and also constrain interaction in the national "civil society." Fifth, it enlarged and standardized the educational system, to train up cadres and to develop at least a minimally qualified and disciplined labor force and citizen-soldiery.

Finally, the nation-state underwrote the construction of a hegemonic national culture, drawing on a new elite of school-trained intellectuals in place of the absolutist nobilities of sword and pen. This new hegemonic national culture was conveyed through a newly standardized national language; through a literature that celebrated a patriotic national history of real and imaginary glories won and grievances suffered, and that defined a common national project growing out of that history; and through symbolic performances and emblems that extolled both that history and that project. These celebrations of nationhood pumped blood into the structure of the state, Friedrich Nietzsche's "cold monster."

The aim was to replace an inherited social and cultural diversity with a unifying homogeneity, to transform England's "amphibious ill-born mob" in Defoe's words) into "that vain, ill-natured thing, an Englishman"; to change "peasants into Frenchmen"; to merge "community" – such as Ferdinand Toennies's native Schleswig-Holstein – into "society," in his case represented by bureaucratic and militaristic Prussia. This nation-building project was doubly revolutionary. It would override inherited distinctions and subsume them under a new symbolically created unity; but under the aegis of that new unity it would also install new distinctions. It not only strove to create a new type of man and woman; these new men and women would also take up their stations in new roles and statuses in a new social division of labor.

All nation-states since 1800 have striven to install these features – or their functional equivalents – but they have of course differed greatly in their effectiveness and in their ability to penetrate and marshal society. Conversely, installing the nation-building project has everywhere generated resistance, "friction" and "noise." We must also remain attuned to distinctions in the nature and course of the nation-building process. The national states that replaced the Spanish empire in Latin America merely reformulated regional identities as national entities, to secure power for the creole elites, not to commit their peoples to constructing real nation-states. The nation-states that proved successful were first the core states of Europe and North America, and then Japan, mostly states that had enriched themselves during the nineteenth century by adding new markets and colonies. The next wave of nation-states, created in the shatter zones of the Habsburg, Tsarist, and Ottoman empires, showed real economic growth, but were then mostly ground into the dust by the political-military dinosaurs on their borders.

Still another wave of nation-states, drawn primarily from Europe's former colonies, joined their predecessors after World War II. These include many of the states under siege discussed in this volume. Many were colonial entities that had originally come into being only as a result of ad hoc military and political power grabs, which brought together peoples of very diverse social and cultural backgrounds into seemingly unified colonial state enclosures. The managers of the newly independent "nation" states inherited these diverse congeries of peoples. They also had to cope with poorly articulated extractive economies and societies, and with the problematic role of the social strata that linked colony to metropolis and markets.

To oversimplify, both old and new states had essentially two political options: a "liberal" option and an "autocratic" (really "kentrocratic," run from a center) option. These two options helped to shape the internal structures of the new states in the course of their development; they also conditioned the kind of crises the states face in the present. In the "liberal" option the state apparatus is structurally severed from the economy and society. The incumbent power blocs are subjected to elections, which allow some claims and grievances to be managed through the play of politics. This functions, in turn, to contain the struggle of classes through "an unstable equilibrium of compromise" (Poulantzas 1973:192). In the autocratic (or kentrocratic) state a body of cadres takes charge of both economy and society, and runs them as a "war economy." They allocate resources to strategic goals by command, and limit alternatives through the exercise of a "dictatorship over needs," as exemplified by the former Soviet Union. Many of the new nation-states, especially those with economies and societies cut up into isolated sectors articulated with external markets within only poorly integrated regions, favored the autocratic model as a ready means to achieve rapid integration and development.

Both models are now in difficulty. The "liberal" model has run up against limits to further accumulation; resistance to intensified taxation has, in turn, produced a "fiscal crisis of the state" (O'Connor 1973). In response, many states have dismantled the Keynesian welfare apparatus, cut the work force to raise productivity, and launched policies to offset internal stagnation of demand by widening the scope of transnational trade, in competition with other nations. Some of these goals may be contradictory: efforts to maintain the pace of accumulation by securing stable and peaceful markets may run counter to the effects of arms exports to political entities likely to disturb the peace. The pressures and contradictions have global ramifications. As we know, the end of the Cold War witnessed not only the implosion of the Soviet bloc but also the end of superpower patronage and supervision over political and military clienteles. Some of the former client states or factions have realigned their allegiances; others have seized the opportunity to gain points or eliminate real and imaginary rivals. These responses have further accelerated the pace of militarization in state systems worldwide, and have greatly expanded the field of opportunities for vendors of armaments, soldiers of fortune, and grave diggers.

Other pressures upon liberal and autocratic states alike derive from the increasing mobility of both capital and labor. Transnational capital has achieved unparalleled liquidity through the development of new financial instruments and arenas, which allow it to abandon areas of stagnant accumulation for areas of new and "flexible" accumulation at a moment's notice. This process is being carried forward not only by multinational corporate organizations but also by globally distributed ethnic networks, both old and new, which combine cosmopolitan know-how with ethnically defined sentiments of mutual dependence and trust. Joel Kotkin (1992) has focused on the British, Chinese, East Indian, Japanese, and Jewish "global tribes" in a controversial book; he lists Armenians, Cubans, Greeks, Ibos, and Palestinians as others that would reward attention. I would add Lebanese and Colombians to the list, as well as several ethnically based mafias in the former Soviet Union. The proliferation of such networks allows capital, people and goods to move through informal as well as formal channels, bypassing the officially legitimated economic arenas of the nation-states.

At the same time, transnational labor migrations are intensifying everywhere, partly to escape the unleashed horses of the apocalypse, partly to follow capital as it moves from one region to another. But immigrants are moving across national boundaries just when capitalism has won some major battles against labor. It has done so in part by scrapping Keynesian welfare policies, in part by turning its back on old-fashioned "smokestack" industrialism, which concentrated labor and facilitated its organization. Instead, the computer revolution in technology and organization now allows capital to become vastly more "flexible" in its arrangements. These arrangements decentralize the labor force. They also create more personalized networks of production and distribution that resemble the "shape-ups," "sweatshops," "family workshops," and "putting-out systems" that predated centralized industrialism. The new technology of communication can, furthermore, greatly reduce interruptions in the flow of production and distribution, while at the same time enhancing control over an individuated labor force. In this transition, business can take advantage, now as in the pre-industrial period, of a superabundance of labor.

In recent years, appeals to one or another kind of segmentary "ethnic" identity have become more audible and visible, even in once strongly unified and homogeneous nation-states. Many of the papers in this collection focus on cases in which states have experienced turmoil, due to intensified "ethnic" claims to power and resources from the state, or to outright ethnic rebellions and calls for secession. Suddenly, everybody seems to be looking for identities that are antagonistic to the identities sponsored by nation-building projects.

These intensifications of "ethnicity" have revived discussions among anthropologists and sociologists on whether ethnicity is "primordial" or – alternatively – "invented" and "constructed." It may in fact be both, as John Comaroff and Paul Stern (1995) have acknowledged. Clearly, humans exhibit a biopsychological proclivity to form bounded identity groups under determinate circumstances. The puzzle lies rather in what these circumstances may be, and how the construction of identities actually proceeds. These identities often seem to surface suddenly, connected with seemingly "instant" traditions, even while they project an aura of persistence since time immemorial. As in all cultural phenomena, those "shreds and patches," as Lowie called them, are clothed by secondary rationalizations with "such an aura of factuality that the moods and motivations seem uniquely realistic." Geertz said this of religion (1973: 90), and the question there, as here, was how this gets accomplished.

I want to suggest that such identities are constructed over time, sometimes over several generations, in a particular dialectical interplay between claims to greater universality and cosmopolitanism on the one hand, and claims to a narrower parochialism of descent and territorial fixity on the other. What is crucial is that these claims do not merely define cognitive distinctions; they also embody rival claims to power, rival claims over who has power over whom, and how.

The course of nation building offers an example. The French Revolution spoke in the name of universal human ideals, which it then inscribed in the banners of the Grande Armée in its conquests of Europe. This, in turn, produced a reactive nationalism in the Germanies, which adopted the new French notions of the nation-state but also constructed a Teutonic primordialism from the detritus of real and imaginary codes of ancient customary law. Once the nation establishes its aggressive and encompassing sway, countervailing "ethnic" interests make themselves heard to invoke mythical golden ages of primordial republics or kingdoms, which they then celebrate by enacting potpourris of supposedly remembered ancient customs. In these "instant" resurrections and remembrances previous resurrections and remembrances may play a significant part. Yet these elements are not stored in some primordial unconscious and then rendered manifest in some enduring cultural structure; they are remembered, added to, and reshaped in social gatherings and cultural productions that represent claims and interests of particular people under definable circumstances – against existing states, for states of their own.

The proliferating claims on behalf of ethnicity must be understood in relation to the nation-states in which they appear, and in relation to the world system formed by these states. Given the expansion of global capitalism and its marshalling of all kinds of resources, ethnic sectional or secessionist movements can also be seen as attempts to bypass the nation-state that oversees local politics, regulates and taxes, controls currencies, and drafts the young men. Sloughing off the nation-state may assist the ethnic claimants in forming more direct ties to the outside world, so as to lay hold of greater opportunities for the home folks and the home region. Conversely, in a world where capital is looking for openings to invest in more flexible arrangements of production – more personal in the familial or patron-client mode, less subject to bureaucratic regulation and interference, less exposed to demands from organized labor – an alliance with local or regional forces can seem inviting to outsiders. The new labor-management relations, too, put a premium on being local home folks, managing one's affairs in "traditionally" understood terms.

In the larger scenarios of global labor flows, issues of ethnicity appear in questions of citizenship and rights to work, as well as in work opportunities within particular segments of the greatly divided and heterogeneous markets for labor. Who gets work and with whom often has ethnic parameters, both for skilled and unskilled labor. Skilled labor – mobilized either for particular jobs or through a brain drain – may move through special, ethnically marked transnational circuits; unskilled labor may similarly encounter ethnically marked labor exchanges and market segments. Economy and society may also become more intensely hierarchical along ethnic and "racial" lines, as national cadres of citizens who remain ethnically unmarked are offered privileges and preferences over non-citizens and temporary "guest workers" whose identity is ethnically defined.

Finally, as the resources that states can distribute socially among their citizens grow increasingly scarce, ethnically defined communities may intensify their mutual competition. The United States seems to be now witnessing a proliferation of increasingly competitive and hostile "communities" of African Americans, Asian Americans, Hispanic Americans, and Jewish Americans, who will also have to compete for places in the budget with non-ethnic "communities", such as the defense community, the intelligence community, and the community of the "physically challenged." In these encounters, nation-state and ethnic claimants are mutually implicated; one could not exist without the other. By playing the game of divide and rule, the state may emerge as the ultimate beneficiary of a lot of friction, toil and trouble. Hear about it on the evening news.

References

Comaroff, John L. and Paul C. Stern (1995) "Introduction: New Perspectives on Nationalism and War." In John L. Comaroff and Paul C. Stern (eds), *Perspectives on Nationalism and War*. Luxembourg: Gordon & Breach.

Geertz, Clifford (1973) "Religion as a Cultural System." In *The Interpretation of Cultures*. New York: Basic books.

Kotkin, Joel (1992) *Tribes: How Race, Religion, and Identity Determine Success in the New Global Economy*. New York: Random House.

Mann, Michael (1993) "Nation-States in Europe and Other Continents: Diversifying, Developing, Not Dying." *Daedalus* 12(3).

O'Connor, James R. (1973) *The Fiscal Crisis of the State*. New York: St. Martin's Press.

Poulantzas, Nicos (1973) *Political Power and Social Classes*, trans. Timothy O'Hagan. London: Sheed and Ward.

Tilly, Charles (1990) *Coercion, Capital, and European States, AD 990–1990*. Cambridge, MA: Basil Blackwell.

2 Forces of reaction and changes of scale in the world system of states

Joseph A. Tainter

Over 200 years ago, Edward Gibbon noted that the problem in studying the Roman Empire is not that it collapsed but that, with all the problems it faced, it lasted so long. It is significant but curious that Gibbon is rarely remembered for this observation. This oversight reveals important things about how we think of complex political systems. It is a truism of anthropology that in the socialization process, a child is taught to regard a cultural order as a natural order. To those who are born, socialized and live their lives in a state organization – a group that includes all of Gibbon's readers – complex political organization seems normal and inevitable. The possibility that any state would not go on and on, perpetuating itself indefinitely, is to most people inconceivable. Thus Gibbon's great insight, that the Roman Empire was not intrinsically a sustainable institution, has been overlooked for generations.

In a society that lacks historical knowledge, each crisis is perceived as unprecedented, requiring a novel response. As Brian Ferguson has described so well in his Introduction to this volume, the diplomats and policy-makers who manage today's crises of cultural violence and political disintegration do so largely without adequate information. Many do not understand the background to today's events well enough even to realize how little they know. This has practical consequences: decisions that are based on an incomplete or incorrect understanding of events are as likely to exacerbate a problem as they are to be merely ineffective. Unfortunately we cannot know the full consequences of popular and professional misunderstandings of cultural and political conflict. Such misunderstanding is great, however, and its effects are likely to be of equal magnitude.

Some brief historical commentary will show readily the extent to which common understandings of today's events are misinformed. The points to be made are as follows: First, tendencies toward disintegration are normal and inevitable, and should never surprise us. Second, integration, disintegration and violence are substantially reactive processes, and respond to the actions of external powers. Third, conflict is not intrinsic to cultural differentiation. And fourth, contrary to the writings of some pundits and scholars, today's centripetal tendencies do not presage a global collapse of states.

As Brian Ferguson and Yale Ferguson have indicated in their contributions to this volume, the concept of the state has multiple and problematical meanings. It is commonly taken to indicate a governing and administrative institution within set borders, superordinate to all other governing and administrative institutions within those borders, and reserving to itself the right to use force. It can also have an evolutionary meaning, as a specific type of political institution that developed late in human history. Some scholars see states as fictive actors, who can be favored or harmed just as a person can be. Yet others focus on the individual actors whose activities collectively comprise state behavior, and whose interests frequently conflict.

A primary focus of this chapter is complexity, a neutral and measurable dimension that supersedes much of this conceptual diversity. Complexity is differentiation in structure and organization, combined with behavioral constraint. More complex systems are characterized by greater differentiation in structure and organization, and by greater constraint. Following from this, the term "state" is used here to mean a highly complex political system that exists within a proclaimed territory, is preclusive within that territory, and reserves to itself the right to use force. The focus is complexity, rather than viewing the state as an institution, an actor, a concentration of actors, or an abstract type.

Tendencies toward disintegration

From a historical viewpoint, the emergence and persistence of complex political institutions is not something that we would intuitively expect. Complex societies such as states are recent in our history, and statistically they are rare. There is a simple reason for this: complexity costs. In the realm of complex systems there is no such thing as a free lunch. Complex living systems of any kind – whether organisms, societies of ants, or societies of people – are costly, requiring high support levels *per capita* (Tainter 1988, 1995, 2000). The cost of complexity is the energy, labor, money or time that is needed to create, maintain and replace systems that grow to have more and more parts, more specialists, more regulation of behavior, and more information. Before the development of fossil fuels, increasing the complexity and costliness of a society meant that *people* worked harder. Thus the development of complexity is one of the wonderful dilemmas of human life. Over the past 12,000 years, we have developed increasingly complex institutions that cost more labor, time, money and energy, and that go against our aversion to such costs. We have done this for a simple reason: most of the time complexity works. It is a basic problem-solving tool. Confronted with problems, we often respond by such strategies as developing more complex technologies, establishing new institutions, adding more specialists or bureaucratic levels to an institution, increasing organization or regulation, or gathering and processing more information. Such increases in complexity work in part because they can be implemented rapidly, and typically build on what was developed before. While we usually prefer not to bear the cost of complexity, our problem-solving efforts are powerful complexity generators. Thus, contrary to common assumptions, there is no latent or inherent tendency toward complexity in human societies, and pressures toward greater complexity are always tempered by the cost of supporting more complex institutions. Complex political systems are maintained through a continuous flow of resources, which are used for problem solving, institutional maintenance, legitimation, or coercion (Tainter 1988).

We should not be surprised that complex political systems are liable to disintegrate. The surprise is rather that they do so infrequently. Complex political systems are prone to collapse, and have been collapsing for nearly as long as they have existed. Gibbon's observations on the essential instability of the Roman Empire bring to the foreground a basic impediment to understanding such matters. For lack of a more elegant term it may be called *the bias of valuing complexity*. The bias of valuing complexity is the normal result of the socialization process, and most of us, even social scientists, incorporate it unconsciously. In essence, the bias is that we value complex state organization and its correlates in the political, intellectual, literary and artistic spheres. We assume that state organization is normal, inevitable, desirable and enduring. It is regarded as a commendable condition of human affairs, for which we are prone to congratulate ourselves (Tainter 1988: 197–199). Given this framework, when states disintegrate we are led automatically to ask "What went wrong?" In many cases this may be the wrong question. To those of us who have been socialized in a state system, it rarely occurs to ask whether statehood itself is endurable. Rather than assume that state political organization is naturally persistent, we would do well in many cases to ask how it is maintained in the face of so many factors that weigh against it.

In the international political arena, the bias of valuing complexity has led to significant misunderstanding and tragic blunders, and it continues to do so. It has been assumed without discussion that the peoples of the world *must* be organized into states, and that these have to be structured precisely in the Euroamerican image. Complex political systems abhor vacuums, and political actors in states always feel compelled to arrange the world in their own image. When the great powers gave up their colonies in this century, they naturally organized the formerly subject peoples into states. In the intervening years it has become clear that this process was poorly conceived, that it is a triumph of form over substance. Many of the states thus created have been unraveling ever since. Many have continued to exist only through continuous inputs of outside resources, such as petroleum and money, and increasingly through the intervention of outside military forces. Control over such inputs has come to be a major instigator of conflict, as Catherine Besteman shows in her discussion of Somalia in this volume. As these states disintegrate, political leaders in the United Nations and the great powers apply the only thing they know: further exercises in state building.

The bias of valuing complexity leads politicians and journalists to see the demise of states as a fall into primordial chaos, the Hobbesian war-of-all-against-all. Seen thus, the disintegration of states takes on the trappings of an apocryphal struggle: good versus evil, light versus dark, liberal values versus ethnic intolerance, statehood versus chaos. Unfortunately, political actors in places such as Lebanon, the Balkans, Somalia and Rwanda have created situations that reinforce these superficialities. In response, political leaders treat the symptoms of imposed statehood with further exercises in state building, not understanding that the events of today are the consequences of similar decisions taken decades ago.

Yet the building of states in this century has accomplished what, in the Middle East, would be labeled as "creating facts." While specific new states may become undone, statehood itself now cannot be. As argued below, the emergence of a world filled with states is substantially irreversible. Statehood likely cannot disappear from some parts of the world unless it disappears everywhere.

Reactive processes

Archaeologists and historians can identify, in all of human history, only between two and five cases of primary state formation. Every other state, over the past 5,000 years, has formed as a response to the existence of other states. The formation and continuance of states is fundamentally a reactive process. This process is still in operation today, and probably always will be. It is especially pertinent to understanding today's events. A period of over 500 years of colonial expansion, followed by a century of deep Western economic and cultural penetration of all parts of the globe, has created a situation where most of the world's peoples must define themselves partly in relationship to Europe and North America (see, for example, Friedman 1993: 229; Marx 1993: 159). It was inevitable that many such peoples would come eventually to define themselves in opposition to Euroamerican dominance, leading to such things as reactive ethnonationalism, religious fundamentalism, and millenarian movements such as *Sendero Luminoso*. These reactions have exploded recently in a contagious manner, a process facilitated by global communications and travel, and by the media. It becomes a dialectical ingredient of such reactive nationalism to reject arrangements imposed by dominant powers. For this reason, and others, we should not be surprised that pressures to realign borders are evident in so many places today.

It is clear in this volume, and from other research, that many of today's conflicts are the outcome of great power expansion and meddling. Disillusionment with Western-derived models of "modernity," for example, has contributed to the rise of Hindu, Sikh and Moslem nationalism in South Asia (Spitz 1993), and to the violence described well by Johanna Lessinger in this volume. In other contexts, Brian Ferguson has made exactly this point in regard to conflict among the Yanomami, and to the broader phenomenon of indigenous conflicts during the period of colonial expansion (1992; Ferguson and Whitehead 1992).

Today, territorial and political arrangements in the areas of former colonies, and in the territories of the former Ottoman, Austro-Hungarian and Soviet empires, have created conditions that lead societal subgroups rapidly to become more sharply defined. Cultural groups that once coexisted now begin to stress their differences, even considering themselves to be "traditional" enemies. In a contrary but parallel process, new identities of unity are emerging where previously they have not existed, as among the Maya of Guatemala (LeBaron 1993; Warren 1993).[1] In some cases there is actual ethnogenesis, which was apparently a policy of the Soviet Union (see, for example, Entessar 1993: 117; Schoeberlein-Engel 1994; see also Aklaev 1992; Rudensky 1992). This process has a self-perpetuating aspect to it: in a competitive environment it is vital to be a member of a competitive group.

We are presented here with a dilemma. States are often inhibited in their cohesion by ethnic differences, but in many cases, ethnic distinctions are a product of, or are reinforced by, states. This dilemma both illustrates the problematic nature of statehood, and points to the need for historical analysis. A primary lesson of this volume is that we cannot understand today's conflicts unless we know about pre-conflict organizations and the distributions of cultural characteristics. Regrettably, outside of anthropology, such knowledge seems to be limited.

It is illustrative of the reactive process that where conflict involves disenfranchised groups (as to some degree it always must), among those without access to the benefits of so-called modernization and Western-style economies, an ideology emerges that transforms disenfranchisement into denial. Modernity and Western influence become evils to be purged, as seen today in Islamic fundamentalism (e.g., Denoeux 1993) and Hindu nationalism (Lessinger, in this volume). What one cannot have is not right to have anyway.

Cultural relations and the organization of competition

If one learned of today's conflicts only through news media, one might think that conflict is an *intrinsic* aspect of ethnic relations, that it is somehow inherent in the nature of cultural identity. Certainly in the media today it is common to account for such violence as that in Rwanda by reference to "ancient tribal feuds," and to refer to ethnic antagonisms in the Balkans as the product of generations of socialization – "drunk with the mother's milk" is a common metaphor.

Political breakdowns must be legitimized culturally by symbols of differentiation. These cultural symbols must be understood, yet analytically they must also, for some purposes, be transcended. In the absence of strong forces favoring integration, and in the presence of similar forces favoring disintegration, any symbol of cleavage, such as religion, kinship, class or ethnicity, may serve to legitimize a breakup, and certainly one can always be found. While the symbolism of cultural differences is endlessly intriguing, and of the greatest importance in individual ethnographic cases, there is also much to be learned on another level of analysis: understanding what forces favor integration or disintegration, and how they are expressed in individual cases.

In the chapters in this volume, conflict can be seen to have arisen over access to resources, economic or political or both, either presented by or otherwise linked to the outside world. In each case, the competition is over a resource perceived to be desirable and scarce, or inequitably distributed. The resource may be economic opportunity, political power, or self-interest masquerading as a cultural movement. In no case do we see the kind of *inherent* conflict between ethnic groups that seems to be assumed by journalists and the public. Although media depictions have tended both to glamorize and to demonize the worldwide upsurge in ethnic identity, ethnicity in this context is merely one criterion for organizing competition in a society. In different contexts, competition is organized equally well by other criteria, such as class or religion.

Bette Denich's account of the violence in the former Yugoslavian states is particularly illustrative. She shows that the current outbreak of conflict can be traced to economic decline in the 1980s, which was brought on by mismanagement and the need to repay international debts. These debts were acquired in the 1970s in the era when massive, questionable loans were being made to developing countries. This aggressive loan-making was a response to the huge deposits of petrodollars arising from the quadrupling of oil prices in late 1973. It is a great irony that the economically marginalized young men of Denich's account are fighting a war instigated by an economic event that happened at roughly the time of their births. Most of them are undoubtedly unaware of the connection of this remote event to their current cause, preferring to believe, and proclaiming to the world, that cultural differences are the sole reason for their war.

There is nothing in cultural differentiation that leads inherently to violence. The inland Niger River delta of Mali, for example, contains what must be one of the world's most complex ethnic mosaics. The groups that occupy this area – Bozo, Somono, Bambara, Marka, Bobo and Fulani – tend toward specialization in their subsistence production and settlement locations. Bambara millet farmers favor high levies and dunes. Bozo fish shallow waters, while Somono fish the mid-river with nets. Marka tend to be rice cultivators, and the Fulani pastoralists. As the floodwaters in the Niger Delta rise and recede, these groups have different peak labor periods. A group that is inactive for part of the year may assist others, as Bozo may help Marka rice cultivators as the waters recede. Fulani graze harvested millet fields, and their animals deposit manure that aids soil fertility.

Although these groups tend to specialize, their subsistence pursuits are generalized enough to reduce the dangers of monocropping. And while they tend to occupy discrete landforms within the delta, there are still conflicting claims to subsistence uses of some lands, and to water rights. Yet owing to a degree of subsistence specialization, and to a complex system of exchanges of labor, products and services, these groups interact with few conflicts, and with minimal governmental supervision (Gallais 1967; McIntosh and McIntosh 1980: 338–344). The conflicts that do arise are attributable to concrete disputes over land, water, and the timing of their use – not to cultural differences, which are substantially a means to organize use of the land.

Disintegration and the future of states

Even taking into account the poor quality of media reporting, it certainly does seem that the world is unraveling everywhere. Some scholars have foreseen a continuing balkanization process, and perhaps the development of a new kind of post-colonial state based on centers of power commanding fairly small territories. Certainly it is not hard to foresee that this could be the outcome of processes underway now in parts of Africa and central Asia. Going further, some have suggested that what we see today may be the start of the breakdown of the post-colonial world system, and the beginning of a global collapse (e.g., Ferguson 1993; Kaplan 1994). Such ideas are not to be taken lightly. Collapse is a recurrent historical process, and no complex society is immune to it. In a survey a few years ago about two dozen historical collapses were found (Tainter 1988: 5–18, 1999). There must be dozens more, perhaps even hundreds, that are simply not documented in historical records.

Perhaps the most influential advocate of this view is the prominent military historian Martin van Creveld (1991). His argument is that war in the future will be waged by amorphous, non-state entities organized on the basis of religion or ethnicity. Such groups tend to pursue what is often called "low-intensity conflict," which involves small, flexible forces, low-technology weapons, use of terrain for tactical advantage, lack of distinction between combatants and civilians, and an overall conception of conflict that nation-states tend to label "criminal" or "terrorist." Since the end of World War II the forces of nation-states, with their ungainly, imprecise weapons, lack of maneuverability, and high logistical requirements, have rarely been successful against such forces. Van Creveld extrapolates from this experience to suggest that as nation-states lose the ability to fight effectively, and to protect their citizens, they will lose legitimacy. People will not be loyal to organizations that cannot protect them. Van Creveld asserts that "[t]he use of low intensity conflict may, unless it can be quickly contained, end up destroying the state. Over the long run, the place of the state will be taken up by warmaking organizations of a different type" (1991: 192).

The characteristics of such new organizations are hard to foresee, but Van Creveld suggests that they may in various places resemble tribal organizations, robber baronies, or the feudal organizations of sixteenth-century Japan (1991: 197). These entities, moreover, will be unable to control large, contiguous pieces of territory (Van Creveld 1991: 203). Thus Van Creveld foresees what would truly amount to a global collapse[2] – a shift to a lower level of complexity – as nation-states disappear and are replaced by smaller, localized, less complex organizations.

Van Creveld's analysis is based on an erudite knowledge of military history and parts of his assessment are compelling. Journalists such as Robert Kaplan (1994), as well as military planners, have been influenced by Van Creveld's views, and have helped to disseminate them. His forecast for the future of the nation-state is undermined, however, by too narrow a view of the functions and evolution of states. Given that complexity is costly, and that states always encounter tendencies toward disintegration, the continuance of state organization is a benefit/cost function (Tainter 1988: 91–126). If protection of citizens was the only benefit of state organization, the weakening of this function would clearly undermine statehood and engender collapse. While organization for competition has certainly been a factor of the highest importance in the history and evolution of states (see, for example, Tainter 1992), states do much more than merely this. They provide a variety of organizational, ideological, economic and information-processing functions as well. These include maintaining order and adjudicating disputes, reinforcing value systems, building and maintaining infrastructure, regulating economic transactions, monitoring the state of the society and its environment, and many more. All of these functions reinforce statehood, even in the absence of a credible national capacity for war.[3] To these must be added the "top-down" factors that also reinforce statehood, including the political manipulations of elites and the interests of multinational corporations.[4] While low-intensity conflict may indeed, as Van Creveld suggests, be the future of war, the fact that the great powers have not yet mastered it does not foretell the demise of state organization. Threats to specific states, especially in the Third World, are another matter, and many of these may be reorganized in coming years.

Having suggested that many contemporary states were poorly conceived, and that complex political organization is both improbable and unstable, I will also argue that we should not expect any wholesale demise of states in the near future. Those that are faltering will be propped up or reconstituted in some manner – or their disintegration, like that of Lebanon recently, will be contained. There are two reasons for this, both of which convey important historical lessons.

The first reason is that, despite the dysfunctional nature of many governments, state organization continues to have a role today. Consider a simple illustration of this point. Imagine a situation where parts of the world – in Africa, say – cease to be organized as states. Even in such areas, processes of reacting to external influences would continue in force. The peoples of such areas would still know about, and want, industrial goods. Some of them would know about and want education; others would desire to travel. Having communication with the rest of the world, their elites would emulate the political behavior and consumption patterns of elites elsewhere. This means that there would be a continuing need for air and sea ports, internal transportation, other infrastructure, maintenance, schools, teachers, technicians, regulations, passports, currency, taxation to pay for these things, and agencies to administer them. Governmental institutions would emerge indigenously, and might be more legitimate than those imposed from without.

The second reason is that political collapses can only occur in power vacuums (Tainter 1988: 200–203). Historically, collapses have taken place under one of two kinds of political situation, which it is worthwhile to illustrate. The first is where an isolated, dominant state is surrounded by societies at lower levels of complexity. The collapse of the dominant state leaves a power vacuum that no equivalent competitor can fill. The premier example is the collapse of the Western Roman Empire, which I describe first.

As a solar-energy based society which taxed heavily, the Roman Empire had little fiscal reserve. When confronted with military crises, Roman Emperors often had to respond by debasing the silver currency and trying to raise new funds. In the third century AD, constant crises forced the emperors to double the size of the army and increase both the size and complexity of the government. To pay for this, masses of worthless coins were produced, supplies were commandeered from peasants, and the level of taxation became oppressive (up to two-thirds of the net yield after payment of rent). Inflation devastated the economy. Lands and population were surveyed across the empire and assessed for taxes. Communities were held corporately liable for any unpaid amounts. While peasants went hungry or sold their children into slavery, massive fortifications were built, the size of the bureaucracy doubled, provincial administration was made more complex, large subsidies in gold were paid to Germanic tribes, and new imperial cities and courts were established. With rising taxes, marginal lands were abandoned and the population declined. Peasants could no longer support large families. To avoid oppressive civic obligations, the wealthy fled from cities to establish self-sufficient rural estates. Ultimately, to escape taxation, peasants voluntarily entered into feudal relationships with these land holders. A few wealthy families came to own much of the land in the western empire, and were able to defy the imperial government. The empire came to sustain itself by consuming its capital resources: producing lands and peasant population. Finally the empire collapsed, and the political organization of the western Mediterranean was greatly reduced in scale and complexity. In some places, war-making organizations emerged not unlike those that Van Creveld foresees.

The lesson of the Western Roman Empire for our purpose is that, because it existed in a power vacuum, it *could* collapse. It was surrounded by societies of lower complexity, none of which was able to reconstitute the scale and complexity of Rome. In the eastern Mediterranean, conversely, the Eastern Roman Empire could not collapse for the simple reason that a rival power – Sassanian Persia – was powerful enough to fill the void, and would have done so. The Eastern Roman polity might have disappeared but the complexity of its organization would not. An equally complex state would simply have taken its place (Tainter 1988, 1994, 1999).

In the second situation, one finds clusters of societies organized at about the same political, economic and technological levels (as described by Price (1977)). Such clusters have been termed "peer polities" in the archaeological literature (Renfrew 1986). In such cases, as we see among the Classic Maya and the Mycenaeans of Bronze Age Greece, clusters of these societies tend to collapse *simultaneously*. Again this has happened historically in the context of power vacuums: in these cases collapse occurred because there was no dominant power nearby to fill the political void (Tainter 1988: 202–203). The famous case of the Southern Lowland Classic Maya exemplifies this type of collapse.

A rising population during the last millennium BC forced the Southern Lowland Maya to clear the rainforest, initiate projects of intensive agriculture, and become enmeshed in a pattern of warfare that led ultimately to the building of massive fortifications and to a tradition of art that heavily emphasized conflict. Inscriptions and graphic art depict a society with intense rivalry among polities, the formation and dissolution of alliances, and the emergence of regional hierarchies. It was a competitive spiral from which no polity could withdraw. Yet Mayan cities could not support either large standing armies or campaigns of sufficient length and intensity to resolve conflicts. Lacking real force, Mayan centers signaled the size and strength of their support populations by the massive, exquisite public architecture for which they are famous. The cost of this competitive system increased over time, culminating in the period called the Late Classic (ca. 600–800 AD), just prior to the collapse. Across the Southern Lowlands, 60 per cent of all dated monuments were built in a period of sixty-nine years, between 687 and 756 AD. Yet the brilliance of the Late Classic period was supported by a peasant population that was impoverished and in poor health. Malnutrition and tropical illnesses spread as people were called upon to support increasing construction and competition. Suddenly the southern cities collapsed, within a few decades of each other, and at least one million people died (Tainter 1988, 1992).

Stalemated military conflicts are among the most damaging of human circumstances. Each polity must maneuver continuously to expand at a neighbor's expense, or deter the neighbor from doing likewise. Defeated powers are typically soon ready to fight again, so that victories are symbolic and short-term. A polity that threatens to dominate will soon find powerful alliances arrayed against it. The costs of military preparedness escalate, as the competitors search continuously for an advantage. More and more resources must be allocated merely to maintain the status quo. As diminishing returns degrade well-being, the participants in such a system must in time either find new energy subsidies to support growing complexity, or collapse (Tainter 1992, 2000). Among the Maya, the collapse of so many polities was completed across the Southern Lowlands within just a few decades. It appears that when peer polities, under competition, evolve greater complexity in a lockstep fashion, they are likely to collapse in the same manner. Together they reach a state of fiscal exhaustion. In the Mayan case, no outside state had the reach or power to take advantage of the vacuum.

The lesson again is that state organization cannot and does not disappear where there are neighbors or competitors strong enough to fill the void. The expansion and contraction of states is a reactive process. Where a state appears to be disintegrating, other states are drawn in almost like insects to light, or matter to a black hole. They are drawn in to seek advantages for themselves, as we see in the involvement of Libya in Chad. They are drawn in if only to preclude a competitor gaining an advantage, as we have seen in the involvement of Syria and Israel in Lebanon. They may even be drawn in for humanitarian reasons, as in Somalia. If none of these conditions applies, they will be drawn in from the bias of valuing complexity, and from the corollary abhorrence of a lack of perceived structure. Although no politician will admit to it, and perhaps none even recognizes it, this last is no doubt much of the reason for the outside world's involvement in places such as Chad and Somalia.[5]

Thus the complex political systems that we call states are unlikely to disappear from substantial parts of the globe while remaining in the rest. Where specific states disintegrate, statehood itself would be reconstituted indigenously or reimposed from outside, or the territories of former states would be absorbed or at least administered by states that remain. Only the low cost/benefit ratio of administrative investment in places such as Chad and highland New Guinea prevents this in a few, isolated areas. Overall, for statehood to disappear, it must, as with the Maya, disappear globally.

Although the factors favoring the continuing existence of states are now very strong, current policies of shoring up political and territorial stasis may sometimes be ill-conceived. The genie of ethnonationalism is out of the lamp, and however much political leaders might wish otherwise, it cannot be put back. The forces of change that have been unleashed can be resisted or they can be accommodated. Thus the prospect in many parts of the world today is to choose between violence arising from attempts to resist change, and violence arising from the enactment of change. The difference between the two may be that while the former could continue indefinitely, the latter holds at least the hope of ultimately satisfying some of the causes of violence, and the potential for an ultimate equilibrium. Since the early 1990s, it has seemed like that equilibrium might involve the formation of dozens or even hundreds of new nations, which would necessarily be much smaller on average than those of today. But it should be understood that, however small they might be, these would still be state-organized societies with governing institutions.

The point is not to recommend balkanization as a policy. It is offered only as a scenario that seems more likely than global collapse to characterize the world over the next century. Of course such a scenario implies a host of new challenges to be resolved. The proportion of such small states that would prove economically, politically and militarily sustainable is uncertain. History suggests that competition and economies of scale would in time favor the formation of larger states again (see, for example, Tainter 1992). Thus when the possible formation of small states is referred to as an equilibrium, that term is meant only in the most transitory and relative sense: a system less chaotic than that which exists today and is foreseeable tomorrow.

While conflicts over states, territories, and resources seem the norm today, there is a contrary effort worth noting. It is ironic that today we applaud steps toward decentralization in firms and governmental agencies, but not in paramount institutions. An experiment in decentralization has been adopted as the policy of Mali, under the leadership of President Alpha Oumar Konaré (Mission de Décentralisation 1997, n.d.). In principle, nearly all responsibilities for administration will devolve to localities, as will the revenues for government. Localities will become responsible for such matters as roads, policing, and land-use management, and will control whatever resources are available for these. The state, conversely, will become relatively powerless and penniless. It will presumably remain responsible for national defense (although in early 2000 the Malian army was reported to have been reduced to about 3,000 soldiers, who are poorly equipped). The level of responsibility for large projects, such as the *Office du Niger*, is unclear.

The details of how to implement this idealistic policy remain uncertain, and President Konaré is, at the time of this writing (December 2000), in his last term. While doubtless there will be many problems of implementation, it is in one way an astute move. President Konaré is a historian by profession, and certainly understands well the factors underlying African conflicts. If the policy of decentralization can succeed, he will have created an African state that is not worth fighting over.

Concluding remarks and implications

Three points concerning the future of states seem to be strongly warranted by our knowledge of history and the evolution of human societies, and by this discussion.[6] They seem largely to be unknown to today's leaders, yet have significant implications for understanding today's events. First, instability is normal in states. It cannot be shown that states are ever stable for more than short periods.[7] Today's instability is a condition that is normal and expectable in the broad context of the history and evolution of states. It appears abnormal only because the improbable nature of statehood is not widely understood.

Second, reactive processes of state formation and disintegration will continue. The process of reacting to dominant states has been one of history's most salient characteristics for the past 5,000 years, and is the reason why the world today is filled with states. It is also a major cause of today's violence. Most of the world's peoples must now define themselves in relation to Euroamerican dominance. That some would come to define themselves in opposition to Westernism was predictable from simple dialectics. Continued meddling and arranging of the world by great powers may make affairs worse by provoking further reactionism.

Third, it is not clear that great powers should always oppose breakdowns into smaller states. Such breakdowns could alleviate some of the problems of reactionism. It is not a question of a world without states, or with some peoples organized into states and some not. Nation-states will still exist, however small. The small states that emerge will evolve according to their own economic viability and competitive position in respect to other states.

In the near future, then, it is unlikely that we will see complete political breakdowns that last for very long. We can foresee in the world system of states changes in scale, but not collapse. Political actors in dominant states feel compelled to fill political vacuums, and this essential attribute of statehood will not disappear soon, if ever. Despite the costs of statehood, the factors underlying it are very strong. Weak states will continue to be supported (at least minimally) by outside resources, unless industrial economies weaken to the point where support has to be suspended. Specific states may be under siege, but statehood itself is not.

Acknowledgements

I should like to thank Bonnie Bagley Tainter for comments on this paper and its earlier versions, R. Brian Ferguson for the invitation to prepare it, Barbara Price for suggestions during the meeting at the New York Academy of Sciences, and two anonymous reviewers for their thoughtful recommendations.

Notes

1 In an interesting case study, Longina Jakubowska describes how contemporary Bedouin resist Israeli attempts to assign an ethnic classification to them. She quotes the principal of a Bedouin school as complaining: "if it was not enough what they [i.e., the Israeli administration] are doing to us, now they tell us we are an ethnic group" (Jakubowska 1992: 85). Yet despite this sentiment, the Bedouin are developing increased religiosity, political identity and identification with the Arab cause, in reaction to Israeli domination (Jakubowska 1992: 100).
2 That is, the loss of an established level of social, political, and economic complexity (Tainter 1988: 4).
3 Most nations have little capability to protect their nationals beyond their borders, against low-intensity conflict or any other kind of violence, yet are not in danger of collapse. Van Creveld's analysis does not take into account either the multiple functions of state organization, or the ideological commitment of citizens to nationhood.
4 I am grateful to Barbara Price for pointing out to me the importance of multinational corporations in this context.
5 This reasoning, derived from the bias of valuing complexity, was once used to legitimize colonialism. It has reappeared recently in arguments that only the reimposition of colonial-like arrangements can save Third-World nations from themselves.
6 I will not reiterate here the point that conflict is not inherent in cultural identity. That message emerges clearly in the chapters of this volume.
7 Relative, that is, to the roughly 99 per cent of human history characterized by small, independent, acephalous, kinship-based organizations (Carneiro 1978: 219).

References

Aklaev, Airat (1992) "War and Social Stress and Their Effects on the Nationalities in the U.S.S.R." In G. Ausenda (ed.), *Effects of War on Society*. San Marino: Center for Interdisciplinary Research on Social Stress, pp. 194–210.

Carneiro, Robert (1978) "Political Expansion as an Expression of the Principle of Competitive Exclusion." In Ronald Cohen and Elman R. Service (eds), *Origins of the State: the Anthropology of Political Evolution*. Philadelphia: Institute for the Study of Human Issues, pp. 203–223.

Denoeux, Guilain (1993) "Religious Networks and Urban Unrest: Lessons from the Iranian and Egyptian Experiences." In Kay B. Warren (ed.), *The Violence Within: Cultural and Political Opposition in Divided Nations*, pp. 123–155. Boulder: Westview Press.

Entessar, Nader (1993) "Azeri Nationalism in the Former Soviet Union and Iran." In Crawford Young (ed.), *The Rising Tide of Cultural Pluralism: the Nation-State at Bay?* Madison: University of Wisconsin Press, pp. 116–137.

Ferguson, R. Brian (1992) "A Savage Encounter: Western Contact and the Yanomami War Complex." In R. Brian Ferguson and Neil L. Whitehead (eds), *War in the Tribal Zone: Expanding States and Indigenous Warfare*. Santa Fe: School of American Research Press, pp. 199–227.

—— (1993) "The World System and Violence: Retrospect, Prospect?" Paper prepared for the Symposium *Issues Surrounding Violence in Africa*, Institute of African Studies, Columbia University.

Ferguson, R. Brian and Neil L. Whitehead (1992) "The Violent Edge of Empire." In R. Brian Ferguson and Neil L. Whitehead (eds), *War in the Tribal Zone: Expanding States and Indigenous Warfare*. Santa Fe: School of American Research Press, pp. 1–30.

Friedman, Edward (1993) "Ethnic Identity and De-Nationalism and Democratization of Leninist States." In Crawford Young (ed.), *The Rising Tide of Cultural Pluralism: the Nation-State at Bay?* Madison: University of Wisconsin Press, pp. 222–241.

Gallais, J. (1967) "Le Delta Intérieur du Niger." *Mémoire de l'Institut Fondamental d'Afrique Noire* 79.

Jakubowska, Longina (1992) "Resisting 'Ethnicity': the Israeli State and Bedouin Identity." In Carolyn Nordstrom and JoAnn Martin (eds), *The Paths to Domination, Resistance, and Terror*. Berkeley: University of California Press, pp. 85–105.

Kaplan, Robert D. (1994) "The Coming Anarchy." *The Atlantic Monthly* 273(2): 44–46, 48–49, 52, 54, 58–60, 62–63, 66, 68–70, 72–76.

LeBaron, Alan (1993) "The Creation of the Modern Maya." In Crawford Young (ed.), *The Rising Tide of Cultural Pluralism: the Nation-State at Bay?* Madison: University of Wisconsin Press, pp. 265–284.

McIntosh, Susan Keech and Roderick J. McIntosh (1980) "Prehistoric Investigations in the Region of Jenne, Mali: a Study in the Development of Urbanism in the Sahel, Part ii: the Regional Survey and Conclusions." *British Archaeological Reports International Series* 89(ii).

Marx, Anthony W. (1993) "Contested Images and Implications of South African Nationhood." In Kay B. Warren (ed.), *The Violence Within: Cultural and Political Opposition in Divided Nations*. Boulder: Westview Press, pp. 157–179.

Mission de Décentralisation (1997) *Guide Pratique du Maire et des Conseillers Communaux*. Bamako: Republique du Mali, Mission de Décentralisation.

—— (n.d.) *La Commune en Questions*. ... Bamako: Republique du Mali, Mission de Décentralisation.

Price, Barbara (1977) "Shifts of Production and Organization: a Cluster Interaction Model." *Current Anthropology* 18: 209–234.

Renfrew, Colin (1986) "Introduction: Peer Polity Interaction and Socio-Political Change." In C. Renfrew and J.F. Cherry (eds), *Peer Polity Interaction and Socio-Political Change*. Cambridge: Cambridge University Press, pp. 1–18.

Rudensky, Nikolai (1992) "War as a Factor of Ethnic Conflict and Stability in the U.S.S.R." In G. Ausenda (ed.), *Effects of War on Society*. San Marino: Center for Interdisciplinary Research on Social Stress, pp. 181–193.

Schoeberlein-Engel, John (1994) "Toppling the Balance: The Creation of 'Inter-Ethnic' War in Tâjikistân." Presented at the Conference "The State Under Siege: Political Disintegration in the Post-Cold War Era," 22–23 April 1994, New York Academy of Sciences, New York.

Spitz, Douglas (1993) "Cultural Pluralism, Revivalism, and Modernity in South Asia: the Rashtriya Swayamsevak Sangh." In Crawford Young (ed.), *The Rising Tide of Cultural Pluralism: the Nation-State at Bay?* Madison: University of Wisconsin Press, pp. 242–264.

Tainter, Joseph A. (1988) *The Collapse of Complex Societies*. Cambridge: Cambridge University Press.

—— (1992) "Evolutionary Consequences of War." In G. Ausenda (ed.), *Effects of War on Society*. San Marino: Center for Interdisciplinary Research on Social Stress, pp. 103–130.

—— (1994) "La Fine Dell'Amministrazione Centrale: Il Collaso Dell'Impero Romano in Occidente." In Jean Guilaine and Salvatore Settis (eds), *Storia d'Europa, Volume Secondo: Preistoria e Antichità*. Turin: Einaudi, pp. 1207–1255.

—— (1995) "Sustainability of Complex Societies." *Futures* 27: 397–407.
—— (1999) "Post-Collapse Societies." In Graeme Barker (ed.), *Companion Encyclopedia of Archaeology*. London: Routledge, pp. 988–1039.
—— (2000) "Problem Solving: Complexity, History, Sustainability." *Population and Environment* 22: 3–41.
Van Creveld, Martin (1991) *The Transformation of War*. New York: The Free Press.
Warren, Kay B. (1993) "Interpreting *La Violencia* in Guatemala: Shapes of Mayan Silence and Resistance." In Kay B. Warren (ed.), *The Violence Within: Cultural and Political Opposition in Divided Nations*. Boulder: Westview Press, pp. 25–56.

3 The state concept and a world of polities under perpetual siege

Yale H. Ferguson

As the only political scientist among so many distinguished anthropologists, participating in "The State under Siege" conference was an unusually enjoyable and enlightening experience for me. I felt entirely at home, not only because my conference colleagues were so generous in welcoming an alien ("the other") from a different discipline in their midst, but also because they and I are obviously wrestling with many of the same issues.

Polities, nationalism and ethnicity

My own specialization most would describe as international relations (IR) theory. That used to be thought to imply a focus on relationships *among* states rather than on what happens *inside* states, with the possible exception of the foreign policy-making process. However, as our conference made clear and I shall reiterate, structures and trends at the global level are crucial to explaining contemporary challenges to the state. Moreover, my own work and that with my longstanding co-author, Richard W. Mansbach at Iowa State University (cf. Ferguson and Mansbach 1991, 1996, 1999a, 1999b; Ferguson *et al.* 2000), on what we term the "polities" model argues that international relations is inseparable from politics at all levels. In fact, we therefore prefer to use the term "global politics" rather than "international relations" to denote the subject of our study. We are interested primarily in patterns of authority (which we define as substantial influence or control) and their relationships to identities, ideology and loyalties; and what such relationships have to tell us about why political entities of all kinds prosper, decay, or die.

Our intellectual perspective is perhaps closer to that of anthropology, archaeology or sociology than of traditional IR scholars in political science. We regard the world of global politics as not exclusively or even primarily one of states, rather one of many different types of polities[1] – layered, overlapping and interacting – that coexist, cooperate, compete and conflict. "The state" in our framework is "just" one type of polity, distinguished by its particular "independent" legal status, emphasis on boundaries and territoriality, and normative claim to be the highest authority and symbol of identification in the modern international system. Where we differ strongly with most archaeologists and anthropologists is with regard to their persistent use of the term "state" to refer to a host of different polities in the ancient and medieval (pre-Westphalian) worlds (e.g., the Hittite state, the Athenian state, the Aztec state, and the like). Such entities were actually, variously, kingdoms built on aristocratic relationships in a feudal-style society, cities, empires, and so on. To call them "states" or even "proto-states" before Westphalian Europe invented the whole notion of "state" is to interject a present-day cultural bias into a much earlier context. It is the political equivalent of talking about the wheeled carts on Roman roads being automobiles. For that matter, as I shall explain, there are plenty of problems that arise from using "the state" as an analytical concept even in the twenty-first century – it is an ideal type or reification that can be very misleading – but at least most educated persons today understand more or less what is connoted by the term.

In fact, events and global trends over the last decade or so are convincing even an increasing number of political scientists and international relations scholars that there is a great deal more to the world than states. The role of transnational corporations, banks and hedge funds in processes of globalization, and that of ethnic identity, religion and culture in the flip-side of globalization – fragmentation and localization – make non-state actors more difficult than ever to ignore. I like to tell the story of a panel on "Non-state Actors in World Politics" that I participated in at a meeting of the International Studies Association in the mid-1970s. A few of the panelists, who rightly thought of themselves as being pioneers in those days because of their interest in things such as firms and terrorist groups, privately expressed their amusement that one of the papers was about the Kurds. Who, indeed, were the Kurds? Who could possibly care? Political scientists then regarded ethnic groups as quaint residues of benighted "tribal" times, amorphous identities that the political socialization campaigns of modern governments were inexorably erasing. Since the "nation-state" was ascendant almost everywhere, we could safely leave the Kurds and other such exotica to anthropologists or ethnomusicologists.

Not long ago "nationalism," too, was a phenomenon associated almost entirely with states. The "new nations" were insisting upon their "right" to "national self-determination"; colonial empires were crumbling; and new "nation-states" were emerging with boundaries that normally reflected former colonial divisions. In a broader sense, nationalism was seen as the characteristic assertive behavior of all old and new states in international politics. "Realists" (a school of IR theory that should always be written with a capital "R" and quotation marks) confidently assured us that we now had a world of billiard-ball states, with no "insides" worth considering except for power capabilities. Each state pursued its "national interest" objectively as those goals enhancing its power and security in an "anarchical" international system. Therefore, what we mainly needed to worry about was ameliorating interstate conflicts.

Today, as Brian Ferguson notes in his Introduction to this volume, we are far more likely than we used to be to appreciate the difference between "state" and "nation." But the confusion still persists insofar as some commentators continue to insist that one of the pieces of evidence that the state is alive and well in our world of globalization and fragmentation is that so many "nations" are still agitating for their own states. This is doublethink of the worst kind: existing states are facing demands for secession, so all must be well with states! It is also wrong-thinking in other respects: many nationalist groups "only" want or will settle for various forms of autonomy rather than independent statehood, and most of those whose demands are not met will go on causing serious trouble for existing states indefinitely. Some groups want full control of the states they are already in. Any way we look at it, a substantial number of states around the globe are under siege from restive nations or "ethnicized" political groupings, whether that siege is through orderly political processes (as in the UK or Quebec or Catalonia) or is taking the form of violence (as in the former Yugoslavia, Spain's challenge from the Basques, some of the former Soviet republics, the Middle East, or many parts of Africa).

In retrospect, IR theories were far more "primitive" and benighted than ethnicity, which these days in any event has risen in status in various scholarly quarters in the name of multiculturalism or saving local cultures from the globalizing homogeneity of McWorld. IR theorists simply did not grasp how long and contingent the process of state-building was, even in Europe (Hall 1999; Krasner 1999; Spruyt 1994; Thomson, 1994; Tilly 1975), and that it was not firmly linked there with "nation" and "nationalism" until the nineteenth century. Nor did we appreciate how different most of the new "nation-states" in much of the rest of the world were from their European progenitors. And we did not understand that the relative quietude of "ethnic" strife even in the heart of Europe reflected at least as much the dampening effect of bipolar post-World War II *empires* as it did the triumph of the state as an institution. Francis Fukuyama (1992) got it at least partially reversed: it was the Cold War rivalry, not its demise, that temporarily made "history" seem to "end." Now that the Soviet Union and its empire have deconstructed and the East–West contest in its old form appears to be over, history has definitely not ended – it is reasserting itself. Historical memories are being resurrected. Age-old hatreds, as well as affinities such as the Russians' identification with "Slavic" Serbs, are being revived. Ethnic identity has come out of the closet, and no one is laughing about the likes of the Kurds anymore. Yet, given their continuing internecine conflicts, is it still appropriate to wonder: who are the Kurds? For that matter, is "Slavic" a meaningful category? Ethnicity, too, is obviously an exceedingly troublesome concept.

Give the state its due

A theorist's responsibility is to insist that we cannot get the most out of our cases or begin to generalize effectively without first getting our concepts in order. Postmodernists rightly warn us that it is impossible to get consensus about anything like a concept. However, we have at least to become more self-conscious about the terms we use and the extent to which they help or hinder analysis and genuine understanding. Concepts, like all theoretical constructs, oversimplify "reality" and tell us what is important and what we can safely ignore. One of our conferees, in discussion, suggested that "the state" is a concept that we would have to invent if it did not already exist. But the facts are that the state as a concept *does* already exist and thinking about the world of the twenty-first century, let alone the pre-Westphalian world, as a world of states confuses at least as much as it clarifies. What exactly do we mean by "the state" – who or what is it? "The state" has so many different, competing, and loaded meanings that its utility for theory-building and case analysis is marginal at best. Catherine Besteman, in her essay in this volume, speaks of Somalia as being perhaps "the most stateless place on earth." Today there are many "places" around the globe – within states, "offshore" or transcending state boundaries like religions, markets or cyberspace – that might vie for that dubious distinction. But I do like her characterization because it implies that the state is a variable, highly contingent and subject to prevailing conditions. The state's degree of coherence, resources, and control over civil society and the external universe varies dramatically by place, time and the issue at hand.

However, let us be fair and give fans of the state concept their due. From one perspective, the state is a legal-normative ideal, a modern symbol and institutional expression of the "common good" that has been dear to the hearts of democrats, venal personal dictatorships, military juntas, and totalitarians alike. For many around the world, identification with one's "country" is still regarded as the highest and noblest identification of all, at least in principle. That qualification is extremely important, because in practice, as Susan Strange (Strange 1996: 72) points out, "it is much more doubtful that the state – or at least the great majority of states – can still claim a degree of loyalty from the citizen substantially greater than the loyalty given to family, to the firm, to the political party or even in some cases to the local football team." The clear exceptions, as she recognizes, "are the few states whose very survival is at stake," such as Israel. With the marked decline in interstate wars in recent decades, the citizens of most countries – in contrast to professional soldiers, who may be sent on dangerous peacekeeping missions – are not very often called upon to die for the state anymore. As Strange puts it: "[l]oyalty of that kind that is ready to die for a cause is more often found among ethnic or religious minorities" such as the Tamil Tigers or Hamas.

That said, we must acknowledge that the state is not just about symbols and rallying citizens for war but also has considerable substance in other day-to-day respects. Some governments of states have an impressive capacity to tax, and large treasuries, the monies from which help to fund infrastructure projects such as highways and services such as education and healthcare. Even in fragile states there is often some concentration of resources at the center, control of which, unfortunately, can be the main object of violent rebel forces. Also, alas, a substantial portion of the national treasury of numerous countries resides in foreign bank accounts of the president or ministers. States typically have standing military and police forces of varying reliability, including some that are more likely to threaten the government than defend it. Politicians and bureaucrats claim to have a Weberian monopoly of the legitimate use of violence and other "sovereign" powers within state boundaries. They are supposed to establish and guarantee an effective legal system to punish criminals and ensure stable property rights. They act in the name of the state, assuring everyone that their policies embody, yes "Realists," the national interest, however vehemently opposing politicians and interest groups may deny it. We should all ask ourselves how many of the world's states actually live up to such standards.

From the perspective of the global system, the sovereignty principle posits a universe of truly independent states. As Robert Jackson (1990) has reminded us in his work on "quasi-states," with particular reference to Africa, the shield of sovereignty has given many shaky and corrupt governments a measure of freedom from external interference they might otherwise not have had. He says it has been a sort of "negative sovereignty," protecting elites and their privileges at the expense of the vast majority of citizens. The response of most governments to Saddam Hussein's invasion of Kuwait does reaffirm that state boundaries do still matter when someone marshals an army and marches across them in the stance of a naked aggressor. Moreover, most states do have some control – often not nearly as much as they would like – over the movement of persons and trade across their boundaries. Also, only states are allowed to be members of most international organizations. Policies emanating from governments (or parts of governments) do affect the evolution of international law, formal and informal regimes, and a host of global issues.

A variety of states

Thus, as we have seen, the state is not without considerable substance, albeit quite varied substance. Nevertheless, fans of the state concept cannot escape four essential points: First, when it comes to the world's two hundred or so states, one size certainly does not fit all, except with regard to some of the standard claims mentioned earlier. Actual states run the gamut from the world's one remaining superpower, to the varied older (and not so old states) of Europe and Latin America, to the restive conglomerates of India and China, to the trading city-state of Singapore and other somewhat troubled Asian economic powerhouses, to the oil emirates of the Middle East and conservative monarchy of Saudi Arabia, to the shaky republics spun off from the former Soviet Union, to the Taliban's Afghanistan and the Iran of the mullahs, to several failed states in Africa, and so on and so on, down to numerous mini-states such as Nauru or Tuvalu (whose main asset, that provides about half of its GDP, is its possession of "tv" as a web address). The fact that all these various entities are sovereign states is worth knowing, but is much less helpful than a lot of other information we need to have some real-world sense of what sort of polities we are dealing with!

Multiple identities and loyalties

Picking up again upon Strange's observation and one that myself and Richard Mansbach have repeatedly stressed in our own work, we come to a second essential point: the state is only one of many group symbols with which persons identify, and it is a profound error to overestimate the extent to which loyalty to the state, anywhere, always or often, comes first (or much farther down the list). All of us humans have multiple identities and loyalties, most of which coexist without serious conflict most of the time, but which under certain conditions can be the source of cross-cutting pressures or prove entirely irreconcilable. Loyalties to self and such extensions of self as family, clan, village, city, ethnicity, religion, profession, firm, political party, faction or ideology regularly undermine the political stability of states and everywhere limit support for government policies. Current public opinion polls around the world, not least in democracies, reflect an almost universal disillusionment with the governments in power. That suggests that citizens are entirely able to separate in their own minds loyalty to country from anything owed to the politicians who are widely thought to be a national disgrace.

An essential puzzle is not whether individuals have many identities – of course they do – but rather why some identities and loyalties come to the fore at certain times and not others. This question speaks directly to the concerns of our conference. Why are most Yugoslavians reasonably content to be Yugoslavians one year, and the next year violently divided into Serbs, Bosnians, Croatians, Slovenes, and so on? Bette Denich addresses this issue directly in her essay on the former Yugoslavia. Elsewhere, why are Ukrainians reasonably content one year to be part of the Soviet empire, and the next year in open revolt, and soon thereafter electing a leader pledged to closer ties with Russia? It appears that multiple identities and loyalties can coexist for long stretches of time, but then situations or issues arise that force individuals and groups to make invidious choices. The political change that results from such choices is continuous, although in some periods it proceeds so slowly that it is almost imperceptible.

At this juncture, we need to return to that other fuzzy concept, ethnicity – that is, the nation that the UN Charter proclaims has a right to national self-determination. This nation is distinct from, although often related to, the legal "nationality" recognized by states as well as the more restrictive category of "citizen." I tell my students that the only wholly secure definition of "nation" is "a people who think they are one." That is actually about all one can say with certainty, but the question remains: *why* do they think they are one? There is considerable literature on this subject, which boils down to those writers who stress the ancient "primordial" and/or historical roots of "nation" (e.g., Smith 1986) and those (e.g., Gellner 1983) who determinedly argue that nations are the essentially artificial creations of the modern state.

This intellectual controversy seems to me to be much ado about little. To be sure, nearly all governments – as well as many elites who oppose them – are hard at work, for their own ends and with greater or lesser success, trying to socialize persons politically. The American government over time did an impressive job convincing an ethnic hodgepodge of citizens that they were "American" and nonetheless could maintain some of their ethnic heritage, a compromise symbolized today by hyphenated Italian-Americans, African-

Americans, Mexican-Americans, and others. Rwandan government political socialization efforts failed, even as tribal elites succeeded in sharpening the Hutu/Tutsi division, which remained incomplete anyway (as Brian Ferguson emphasizes in the Introduction to this volume). However, writers stressing the ancient roots of nations are correct, too, because national myths (and myths they are) almost always draw together some bits and pieces of common history or culture. It is a very selective process and hard to predict which bits and pieces will prevail. Why do these myths take the form they do? Why does political socialization work sometimes, or for a time, and not other times? We're back to fundamental questions: What identities are important for what purposes? Why are persons loyal? Why do old political affiliations wane and die, and new ones emerge?

Part of the reason that states persist, of course, is that their governments all exercise some coercion along with attempts to persuade. Some governments exercise a lot of coercion, Pinochet, Haitian leaders, or the KGB spring to mind. An identity can to some extent be imposed, although most are not. For example, you might have been told a few years ago that, like it or not and whatever your other identities (e.g., Armenian Catholic), you were a citizen of the Soviet Union. But, Mansbach and I argue, loyalties are largely an exchange phenomenon and cannot be imposed. Persons are loyal when they are getting benefits in exchange, including the not-to-be-underestimated psychological satisfaction that may come from being associated with a group and its ideology. Conversely, loyalty tends to diminish when the costs of association persistently seem to exceed benefits. Linda Seligmann thus correctly asks in her essay on Peru: how does what Peruvians have been getting from the government of Peru compare to what they have been getting from its competitors, such as Sendero Luminoso and drug plantations. Peru is one of many extreme cases, but nearly everywhere around the world a better educated and "wired" citizenry is getting harder to fool, making more demands of government, and insisting that political elites honor their promises. Unfortunately, this is happening at a stage in world history when governments are losing their grip and are less and less able to deliver (more on this shortly).

Limitations of sovereignty

A third major point anyone impressed by the state concept must come to grips with is that legal sovereignty, either in its domestic or its international dimensions (if we can separate these two realms, which we increasingly cannot), has at most only modest consequences. Brian Ferguson has commented that "states are both objects and subjects of struggle" (in the conference that led to this volume). As we too have observed, whatever resources the government has, which sometimes is not all that much, different groups may want. Far from possessing a monopoly on the use of violence, governments that are widely regarded as illegitimate and/or incompetent and/or vulnerable often are unable to preserve a modicum of domestic tranquillity. They are routinely challenged by military coups, roving bands of rogue military, street demonstrations, guerrillas in the mountains or jungles, urban terrorists, ethnic warfare, warlord gangs, criminal cartels, and so on. Control of violence and crime is a major preoccupation even for many popular governments. In all cases, *pace* Weber, the existence of the violence and criminal behavior itself is as significant as its "illegitimate" or "outlaw" nature. Indeed, some anti-government behavior may be seen by the general populace as being much more legitimate than the government.

Our examples also highlight the important fact, which statist theorists tend to neglect, that groups other than governments have major resources as well. For years social science literature has perpetuated the false impression (which perhaps can be traced to *laissez-faire* economists) that there is a clear distinction between "public" and "private" sectors, and that those interested in politics are primarily concerned with the state. In fact, the line between public and private is continually shifting, and in most open economies the "private sector" has had far more total wealth at its disposal than governments. So if politics, authority and governance have to do with the effective allocation of values, we cannot afford to ignore the likes of value allocators such as firms and banks (cf. Cutler *et al.* 1999). They may not be inclined to physical violence, but they have much to do with the fortunes of states and citizens. In most countries, arguably, the value of a national currency is more dependent upon the behavior of local entrepreneurs, investors and consumers – and global financial market speculators – than it is upon the actions of central banks (Greenspan nothwithstanding), let alone anything a national legislature does. Daily currency flows vastly exceed the amounts needed for actual trade in goods and services, and in any event most trade is already managed and accounted for intra-firm.

The essays in this book demonstrate that many of the challenges states face are from the unsettling effects of broad trends in global politics and the world economy. If, as Brian Ferguson has always asserted with reference to the Yanomamos, conflict tends to be conceived in local terms but, in fact, responds to changes in the external environment, then there must be an awful lot of change "out there"! What then are we to expect but escalating conflict? For example, although the world has obviously gained in other ways from the end of the Cold War, we have lost whatever stability emanated from the two blocs. Is US hegemony an effective substitute? The Cold War left dangerous things behind, from automatic weapons in the hands of Somali teenagers to bloated military establishments (some with nuclear arsenals), old Communists, and inexperienced non-Communist political elites. The Cold War's demise also – this is where Fukuyama was correct – left us with the apparent normative triumph of free market capitalism and the political ideal of democracy. Whatever their merits, both have led to a great deal of economic and political turmoil in parts of the world where they had been practiced not at all, to a lesser degree, or in non-Western forms. Now we have the additional disturbance of a backlash against "globalization" that afflicts developed and developing countries alike (cf. Friedman 2000; Held *et al.* 2000; Scholte 2000).

Most important, as the whirlwind of events over the last decade suggests, change in the world at all levels seems to be speeding up. We're experiencing more and more of what James Rosenau (1990, 1997) has termed general "turbulence." Most governments – not just those in the developing world – are facing growing problems arising from such sources as the technological and communications revolution, a better-informed and less passive citizenry, and the transaction flows controlled by transnational firms and banks (not to mention individual investor day-traders). The world with respect to markets has moved from national capitalism to alliances and networks among firms. Governments hardly understand the full dimensions of what is happening, and therefore even what data to gather, which of course is a prerequisite to designing policies for effective regulation. Some analysts, such as myself, doubt whether substantial regulation of markets (even if desirable) can ever be accomplished by governments, because they each operate in too small an arena, intergovernmental cooperation is so cumbersome to build, private firms are light-years ahead in thinking globally, and market structures and practices are evolving at a bewildering pace. Whatever reforms are required will probably have to come (if at all), as they did in the wake of the 1930s stock market collapse and depression, in the wake of crises and at the behest of the private sector itself. That, of course, raises the question of who is the servant and who is the master, which the tail and which the dog. In fact, if governments are going to act at anybody's behest, they will have to do so in concert, because the problems to be addressed obviously transcend the boundaries of individual states.

Among the changes out there in the world is the rapid growth of larger and larger units, international organizations and regimes and a host of non-governmental organizations (NGOs), as well as the transnational firms, banks, alliances and networks we have already mentioned. We also have increasing political fragmentation. The two trends (Rosenau's "fragmegration") are going on simultaneously and are related. For example, the very existence of larger entities such as the European Union, NAFTA, and transnational business and finance – not to mention some older organizations such as the UN and NATO – seems to make smallness a more viable alternative for breakaway mini-nationalisms such as the Croatians or Quebeçois. They think they may have new affiliations to fill some of the gaps left by the ties they chose to sever. Also, preserving and enhancing one's small group may provide a last refuge for the familiar in the midst of global change. Yet small is often vulnerable, and a radical decline in living standards – let alone death at the hands of ethnic cleansers – may well be too high a price to pay for reaffirming small group identity.

The state is not an actor

A fourth major point that devotees of the state concept have to recognize is that states, as such, do not behave. The state is not an actor, certainly not a unitary actor. Individuals, bureaucracies, parties, self-interested military establishments – a wide variety of groups within, without, and extending across state boundaries

– act. States do not. Policies may be attributed to states (e.g., US policy on such-and-such), but given adequate information we can and should trace the source of every so-called state policy to non-state sources. Those non-state sources are sometimes embarrassingly in evidence when different politicians and bureaucrats offer strikingly different interpretations of what the policy actually is. There is competition *within* virtually every government in the world both when each significant policy is being made and when it is implemented. If anything, the internal competition has grown more severe, sometimes to the point of gridlock, as modern governments have become increasingly bureaucratized and otherwise more institutionally complex.

De-reifying the state has an additional analytical virtue, forcing us to ask again: who or what is the state, and whose interests does it really serve? Despite all the propaganda to the contrary, government elites are rarely representative of the populace at large. Under-representation of particular ethnic or other groups in the institutions of government makes it difficult for the state even to pose as a "higher" and "neutral" defender of the public interest. The general citizenry does not benefit equally, and many are benefiting hardly at all, from either the direct largesse or trickle-down from state programs. Nevertheless, no government will survive for long if it is not benefiting someone, at the minimum a corrupt elite stratum (e.g., an old-style Latin American dictatorship). We should not leap to accept the dubious old argument that poverty and oppression are the major causes of violence. Throughout history, most violence has been perpetrated by elites who are doing quite well, thank you, via the states and empires that they dominate – motivated by greed rather than need. The scholarly literature on the subject tells us that those who have most to gain from violence are normally the slowest to resort to it, except when conditions suddenly go from bad to intolerable. Much more volatile are middle-class setbacks after a period of rapid progress. Ironically, then, the more economic and social progress we make, the greater the risk of explosive downturns, and all the turbulence on the world economy certainly does not help in that regard. We should also keep in mind that elites exist at all levels of society, not just in an upper stratum. Once a pattern of violence sets in, it is often difficult to stop, not only because violence can evolve into a "culture" or way of life (death) but also because elites among the group(s) involved tend to develop significant status – psychological, and sometimes material, stakes in the continuation of violence. Just as governments of states may serve narrow interests, the same can be true of anti-government leadership.

In sum, in the sense that the government of a state is typically divided against itself and must compete both with a highly variegated civil society and with transnational actors, the besieged state is hardly a new phenomenon. Indeed, polities of all kinds have been under siege since the beginning of human association, insofar as they have continually had either to oppress and/or to justify their existence by meeting the demands of their constituents. However, for the reasons we have discussed, the challenges for the state do appear to be intensifying in the present era.

The future of the state

Another key theme considered by the conference was the future of the state. As Brian Ferguson suggested in his opening address, the Westphalian state has had a pretty good run as a model for a few hundred years and it may be that the world is moving on – perhaps even hurtling on. In fact, the Westphalian state model has been realized to a large extent only in Europe and not everywhere, satisfactorily, there. It is instructive to think of Italy, caught in the identity crossfire among cities, regions and the Mafia. Be that as it may, where do we go from here, both within and beyond existing states? Rearranging boundaries forcibly from the outside is still likely to meet widespread resistance, but the increased cost of war versus the decreasing value of territory (except as regards ethnic "homelands") should mean the incidence of interstate war will continue to decline. Nevertheless, as we have noted, boundaries are being rearranged in a number of places from the inside and, in any event, are constantly being transcended.

States are surely not going to disappear, not least because they still have considerable utility and capacity to attract allegiance. Anyway we look at it, however, the role of the state is going to have to adapt and change. That said, the entire world is in urgent need of new political arrangements for which we do not always have the appropriate ideas or forms or words to describe. There are hundreds of international functional regimes, including many that never make the headlines, that are exercising significant amounts of control over particular issues such as fishing, telecommunications, transportation and river pollution. In the very birthplace of the Westphalian state, the Europeans have forged a European Union, a still-evolving mixture of state, community, region, city and network governance, which traditional notions of federal, confederal, consociational or subsidiarity do not seem to capture. The experiment is, in many respects, unprecedented and is at best of limited relevance to what may yet be fashioned elsewhere in the world. When the smoke clears on the battlefields of breakaway polities, there will have to be formulae invented to knit smaller units together in selective ways to form larger ones. One can foresee autonomy arrangements for certain minorities and economic (re-)integration for limited sectors of the economy. Fission and fusion will occur in the future as it has in the past, although with innovative forms and increasingly complicated interrelationships that are appropriate for our highly interdependent and incompletely "globalized" world.

What, then, are the policy implications for those established governments and international organizations that are watching so much of the rest of the world in turmoil? Helio Belik observes in his essay in this volume that both the UN and the OAU seem to be unable to have a significant effect on political conflict in Angola. While we are innovating institutionally in more limited arenas, are we not also going to have to fashion some new sorts of overarching global, regional or subregional arrangements to encourage peaceful settlement of disputes and to help guarantee whatever agreements can be reached with regard to minority rights? And how should the major powers respond when faced with future calls for humanitarian intervention in countries such as Somalia, Rwanda or Haiti, where conditions, by any measure, are truly appalling? Like the liberal social scientists most of our conferees are, we have been content – and perhaps a little too eager, I believe – to blame foreign influences for many of the difficulties experienced by indigenous regimes. To be sure, colonialism, neo-colonialism, Monroe Doctrine-style interventions and Cold War competition all have a terrible negative balance sheet to weigh against any positive contributions they may once have made. Should the rest of the world, then, take refuge in the argument that experience reveals that their involvement in local conflicts can do little good and may make matters worse? We scholars have tended to avoid this distasteful issue in our deliberations, but it remains a pressing one. Thus I will close with the observation that studying state identity and violence, in my opinion, carries with it a serious obligation to engage in the policy debate.

Note

1 In our conception, a polity is any entity that has a significant measure of identity, a degree of hierarchy (leaders and followers), and the capacity to mobilize persons for political purposes (that is, for value satisfaction or relief from value deprivation). There are many types of polities: families, clans, tribes, chiefdoms, cities, "states" in federal systems, cantons, religious entities, Westphalian or putative nation-states, regional international organizations, empires, and so on. Each of these is only an ideal type, while actual polities even of the same type obviously differ widely in the discreteness of their identity, organization, and capacity.

References

Cutler, Claire, Virginia Haufler and Tony Porter (1999) *Private Authority and International Affairs*. Albany: State University of New York Press.

Ferguson, R. Brian (1999) "A Savage Encounter: Western contact and the Yonamami War Complex." In R. Brian Ferguson and Neil L. Whitehead (eds), *War in the Tribal Zone: Expanding States and Indigenous Warfare*. Santa Fe: School of American Research Press, pp. 199–227.

Ferguson, Yale H. and Richard W. Mansbach (1989) *The State, Conceptual Chaos, and the Future of International Relations Theory*. Boulder: Lynne Rienner.

—— (1991) "Between Celebration and Despair: Constructive Suggestions for Future International Theory." *International Studies Quarterly*, 35(4): 363–386.

—— (1996) *Polities: Authorities, Identities, and Change*. Columbia, SC: University of South Carolina Press.

—— (1999a) "History's Revenge and Future Shock: The Remapping of Global Politics." In Martin Hewson and Timothy J. Sinclair (eds), *Approaches to Global Governance Theory*. Albany: State University of New York Press, pp. 197–238.

—— (1999b). "Global Politics at the Turn of the Millennium: Changing Bases of 'Us' and 'Them'," *International Studies Review*, Special Issue 1(2): 77–107. Also in Davis B. Bobrow (ed.) (1999) *Prospects for International Relations: Conjectures about the Next Millennium*. Malden, MA: Blackwell Publishers, pp. 77–107.

Ferguson, Yale H., Richard W. Mansbach, Robert A. Denemark, Hendrik Spruyt, Barry Buzan, Richard Little, Janice Gross Stein and Michael Mann (2000) "What Is the Polity? A Roundtable," *International Studies Review*, 2(1): 3–31.

Friedman, Thomas (2000) *The Lexus and the Olive Tree*. New York: Anchor Books.

Fukuyama, Francis (1992) *The End of History and the Last Man.* New York: The Free Press.
Gellner, Ernest (1983) *Nations and Nationalism.* Ithaca: Cornell University Press.
Hall, Rodney Bruce (1999) *National Collective Identity: Social Constructs and International Systems.* New York: Columbia University Press.
Held, David, Anthony McGrew, David Goldblatt and Jonathan Perraton (2000) *Global Transformations: Politics, Economics and Culture.* Oxford: Polity Press.
Jackson, Robert H. (1990) *Quasi-States: Sovereignty, International Relations, and The Third World.* Cambridge: Cambridge University Press.
Krasner, Stephen D. (1999) *Sovereignty: Organized Hypocrisy.* Princeton: Princeton University Press.
Rosenau, James N. (1990) *Turbulence in World Politics: A Theory of Change and Continuity.* Princeton: Princeton University Press.
—— (1997) *Along the Domestic-Foreign Frontier: Exploring Governance in a Turbulent World.* Cambridge: Cambridge University Press.
Schoulte, Jan Aart (2000) *Globalization: A Critical Introduction.* New York: St. Martin's Press.
Smith, Anthony D. (1986) *The Ethnic Origins of Nations.* Oxford: Blackwell.
Spruyt, Hendrik (1994) *The Sovereign State and Its Competitors.* Princeton: Princeton University Press.
Strange, Susan (1996) *The Retreat of the State: The Diffusion of Power in the World Economy.* Cambridge: Cambridge University Press.
Thomson, Janice E. (1994) *Mercenaries, Pirates, and Sovereigns.* Princeton: Princeton University Press.
Tilly, Charles (ed.) (1975) *The Formation of National States in Western Europe.* Princeton: Princeton University Press.

4 Tribalism, ethnicity and the state

David Maybury-Lewis

Tribal or indigenous peoples do not occupy a prominent place on the world's agenda, so it might seem odd to include them in a discussion of state, identity and violence. After all, if anybody has been under siege, it is tribal peoples and usually at the hands of the state itself. I shall argue, however, that the situation of tribal peoples belongs very much in this discussion, in fact that tribalism, ethnicity and the state are concepts that cannot be properly understood without reference to each other.[1]

According to the evolutionary theories that provided the rationale for colonialism in the nineteenth century, tribal peoples were savages, those same "squalid savages" to whom Teddy Roosevelt referred in *The Winning of the West*, when he wrote that this great continent of ours could not have been left as their playground. In this view, civilized people had no obligation to negotiate with savages. They might have to on occasion, but once they had established their own power and authority they were justified in dealing with savages as inferiors, as people to be civilized, who must on no account be allowed to impede the progress of civilization. These were the attitudes that lay behind the genocidal horrors inflicted by imperialists at the tribal margins of their empires.

Nowadays enlightened opinion is too sophisticated, or too politically correct, to insist on the contrast between our "civilization" and the "savagery" of the indigenous or tribal peoples who bear the brunt of it. We have other discourses, however, that serve similar purposes. There is the discourse of development, according to which tribal peoples stand in its way and cannot be permitted to do so. This implies that, in the name of development, the lands and resources of tribal peoples must be taken away from them and used by others. This ignores the fact that this is by no means a necessity of development, but rather an aspect of power politics. Powerful interests or mainstream populations covet tribal resources. The state backs them and the indigenous groups suffer.

There is the discourse of culture, according to which tribal societies are supposed to possess cultures so fragile that they cannot adapt to the modern world. They are therefore dying out. This is said to be inevitable and even a good thing, for they will then no longer stand in the way of development. This overlooks the fact that indigenous societies have shown remarkable resilience and ingenuity in adapting to modernization while maintaining their own cultures.

Above all there is the discourse of the nation. Indigenous peoples are said to threaten the nation by wishing to secede from it or simply by fragmenting it. This ignores the fact that very few indigenous peoples wish to secede from the states in whose territory they find themselves. The draft declaration on indigenous rights, published by the UN Working Group on Indigenous Populations, makes it clear that self-determination for indigenous peoples refers to autonomy *within* states, for it specifies the rights of such peoples within the state and the responsibilities of the state towards the indigenous groups. The real threat that indigenous peoples are perceived as posing is the threat of fragmentation. If they are permitted to maintain their own languages and cultures and not to blend into the mainstream of the states in which they live, this requires that those states be organized as multi-ethnic polities, yet it is precisely the multi-ethnic state which is so energetically and so widely opposed.

In the west this opposition has been grounded in the enlightenment tradition that has dominated our thinking since the French revolution. According to this tradition the state could and should be the progressive and rational matrix for human social organization. It would, as Rousseau thought, reflect the "general will" of its citizens, dealing with them uniformly and on an equal footing. The state would be the organizational form of the nation, that hard to define entity consisting of a body of people with a sense of belonging together, of having a common history and a common culture.

The idea that the state should correspond to a nation and vice versa has been the source of endless confusion, exacerbated by the United Nations, which is an organization of member states. One of the first pronouncements of the UN after its birth was the Universal Declaration of Human Rights, aimed at protecting the rights of individuals. Meanwhile the organization has, for obvious political reasons, been most solicitous of the rights of states, even when it was those very states that were infringing the rights of the individuals that the UN claimed to protect. The organization has however been notoriously skittish about the rights of peoples who do not control states. This was clearly evident during the political manoeuvering that preceded the declaration of the Year of Indigenous People. The member states were reluctant to give recognition to peoples who were demanding autonomy within their states. Since they had agreed to celebrate the quincentenary of Columbus' first voyage to the Americas, they felt however that they could not reject the demand of indigenous peoples for corresponding recognition. Nevertheless, member states lobbied hard and successfully to change the name of the event from the Year of Indigenous People*s* to the Year of Indigenous People. The omission of the final "s" indicated that the majority of member states would agree to recognize indigenous people as having only individual rights, not group rights.

This antipathy to group rights derives from the enlightenment thinking already mentioned, which considered ethnic attachments archaic and undesirable, exclusionary and divisive. They could be tolerated in properly modern states only if they were secondary and sentimental, as folklore in fact. They could not be tolerated as important markers of identity and were especially to be shunned in the political arena. A corollary of this view was that ethnicity would disappear with modernization. In the meantime it should be ignored, helped to disappear, or actually suppressed. Both the Marxist and non-Marxist versions of western thinking subscribed to this view. Marxists argued that ethnicity was false consciousness, which would evaporate as people understood their true interests under socialism. Non-Marxists argued that ethnicity was an archaic form of tribalism that would vanish as modernization ushered in the liberal state.

Both views have recently been exposed as being glaringly wrong. Ethnicity is not disappearing. On the contrary, it continues to be a powerful force in world affairs and ethnic conflicts are erupting on every continent. This has left yesterday's theorists without explanations, or rather it seems to have left many of them clinging to the wrong explanation. They believed that ethnicity was a kind of atavism which would be eradicated by modernization in the march toward civilization. The pillars of this civilization would be nation-states. If, therefore, nation-states are still plagued by ethnic conflicts, even in the most modern nations of western Europe, it follows that civilization has somehow been unsuccessful there. From this it is only a short step to concluding that the "natural" or "primordial" ethnicity of humankind just bubbles up to create havoc wherever civilization, in the form of the appropriate nation-state, has not taken hold. This kind of reasoning focuses too much on the theory of the liberal state and too little on the experiences of actual states in recent times. The nation-states of western Europe for example are relatively recent phenomena. A German state that would unite all (or even most) Germans has always been problematic and German thinkers such as Fichte and Herder, while they longed for a state that would express the *Geist* or spirit of its German inhabitants, were nevertheless doubtful that it could be realized in practice. Even the French, who exalted the state, could only do so by ignoring the ethnic and linguistic differences among themselves. In 1789 half the population of France did not speak French at all and a century later half of the population considered French a foreign language. Scholars are now re-examining the states of western Europe and concluding that they too have only recently and sometimes partially succeeded in establishing themselves as nation-states. Nor have these states always served as good examples of the values of the enlightenment. Fascism and Nazism arose in western Europe. Stalinism and a number of lesser dictatorships have also plagued European states in recent times. In fact, a close examination of the record makes it harder and harder to determine which European states correspond to the Rousseauesque conception of the state or to the modernizing ideal put forward by our own theorists.

Yale Ferguson notes in this volume that Third World states differ from the European model. To this I would add that perhaps European states also differ from the European model, or at least from the model to which European states are supposed to aspire. It is true, however, that if the correspondence of actual states with this model is dubious in Europe, it is even more so elsewhere.

Latin American states have not been particularly successful in the task of national mobilization, in incorporating their citizens into the state and providing them with reasonable access to social and economic opportunities. At one extreme states such as Peru and Guatemala have historically excluded their indigenous majorities from full citizenship and have paid a severe price for trying to maintain their states as exclusive and oligarchic systems. At the other, inclusionary states such as Mexico and Brazil have insisted that their populations should all join the mainstream. Each nation ostensibly took pride in the racial mixture of its population and the hybrid civilization thus created. Each nation had its own version of *indigenismo*, intended to help its indigenous population to vanish into the mainstream. Mexico's *indigenismo* was intended for just this purpose. So was Brazil's *indigenismo*, but Brazil's indigenous peoples make up a tiny fraction of the country's population. Brazil's hybrid civilization rested instead on an amalgam of black and white citizens. Either way, both Mexico and Brazil left large proportions of their populations marginalized.

The newer African states have shown themselves to be notoriously weak. The colonial powers administered large territories, which normally contained various indigenous polities. After independence, these territories emerged as states, which usually included a number of ethnic groups that had little in common with each other apart from their common experience of colonialism. African leaders have, nevertheless, insisted on the integrity and viability of these inherited states, and stigmatized substatal ethnicity as "tribalism." The result has been either competition between powerful ethnic groups to control the state, or states which have been taken over and run hegemonically by representatives of one ethnic group. Either way, the potential for ethnic conflict has been considerable.

Asia too has been plagued with ethnic conflict. Interestingly enough, two of Asia's most important experiments in multi-ethnic coexistence have taken diametrically opposed tacks. Indonesia succeeded until recently in keeping the peace between its hundreds of disparate peoples by means of an authoritarian system of cultural and religious pluralism. India, on the other hand, worked to become a modern, secular, liberal state, which would refuse special recognition to or accommodation of ethnic groups. Instead it hoped this liberal state would provide the best non-sectarian framework within which India's ethnic groups, particularly those who defined themselves by their religions, could co-exist peacefully. India's traditional syncretism enabled the system to work for a while, but it is now under strain as conflicts between Hindus, Sikhs and Muslims threaten to tear it apart.

The Indian experience shows just how difficult it is to establish a liberal state where ethnic differences become irrelevant. This is an ideal which is seldom realized. This does not mean however that we must revise our ideas about "the state as we know it," but rather about the state as we thought we knew it. We cannot assume that modernization will lead to a certain kind of state, in which ethnicity disappears. It follows therefore that we have to contemplate new kinds of states in which ethnic differences are accepted and incorporated into their ideological and institutional structures.

If we need a new approach to the state, we also need (even more drastically) a new approach to ethnicity. Or rather, we need the world at large to take seriously the approaches to ethnicity that scholars have been developing for over twenty years. Ever since Fredrik Barth's book on *Ethnic Groups and Boundaries* (1969), anthropologists have been deconstructing ethnicity. We have long since established that ethnicity is neither inherently primordial, nor purely circumstantial. It is the potential, possessed by all human beings, of feeling a special kind of solidarity, analogous to kinship with their fellows. People may feel "ethnic" solidarity on the basis of race, language, religion, history, custom, or a combination of these. It is equally important to remember that ethnicity is not invariably activated and, even when it is, it need not lead to conflict.

Yet these insights, long known and documented, are currently being drowned by a cacophony of voices, insisting on a kind of sociobiology of ethnicity. Such a view considers ethnic conflict to be the result of a natural human tendency to band together with one's fellows and fight and kill those unlike oneself. According to this view the horrors taking place in the Balkans and Rwanda and elsewhere are no more than the continuation of primordial conflicts that have taken place since time immemorial. This is a convenient doctrine, for it enables those who espouse it to wash their hands of these "atavistic" conflicts and to ignore their own role in them.

The grimmest findings of recent anthropological research, as the chapters in this volume document only too clearly, are that ethnic conflicts are frequently the result of deliberate instigation and manipulation. Nor is this only a game for insiders. States inflame ethnic conflicts in other countries, as do terrorists, fanatics, and even entrepreneurs, dealing in drugs, armaments and other profitable ventures. The dirty secret of ethnic conflict is that it is not the result of human tribalism, nor of unquenchable historical passions. On the contrary, it is normally fanned into flame by interested parties.

If tribalism is not the cause of ethnic conflict, modernization is not the solution for it either. In fact, the globalization of the world's economy and the increasing internationalization of its processes and institutions is sapping the power of the state and increasing the possibility that people will seek refuge with their own kind. In many parts of the world, it is not only the political realignments, or attempted realignments that have led to conflict. It is these in combination with economic hard times, with social dislocation and its attendant alienation. In the best of times and in the most fortunate places the liberal state guaranteed political liberty to the individual and was the scene of intense struggles for equality. The fraternity that was supposed to accompany them did not often materialize. So people struggle for a sense of community, of belonging, and it is precisely in periods of change and modernization, when people feel most uncertain and fearful, that this quest becomes most urgent. It is in times like these, such as we are now experiencing, that the state appears unresponsive or actually alien to individuals, and citizens are therefore left to seek protection elsewhere. These are the times that offer the greatest opportunities for unscrupulous ethnic politicians. They offer the most dangerous solution of all – the ethnic state, corresponding to a single people. In such states those who do not belong to the dominant group must be eliminated: killed, driven out or suppressed.

It is this stark reality that indigenous peoples have always understood, for they are by definition peoples who have been subjugated by alien states. Since they have always been regarded as inferiors and outsiders, their rights have normally been neither much considered nor much respected by the states in which they find themselves. Indigenous peoples have always known what it was to be treated as ethnic undesirables by the states that claimed them as citizens, and they have learned that even liberal and democratic states do not always do justice to them. Indigenous peoples are thus a special instance of ethnic minorities, but one which highlights the problems minorities face in states that refuse to make a place for them.

This chapter sets out arguments and conclusions that are extensively documented in the case studies presented in this volume. These findings show that social scientists in general and anthropologists in particular have an urgent task to perform, namely to make these facts better known and to use them to counteract the commonly accepted falsehoods of the conventional wisdom. We must insist that indigenous peoples are not savages, that they do not stand in the way of development, and that they are capable of changing with the times even as they maintain their own cultures. We must insist that ethnicity and ethnic conflict are neither given in our genes nor atavistic peculiarities of certain societies. We need to show instead how a clearer understanding of the political economy of such conflicts demonstrates who instigates them and how and which outside forces are involved. Such an understanding is an essential first step if there are ever to be effective national and international efforts to prevent ethnic conflict. Finally, we need to show that it is necessary to rethink the theory and practice of the state. The traditional antidotes to ethnic divisiveness – a liberal state that tries to make ethnic attachments irrelevant or an authoritarian state that tries to suppress them – have not worked well, and the need for greater attention to the theory and practice of the multiethnic state is glaringly apparent.

The problem we face as social scientists is however more than a matter of giving the lie to the many misconceptions that surround these emotionally and politically charged issues. We need to understand why these misconceptions endure, in spite of the evidence against them, and to develop a clearer idea of what to do about it. We need, in fact, to mount the kind of challenge that Franz Boas and his students did to the racist ideas of their time. That challenge did not of course abolish racism, but it destroyed its respectability among serious people. We have yet to destroy the respectability of current misconceptions about tribalism, ethnicity and the needs of the state, and these are ideas whose consequences can be as devastating as racism.

Note

1   This argument has been set out at greater length in Maybury-Lewis 2002.

References

Barth, Fredrik (1969) *Ethnic Groups and Boundaries*. Boston: Little, Brown.
Maybury-Lewis, David (2002) *Indigenous Peoples, Ethnic Groups and the State*. Boston: Allyn and Bacon.

5 Culture, violence, and ethnic nationalism

Weighing alternative strategies of explanation and media representation

Kay Warren

What are the contending perspectives for the analysis of conflicts that involve ethnic intensification? Recent studies of conflict and violence have generated very different framings and languages of analysis which reflect discordant research paradigms in the social sciences.[1] Political scientists and sociologists often speak in term of leaders' self-interests, competition over scarce resources, and patterns of rational choice when they discuss politicized ethnicity (Horowitz 1985; McAdam *et al.* 1996; Young 1976, 1993). At issue in nationalist movements is the motivation of rivals for state power, particularly those who defy political systems and seek to undermine the integrity of the state.

As a result of the ubiquity of this framing, public commentators – be they academics, journalists, or policy makers – now routinely question political leaders' self-declarations in order to unmask opportunists willing to manipulate and inflame populations to their personal advantage. We find in these descriptions of "strongmen," "warlords" and "ethnic rebels" a willingness, sometimes a frightening eagerness, to promote the radical fracturing of society into antagonistic groups. The strategy is the unification of one's own group through wider divisive antagonism.

An alternative line of social analysis – used more commonly by anthropologists, social movement analysts, and culturally inflected political scientists – isolates patterns of cultural resistance to domination and oppression. This is less of a top-down formulation. Rather than ignoring those with limited access to power, this perspective seeks to diversify agency by including subaltern voices, local cultural practices, and distinctive hermeneutics. Resistance perspectives examine the way local communities, ideologies and actions reject the terms established for subordinates by state authorities and regional powerbrokers (see Carmack 1988; Corradi *et al.* 1992; Fox and Starn 1997; Hale 1994; Holland and Lave 2001; Sluka 2000; Warren 1993; Warren and Jackson 2002).

As has become clear in this literature, resistance takes many highly coded forms. James Scott (1990) argues that a tactical dual consciousness allows subordinates to feign submission yet hold subversive beliefs – in his terms behind-the-scenes "hidden transcripts"; Richard Falk (2001) observes that movements, particularly indigenous ones, often combine radical separatism and cultural autonomy with the fall-back position of working within state-centric systems for recognition, direct representation, and rights. Resistance literature tends to be less leadership focused and more concerned with cultural forms through which local populations keep their veiled social critiques alive. Most of this literature explores agency in the face of seemingly overwhelming domination and the ironies of dual (or multiple) consciousness (Aretxaga 1997; Das *et al.* 2000; Greenhouse *et al.* 2002; Nordstrom and Martin 1992). Obviously, one cannot read these codes of resistance from afar, that is, without knowledge of particular cultural circumstances and access to how people rework cultural forms to deal with the raw existential dilemmas they face.

The mix of opportunism and resistance approaches chosen for interpreting a particular conflict depends on a range of factors, including the historically and politically conditioned gaze of researchers working in regional studies traditions. Latin America – with its long colonial history, recent decades of military and authoritarian regimes, and rocky transitions to democracy along the path of jarring neoliberalism – has drawn the attention of resistance theorists. The transition from authoritarianism to democracy has generated a concern with low-intensity peace and with new hybrids of post-Cold War political resistance. Former guerrilla leaders who now seek structural change through party politics rather than rebellion are but one example. Counter-insurgency tensions have not disappeared in this transition, nor have anti-communist ideologies and clandestine Cold War institutions. Rather, polarized tensions created through earlier conflicts live on in dramatically transformed circumstances (Warren 2002a, 2002d).

Other world regions are involved in very different transitions, which create new authoritarianisms as often as new democracies. Africa, the Former Soviet Union, the Former Yugoslavia, and India – with their cultural mosaics, nationalisms on the right and left, religious fundamentalism, and fragmenting states – have drawn the attention of analysts who now stress opportunism and the capacity of leaders and elites to polarize conflicts (Huntington 1996; Kaplan 2000). I wonder if, in the rush to understand the intentions of leaders and the top-down perspective this induces, some analysts are missing the ways in which local culture influences the politics and persuasiveness of different forms of counter-nationalism – some ethnically charged and others not (Nordstrom 2000, n.d.; Sluka 2000).

The turn to politics, manipulation, and corruption; the legacies of great power involvement in national affairs; and the role of international arms trade in national and regional affairs – all mark a coming of age of anthropology as a field that, like comparative politics, speaks to current political crises. It is interesting that both fields seem to be taking the nation-state as the locus of anxiety. The "failed state" is one that loses control rather than one that fails its citizens in innumerable ways. Brian Ferguson's multilayered sovereignty (see the Introduction to this volume) and Aihwa Ong's (1999) graduated sovereignty are continually compromised and transformed by states' involvement in regional trade agreements and by wider patterns of international intervention throughout the world.

The mass media has been an important conduit of globalization. The media's focus on political instability and state fragmentation is made even more credible by the rapid circulation of graphic media images of mutilated bodies that represent "ancient ethnic hatreds." By looking at the production of news for particular markets, analysts have singled out the constraints that inhibit more comprehensive coverage: storyline conventions that influence how the news is told, organizational structure of the media industry that produces programming, and economic pressures that stem from reliance on advertising revenues (Allen and Seaton 1999; Moeller 1999). Over and over again, official media consumption promotes dangerously simplified and essentialized ethnic readings of conflicts, ones that reinforce primordialist readings of "the other".

If one looks more closely, for instance, at US news accounts of Bosnia, Chiapas or Rwanda, in fact one finds appalling initial ignorance and, as a story matures, more nuanced explanations of the conflicts. But subtle explanations are often lost in the persistent journalistic drum beat of "ancient ethnic hatreds," "centuries-old enmities" and "tribal antagonisms," and by photographs of primordial violence with little or no explanation of events from the participants' point of view. How the muting of combatant and civilian voices has become a conventional practice, accepted by wider publics, is an important issue. Wartime reporting by the Western press only seems to amplify these effects, especially when reporters mirror state norms for patriotism.

Such presentations in our mass media deflect attention away from the reality that the West has been directly involved in many "localized" conflicts through a history of colonial engagements (Mamdani 2001) and more recent economic and political interventions (Escobar 1995; Ferguson 1994). Thus, the move to examine the media coverage of conflicts is a welcome one because it reveals the political stakes of imposing a particular ethnic construction on a flux of events initially experienced by participants in much more diverse ways.

Further research on the media might examine the role of Western nationalism and the ways in which the audience reception of news of foreign conflicts reflects Western fears of its own internal diversity – so often naturalized biologically and redeployed in the language of euphemisms. Media research might also look for differential treatment based on our nation's definition of "spheres of influence," "strategic concerns," and "national security" – other legacies of the Cold War that continue in ever evolving ways to shape what policy makers know and journalists treat in the news. These discourses have been explicitly deployed, for example, in responding to the 2001 terrorist attacks on the World Trade Center and the Pentagon.

Additionally, studies of violence are examining the ways in which the leaderships of opposition movements use media to gain international leverage, as in the case of the Zapatistas' use of the internet (Nash 2001); how competing elites use the media to incite locally enforced genocidal violence, as in the case of Rwanda where radio was used to stir incendiary hatred between ethnic groups (Li 2001; Mamdani 2001); how militaries create training manuals with images of the "savage" other that justify preemptive violence (Schirmer 1998); and how personal oral narratives of violence are recrafted into different media for different uses, from *testimonio* literature to truth commission reports (Arias 2000).

In contrast to the overdetermined language of ethnic antagonism, recent research in anthropology on ethnicity demonstrates that many social systems involve the coexistence of diverse groups and hybrid identifications, and that politics in various parts of the world crosscuts ethnic, religious and linguistic difference (Hernández Castillo 2001; Kearney 1996). An important deconstruction of ethnicity is occurring through these analyses. In part this is a very old argument; in part it is a very novel one.

Discrediting primordialist readings of ethnicity – certainly an important step – need not, however, lead to a marginalization of the cultural stakes of these conflicts. The classical approach was to discredit ethnicity in order to uphold class or religion as the prime factor.[2] A more recent academic counter-trend is to widen the field of identities and identifications under consideration and to understand class as a creation of particular cultural and historical circumstance rather than a pre-established or transcultural set of categories (Warren 1998).

In some quarters, however, scholars have grown impatient with the direction of contemporary cultural analysis, particularly with postmodernist discussions of cultural hybridity and borderlands (Appadurai 1996; Ong 1999; Rosaldo 1989). Overflowing depictions of bicultural or multicultural identities are seen as instances where the hyper-real displaces a reality of violence, poverty, unemployment, blockades, state surveillance, repression, and social fragmentation. The indictment, advanced in these terms by scholars such as Victor Ortiz (personal communication) and Michael Kearney (1996), charges that our superficial fascination with mobility and change trivializes and effaces concrete situations of violence. But does this have to be the case?

By contrast, I would argue that a fuller cultural analysis, which pursues the multiplicity of identities and the flow of ideas and signs across borders (Gupta and Ferguson 1992), is central to interpreting conflict and the directions it takes. Deconstructing ethnic and primordialist arguments leaves a more complex, current and dynamic cultural field. To paraphrase Begoña Aretxaga (1997), the issue is not just meanings that mediate reality, but images that make imagination – in this case violence, fragmentation and/or coexistence – possible. Instead of assuming that people internalize the ethnic hatred and opportunist politics sold by corrupt leaders and the media – an assumption left unchallenged in US journalism by repeated photographs of armed mobs or irregular soldiers without any sense of people's reasons for their participation – we need to understand the playing out of contradictory consciousness in people's daily lives and the political consequences of these understandings. To make sense of low-intensity peace or nationalist crises, one must historicize and contextualize these forms of violence and the common denial of its institutionalization by governments engaged in counterinsurgency warfare (Warren 1993).

I am suggesting that we see conflict and violence not as exceptional moments and crises but as integral parts of a social fabric already fragmented in innumerable ways. I am also suggesting that we widen the scope of our analytical analogies so that in recognizing the dialogical character of identity, we do not reduce it simply to a practical competition over resources. To complicate the opportunist approach, more needs to be known about people's understandings of the contradictory tensions and the personal as opposed to collective interests in their lives. We also need to study the concrete forms of resistance and dominance people use to constitute their social worlds. Struggles over memory and history, culturally specific non-realist narratives for the expression of grievances, and the local constructions of "choice," "competition," and "opportunism" are all doors to a fuller cultural analysis (see Arias 2001; Malkki 1995; Tambiah 1986, 1996; Warren 1998). At issue in moments of crisis is the intensification and redirection of what is already there, what already generates cultural understandings. It is crucial to show the local terms of complicity in and resistance to violence.

For democracies and fragmenting states, duplicity, denials of wide-spread violence, and the displacement of blame are foundational strategies, whether it be in the urban US, rural Guatemala, or Afghanistan. Culturally informed analyses call for an array of strategies for studying representation, control, resistance and complicity – the violence within and beyond state borders. Significantly, these same strategies can be used to explore unexpected alliances and avenues of negotiation that might successfully challenge violence and its grammar of oppositions. Cultural analyses have direct bearings on how Western powers envision their political options: why has bombing been our prime solution in so many countries; why are we not promoting all sorts of options for negotiating violent conflict in Mexico, Ireland, Israel/Palestine, Afghanistan, Colombia, and elsewhere?

Chiapas, Mexico and Guatemala: an emerging contrast

Research on the Zapatista rebellion in southern Mexico and on cultural nationalism in neighboring Guatemala mirrors many of the same tensions and dilemmas I have discussed. Explanations of the Zapatista rebellion stress the corruption of local leaders by a one party system (the PRI) and state policies that rewarded mid-twentieth century cooptation with the power to redirect development resources and extend patronage systems locally (see Collier and Quaratiello 1994; Harvey 1994). As a result, the small Mayan corporate communities – the product of a historical interplay of colonial domination and highly localized indigenous resistance – were transformed into a troubling and very intolerant political form (which, it is important to add, did not have ethnic nationalist aspirations). With expanding populations and dwindling land bases, strongmen (*caciques*) pushed the poor and protestant converts out of their communities, forcing some into zones of recent colonization, where a mix of ethnicities and politics prevailed. Chiapas is a region in which people have had a long history of exposure to religious and class-based ideologies that have informed their political interests.

The historical moment for rebellion is a crucial element of this story: the 1994 Zapatista revolt occurred just as the Mexican government and urban middle classes were looking forward to the collegiality of NAFTA (the North American Free Trade Agreement) and, consequently, wanted to project the media image of a modern society with its own variant of democracy. Yet NAFTA brought with it new tensions for the rural poor, including subsistence shocks with cuts in government subsidies for staples and the repeal of *ejido* law that protected communal lands in rural Mexico. The rebellion has had many repercussions, among them the unmasking contradictory effects of national development policies, one-party democracy, and international economic integration.

The Zapatistas sought to expand their organization around these political and economic issues. The state responded with severe repression of rural communities and the creation of death squads that fractured rural communities and led to assassinations of local leaders and massacres of Zapatista sympathizers by others in their communities. Although Zapatistas quickly moved to negotiated peace and government reform (see Autonomedia 1994), even the subsequent Fox administration has not been able to garner political support for a peace process and truth commission or for the Zapatista demands for regional autonomy in a federalist system.

When the Western media shifted from calling the rebellion a "peasant" uprising to a "Mayan" one, I wondered if they had fallen into the trap of reinscribing ethnicity onto a conflict that, in reality, had diverse politics and identities. As Nash (2001) and Stephen (2001) argue, the Zapatista movement is at once an ethnic nationalist movement that has been shaped by Mayan community norms for participatory decision making and a heterodox multi-ethnic agrarian movement that uses the imagery of Mexican grassroots nationalism, neo-Marxism, and human, cultural, and gender rights. The model is ethnically inclusive and highly egalitarian, struggling with internal tensions, for instance, over gender issues. Nash (1967, 2001) and Stephen (2001) show the diverse impacts of growing rural impoverishment with NAFTA reforms and the ways resistance is expressed in local narratives of oppression. Their work makes a provocative case for a process of ethnic intensification in the face of regional and state violence which has involved the reweaving of neo-Marxist ideologies into culturally rooted Mayan ones, along with a transethnic concern for multiple dimensions of inequality and new models of participatory democracy. Peace has proved elusive.

Across the porous border in Guatemala, the struggle was in a different phase in the 1990s: the question was how to negotiate peace after the intense army-insurgent warfare which dominated the Mayan highlands from 1978 to 1985, displaced 20 per cent of the national population and killed an estimated 100,000 civilians. In fact, institutionalized ethnic intensification became part of the peace process, much to the surprise of many officials and citizens. The international human rights community and the leftist guerrilla insurgency – represented by the URNG rebel coalition – along with an assembly of the civil organizations pressured a recalcitrant government and army to negotiate a settlement that demilitarized the countryside, gave amnesty to combatants, outlined important democratic reforms, organized the return of tens of thousands of refugees, and recognized indigenous rights.

Two social movements converged across the peace process that lasted from 1988 to 1996: the *popular*, class-based transformation of the left; and the culturalist movement for the revitalization of Mayan identity. For a wider say in national politics, both movements engaged in projects of cultural and political standardization – a transformation of community identities into larger political blocks. Both concentrated on unmasking the public secret that state authorities supervised a policy of genocidal violence in the 1970s and 1980s during which the military destroyed hundreds of rural communities as it sought to punish civilians for their real or imagined support of the insurgents. To be indigenous was to be treated as the dangerous "other."

Activist groups lobbied for the creation of a truth commission to produce an accounting of the violence that focused on recognizing the victims and their stories, and documenting the high proportion of Mayan civilians killed by the army (CEH 1999). The Catholic church collected narratives of violence for their report (REMHI 1998). The courts have not been the focus of retribution since a general amnesty was declared for the combatants.

One response to this violence, which drew power from corrosive and very public racism, has been the revitalization of indigenous identity (Cojtí Cuxil 1991, 1995, 1996, 1997). Mayas are now attempting to create novel identifications to push not only for recognition and self-determination but also for a reconfiguring of national culture and state policy to promote federalism and the support of Mayan schools, the legitimacy of customary law, and the right of Mayas to have access to court interpreters so they can follow legal proceedings.

The question is whether the state will embrace democratic models for political representation. Mayan leaders are concerned about two kinds of representation: first, the democratic representation of formerly marginalized and disenfranchised peoples in all national social institutions; and second, a Maya role in the mass media through which citizens constitute their politics and identities. Until the peace negotiations, the Guatemalan nation-state had not conceived of itself as a multicultural one, and there is still great ambivalence about this recasting of the nation-state. The defeat of the 1999 indigenous rights referendum three years after the signing of the peace accords demonstrated the unfinished business of creating a consensus to reflect the peace accord motto of Guatemala as a "multi-cultural, ethnically plural, and multi-lingual" state and society (Warren 2002c).

In both countries, politicized identity and local culture are highly salient for understanding community responses to authoritarian politics and repression. Not surprisingly, local culture brings other conflicts and cleavages to the agenda of national politics. Obviously, these observations are only the beginning of what can be said comparatively about Chiapas and Guatemala.

Let me close this brief illustration by underscoring that, in this Mayan culture area, ethnicity is not a constant; nor has it been an unproblematic source of pan-community political mobilization in the past.[3] At one point, in conjunction with the conference, Brian Ferguson worried about the "dark side of multiculturalism" through which "robust cultural traditions are turned [by intellectuals] from mutual respect to mutual intolerance." In contrast, I would suggest we imagine diverse kinds of public intellectuals in other cultural systems and many roles for them – both complicit with and critical of polarizing violence.[4] The Zapatistas, who have a multi-ethnic constituency, have caused other indigenous groups to rethink their relation to the state and to press for regional autonomy and decentralized federalism. In Guatemala, by contrast, cultural nationalism operated as a source of social critique largely within the system or in parallel institutions such as private Mayan schools.

In Guatemala, full-time Pan-Mayanists are often educated urban-based elites, whose authority is, nevertheless, shaped and limited by Mayan leadership conventions from the rural communities where they maintain strong family ties. Older incarnations of the *kamol b'ey* (leaders, or "takers of the path" in Kaqchikel) have been revitalized by cultural nationalists in a way that places limits on individuals' powers. Community *kamol b'ey* have a continuing intellectual presence in Mayan society, part human archive of esoteric knowledge, part conciliator in the face of interpersonal conflicts, part choreographer of family and community religious life. Now national *kamol b'ey* are theorizing racism in books, creating local libraries, and dreaming of a Mayan university (Warren 1989). Their social criticism involves a complex interplay of tolerance and intolerance. As with the Black Consciousness Movement in South Africa, activists are theorizing the scars of racism, alternative political futures of the movement, and the legacies of local complicity in state violence.

Continuities in the social construction of authority and novelties in the ways in which new works are borrowed and reworked in the political quest for collective rights are important aspects of ethnic nationalist history. The status and mobility of Mayan elites, a benefit of their employment in internationally funded peace building and development work has resulted in the emergence of a parallel middle class. Upward mobility, however, has created new dilemmas for professionals whose reference group is not only their own people; they also strive to match the living standards of Ladino professionals (Montejo 2002). Montejo notes that the question many Maya professionals ask each other directly or indirectly is: "Are you *nivelado* yet?" (Have you caught up with the Ladino professionals in material measures of success and prestige? Have you arrived?) This competition puts intense economic pressure on emerging elites, many of whom come from humble backgrounds. For their efforts, they are rewarded with heightened *envidia*, with corrosive envy which has a long and painful history of fragmenting social relations and generating interpersonal violence in rural communities. Class differentiation and new ethnic cleavages are a particularly charged facet of the second generation of ethnic nationalists.

Conclusions

Anthropology can make several important contributions to the analyses of ethnic resurgence and state, identity and violence. One is to widen the range of states and situations under consideration. Another is to continue the postmodern examination of ethnicity. I would argue, however, that analysts risk making a strategic mistake if they cynically dismiss ethnicity (read "identity," read "culture") as only a mask for manipulation. Instead, I would argue for a widening of the scope of identity-politics in our analyses. Certainly, it would be a mistake to reduce culture to ethnicity, formal ideology or universal psychology (Beck 1999; Huntington 1996; Kaplan 2000). Rather analysts can show that leadership has its own cultural meanings, styles and cleavages, and that "self-interest" and its calculation are culturally and situationally constituted in states with different histories, as this Mexico–Guatemala comparison has revealed.

To address these issues more fully, anthropologists also need to follow their reflexive impulses and consider the factors – political, cultural and academic – that shape the analyst's gaze. How does the Western academic division of the world into conventional regions – which receive differential attention and funding both in academic research and international relations – influence our generalizations about and definitions of conflict and ethnic intensification? More needs to be done to deconstruct our categories for and explanations of conflict. We need also to recognize the courage of those who buck entrenched trends.

A final anthropological contribution is to expose ideologies that channel corrosive hatred and justify the treatment of "the other" as something less than fully human. Anthropologists need to spell out the internalized, often contradictory, cultural scripts and tacit knowledge that people bring with them – the capacity to orientalize and stigmatize (Prakash 1992) – and trace their impact on conflicts over resources, politics and community. The problem is not just self-interested and corruptible rivals seeking power, but also the complex collective contexts in which people live their lives and find their own agency and its negation.

Thus, when the violence of high- or low-intensity conflict is directed at civilian populations, it is important to understand people's experiences and their narratives – personal and historical, realist and non-realist, personal and institutional – for making sense of disorienting uncertainty, fragmented realities, and the widespread tactical use of violence as a weapon. How do people come to be persuaded to stigmatize particular differences – to channel hatred that justifies the extinction of particular "others" – while accepting the legitimacy of a wide variety of other differences in daily life? When do differences start to make a difference? And *which* ones? At the heart of this analysis is a conundrum: are we fated to live in social worlds that recreate negative and threatening others? Or, can we imagine a self-correcting post-orientalist social order, one where a variety of differences coexist? It is as crucial to discern who is trying to answer these questions for us in the contemporary world as it is to pay attention to the substance of the current answers to these questions.[5]

Notes

1 My thanks to the participants in the 1994 "The State Under Siege" conference for their extremely thought-provoking presentations and seminar discussions, to June Nash for sharing her comparative Chiapas–Guatemala analyses over the years, and to Stephen Jackson and Begoña Aretxaga for useful feedback on the draft of this ana-

lysis. In recent years, I have learned a great deal from other collaborative research networks that I have been involved in, especially from those chaired and co-chaired by Carol Greenhouse, Jean Jackson, John Watanabe, Arturo Arias, Jeff Sluka, Sonia Alvarez, Evelina Dagnino, and Arturo Escobar. I have written a series of essays and a book on violence which are echoed in this piece (see Warren 2001a, 2001b, 2002d) and have taken up additional issues, such as ethical and positional concerns, *testimonios*, the Cold War/post-Cold War transition, ethnically identified social movements, and the unfinished business of healing (Warren 1998, 2002c). Funding for my research has come from the Wenner-Gren Foundation, the John Simon Guggenheim Foundation, Princeton University, and Harvard University.
2 For instance, it is interesting to contrast Wolf (1969), Stoll (1993), Escobar and Alvarez (1992), and Alvarez *et al.* (1998).
3 For more on violence, nationalism and ethnicity in Guatemala, see Diane Nelson (1999) and Greg Grandin (2001). For more on Chiapas, see Neil Harvey (1998) and Gary Gossen (1999).
4 See Warren and Jackson (2002) for comparative case studies of ethnic politics in Guatemala, Colombia and Brazil.
5 See Prakash (1992); Zulaika and Douglas (1996).

References

Allen, Tim and Jean Seaton (eds) (1999) *The Media of Conflict: War Reporting and Representations of Ethnic Violence*. London: Zed Books.

Alvarez, Sonia, Evelina Dagnino and Arturo Escobar (1998) *Cultures of Politics/Politics of Cultures: Re-visioning Latin American Social Movements*. Boulder: Westview Press.

Appadurai, Arjun (1996) *Modernity at Large: Cultural Dimensions of Globalization*. Minneapolis: University of Minnesota Press.

Aretxaga, B. (1997) *Shattering Silence: Women, Nationalism, and Political Subjectivity in Northern Ireland*. Princeton: Princeton University Press.

Arias, Arturo (2000) *The Rigoberta Menchú Controversy*. Indianapolis: University of Minnesota Press.

Autonomedia (1994) *Zapatistas! Documents of the New Mexican Revolution*. Brooklyn: Autonomedia.

Beck, Aaron T. (1999) *Prisoners of Hate: The Cognitive Basis of Anger, Hostility, and Violence*. New York: HarperCollins.

Carmack, Robert (ed.) (1988) *Harvest of Violence: The Maya Indians and the Guatemalan Crisis*. Norman: University of Oklahoma Press.

CEH, Guatemalan Commission for Historical Clarification (1999) *Guatemala: Memory of Silence Tz'inil Na'tab'al*. Washington: American Association for the Advancement of Science. http://hrdata.aaas.org/ceh/report

Cojtí Cuxil, Demetrio (1991) *Configuración del Pensamiento Político del Pueblo Maya*. Quetzaltenango, Guatemala: Asociación de Escritores Mayances de Guatemala.

—— (1995) *Ub'aniik Ri Una'ooj Uchomab'aal Ri Maya' Tinamit; Confirguración del Pensamiento Político del Pueblo Maya*, Part II. Guatemala: Seminario Permanente de Estudios Mayas and Editorial Cholsamaj.

—— (1996) "The Politics of Mayan Revindication." In Edward Fischer and R. McKenna Brown (eds), *Mayan Cultural Activism in Guatemala*. Austin: University of Texas Press, pp. 19–50.

—— (1997) *Ri Maya' Moloj pa Iximulew; El Movimiento Maya (en Guatemala)*. Guatemala: Editorial Cholsamaj.

Collier, George and Elizabeth Quaratiello (1994) *Basta! – Land and the Zapatista Rebellion in Chiapas*. Oakland, CA: Food First Books.

Corradi, Juan E., Patricia Weiss Fagen and Manuel Antonio Garretón (eds) (1992) *Fear at the Edge: State Terror and Resistance in Latin America*. Berkeley: University of California Press.

Das, Veena, Arthur Kleinman, Mamphela Ramphele and Pamela Reynolds (eds) (2000) *Violence and Subjectivity*. Berkeley: University of California Press.

Escobar, Arturo and Sonia Alvarez (1992) *The Making of Social Movements in Latin America: Identity, Strategy, and Democracy*. Boulder: Westview Press.

Escobar, Arturo (1995) *Encountering Development: The Making and Unmaking of the Third World*. Princeton: Princeton University Press.

Falk, Richard (2001) "Self-Determination Under International Law: The Coherence of Doctrine Versus the Incoherence of Experience." In Wolfgang Danspeckgruber (ed.), *The Self-Determination of Peoples*. Boulder: Lynne Rienner, pp. 31–66.

Ferguson, James (1994) *The Anti-Politics Machine: "Development," Depoliticization, and Bureaucratic Power in Lesotho*. Minneapolis: University of Minnesota Press.

Fox, Richard and Orin Starn (1997) *Between Resistance and Revolution: Cultural Politics and Social Protest*. New Brunswick, NJ: Rutgers University Press.

Gossen, Gary (1999) *Telling Maya Tales: Tzotzil Identities in Modern Mexico*. New York: Routledge.

Grandin, Greg (2001) *The Blood of Guatemala: A History of Race and Nation*. Durham, NC: Duke University Press.

Greenhouse, Carol, Beth Mertz and Kay Warren (eds) (2002) *Transforming States: Ethnographies of Subjectivity and Agency in Changing Political Contexts*. Durham, NC: Duke University Press.

Gupta, Akhil and James Ferguson (1992) "Beyond 'Culture': Space, Identity, and the Politics of Difference." *Cultural Anthropology* 7: 6–23.

Hale, Charles R. (1994) *Resistance and Contradiction: Miskitu Indians and the Nicaraguan State, 1894–1987*. Stanford: Stanford University Press.

Harvey, Neil (1994) "Rebellion in Chiapas: Rural Reforms, Campesino Radicalism and the Limits to Salinismo." *The Transformation of Rural Mexico*, number 5, second edition. La Jolla: Center for US–Mexican Studies, University of California at San Diego, pp. 1–49.

—— (1998) *The Chiapas Rebellion: The Struggle for Land and Democracy*. Durham, NC: Duke University Press.

Hernández Castillo, R. Aída (2001) *Histories and Stories from Chiapas: Border Identities in Southern Mexico*. Austin: University of Texas Press.

Holland, Dorothy and Jean Lave (2001) *History in Person: Enduring Struggles, Contentious Practice, and Intimate Identities*. Santa Fe: School of American Research Press.

Horowitz, Donald (1985) *Ethnic Groups in Conflict*. Berkeley: University of California Press.

Huntington, Samuel (1996) *The Clash of Civilizations*. New York: Simon and Schuster.

Kaplan, Robert (2000) *The Coming Anarchy: Shattering the Dreams of the Post Cold War*. New York: Random House.

Kearney, Michael (1996) *Reconceptualizing the Peasantry: Anthropology in Global Perspective*. Boulder: Westview Press.

Li, Darryl (2001) "Echoes of Violence: Radio and Genocide in Rwanda." Senior Thesis, Harvard University.

McAdam, Doug, John D. McCarthy and Mayer N. Zald (1996) *Comparative Perspectives on Social Movements: Political Opportunities, Mobilizing Structures, and Cultural Framings*. New York: Cambridge University Press.

Malkki, Liisa (1995) *Purity and Exile: Violence, Memory, and National Cosmology among Hutu Refugees in Tanzania.* Chicago: University of Chicago Press.

Mamdani, Mahmood (2001) *When Victims become Killers.* Princeton: Princeton University Press.

Moeller, Susan (1999) *Compassion Fatigue: How the Media Sell Disease, Famine, War and Death.* New York: Routledge.

Montejo, Victor (2002) "The Multiplicity of Mayan Voices: Mayan Leadership and the Politics of Self-Representation." In Kay B. Warren and Jean E. Jackson (eds), *Indigenous Movements, Self-Representation, and the State in Latin America.* Austin: University of Texas Press.

Nash, June C. (1967) "The Passion Play in Maya Indian Communities." *Comparative Studies in Society and History* 10: 318–327.

—— (2001) *Mayan Visions: The Quest for Autonomy in an Age of Globalization.* New York: Routledge.

Nelson, Diane (1999) *The Finger in the Wound: Ethnicity, Nation, and Gender in the Body Politic of Quincentennial Guatemala.* Berkeley: University of California Press.

Nordstrom, Carolyn R. (2000) "Shadows and Sovereigns." *Theory, Culture, and Society* 17(4): 35–54.

—— (n.d.) *War, Peace, and Shadow Powers: The Licit, the Illicit, and the Unknown.* Unpublished ms.

Nordstrom, Carolyn and JoAnn Martin (eds) (1992) *Paths to Domination, Resistance and Terror.* Berkeley: University of California Press.

Ong, Aihwa (1999) *Flexible Citizenship.* Durham, NC: Duke University Press.

Prakash, Gyan (1992) "Writing Post-Orientalist Histories of the Third World: Indian Historiography Is Good to Think." In Nicholas B. Dirks (ed.), *Colonialism and Culture.* Ann Arbor: University of Michigan Press, pp. 353–388.

REMHI, Proyecto Interdiocesano de Recuperación de la Memoria Histórica (1998) *Guatemala: Nunca Más.* Guatemala: Oficina de Derechos Humanos del Arzobispado de Guatemala (ODHA).

Rosaldo, Renato (1989) *Culture and Truth: The Remaking of Social Analysis.* Boston: Beacon.

Schirmer, J. (1998) *The Guatemalan Military Project: A Violence Called Democracy.* Philadelphia: University of Pennsylvania Press.

Scott, James C. (1990) *Domination and the Arts of Resistance: Hidden Transcripts.* New Haven: Yale University Press.

Sluka, Jeffrey (ed.) (2000) *Death Squad: The Anthropology of State Terror.* Philadelphia: University of Pennsylvania Press.

Stephen, Lynn (2001) *Zapata Lives! Histories and Cultural Politics in Southern Mexico.* Berkeley: University of California Press.

Stoll, David (1993) *Between Two Armies in the Ixil Towns of Guatemala.* New York: Columbia University Press.

Tambiah, Stanley (1986) *Sri Lanka: Ethnic Fratricide and the Dismantling of Democracy.* Chicago: University of Chicago Press.

—— (1996) *Leveling Crowds: Ethnonationalist Conflicts and Collective Violence in South Asia.* Berkeley: University of California Press.

Warren, Kay B. (ed.) (1989) *The Symbolism of Subordination: Indian Identity in a Guatemalan Town.* Austin: University of Texas Press.

Warren, Kay B. (ed.) (1993) *The Violence Within: Cultural and Political Opposition in Divided Nations.* Boulder: Westview Press.

—— (1998) *Indigenous Movements, and their Critics: Pan-Mayan Activists in Guatemala.* Princeton: Princeton University Press.

—— (2001a) "Violence, In Anthropology." Entry A3/1/042 in *International Encyclopedia of Social and Behavioral Sciences.* London: Elsevier.

—— (2002a) "Epilogue: Toward an Anthropology of Fragments, Instabilities, and Incomplete Transitions." In Carol Greenhouse, Beth Mertz and Kay Warren (eds), *Transforming States: Ethnographies of Subjectivity and Agency in Changing Political Contexts.* Durham, NC: Duke University Press, pp. 379–392.

—— (2002b) "Introduction: Theory and Politics in the Study of Indigenous Movements." Co-authored with Jean Jackson. In Kay B. Warren and Jean E. Jackson (eds), *Indigenous Movements, Self-Representation, and the State in Latin America.* Austin: University of Texas Press.

—— (2002c) "Voting Against Indigenous Rights in Guatemala: Lessons from the 1999 Referendum." In Kay B. Warren and Jean E. Jackson (eds), *Indigenous Movements, Self-Representation, and the State.* Austin: University of Texas Press.

—— (2002d) "Notes for an Essay on the Perils (and Promises) of Engaged Anthropology." In Victoria Sanford and Asale Ajani (eds), *Engaged Observer: Advocacy, Activism, and Anthropology.* Tucson: University of Arizona Press.

Warren, Kay B. and Jean E. Jackson (eds) (2002) *Indigenous Movements, Self-Representation, and the State.* Austin: University of Texas Press.

Wolf, Eric R. (1969) *Peasant Wars of the Twentieth Century.* New York: Harper Torchbook.

Young, Clifford (ed.) (1976) *The Politics of Cultural Pluralism.* Madison: University of Wisconsin Press.

—— (ed.) (1993) *The Rising Tide of Cultural Pluralism; The Nation-State at Bay?* Madison: University of Wisconsin Press.

Zulaika, Joseba and William Douglas (1996) *Terror and Taboo: The Follies, Fables, and Faces of Terrorism.* New York: Routledge.

Part II
Cases

6 Civil war in Peru

Culture and violence in historical perspective[1]

Linda J. Seligmann

Bridges over deep rivers

José María Arguedas, one of Peru's best-known literary figures and an early ethnographer of Andean society of the central highlands, repeatedly invoked the apt metaphor of deep rivers, also the title of one of his novels, to describe Peru's sociocultural reality, particularly its ethnic landscape. Deep rivers: multiple strata, swirling in pools, tranquil at times, overflowing their banks in torrential floods at others, unfathomable and mysterious, loudly speaking in multiple tongues, and capable of carrying away all human impurities. In Arguedas's novel (1978), "the plague," typhus, kills in droves the poorest and most down-trodden Quechua[2] hacienda Indians as they seek to flee a hacienda (large landed estate). The concrete bridge across the river that divides the mestizos[3] from the Indians is also the means by which the plague spreads to the rest of the population. For the hacienda Indians who have internalized their subordinate status, the only way to combat the plague is through magico-religiosity. Arguedas believed nevertheless that some day these poorest of the poor would rise up, risk death, terrible repression and violence, and challenge the material and ideological cruelty they confronted in their daily lives. At the same time, Arguedas also rejected the future of Peruvian society as a simple polarization between dominant and subordinate forces. He himself was a product of miscegenation and self-consciously recognized it with a potent degree of ambivalence and discomfort. He envisioned a future in which room for difference without imposed integration or assimilation coexisted with equality. He committed suicide but his ideas have lived on.

The tension between these two perspectives – one in which violence would be necessary to bring forth a new age of justice, the other in which Peruvians would come to respect the value of living in a multiethnic society and recognize that bridges created a constant flow across multiple sectors of the society – helps to explain the historical context for Peru's civil war in the 1980s. This article discusses some of the most salient causes for the civil war in Peru. It also implicitly compares and contrasts the situation in Peru with others considered in this volume, concentrating upon the organizational forms that different ideologies of ethnicity have taken and their relationships to wider economic and political forces. Finally, it moves to an appraisal of actions the civilian population has taken to diminish the level of violence, in particular, the growth of a variety of peasant-managed civil defense patrols and social movements.

State–society relationships in Peru resemble those of other post-Cold War nations, characterized by a violent movement in the name of ethnic vindication, the imposition of neoliberal economic policies, and a rhetorical concern with democracy by a civilian president who nonetheless abolished the judiciary and legislature, made a pact with the military, and transformed himself into an "autodictator." However, important differences also exist, namely that the Shining Path guerrilla movement began organizing in the 1950s long before the formal end to Cold War geopolitics, popular support for the guerrilla movement was weak, an extralegal economy provided foreign exchange and weapons, thereby creating conditions for an extreme degree of corruption and cooperation among political forces normally at odds with one another, and substantial civilian support existed for Fujimori's regime (1990–95; 1995–2000) until his bid for a third term in office.[4]

While there are global forces and structural conditions common to Peru and other regions facing conflict and violent upheaval following the end of the Cold War, it is equally important to consider how these structures and forces are actually experienced by people as *processes*. How do they apprehend economic and political forces in the light of their existing cultural, economic, and political values and practices? How do their interpretations then contribute to the subsequent choices they make and the constraints upon them? In this chapter, I wish to move beyond describing violent conflict to examining the phenomenology of violence in Peru. More specifically, I address the following questions: Why was Sendero so successful? What led to the odd twist of fate in which a democratically-elected president, Alberto Fujimori, son of Japanese immigrants, abolished the legislature and judiciary and declared himself an autodictator, finalizing the extraordinary powers he gathered to himself by establishing a formal pact with the military? And in yet another ironic twist, why did the majority of Peruvians welcome his actions in obvious disregard for what is usually taken to be democratic process? Did the steps that Fujimori took, in conjunction with the military, the IMF, and transnational sources of capital, represent the evolution of a new form of governance, perhaps a rejection of the state as a prototypical institution, deeply engrained in philosophical notions of what constitutes democracy?

Theoretical considerations and methods

My analysis derives from interviews with a wide spectrum of Peruvians in urban and rural areas, archival research, news reports, and, most significantly, five years of field research in different Andean highland communities of southern Peru. In particular, I draw in this chapter on a year and a half of field work in one region (1984–85, 1991, 1993, 1998), Huanoquite, that was pulled into the conflict between Sendero Luminoso and the police and armed forces during the civil war.[5] Huanoquite is located in very rugged terrain 65 kilometers southwest of the departmental capital of Cuzco. An Inca road passes through the district, continues on to the central highlands, crossing the Apurimac River, and eventually reaches the coast. With a population of 4,082, it is the largest of six districts of the Province of Paruro. Most of its inhabitants speak Quechua, though many of them also speak Spanish. Home to a number of powerful landlords, and multiple ethnic polities, forcibly resettled during the sixteenth century, it has a long history of resisting dominant regimes and was one among many regions targeted by a major agrarian reform in 1969.

While many of the examples below of why and how violence unfolded the way it did in Peru come from my ethnographic interpretations of the experiences of Huanoquiteños, I demonstrate how structures, policies and events from far outside Huanoquite have become part of their cultural, economic and political praxis. Likewise, I consider how others perceive the stance and value systems of Huanoquiteños and how those perceptions have affected their actions.

F.G. Bailey (1963), in setting forth his political action theory, initially distinguished three levels of analysis – the cultural, sociological and external, equated with the individual, the group or village, and national or transnational relationships, respectively. In 1969, in *Stratagems and Spoils*, he moved away from equating structure with bounded units of analysis to structure as constituted by systems of interaction and the rules upon which they were based. The emphasis in Bailey's political action theory on face-to-face encounters of particular individuals within particular settings, and their manipulation of material resources and symbols is heuristic for my purposes, especially in understanding why certain sectors of the population became adherents of Sendero. However, Bailey's approach tends to underplay how structure, history and cultural interpretations may destabilize existing systems and shape the stratagems that individual actors employ, especially in inciting unintended consequences. Below I address the dialectical interaction of structure and process within an historical context. I consider how different political actors have made sense of the same history, using in abbreviated fashion the methodology Jean Comaroff applies to her study of the history of the Tshidi in South Africa. She argues that while distinctions may be made between "the internal dynamics of a precolonial system and the developing forms and agencies of capitalism and the state," in reality, the interaction of these structures as constitutive of history is now part of an encompassing political economy (Comaroff 1985: 17–18).

The challenge, of course, is how to use a linear narrative form to depict the simultaneity of processes emanating from different sources, all subject to structural constraints and interpretations, yet carrying different weights. Jean Comaroff puts it well in her description of the methodology of event history:

> while events are the realization of structure, they cannot explain its form or its existence in time. Rather, they are themselves the outcome of social practice, whose motivation is configured by an underlying system of principles ("structure"). The latter shapes human consciousness through the mediation of symbols; yet its implications for practice are seldom free from conflict, and practice, in any case, occurs within material circumstances that impose

constraints of their own. Social action is thus not merely an "expression" of structural principles, it is an attempt to reconcile contradictions inherent in these principles and in the relationship between them and embracing material realities. Events ... may either reinforce the system in place or undermine it ... they have cumulative consequences, and sometimes give rise to irreversible change in the conditions of practice which are unintended at the level of individual motivation.

(1985: 17)

Anthropologists have the tools to cross disciplinary boundaries. In historicizing cultures of conflict and violence, and in recognizing that self-interest and the maximization of material values are mediated by cultural considerations, I think that they may be able to meet the challenge of this kind of complex analysis and provide considerable insight into seemingly chaotic and otherwise obscure turns in political behavior that cannot be adequately explained solely by the collection of data, attitudinal surveys, interviews, game theory models, questionnaires, the elaboration of ideal types, and a reliance solely upon macro- or microlevel explanations.[6] I also argue that anthropologists must abandon for once and for all the notion of self-enclosed or homeostatic systems but rather must account for inequalities and hierarchies that emerge historically and across a vast terrain of differentiated social and physical space.

Culture, ethnicity and violence

Warren (1993a: 2) argues that in trying to understand cultures of terror and violence, we must heed "how conflict produces culture, not just ... how cultural differences promote conflict." And Eric Wolf, in his role as discussant in this symposium, observed a close relationship between the rise of capitalism and the rise of violence in which the nation-state itself often becomes a machine of violence. Functioning in the capacity of authorizing or repressing violence through a variety of means in order to ensure that capitalist relations take root and thrive, Wolf argued that violence becomes integral to the state itself, leading to a situation in which "violence is just around the corner and you drink it with mother's milk." As violence becomes the mechanism by which honor is upheld, conflicts decided, and particular economic paths followed, it may become daily cultural practice, taken for granted, and transmitted from one generation to the next.

Finally, as Andrew Strathern, one of the participants in this symposium, observed, even though ethnicity and "age old hatreds" may be reified concepts used by the media and many governments to explain sudden and extraordinarily violent moments of genocide, the notion of ethnicity, once it has become part of the fabric of the society – essentialized within the society, so to speak – indeed produces extreme violence. The use of ethnicity in order to create social categories and divisions thus becomes a form of structural violence. The constructive efforts of political leaders and social movements (or the state, occasionally) to eradicate factionalism and racism confront a long history of racial ideologies and ethnic characterizations that have been wielded by people (and bureaucracies) as a means of shoring up distinctive identities and, usually, differential access to resources. Therefore, while recognizing that the common practice of rationalizing violent conflict in terms of primordialist ethnic hatreds should be abandoned, in explaining the course of Peru's civil war, we must pay attention to how ethnicity takes on a life of its own and fuels conflict.

Dystopic utopias: The Shining Path

Peru began to gain notoriety in the 1980s because of the actions of the Communist Party of Peru – Sendero Luminoso, one of the few wholly orthodox Maoist guerrilla movements still active in the world. The group began their work in the central highlands, not far from Arguedas's home. They were inspired by Marx, Lenin, Mao and, specifically, China's Cultural Revolution. They also found guidance and the name for their movement in the writings of the early-twentieth-century Peruvian philosopher and founder of Peru's Communist Party, José Carlos Mariátegui. Mariátegui wrote *Seven Interpretive Essays of Peruvian Reality*, a classic read by almost all Peruvian school children. He was convinced that Peru's future lay in establishing a socialist form of government, but he also cautioned that European socialism could not be transplanted wholesale to Peru. Rather, its tenets and praxis had to be modified to conform to the sociocultural reality of Peru's indigenous Quechua communities. Abimael Guzmán Reynoso became Sendero's living leader, better known as Presidente Gonzalo. He was a Kantian philosopher, one time university professor at the University of Huamanga in Ayacucho, and a scholar of democratic socialism. He, other leaders of Sendero, and hundreds of supporters are now behind bars along with many others who had nothing to do with Sendero at all.

By 1993, close to 30,000 people had died in the civil war between Sendero and state forces represented by the military and national police. Hundreds had disappeared, some discovered later in a tortured and mutilated state in mass graves located near hamlets in valleys between the high and isolated Andean peaks. Even in the midst of physical dislocation, political uncertainty and general economic hardship, daily life continued during the civil war as people tried to survive, feed themselves and their children, cultivate a sense of human community, and fortify their political organizations.

Perhaps a total of 5,000 active participants who had a network of sympathizers and passive supporters in both rural and urban regions of Peru, members of Sendero succeeded in creating terror and chaos, and causing extensive economic damage to a country already in bad economic shape. They began organizing in the late 1950s and initiated their armed struggle in the central highlands in 1980.[7] They upset any remaining political stability in an already politically unstable environment. Their success was in part attributable to the policies of short-sighted governments, a society that has refused to treat highland peasant and lowland Indian populations as equal citizens, and inept security, police and intelligence forces, who have also felt few qualms for many years about mistreating Quechua peasants and using them as cannon fodder.

Once Sendero's struggle was underway, it was strengthened by the insidious effects wrought by any culture of violence and terror. The centuries of fear that underlie relationships between mestizos and Quechua people created paranoia, panic, and the assumption by mestizos of opposition, uprising and rebellion on the part of *all* Quechua inhabitants. Kay Warren (1993b: 33) describes a similar dynamic in Guatemala among Mayas and *ladinos*. As different sectors of Peruvian society responded to and acted upon these fears, a situation of "crafted ambiguity" arose in which self-censorship and pervasive mistrust rent asunder the workings of reciprocity and community, and the capacity for effective political organizing (Warren 1993b: 47).

Setting the stage for Sendero

Peru's economy has relied heavily upon extraction and commodity production without being able to achieve expansion and industrialization or domestic agricultural self-sufficiency. Even when it has experienced economic growth, income distribution has been alarmingly skewed with Quechua peasants at the bottom of the economic ladder, this despite differentiation among peasants themselves. In addition, although formal "democracy" was restored to many Latin American countries in the decade of the 1980s, governments were faced with implementing highly unpopular politico-economic measures to ensure the steely benevolence of the International Monetary Fund. The effects of austerity measures were keenly felt by the lower classes who experienced increasing immiseration; they placed in jeopardy the aspirations of the middle classes and elite; weakened (at least initially) the economic competitiveness of underdeveloped nations within the world market; and generally enhanced the probability for social violence.[8] This violence was met with repression. Even while austerity measures ultimately led to economic growth, the income discrepancy between rich and poor contributed to a deep sense of resentment and dissatisfaction that had the capacity to fuel violence. Especially important to remember is that such events, as they are experienced, become part of people's cultural repertory.[9]

The conditions described above help to explain a predisposition for violence in Peru but it is important to recognize that many other nations faced with a long history of colonialism, racial discrimination, exploitation of indigenous populations, and chronic underdevelopment, debt and austerity measures did not take the particular path of violence that Peru did. Below, I elaborate upon several processes that are more unique to Peru and help to explain the emergence of Sendero and the degree of violence that characterized Peru's civil war. Specifically, I discuss the consequences of Peru's 1969 agrarian reform, arguing that the emergence of a new stratum of regional intermediaries and the failure of rural education contributed greatly to the ensuing violence. I also examine how national policies and anti-drug trafficking policies, most of which originated in the USA, also contributed to the success of Sendero and, eventually, to the downfall of the Fujimori regime and a more general state crisis.

Reform in Peru

Peru's 1969 agrarian reform, a watershed in transforming peasant–state relations,[10] made an undeniable impact upon the course of political events that would soon transpire. The reform dramatically revealed Peru as a state whose legitimating rhetoric and military power were far more in evidence than its viability as a nation, institutionalized in people's hearts and minds. The nation as an "imagined community" remained far more a dream than a reality, thus causing the Peruvian state to confront the problematic of maintaining control and projecting an ideology of shared concerns, beliefs and perceptions (see Marx 1993: 159–60).

In 1968, a military junta, headed by General Juan Velasco Alvarado, seized power in Peru. On 24 June 1969, Velasco announced one of the most ambitious agrarian reforms in Latin America with his now famous proclamation:

> From today onwards, the peasants of Peru will no longer be pariahs or the disinherited, living in poverty from birth to death, and viewing themselves as powerless before a future that appears equally dismal for their children. From the time of this fortuitous day, the peasants of Peru will truly be free citizens for whom the nation will finally recognize their right to the fruits of the earth that they cultivate and a place of justice within a society that will never again treat them as diminished citizens, men to be exploited by other men. ... Peasants, the landlords will no longer eat your poverty.[11]

The passage of the agrarian reform law was motivated by peasant uprisings, fear of revolution, a genuine desire on the part of the government to improve the livelihood and treatment of Peru's indigenous population, and the dream of modernization and development. At the same time, "the agrarian problem" was, as William Roseberry (1993: 323) has pointed out,

> a question posed *about* the peasantry, not necessarily *of* or *by* them, and it was most frequently posed by urban intellectuals and activists located in universities, development agencies, state bureaus, and party committees. It was asked in conferences, lecture halls, seminar rooms, and roundtables, and the conclusions were presented in memoranda, communiqués, working papers, articles, monographs, and books.

Roseberry cautions that,

> This does not necessarily mean that the answers would have been better had the questions been asked by or of the peasants themselves, or had the conclusions been shared more fully and collaboratively with villagers. But

we need to remember that the agrarian question was simultaneously an urban, or national, or "proletarian" question, that it seemed unavoidable for groups asking other questions and pursuing other (nonrural, nonpeasant) agendas.

This approach to agrarian reform resulted in, at best, policies that did not fit well with the reality of most highland peasants. The reform failed to stimulate agricultural productivity in the highlands though it did distribute a high proportion of lands to peasants in the form of cooperatives, ill-suited to traditional Andean methods of production. Despite the expectation that former landed estate owners would reinvest their earnings and energy in the industrial sector, little evidence shows that they did so, especially since the bonds they received became worthless as inflation skyrocketed. Rather, they entered petty commerce and the service sector, and a few hung on, exerting their informal power in the countryside. Probably more than a few found their niche in the wide and deep coca economy.

In the agricultural sector in the highlands, after the 1969 reform, permanent workers on landed estates were granted control of estate lands, which were transformed into government managed cooperatives, but Peru's native communities were almost entirely excluded from the reform, thus catalyzing bitterness between these two sectors of the rural population.

Within a single highland district, Quechua peasants were differentiated in terms of their land tenure and labor relations, territorial affiliation, their integration into the market economy, and their political orientations. The reform did not take account of the various and distinctive kinds of social relations of production that were already well-established among Quechua peasants. A close analysis of what happened in one highland district, Huanoquite, as a consequence of the agrarian reform, reveals that while the reform significantly opened up the space in which native inhabitants could question their subordinate relationship to the Peruvian nation-state, the meaning of legitimate authority, and the nature of the institution of community itself, it also simultaneously generated dramatic transformations in the local authority structure and created (or exacerbated) serious divisions among different groups of peasants. The reform law, because it equated poverty with economic inequities, failed to take account of existing ethnic differences in the countryside based on unequal relations of power and the social construction of cultural identity. Multiple conflicts developed among different groups of peasants; and the changing policies of different national regimes over a relatively short period of time left peasants reeling in their efforts to take advantage of legal measures to defend their land and labor rights. The yawning gap between the already highly capitalized, relatively sophisticated, and urbanized coastal regions and the relatively underdeveloped and rural highland populations also continued to grow. In addition, the government's deliberate lack of attention to the polycultural dimensions of "Indianness" and the problems it presented to national integration left it unprepared to deal with a resurgence of interest among peasants in their ethnic identity and their efforts to struggle openly against racial discrimination.

The conditions in the countryside accelerated the rate and numbers migrating between rural and urban centers. The explosion of the urban informal sector attested to the lack of real jobs in cities, however much ingenuity the popular classes of the cities showed in creating something out of nothing. Figures on unemployment and underemployment have ranged from a low of 60 per cent to a high of 90 per cent of the active working population (see Burt and Panfichi 1992). On the other hand, in moving back and forth between rural and urban sectors, Quechua people experimented with new kinds of knowledge, became exposed to new kinds of exploitation and forms of political organizing, became more astute about the politics of the Peruvian nation-state, and saw their rural communities from a fresh perspective. Migration exacerbated intergenerational conflicts and incited debates about the uses of cultural knowledge.

The local political face of reform

Many Quechua peasants, especially those who resided in communities and benefited less from the agrarian reform, enthusiastically welcomed the opportunity to participate politically in order to influence national policies and priorities. In addition, the visible and audible presence of peasants in local governance stemmed directly from the legal measures of the reform which formally endorsed peasant electoral politics at the district level. In Huanoquite, for example, the district's mayors, heavily pressured by peasants, began lobbying in Cuzco for roads and health posts; they demanded that the district be formally recognized as an archaeological zone with resources valuable to Peru's patrimonial heritage; and they formed a united defense front with other mayors from Paruro to send a commission to Lima requesting rural services. Independently of their official representatives, Huanoquite's peasants also began to make demands upon the state. Together with peasants from other provinces in Cuzco, they sent a delegation to the Ministry of Agriculture requiring, above all, that reform officials know Quechua so they would not have to use interpreters in their contacts with peasants. They also participated in a department-wide demonstration in Cuzco in 1970. There, they denounced the "myths of support from the actual government." They asked that "bad functionaries be ousted." They insisted that a "process of moralization of government authorities take place."

The district council constituted the principal local political entity that could channel the demands of multiple peasant collectivities to the state. In the late 1970s, almost a decade after the passage of the reform law, Huanoquite's peasants began to seek control of the district council. In 1975, a conservative military government had seized power in a coup. The effects of new government policies, particularly the reversal of the reform, only gradually reached Huanoquite, which was still deeply involved in adjusting to the effects of the reform itself. In 1977 a typical conflict over the office of district mayor ensued, pitting two members of the landed elite against each other. Romero, an intimidating absentee landlord, represented the old-style landed oligarchy. Gamboa represented a younger generation of intermediaries that had emerged during the reform and emphasized the incorporation of peasants into processes of modernization and development.

At this juncture, for the first time, the voices of Huanoquite's peasants were raised and played a role in decision-making about control of the district council. In an action possibly encouraged by Gamboa, they took to the streets and burned effigies of the local landed elite. Romero refers to that moment as "the inception of class warfare."[12] In an extraordinary assembly held in 1978, attended by peasant representatives from the entire district, as well as by provincial authorities from Paruro, peasants openly proposed that the position of mayor be filled by a peasant. In one man's words:

> So long as these mayors are in office, no one can work in peace. Furthermore we condemn the teachers for holding festive lunches on school days. We would like them to understand that the National Education Center that has been established is not for stars but for the pueblo of Huanoquite.[13]

Two years later, in 1980, Sendero embarked upon its campaign of armed struggle. Among its first actions was the desecration of General Juan Velasco Alvarado's tomb (see Arce Borja 1989). Also in 1980, all members of Huanoquite's district council resigned, stating that, "This council does not have the necessary support from the provincial authorities and from the pueblo."[14] That same year, Juan Bautista Quispe Antitupa, running on the United Left Front slate, became the first peasant ever elected to the office of district council mayor in Huanoquite.

Once the district council was in their hands, a great optimism characterized Huanoquiteños' sentiments about their own march toward development. They sent representatives to the Pachacutec Agrarian League; they elected "peasant students" to participate in SINAMOS training courses in Cuzco. They demanded schools that functioned in their interest, especially an agronomy school; a medical post; the renovation of their plaza; a Sunday regional market; trucks and truck drivers who would follow enforced rules of scheduling; new roads; tractors; credit; electricity; the establishment of a local chalk industry; and a small factory for making brick gables for roofs. They formed into sub-committees and relied heavily upon the new local powers that had appeared in Huanoquite to press their demands with state agencies.[15]

This history is worth recounting because it signalled qualitative changes in Huanoquiteños' (and many other peasants') relationships to the state; their resistance to dominant ideologies and elites; and their ideas about the kinds of steps they should take to defend their autonomy. The incident above indicates the growing impotence of the old landed elite in the face of the reform law and a rupture in the subservient behavior of Huanoquiteños' toward mestizos. It also revolves around three key processes that were intimately related to one another in the eyes of Huanoquite's peasants and that have been the focus of political struggle in the district ever since: education, progress and peasant unity. They saw both education and progress as the bases for their integration into national society and as the means by which their children could achieve upward mobility. How to get resources for the purposes of education and progress, of what education and progress should consist, and who would control these developments were crucial issues for Huanoquiteños.

A decade later, few of their aspirations had taken on material form. The truck road between Huanoquite and Cuzco was described as "a road of death. ... Traveling to that zone was a veritable odyssey";[16] and a medic sent from Cuzco to man the post in Huanoquite abandoned his duties, characterizing Huanoquite as "an almost deserted pueblo ... a barbaric pueblo which deserves no attention from the Department of Health."[17]

In 1982, Sendero attacked Huanoquite for the first time. A column of three men and three women blew up the cooperative's tractor, essential to the cultivation of its 800 hectares of relatively flat land. Before disappearing, they painted the walls of the colonial church with slogans proclaiming the glory of the coming revolution, identifying themselves by the now familiar hammer and sickle. The destruction of the cooperative's tractor sent the cooperative, which had already suffered from mismanagement, into bankruptcy. The Senderistas were caught as they fled to Cuzco by way of the Inca road. Shortly thereafter, the sinchis, a special military shock force similar to the Green Berets, occupied Huanoquite and remained for almost a year. The failure of the cooperative left many of its lands fallow, and intensified conflict between cooperative members and community members. The latter, who had received little from the reform, repeatedly sought to invade the cooperative's lands. Sendero, taking advantage of the growing animosity between the cooperative and communities, sought to gain support from communities for their movement. Cooperative members, in turn, began to perceive the community as allies of Sendero.

In 1986, Engineer Edgar Hurtado, a representative of President Alán García's government and head of the Paruro microregional development scheme, journeyed to Huanoquite. He offered them loans, doctors, funds toward an electricity project, a high school, an agrarian security force, and a tractor. He returned several months later to encourage Huanoquiteños to attend the *rimanakuy* or direct dialogue in Quechua between the President and peasants in Cuzco. These events can best be characterized as the belated albeit innovative efforts on the part of the state to alter peasant perceptions of it as an ineffectual, hypocritical entity that had reneged on most of its rhetorical commitment to Peru's peasants. Despite the ostensible renewed interest of the government in Huanoquite, it never delivered on the promises Hurtado had made.

In July of 1991, Sendero had gathered momentum in the region. Authorities confided to me that they were sleeping at night in other people's homes for fear that guerrillas would attack them. One teacher had been killed. Huanoquiteños had formed themselves into a civil defense patrol. The number of attacks defined as "banditry" had soared; and Huanoquiteños disparaged the protection of the police and military units that had entered the district. In another extraordinary general assembly attended by all district representatives, the president of one community announced, "The Civil Guard only commits abuses. There is no legal justice here."[18]

What happened? The notable absence of the state in supporting Huanoquite in its own desires for development until 1986 requires an explanation. Four processes conspired to undermine the incipient unity Huanoquiteños had begun to forge. The reversals of the reform, ushered in by the military coup in 1975, affected all highland communities. These were compounded by a severe economic and fiscal crisis that began in 1980. Third, the reform law catalyzed bitter land conflicts between communities and cooperatives, especially since cooperatives were favored by the reform (see Seligmann 1995), and last but not least, a new stratum of "progressive" regional intermediaries crucially intervened in village political life.

Power and violence: the rise of regional intermediaries

The disappearance of large landholders as a socially accepted, privileged and protected class left a political vacuum in Huanoquite. This vacuum became an arena in which Huanoquiteños vied for control over the channels that the landed elite had dominated. Huanoquiteños became especially concerned about the value of a new generation of regional intermediaries who emerged in the 1970s as an important political force, supplanting the old landed oligarchy. The activities and profiles of these brokers are, I believe, key to understanding the character of Sendero.[19] Members of this group were not homogeneous in terms of class or ethnicity. They primarily held occupations as teachers, bureaucrats, entrepreneurs, and as lawyers and judges in a few cases. Their class backgrounds differed. Some were the children of the landed elite, while others, particularly teachers and entrepreneurs, were the children of wealthier peasants who had obtained an education and migrated permanently to Cuzco. Still others, such as truck owners, were members of the landed elite who had experienced downward mobility during the reform.

Despite their success in acquiring many of the trappings associated with belonging to the stratum of mestizos, including access to higher education, they had difficulty achieving upward mobility. For many of them, owning land had been inextricably intertwined with high status. After the reform, they could no longer depend upon that resource to ensure a respectable place for themselves in Peruvian society. The agrarian reform itself, the interpenetration of rural and urban spheres, and the dynamics of migration contrasted sharply with the availability of economic opportunities and led to growing tension between rural producers and urban elites, and increasing dependence upon the state. These individuals, within Peruvian society, found themselves struggling to improve their economic status and accumulate greater political power. Despite their best efforts, they were increasingly marginalized and made "superfluous."

Jobs were scarce; and the government cared little about improving the livelihood of rural teachers.

Many of these brokers could be characterized as suffering from severe identity conflicts, whether they hailed from the Quechua peasantry or the landed elite, and they struggled to resolve them by creating an alternative social and economic niche for themselves through mediating functions in the local and regional offices of government, in the markets, and in the schools. They took advantage of existing cleavages within Huanoquite to enhance their own opportunities. Despite the different values they espoused, often their behavior differed little from that of the old landed elite. The efforts of Huanoquiteños to revise existing relations of authority by coopting or attempting to appropriate the discourse of the national regime thus often met with failure. The ensuing struggles over the bases of legitimate local level political authority and the intervention of these new brokers helped pave the way for Sendero.

The criteria for becoming an authority in Huanoquite in either the political or religious domain intersected with new criteria established after the reform. Differential control over land overwhelmingly began to determine who held office. Modern education enhanced villagers' possibilities. Younger, more educated authorities were situated in a much wider social network than previous authorities had been. One man's assessment of the elders was curt: "they are useless, illiterate." Control over land, literacy, and the capacity to manipulate ties to the regional and national bureaucracies became important to villagers as channels through which they could become recognized as powerful, authoritative and necessary to the well-being of the district. Those who were most successful at mediating these demands were the well-to-do who could be at once both more modern and more traditional than their less-fortunate relatives. Thus, an irresolvable tension arose between the idioms and consequences of constructive hierarchy, on the one hand, and destructive competition, on the other. The fault lines that developed within districts such as Huanoquite were particularly useful to Sendero. Its members showed great skill at allying themselves with one faction and then eventually taking control, or destroying it.

Rural education and violence

Another critical area in which regional intermediaries intervened to exacerbate existing conflict was education. Anderson (1983) specifies that for the imagined community of the nation to come into being, literacy, the print media, perhaps now, television, and certainly, a national educational program, become crucial vehicles in the service of fostering nationness. The Velasco regime implemented an educational reform in 1970 because it saw literacy and education as essential to modernization and national integration. The Minister of Agriculture, for example, stated, "It would be difficult to speak of anyone with more social emotion than the students. They should apply the excess of their emotions in favor of the Agrarian Reform in order to provide assistance to peasant communities." He added, "The new system of national education will be implemented next year. ... Peasant schools will be established, staffed by professionals who will repay society for their education." These decrees threatened many Peruvians who harbored little ethnic identification with Quechua-speaking peasants.[20]

The Velasco regime proceeded to employ a number of young men and women as clerks and bureaucrats in government offices. The access to education and bureaucratic officialdom led to a situation in which for many of those who would eventually become members of Sendero a utopian idealism became coupled with some, but not very much, education. The state's failure to support sufficiently rural education redounded negatively upon both peasants and teachers. The teachers, condemned by the peasants for their lackadaisical and racist behavior, and ignored by the state in their demands for better working conditions, despite their formation into a powerful union, SUTEP, eventually turned against the state altogether, becoming the intellectual and military vanguard of Sendero. In fact, one of Sendero's most important tactics during its early evolution was to infiltrate and gradually take over control of particular unions.

SUTEP was one of the most important unions that Sendero members penetrated. In doing so, however, they constructed their own rigid views of ideal Peruvian society. They had become quintessential hybrids themselves. Unable to achieve assimilation into either rural Quechua society or the dominant urban mestizo society, they forged their own path. Their ideology assumed that peasants were unable to fend for themselves, that they could not accurately identify their enemies, and that "the party" would have to take on the burden of "guiding the peasants" into violent overthrow of the state.[21] It is interesting to note, in this respect, the comments of one Huanoquite teacher, echoed by many others. A Sendero sympathizer, the teacher was an active member of SUTEP; he had participated in the 1960s uprisings in the La Convención valley and in Antapampa, and had worked with SINAMOS in setting up training courses for peasants. At the same time that he denounced the landed elite and the factionalism within the district, commenting that, "only when the elite is killed will life change in the countryside," he also denounced the Huanoquiteños, stating, "they are very indifferent ... they are not interested in education. They are conformists, alienated from the progress of their own community. As long as the community does not understand what education is, things will be difficult."[22] In the hundreds of pages of public documents and interviews issued by Sendero, not once do they make mention of Andean cultural traditions or values except to condemn them harshly as an impediment to their own project. Scholars who have read messianism into Sendero's agenda are thus imagining it. A position for which equally little evidence exists is that peasants themselves were interpreting Sendero as a messianic movement.[23]

Huanoquiteños saw education as paramount to the benefits that development could bring them as individuals and communities, as did the state. Although the education Huanoquiteños received rarely served their interests and was provided to them by often unqualified teachers who were ambivalent about their own identity within the national society, Huanoquiteños continued to consider education crucial to the future well-being of their children. By 1980, however, many of them had turned against the teachers and threw them out temporarily. (This coincided with the election of Quispe as Huanoquite's peasant mayor.) The form and content of education that they had hoped for did not coincide with what they received. The teachers had constantly denigrated the students with racial slurs, calling them "lice-bitten" and "smelly." They presented children with a formal rendition of Peruvian history and with knowledge that held little meaning for them. They refused to allow the students to speak Quechua. They encouraged individual competition, an idea antithetical to the value that Huanoquiteños placed upon cooperation. They were not loath to use corporal punishment. And, ignoring the demands of agricultural labor cycles, they severely sanctioned students for absences at the same time that they themselves were frequently absent without notice. The Huanoquiteños characterized them as lazy and immoral. The district council, headed by Mayor Quispe, supported the Huanoquiteños' condemnation of the teachers. It denounced them in *El Sol*, the regional Cuzco newspaper, and on a major Cuzco radio station, "Tawantinsuyu," stating that, "We have no reason to hide the abuses of the teachers that are against the law." Most remarkable was the immense gap between the expressed desire for education on the part of Huanoquiteños and the teachers' repeated declarations that Huanoquiteños had no interest in education at all. Clearly, the debate was not about education *per se*, but rather about the kind and quality of education Huanoquiteños were demanding, and, most importantly, the behavior of teachers with respect to Huanoquiteños.[24]

The capacity of Huanoquite's peasants to use their existing political structures in order to incorporate these multiple changes experienced a crisis whose core discourse concerned the viability of these structures and relationships in protecting local autonomy, a sense of legitimacy, and taking advantage of state resources. Despite their efforts to enter into national politics, Huanoquiteños continued to experience obstacles and rejection from state bureaucrats and party officials who, notwithstanding their rhetoric of equal rights for Peruvian citizens, discriminated against "the low ways of peasants" as one bureaucrat put it. These perceptions filtered down to Huanoquiteños who struggled anew with whether or not to accept their own inadequacy as national citizens and depend upon "alternative interlocutors" to the state to make their demands heard. Huanoquiteños' comments in this respect are revealing. Their statements are shot through with a clarity of vision of what was at stake for them in placing their faith in the state, partisan politics, or intermediaries. They were increasingly aware that, in the process of being used by these intermediaries, what they had to say was being compromised.[25]

Taking control

The Velasco regime, threatened by autonomous political organizing among dissatisfied peasants, sought to control it by establishing state-sponsored agrarian leagues and SINAMOS, an army of technical engineers and idealistic bureaucrats. In neither case were these organizations to be identified in terms of class or ethnic struggles. Rather their functions were intended to be technical in nature – providing credit, assisting peasants in learning cooperative management, and introducing agricultural innovations. Peasants who opted for membership in more radical organizations such as the Peasant Confederation of Peru (CCP) suffered represssion from the government. The ill-fated decision on the part of the Velasco, and then the Morales (1975–79), regimes to repress peasant political mobilization led to a greater radicalization of peasants. In turn, as the Velasco regime sought to channel the freedom, aspirations, and conflicts unleashed by reform, different sectors of Peruvian society sought to control these processes as well.

Although Huanoquiteños found it almost impossible to dissociate themselves in any permanent fashion from the uncomfortable alliances in which they found themselves, they did seek alternatives which led to a state of extreme tension in the district. They used formal and informal assemblies which often took place far from the village center in the fields where people were working to sanction intermediaries, to air their grievances, and to prolong debates that did not have easy resolutions. In doing so, they continuously tested shifting political alignments. The social and cultural structure of assemblies became a principal arena in which villagers could manipulate or challenge dominant authority structures. In the course of airing their grievances publicly, Huanoquiteños discovered significant points of commonality among them that they could then use as the basis for collective policy-making and action.

They also sought to combat factionalism and the tension between national incorporation and local autonomy by participating in new kinds of supracommunity organizations, among them the Cuzco Departmental Federation of Peasants, the Revolutionary Agrarian Federation Tupac Amaru, and the United Left Front. Through these organizations, they exchanged information with other peasants, discovered that they were encountering the same kinds of problems, and began to work toward grassroots mobilization that was less compromising and often effective. They participated in high numbers in national strikes, sacrifice marches, and demonstrations against the Ministry of Agriculture, protesting the reversal of agrarian reform policy. In a demonstration in 1984 attended by approximately 4,000 peasants from communities and cooperatives in the department of Cuzco, one man from Huanoquite spoke publicly, expressing forcefully the reasons he was there:

> We, in Huanoquite, have always experienced isolation. Until now, we have suffered in our hearts all the injustices perpetrated by governments of misery and hunger. Now we have come to Cuzco to actually fight against these injustices. Death to the reactionaries. Let us find a new way of life.

Jeffrey Riedinger (1993: 182), speaking of agrarian reform in the Philippines, refers to the paradoxical tension between reformist measures and the efforts of government officials and/or elites to control the course they take as "depoliticizing and disempowering discourse [which] forms part of the continuum of violence and confrontation practiced by elites in resisting redistributive reform." David Maybury-Lewis also calls attention to this as a general practice among states when the idiom of development replaces that of the "expendability of squalid savages." Once development becomes a major goal of nation-building, then the state is bound to consider ethnic identities or cultural rights as obstacles to be overcome. In this sense, the causes of Peru's civil war cannot be wholly explained by relative deprivation theory. It is true that Quechua peasants organized in order to gain more resources, but they did so, not necessarily in order to become like urban "civilized" folks but rather to use them for a variety of their own purposes.

Under these conditions the new regional intermediaries emerged as crucial economic, social and political brokers between peasants and the state. Peasants, with their need for intermediaries and long history of oppression at the hands of the state, remained perhaps the single potentially malleable resource that these individuals could use to enhance their standing. They thought that, by imposing the will of their minds together with strategic military skills, they could engineer a great social upheaval. They believed they could convert science into religion and that it was necessary to use violence to do so since, in their words, "Except for power, all is illusion."[26] One of Guzmán's statements offers a dramatic example of Sendero's cold-blooded appraisal of how to overturn the existing economic and political order:

> The capitalist system condemns 60,000 infants a year to death before the age of one. In comparison, the quota of blood necessary for the revolution is a small price for installing a more egalitarian system.
>
> (Smith 1992: 24)

Peasants, disenchanted by the vagaries of a state that offered them modernization, assimilation, integration, and perhaps even a class identity, rather than recognizing the infinitely more complex topography of the construction of indigenous identities, also turned to Sendero. They joined in higher numbers in the post-Velasco years when the state turned a blind eye to "la mancha India" ("the Indian stain," as some Peruvians refer to their country's most heavily indigenous geographical region in the southern and central highlands) and its economic and political problems, and the national economy began a precipitous decline. Peasant support for Sendero did not constitute a disjunctural moment, however, in the history of peasant-state relations. Rather, it represented a continuity in the thorny issue of genuine versus non-authentic citizenship for the Quechua people whereby, periodically, the state would claim to acknowledge Quechua inhabitants as full citizens but then fail to live up to its own rhetoric. The Velasco regime indeed made greater headway than prior governments in recognizing the needs and rights of Quechua people, including their right to vote and to control to a far greater extent the land they worked. Yet it did so principally to achieve national integration, avoid separatism, and make Quechua peasants into modern farmers. Even these measures were threatening to the many Peruvians who considered them far too radical and who welcomed the halt to agrarian reform initiated by the military coup and dictatorship of Morales Bermúdez in 1975.

Perhaps parallels to these dynamics can be found in other nation-states where earlier reform or modernization policies created a political space or vacuum in the countryside without simultaneously creating economic opportunities. In Peru, this space became a primary resource in struggles for upward mobility and power within a shrinking economy. It fostered the growth of a stratum of regionally educated intermediaries who were unable to achieve their own economic or political mobility but who had placed great hopes in the agrarian reform initiative. Perhaps unwittingly, they had also absorbed many of the same behaviors and attitudes the landed elite had displayed toward peasants. Their own words tell the story best. The first are the words of a man who defected from Sendero:

> We created another social stratum within the same community; another overseer; another owner, because we felt we had more power than other peasants. We created another race, another social problem within the conglomerate of the same community. And thus, we also created those who exploit and those who are exploited. Exploited, the peasants are illiterate and they let others run things who know a little more, who have a little more culture, who have a little higher level of education. We were the ones who began to govern and to exploit our own brothers, and thus we rose as new millionaires, new hacendados. We were too close to them [our own brothers] to know ourselves as we really are. The peasants try to benefit from those who have a little more experience, culture. We leave as millionaires and abandon again the poor who are trying to recuperate their lands, trying to improve themselves. We leave them totally abandoned and even annihilate the community.
>
> (Interview, 1991)

And from a lawyer who had been a member of the Peruvian Communist Party:

> Sendero Luminoso is, perhaps, an exaggeration of good faith. When I was young and also when I became a lawyer and before the Agrarian Reform, I was absolutely certain that when land was given to the peasants, the Peruvian problem would be resolved. I had the idea that every peasant worked, a little lazy, a bit of a thief because he worked for someone else, the hacendado, but if the land were his, he would work it with great eagerness. It was a lie. It hasn't been that way. As a result all my faith in that epoch has crumbled because reality is different. ... A harsh hand is needed. The peasants are cold, they can't walk, they get drunk, man and woman, they lie sprawled out on the ground. How is a country going to develop? How is a community going to grow? We need, now we don't say a whip because this is no longer the epoch of the whip, but something that will obligate them to

work for themselves, something within each person, each community, a spiritual matter that will make them work for themselves. Perhaps it is this faith that belongs to Sendero who has lifted arms because they want to improve things but by a very bloody, drastic and severe path. They are a violent reaction to so much abuse, so much immorality, which can be seen among all of Peru's politicians today.

(Interview, 1991)

And finally, from a formal document published by Sendero:

In these times, the official left in Peru has not simply erred by having chosen the electoral path but it has also deliberately put itself at the service of the democratic bourgeoisie with confusing proposals of reform within a system that was already once attempted by the military government of General Juan Velasco Alvarado and dismantled by the most reactionary sector of the armed forces, headed by General Francisco Morales Bermúdez: "The Stubborn Reformist Leads the Way to the Murderer."

(Mercado 1986: 62)

Deep rivers: breaking bridges

Crawford Young (1993: 22–23) enumerates three orientations to cultural pluralism. One, the instrumentalist orientation, focuses on how ethnicity is used in political and social competition. Although he does not distinguish between the institutions and rhetoric of ethnicity, he points out that ethnicity (in his words, cultural pluralism) becomes "contingent, situational, and circumstantial," given that political factors exist which might activate it; there are cultural entrepreneurs who supply its doctrine; and activists who exploit ethnic solidarities. We have already seen that during the agrarian reform, regional intermediaries took center stage as cultural entrepreneurs and many of them eventually became members of, or sympathizers with, Sendero. Sendero sought to remake Peru by destroying all existing political structures. The regimes of Belaúnde and García sought to eradicate the roots of Sendero. In the following section, I discuss how, despite the very different goals members of Sendero and policy makers of the government held, both wielded ethnicity as a powerful weapon, ultimately against those they perceived as Quechua. For Sendero, if they were not activists or sympathizers, they were enemies. For the government, the same was true. Those who were targeted struggled with their own political and cultural responses to such an alienating and destructive polarization of forces.

The work of revolution

Members of Sendero worked in squatter settlements, infiltrated unions, set up popular schools in rural areas in order to raise the consciousness of Quechua peasants, and generally imposed their vision of an ideal Peruvian society. Despite their labor among peasants and workers, they displayed a surprising misunderstanding or deliberate lack of comprehension of a very different mode of decision making and organization among many Quechua communities and, in the urban squatter settlements, one that was grounded in consensus. Just as the state had traditionally been threatened by the old sack of potatoes problem of peasants (which peasants have used astutely to elude the reach of the state), so was Sendero threatened. They refused to accommodate to the heterogeneity among peasants, preferring to view them as a monolithic, abstract, ideal category. Overinfluenced by the Maoist idea of a vast army of peasant-workers, Sendero resorted to wholly undemocratic, non-consensual measures of terror, threats, killings, and absolutism to impose their will in order to follow through the five stages of revolution Guzmán had specified.

Orin Starn (1998: 229) admonishes with good reason the US scholars who have considered Sendero to be a grassroots peasant movement. Rather, in his words, Sendero

> operated through a rigid hierarchy that replicated the general stratification by race and class in Peru. Dark-skinned kids born in poverty filled the bottom ranks under a leadership composed mostly of light-skinned elites.

Guzmán himself stressed that Sendero was not democratic:

> The Party is not a party of masses. ... the party is a select organization, a selection of the best, of those who have proven themselves, of those who have wood, as Stalin said, being numerically few in proportion to the immense masses, the party defends the interests of the proletariat.
> (Interview with Abimael Guzmán, 31 July 1988, *El Diario*, cited in Burt and Panfichi 1992: 23).

Sendero's failure to realize that peasants would not uniformly respond to policies formulated primarily on ideological grounds helps to explain the extreme violence that its members resorted to when peasants did not display the support for the movement that the former's ideology had predicted. Sendero's utopian model required that Peru's cities be surrounded from the countryside by putting "the noose around the neck of imperialism and the reactionaries ... and garrot[ing] them by the throat," in Guzmán's words (speech delivered on 19 April 1980, at the initiation of the armed struggle, cited in Starn *et al.* 1994: 461).

Few of the events in Peru can be attributed specifically to post-Cold War international phenomena. The exception may well be the further weakness of parties of various orientations or affiliations on the left and right alike. In a case of classic segmentary opposition, the polar stars of communism and American imperialism had held together the startling number of factions on the left and right of traditional political parties and fronts. Without these guiding lights, they splintered into numerous and remarkably ineffectual factions. The demise of traditional political parties as well as the debilitation of unions and federations that represented peasants strengthened Sendero initially. Furthermore, the ineptitude of the government became blatantly apparent during President García's regime (1985–90). Its deliberately extremist measures against what it deemed to be "subversive activity" led to a crucial disjunctural moment when peasants, in far greater numbers, rejected the legitimacy of the state. President Alan García of the APRA party increased repressive activities in the countryside and cities, arresting and "disappearing" numerous innocent civilians, many of whom were Quechua. These repressive measures culminated in the massacre of almost 300 "subversive" prisoners in Lima at point-blank range on 18 and 19 June 1986, a move ordered by García. The García regime endorsed the use of death squads, and after Sendero had attacked a rural community, police and military forces would often indiscriminately kill large numbers of innocent peasants in the region. Even if the "rules of the game" had been broken repeatedly prior to this point in time, these events made many peasants reconsider their willingness to attempt to play the game at all. The ways that Sendero's members and the government used a kind of distorted understanding of ethnicity as a weapon had devastating consequences for all Peruvians.

Cultural interpretations of violence

Members of civil society had several different kinds of responses to state and guerrilla actions that arbitrarily pigeon-holed individuals as "Indians" and potential soldiers of the proletariat. Especially in the countryside and in indigenous communities, one of the most telling cultural artifacts that signalled a rupture with the existing social and political order were the representations of the culture of violence and terror found in the numerous stories circulating of *ñakaqs*. These monstrous beings, usually in the guise of foreigners, killed Indians, tore apart their limbs, and drained them of fat in order to manufacture different things. They were hardly new to indigenous oral traditions or experience and took on various human forms that kept pace roughly with the changing political and economic conditions of Peru. They first resembled priests who made church bells, then foreign entrepreneurs who manufactured oil for airplanes, then foreigners who amputated limbs and extracted organs and eyes from native inhabitants to sell them abroad, and finally, soldiers who made weapons. In the 1980s, ñakaqs leaped out of oral traditions and began to walk the streets of peasant communities, especially in Ayacucho, alternatively leading to heightened terror or to collective attacks upon these beings. Billie Jean Isbell (1992: 74–75) reports that in her interviews, peasants in Ayacucho (where Sendero first began its armed struggle) perceived members of Sendero to be a new form of ñakaq:

> flesh eating beings feeding off a population with no more fat to give ... [peasants] see themselves trapped between flesh-eating ñakaqs, and "foreigners" who know no fear, who are more savage than Peruvians. They

cannot imagine that their own countrymen could act so brutally. ... These figures of power are out of place – not from one's own place and time.

Quechua peasants perceived *both* soldiers and members of Sendero to be ñakaqs. An obvious leitmotif apparent in experiences with and stories of ñakaqs, which are widespread in the Peruvian Andes, is that Indians' lifeblood is sucked from them violently in order to make things. These sentiments are deeply rooted in a historical legacy that has reified Indians into things, refused to recognize their individuality and humanness, and quite explicitly involved events of rape and pillage for purposes of material acquisition. In Wachtel's *Gods and Vampires*, he poignantly traces how ñakaqs (known as *kharisiris* in the Uru region of Chipaya, Bolivia in which he worked) no longer are "foreigners" of one sort or another; rather, they are now sometimes individuals from *within* communities. Wachtel argues that processes of exploitation, modernization and corruption have become internal to Andean peasant communities, disrupting circuits of reciprocity, trust and intergenerational communication.

One can draw parallels between these experiences and narratives and those that Kay Warren (1993: 25–56) describes as taking place among the Mayas of Guatemala: distrust of one's neighbors, friends and relatives; a situation of "betrayal and existential dilemma"; a growing sense of desperate entrapment. Where ethnicity became the primary vehicle used by the forces of law and order and by members of Sendero, one was no longer able to speak or act without fear or mistrust. Especially during the García regime, people, whether they were mestizos or Quechua, did not want to speak of what was transpiring and when they spoke it was in a very circumspect fashion.

Civil defense patrols, soup kitchens, grassroots movements and non-governmental organizations

While ñakaqs were particularly dramatic means that peasants used to express their agony, another response among members of civil society to the polarized state of violence was the growth of social movements grounded in demands for peace and justice. Protests against human rights violations also became alternative channels for resisting violence, condemning brutality on the part of both the government and Sendero, and pleading for greater political and economic representation for Quechua peasants and urban migrants, especially among mestizos in urban areas. In addition, in the urban *barriadas* (also known as *pueblos jovenes*), recently-arrived and well-established migrant households, with great courage, sought to combat the inroads Sendero was making into their existing political organizations. Women organized soup kitchens to ensure their families' sustenance. In the countryside, different kinds of civil defense groups arose, some encouraged by the military, others welcomed by peasants themselves, as a way of overcoming the "existential dilemma" of distrust and of defending themselves against Sendero (see Starn 1991). As Orin Starn (1998: 232) stresses, the government's arming of peasants was a radical departure for the Peruvian state, which considered giving out guns ... as unthinkable ... in the first years of the fight against the Shining Path, as the military was no more trustful than the original band of European conquerors of the real allegiance of the Andean villagers.

Starn (1998: 232) adds that the passage of a national law in 1992 recognizing the right of civil defense patrols to arm themselves, resulted in "codifying the reversal of the colonial withholding the technology of war from Andean peasants, and signalling the confidence of Fujimori and his generals in the strength of their unlikely alliance with the peasantry in the war against the Shining Path."

Sendero reacted to the tentative efforts of peasants and workers alike to create alternative political spaces by engaging in ruthless and measured attacks upon leaders in rural and urban communities. The decision of the government to arm peasants and Sendero's increasingly brutal tactics ironically may have forged a growing sense of pan-ethnic identity among Peru's Quechua people. Leaders of civil defense patrols met together, recognized that they were encountering similar difficulties, talked over tactics and strategies, and shared their experiences.

Sendero's instrumental and extremely violent use of ethnicity, intent upon establishing and discerning polarized enemies where they did not necessarily exist, helps to explain the initial overwhelming support for Fujimori when he was elected to the presidency in 1990 despite the seemingly dictatorial measures he took during two terms in office. For many Peruvians, Fujimori seemed practical rather than ideological, a perception bolstered by his lack of affiliation with traditional political parties. Fujimori, as an autodictator, established a formal pact with the military. Without resorting to a coup, he succeeded in achieving precisely what a military coup had in the past. His autocratic rule, although it certainly served some interests of peasants and workers, just as easily, and even more effectively than ever before, was able to turn against them.[27]

The specter of Uncle Sam, cocaine and spy chiefs

A final, more international, factor continues to contribute to the extreme degree of violence in Peru: coca and coca paste production, together with the antidrug trafficking policies and investments on the part of the USA. The collusion between police, military and antidrug trafficking forces, peasants who grow coca and transform it into coca paste, and members of Sendero who protected peasants and traffickers connected to Colombian cartels from the intrusions of DEA types in exchange for a tax on the coca and weapons has led to an extreme degree of corruption and cooperation among political forces normally at odds with one another. In 1994, some 2,459 policemen, including officers, were punished for misconduct, including excessive use of force and drug-related crimes. As a result 1,113, including 13 senior officers, were fired.[28] These figures only give an inkling of the much higher numbers of law enforcement personnel who are involved in drug trafficking. Anti-drug trafficking campaigns, spearheaded by the US, are greeted by all Peruvians with ambivalence. Funds from the DEA are welcomed despite sentiments of nationalism and an irritation at US intervention in Peruvian affairs. The revenues and employment for different sectors of society created by coca cultivation and drug-trafficking itself perpetuate this illicit and destructive but essential economy.

Limited economic opportunities within Peru, and money and resources from outside exacerbated the violence between and within multiple groups. Not only were Quechua peasants involved in the low-intensity warfare and counterinsurgency that accompany, *de facto*, the war against drugs, but also other Indian groups (see Gonzales 1992: 105–126). In one example, the MRTA, another major guerrilla group, inspired by the Cuban revolution, was active in the jungle and became involved in violent turf wars with Sendero over controlling populations there and who would receive taxes from coca growers. In 1994, Sendero massacred sixty-two Asháninka Indians, one of the largest Amazonian groups, in the jungle region of Satipo, Department of Junín. Fourteen children had their ears cut off, suggesting that Sendero thought they were acting as spies. The Asháninka, faced with pressure from Sendero and not provided with any protection from the state, split into two groups, one allied with Sendero, the other divided into small bands fleeing deeper into the jungles and mountains.

Conclusion

Deep rivers. The causes of extreme violence in Peru predate the Cold War by at least thirty years, dating back to when Sendero first began organizing. The lines between different enemies have grown ever murkier since the end of the Cold War. What now appears in the place of traditional peasant federations or class-based parties and unions is a multiplicity of grassroots organizations, as fluid and unstable as the river. This kind of grassroots democracy tends to be far more meaningful to the people participating in it than the superficial and fragile structures of democracy that Peruvians ushered in in 1985 and, again, in 1990. While the establishment of due process and an independent judiciary are governmental institutions that they want to see put in place once again, they do not want to experience the dictatorship of traditional parties or the terror of Sendero, neither of which has empowered them significantly.

A few words of caution are in order, however. One reason to heed the recent political history of Peru and the curious form of the present Peruvian state is because many social scientists have lauded the current "informalization" of democracy taking place throughout Latin America. Many Peruvians, and especially the Quechua still struggling for citizenship rights, have a pretty clear idea of what democracy means to them, given their history. They are nevertheless persuaded by populist rhetoric, given the few options from which they can choose at present. In a situation where a balance of powers does not exist to offset the executive branch, populist rhetoric may blur rather easily into fascist action.

Participants in this symposium have observed that many groups which have led extremely violent movements, some directly against the state, others against particular groups in such a way that the ensuing chaos threatens the future of the state, occupy a "superficial" or "marginal" structural position in their society. It is important to note, in the Peruvian case, that these individuals were not the *most* impoverished sectors of society, but rather were losing out in the course of changes. They had reasons and opportunities to consider alternative political and philosophical models, and they occupied a privileged enough position to allow them to participate in designing and implementing such models, however violent they might be.

It is difficult to predict the trajectory that Peru's turn away from violence will take. It is hardly a permanent condition, however. The state's legitimacy as an institution has been temporarily restored, in great part due to the rallying of Quechua peasants against the call to violence issued by Sendero (see Starn 1998) and the arrest of the principal leaders of Sendero, including Abimael Gúzman. Whether or not the efforts of Quechua peasants to keep intact both their communities and the nation-state will be transformed into substantive economic and political gains for them remains unknown. The long history of using ethnicity as a primary weapon in political organization and mobilization, the effects of Fujimori's neoliberal economic agenda, and the US drug trafficking policies over the last decade have made for a remarkably precarious foundation upon which to perpetuate any kind of long-lasting peace. It is ironic that the violence perpetrated by the Fujimori regime (together with Montesinos) in the name of law and order did more to nearly bring about the demise of the state than Sendero.

A coda: corruption, cooptation and coercion – the demise of a regime

Fujimori's efforts to seek a third term as president came to an operatic end in November 2000 when his right-hand man and chief of the National Intelligence Service (SIN), Vladimiro Montesinos, was caught on videotape bribing an opposition legislator with $15,000 to switch party affiliations three weeks prior to the run-off election between Fujimori and opposition candidate Alejandro Toledo. Fujimori had lacked a majority in the legislative assembly but shortly after the elections, which were riddled with fraud, he obtained a majority. Seventeen opposition legislators switched parties. Videotapes showed four of them receiving cash bribes from Montesinos. This followed fast upon the revelation of an international arms deal brokered by Peru between Jordan and the Colombian guerrilla group, FARC, of 10,000 AK-47 rifles (the Canary Islands, Guyana, and Iquitos were links along the way). The USA had known of Montesinos' involvement in some measure in this arms deal since 1999, but since it was in the middle of setting up a $1.3 billion anti-drug-trafficking package for the Andean region, it did not respond favorably to Montesinos' unsavory involvement in voter fraud and drug/arms trafficking. Montesinos eventually fled the country, seeking asylum in Panama. The Central Intelligence Agency, which had worked with Montesinos for many years, unsuccessfully attempted to engineer the asylum in order to wash its hands of Montesinos. Montesinos returned to Peru after the government unveiled an amnesty plan for those implicated in the human rights abuses during the civil war, then disappeared from sight again, and was finally arrested in Venezuela and extradited to Peru in June 2001. Fujimori, even after deactivating the National Intelligence Service in response to popular protests and international pressure, was faced by an overwhelming lack of support from civil society and divisions within the armed forces. He subsequently resigned from office and sought refuge in Japan. This scenario of extraordinary complexity grew even more grisly when it was discovered that Montesinos had managed to stow away at least $800 million in Swiss bank accounts. No one doubts that these monies come directly from drug trafficking and international arms dealing, with a little assistance from the CIA in facilitating these connections. A transitional government is now in place in Peru. Popular and international protests and pressure have succeeded in restoring a degree of integrity to the new transitional government, and electoral reforms in anticipation of new elections have begun decentralizing the electoral process. Nevertheless, Montesinos's army peers from Chorrillos Military College permeate the ranks of Peru's bureaucracy at all levels and they have been responsible, with Fujimori's acquiescence, for a reckless disregard of basic citizenship rights among Peruvians.[29]

Interestingly, although peasants suffered the brunt of accusations of being subversives and of being caught in the crossfire of the civil war, recent events protesting the presidential campaign in April 2000 took a different turn. The huge opposition rallies that accompanied the recent events in Peru were in large part due to the infringement of middle-class human rights, such as the extreme government control and censorship of the media, electoral fraud, and the arrests, torture and harassment of opposition candidates and voters. The Fujimori regime had garnered substantial support from peasants by establishing elaborate patron–client ties and dependency upon the regime in the countryside, through handouts and infrastructural projects.

Fujimori, during his rallies, was surrounded by banners proclaiming him as "el chino." Opposition candidate, Alejandro Toledo, the 54-year-old son of Andean peasants turned World Bank economist, and married to a Belgian anthropologist, appeared in his rallies as an Inca emperor with the sun on his chest. During a huge protest with more than 130,000 in the central plaza of Lima alone, people came from all over Peru – the Amazon, the Andean highlands, the coast, and, of course, the capital itself, to participate in "The March of the Four Suyos." The *suyos* symbolized the original four quarters of the Inca empire, *Tawantinsuyo*, as it was known. At the inception of the rally, four Indian representatives from each of the suyos blew on a conch shell, used to call people to war, to gather them together, or to communicate messages. Finally, Toledo issued a proclamation that can only be viewed as racist and nationalistic even as he perceives himself as being exactly the opposite:

> This is the voice of the people echoing through the Andes with more force than the guns of those who do not love their country. If they think they can beat the will of the Peruvians, these Orientals don't understand our Andean roots.
>
> (*New York Times*, 28 July 2000)[30]

Once again, we see the peculiar ways in which indigenous culture and the weapons of ethnicity are skillfully wielded to garner votes from across Peru's class and ethnic divisions and to create the semblance of a nation that remains to be consolidated.

Acknowledgements

I am appreciative of the many individuals who commented on this manuscript as it evolved. Bill Mitchell first gave me the opportunity to prepare a talk for the new York Academy of Sciences, which served as the catalyst for the invitation I received from R. Brian Ferguson to participate in a special symposium at the NYAS on the impact of the end of the Cold War geopolitics upon the dynamics of nation-states. The thoughtful and provactive remarks of David Maybury-Lewis, Andrew Strathern, Kay Warren and the late Eric Wolf, as well as those of the participants themselves were invaluable in helping me think through and refine my ideas. Observations and queries made by my colleagues at George Mason University, in particular, John Stone and Kevin Avruch, and the anonymous reviewers of this manuscript also sharpened my theoretical arguments and focus. Finally, I am grateful Brian Ferguson for shepherding this project through and offering me the opportunity the think in a more comparative fashion about my own research.

Notes

1   Portions of this chapter can be found in greater ethnographic and analytic detail in my book, *Between Reform and Revolution: Political Struggles in the Peruvian Andes, 1969–1991* (Seligmann 1995).
2   The Quechua are a majority native population of the Andean highlands. There are four major variants of Quechua in different regions of the Andes, which are not mutually intelligible. When the Incas established their empire, many native languages were spoken, but the Spanish, after their conquest, made Quechua the *lingua franca* of the empire. Within particular regions, Quechua peoples share a common language, a wide range of cultural practices, and a history of subordination and discrimination, and many have participated together in peasant leagues and federations. Nevertheless, there is a very weak sense of pan-Quechua identity. Rather, people identify themselves with particular territories or valleys and mountain spirits, and they are differentiated by land tenure patterns, labor relations, economic standing, religious belief systems, and their differing degrees of participation in migratory flows.
3   "Mestizo" generally refers to those who are of mixed Hispanic and indigenous ancestry and who define themselves culturally as non-indigenous. Numerous social "markers" serve to distinguish "mestizos" from "indios" – urban clothing, literacy in Spanish, non-manual occupation, and sometimes skin color. However, these markers are also flexible and their meaning is established more often than not relationally through social interactions that themselves are structured by power relations.
4   Fujimori succeeded in challenging the Peruvian constitution, which limits the president to two consecutive terms. The constituent assembly, reorganized by Fujimori himself, upheld his amendment to allow him to run for a third term. Elections were held on 9 April 2000, with a close race between opposition candidate Alejandro Toledo and Alberto Fujimori. Fujimori almost won an outright majority, which would have prevented a run-off, amid accusations of rampant fraud, including pay-offs to congressmen to switch party affiliations, and tampering with signatures and ballots. He handily won the run-off since Toledo refused to actively participate in it. Only

when Fujimori's right-hand man and head of the National Intelligence Service (SIN), Vladimiro Montesinos, was videotaped passing a huge bribe ($15,000) to a congressman, did things begin to fall apart. Montesinos fled the country to Panama and eventually Fujimori himself announced his resignation and fled to Japan on 20 November 2000. A transition government is now in place with new elections to be held in April 2001.

5 I have used pseudonyms throughout in order to protect individuals whose lives might be threatened because of comments they have made about the civil war and/or because they were directly involved in it.

6 As Crawford Young (1993: 27) points out,

> However serviceable general and comparative concepts may be in grasping its dynamics, cultural pluralism in operation is contingent upon its immediate environment. The historical trajectory of a given polity provides one set of defining parameters. The imprint of the past persists through the embedded collective memory of traumatic or inspirational moments or events, patterns over time by which broadening elements in civil society have been incorporated into an actual political realm, and evolving structures of political organization, conflict and cooperation.

7 David Scott Palmer's (1992) edited volume offers a useful overview of Sendero, especially in terms of its operations in the central highland region. Ronald Berg (1986, 1992), Carlos Iván Degregori (1989, 1990), Nelson Manrique (1989), Orin Starn (1991, 1998) and Starn *et al.* (1994) provide first-hand accounts of peasant relationships to Sendero Luminoso. Degregori, who lived and taught in Huamanga, Ayacucho for many years, gives an excellent account of the social background of members of Sendero. Deborah Poole and Gerardo Rénique (1991, 1993) and Enrique Mayer (1991) pay close attention to the broader, historicized context in which peasant politics have unfolded and in which the construction of ethnic identity has taken place in Peru. Stern's (1998) edited volume gives the most impressive historically contextualized perspectives on the emergence and place of Sendero in Peruvian society.

8 Teivo Teivainen's *Enter Economy, Exit Politics* (2000) argues persuasively that the attempt to carry out state policies on the basis exclusively of economic analyses that are supposedly politically neutral is far from neutral. In his analysis of the contemporary political economy of Peru (especially during Fujimori's presidency), he documents how arguments of economism have been used and specifies their political intentions and consequences.

9 Glen Farvin, reporting for the *Miami Herald* (6 April 2000) documents that Peru's Gross Domestic Product had increased in 1998 by 7 per cent, and even more in 1999. Nevertheless, demand in the economy fell so sharply that "it felt like a recession to consumers, manufacturers and banks, even if, statistically, it was not." The men and women in the informal service sector whom I interviewed during this period voiced similar sentiments. By April 2000, economic growth had skyrocketed with $8.8 billion in Peru's foreign reserves, far more than the other Andean countries. President Fujimori was well aware nevertheless of how little impact this had had on most Peruvians, reflected in his decision to make employment his number one concern during his campaign for a third term in office.

10 A substantial corpus of scholarly literature has been devoted to general analysis of Peru's 1969 agrarian reform. I (Seligmann 1995) concentrate upon the political and cultural dimensions of agrarian reform, in particular, how it shaped peasant relations to the state and the subsequent evolution of Sendero. José María Caballero (1980, 1981) evaluates land tenure before and after the reform. Abraham Lowenthal (1975), José Matos Mar and José Manuel Mejía (1980a, b), and Tom Albert (1983) discuss the reform process, policy measures, how they were implemented, and their general conse-

quences. David Guillet (1979) examines similar issues, using a case study of Anta, one of the largest cooperatives established in the southern highlands. Anibal Quijano (1979) and Rodrigo Sánchez (1979) analyze peasant movements and land seizures that took place during the reform. Cynthia McClintock (1981) examines how the reform changed attitudes and political behavior among peasants, primarily in coastal regions. McClintock (1982) and McClintock and Lowenthal (1983) evaluate the impact of postreform policy reversals. Peter Cleaves and Martin Scurrah (1980), Alfred Stepan (1978), Liisa North (1983), and Liisa North and Tanya Korovkin (n.d.) explain how the role and composition of the Peruvian state affected the reform process. Carlos Amat y León (1980) addresses economic and food policies promoted after the reform, and Luís Pásara (1978, 1982) offers detailed studies of changes in the legal order during the reform.
11 Quoted in Pease and Verme 1974: 93.
12 Comunidad de Maska, Libro de actas, 26 April 1975.
13 Concejo Distrital de Huanquite, Libro de actas, 20 July 1978.
14 Concejo Distrital de Huanquite, Libro de actas, 18 June 1980.
15 Numerous references to these undertakings are found in community, cooperative, and district council minutes. See, for example, Concejo Distrital, Huanoquite, Libro de actas, 7 December 1978; 22 January 1979; 25 January 1979; all entries, 1980.
16 *El Sol*, 13 January 1977, p. 1. (*El Sol* is one of Cuzco's principal newspapers.)
17 Comunidad de Maska, Libro de actas, 12 February 1978.
18 Comunidad de Maska, Libro de actas, July 1991.
19 The characterizations of these intermediaries are drawn from formal interviews and conversations I had with such individuals as well as conversations about them with other Huanoquiteños; the proceedings of general assemblies and meetings; and the course of daily life. In reading of the organization and activities of Sendero, it becomes apparent that many of these brokers played key roles in the movement throughout the highlands. Although it is impossible to know with any certainty if these intermediaries were members of Sendero, enough of them made veiled references to their sympathies with the movement that I am willing to take the risk of assuming that they were either sympathizers or activists. That Huanoquite had been targeted for Sendero actions makes it even more likely that they were participants in one fashion or another.
20 Remarks of Minister of Agriculture Jorge Barandiarán, in *El Sol*, 28 June 1969, p. 2; 13 May 1970, p. 2. Velasco was explicit in viewing rural education as critical to creating a unified nation. He viewed "the educational system as a mechanism for integrating the peasantry into the social order" (Velasco 1972: 63).
21 Guzmán, in fact, stressed the key role in Sendero of intellectuals, who, "as high school and university students and professionals, should work in the service of the proletariat and peasantry, specifying and guiding them toward a new scientific national culture, and making them conscious that the only way they will achieve it is through revolution" (Arce Borja 1989: 386).
22 Interview, Huanoquite, 7 April 1984.
23 Primary sources revealing Sendero's ideological orientation can be found in *Guerra Popular en el Perú* (1989), compiled and edited by Luís Arce Borja; numerous issues of Sendero's newspaper, *El Diario*, in particular, 5 July 1989; *Entrevista al Presidente Gonzalo* (1988) and *Desarrollar la guerra popular sirviendo a la revolución mundial* (n.d.), compiled by the Partido Comunista del Perú and Mercado (1986). Gorriti (1991, 1992) offers incisive details of Sendero's strategic planning, biographical accounts of many of its leaders and participants, and a critical appraisal of the contradictory policies and actions of the police, military, and special antiterrorist units as they sought to quell Sendero.
24 Concejo Distrital, Huanoquite, Libro de actas, 18 September 1980; 20 October 1980; 15 January 1981.
25 Take, for example, the following statements made by Huanoquiteños in the 1980s: "The director of the school is a wolf bitch, disguised as kindness and generosity"; "He, a teacher and merchant, seeks to gain the friendship of our pueblo with an eye

toward advancing to a position in the district council"; " When the Vice President of Peru, Javier Alva Orlandini came to Cuzco, we spoke with him. He offered to talk to the President in our behalf and donate a tractor to our village. This was what he said but to this day he has not complied with his promise"; and "His attribution of power to himself is his way of seeking revenge. Now the pueblo has awakened and we will throw off the chains of domination." These statements were made by members of both communities and cooperatives in Huanoquite.

26 This is a favorite Sendero slogan, quoted in Degregori 1990: 10.
27 In 1994, violence, human rights abuses, and scorched earth tactics were once again on the rise in Peru. For two weeks airborne troops strafed hamlets in the central highlands, committing "indiscriminate aggression against civilian targets" (*Financial Times*, 21 April 1994, p. 5). Although the military justified its actions as a search to root out Sendero once and for all, some observed that these extreme measures were not unconnected to Fujimori's growing interest in selling Peru as a fashionable country for overseas investors" (*Financial Times*, 11 April 1994, p. 3). It is also important to note that Guzmán, from his prison cell, twice sought an amnesty with the government for Sendero members, which was rejected out of hand by Fujimori.
28 *Xinhua General Overseas News Service*, 14 April 1994, Item no. 0414030.
29 Most of this is now common knowledge. Detailed reports of the arms deal, and the connections between the CIA, drug traffickers, and Montesinos can be found in the *New York Times*, 6 November 2000, A3; and the *Washington Post*, 7 December 2000, A1, A29. Peru's transitional government has shown remarkable integrity and an article deserves to be written, analyzing exactly why it did not seem to fall into the same terrible mistakes of corruption and paralyzation as other regimes. To its credit, thirteen high-ranking military officials were forced out. It undertook a genuine and much-needed house-cleaning and in a limited amount of time achieved some success, perhaps because so many politicians and members of the military were compromised by the Montesinos videotapes.
30 In a final ironic twist, elections were held in June 2001 between a ghost from the past, Alán García, and Toledo. Although Toledo won by a substantial margin, García too was remarkably skillful in garnering votes. It is not that Peruvians have forgotten the past and García's disastrous presidency, but rather that APRA is the only well-established political party apparatus that exists and that García's campaign relied heavily not on responsible governance but rather on maximizing his popularity.

References

Albert, Tom (1983) *Agrarian Reform and Rural Poverty*. Boulder: Westview Press.
Amat y León, Carlos (ed.) (1980) *Realidad del campo Peruano después de la reforma agraria: 10 ensayos críticos*. Lima: CIC y Editora Ital Perú.
Anderson, Benedict R. (1983) *Imagined Communities: Reflections on the Origins and Spread of Nationalism*. London: Verso.
Arce Borja, Luís (ed.) (1989) *Guerra popular en el Perú: el pensamiento Gonzalo*. Brussells: Luís Arce Borja.
Arguedas, José María (1978) *Deep Rivers*, trans. Francis Barraclough. Austin: University of Texas Press.
Bailey, F.G. (1963) *Politics and Social Change: Orissa in 1959*. Berkeley: University of California Press.
—— (1969) *Stratagems and Spoils: A Social Anthropology of Politics*. Oxford: Basil Blackwell.
Berg, Ronald (1986) "Sendero Luminoso and the Peasantry of Andahuaylas." *Journal of Interamerican Studies and World Affairs* 28: 165–196.
—— (1992) "Peasant Responses to Shining Path in Andahuaylas." In David Scott Palmer (ed.), *The Shining Path of Peru*. New York: St. Martin's Press, pp. 83–104.

Burt, Jo-Marie and Aldo Panfichi (1992) *Peru: Caught in the Crossfire*. Jefferson City, MO: Peru Peace Network.
Caballero, José María (1980) *Agricultura, reforma agraria y pobreza campesina*. Lima: IEP.
—— (1981) *Economía agraria de la sierra peruana antes de la reforma agraria de 1969*. Lima: IEP.
Cleaves, Peter and Martin J. Scurrah (1980) *Agriculture, Bureaucracy and Military Government in Peru*. Ithaca: Cornell University Press.
Comaroff, Jean (1985) *Body of Power, Spirit of Resistance: The Culture and History of a South African People*. Chicago and London: University of Chicago Press.
Degregori, Carlos Iván (1989) *Qué difícil es ser Dios: ideología y violencia política en Sendero Luminoso*. Lima: Zorro de Abajo.
—— (1990) *El surgimiento de Sendero Luminoso: Ayacucho 1969–1979*. Lima: IEP.
Gonzales, José E. (1992) "Guerrillas and Coca in the Upper Huayllaga Valley." In David Scott Palmer (ed.), *The Shining Path of Peru*. New York: St. Martin's Press, pp. 105–126.
Gorriti, Gustavo (1991) *Senxzdero: Historia de la guerra milenaria en el Perú*, volume 1. Lima: Editorial Apoyo.
—— (1992) "Shining Path's Stalin and Trotsky." In David Scott Palmer (ed.), *The Shining Path of Peru*. New York: St. Martin's Press, pp. 149–170.
Guillet, David (1979) *Agrarian Reform and Peasant Economy in Southern Peru*. Columbia: University of Missouri Press.
Isbell, Billie Jean (1992) "Shining Path and Peasant Responses in Rural Ayacucho." In David Scott Palmer (ed.), *The Shining Path of Peru*. New York: St. Martin's Press, pp. 59–82.
Lowenthal, Abraham F. (ed.) (1975) *The Peruvian Experiment: Continuity and Change under Military Rule*. Princeton: Princeton University Press.
McClintock, Cynthia (1981) *Peasant Cooperatives and Political Change in Peru*. Princeton: Princeton University Press.
—— (1982) "Post-Revolutionary Agrarian Politics in Peru." In Stephen M. Gorman (ed.), *Post-Revolutionary Peru: The Politics of Transformation*. Boulder: Westview Press, pp. 17–66.
McClintock, Cynthia and Abraham F. Lowenthal (eds) (1983) *The Peruvian Experiment Reconsidered*. Princeton: Princeton University Press.
Manrique, Nelson (1989) "La década de la violencia." *Márgenes* 5–6: 137–182.
Marx, Anthony W. (1993) "Contested Images and Implications of South African Nationhood." In Kay Warren (ed.), *The Violence Within: Cultural and Political Opposition in Divided Nations*. Boulder: Westview Press, pp. 157–180.
Matos Mar, José and José Manuel Mejía (1980a) *Reforma agraria: logros y contradicciones, 1969–1979*. Lima: IEP.
—— (1980b) *La reforma agraria en el Perú*. Lima: IEP.
Mayer, Enrique (1991) "Peru in Deep Trouble: Mario Vargas Llosa's 'Inquest in the Andes' Reexamined." *Cultural Anthropology* 6(4): 466–504.
Mercado, Roger (1986) *Periodismo para el pueblo y por el pueblo: artículos inéditos silenciados por la prensa burguesa del Perú sobre Sendero y otros temas*. Paris: Ediciones Latinoamericanos.
North, Liisa (1983) "Ideological Orientations of Peru's Military Rulers." In Cynthia McClintock and Abraham Lowenthal (eds), *The Peruvian Experiment Reconsidered*. Princeton: Princeton University Press, pp. 209–44.
North, Liisa and Tanya Korovkin (n.d.) *The Peruvian Revolution and the Officers in Power, 1967–1976*. Occcasional Monograph Series, no. 15. Montreal: McGill University.
Palmer, David Scott (ed.) (1992) *The Shining Path of Peru*. New York: St. Martin's Press.
Partido Comunista del Perú (1988) *Entrevista al Presidente Gonzalo*. Lima: Ediciones Bandera Roja.

—— (n.d.) *Desarrollar la guerra popular sirviendo a la revolución mundial*. Lima: Partido Comunista del Perú.
Pásara, Luís (1978) *Reforma agraria: derecho y conflicto*. Lima: IEP.
—— (1982) *Jueces, justicia y poder en el Perú*. Lima: CEDYS.
Pease, Henry and Olga Verme Insúa (1974) *Perú, 1968–1973: Cronología política*, 2 volumes. Lima: DESCO.
Poole, Deborah and Gerardo Rénique (1991) "The New Chroniclers of Peru: U.S. Scholars and their 'Shining Path' of Peasant Rebellion." *Bulletin of Latin American Research* 10(2): 133–91.
—— (1993) *Peru: Time of Fear*. New York: Monthly Review Press.
Quijano, Anibal (1979) *Problema agrario y movimientos campesinos*. Lima: Mosca Azul.
Riedinger, Jeffrey M. (1993) "Everyday Elite Resistance: Redistributive Agrarian Reform in the Philippines." In Kay Warren (ed.), *The Violence Within: Cultural and Political Opposition in Divided Nations*. Boulder: Westview Press, pp. 181–218.
Roseberry, William (1993) "Beyond the Agrarian Question in Latin America." In Frederick Cooper, Allen F. Isaacman, Florencia Mallon, William Roseberry and Steve Stern, *Confronting Historical Paradigms: Peasants, Labor, and the Capitalist World System in Africa and Latin America*. Madison: University of Wisconsin Press, pp. 318–370.
Sánchez, Rodrigo (1979) *Toma de tierras y conciencia política campesina*. Lima: IEP.
Seligmann, Linda J. (1995) *Between Reform and Revolution: Political Struggles in the Peruvian Andes, 1969–1991*. Stanford: Stanford University Press.
Smith, Michael (1992) "Taking the High Ground: Shining Path and the Andes." In David Scott Palmer (ed.), *The Shining Path of Peru*. New York: St. Martin's Press, pp. 15–32.
Starn, Orin (1991) *"Con los llanques todo barro": Reflexiones sobre rondas campesinas, protesta rural y nuevos momentos sociales*. Lima: IEP.
—— (1998) "Villagers at Arms: War and Counterrevolution in the Central-South Andes." In Steve Stern (ed.), *Shining and Other Paths: War and Society in Peru, 1980–1995*. Durham, NC and London: Duke University Press, pp. 224–257.
Starn, Orin, Carlos Iván Degregori and Robin Kirk (eds) (1994) *Peru: History, Culture, Politics*. Durham, NC: Duke University Press.
Stepan, Alfred (1978) *The State and Society: Peru in Comparative Perspective*. Princeton: Princeton University Press.
Stern, Steve (ed.) (1998) *Shining and Other Paths: War and Society in Peru, 1980–1995*. Durham, NC and London: Duke University Press.
Teivainen, Teivo (2000) *Enter Economy, Exit Politics: Transnational Politics of Economism and Limits to Democracy in Peru*. Helsinki: Finnish Political Science Association.
Velasco, Juan Alvarado (1972) *Velasco: La voz de la revolución: Discursos del Presidente de la República General de División Juan Velasco Alvarado, 1970–1972*, volume 2. Lima: SINAMOS.
Wachtel, Nathan (1994) *Gods and Vampires: Return to Chipaya*. Chicago: University of Chicago Press.
Warren, Kay B. (1993a) "Introduction: Revealing Conflicts Across Cultures and Disciplines." In Kay Warren (ed.), *The Violence Within: Cultural and Political Opposition in Divided Nations*. Boulder: Westview Press, pp. 1–24.
—— (1993b) "Interpreting *La Violencia* in Guatemala: Shapes of Mayan Silence and Resistance." In Kay Warren (ed.), *The Violence Within: Cultural and Political Opposition in Divided Nations*. Boulder: Westview Press, pp. 25–56.
Young, Crawford (1993) "The Dialectics of Cultural Pluralism: Concept and Reality." In Crawford Young (ed.) *The Rising Tide of Cultural Pluralism: The Nation-State at Bay*. Madison: University of Wisconsin Press, pp. 3–32.

7 "Religious" violence in India

Ayodhya and the Hindu right

Johanna M. Lessinger

Introduction

This chapter is an examination of the wave of rightist political violence currently sweeping India. It is an attempt both to describe the shape of that violence and to place it in context, identifying the groups, the political forces and the ideological struggles surrounding the ever more frequent instances of individual and mob violence which have characterized Indian politics since 1992. I go on to suggest how this violence is not simply a temporary aberration but is central to the way the Hindu right in India shapes a new identity, widens its appeal and challenges control by the traditional organs of the state.

The account begins with the "incident" – rightist Hindus' destruction of a large Muslim mosque in the North Indian town of Ayodhya, followed by widespread anti-Muslim riots across North India. These events initiated the current pattern of Hindu sectarian violence, sometimes called "communal conflict" in India, and dubbed ethno-religious mobilization by scholars such as Jaffrelot (1996: 522). My own argument is that the present situation is less about religion than about class conflict under the strains of globalization. The movement employs a discourse of religion and faith as a way to forge political unity among groups otherwise divided by class, caste and regional differences, but the ultimate aim is political power for certain class groupings.

In the wake of the 1992 Ayodhya incident, the Hindu rightist coalition responsible for the first attacks has come to dominate India's central government as well as several state governments. Despite its current grip on power, the coalition has continued to threaten Muslims, but has also turned its terror tactics against Indian Christians (who are often low caste) and against middle-class secular intellectuals. This suggests that a constant level of low-intensity violence is not only essential to the rightist agenda but is also becoming a routine part of Indian politics.

The Hindutva (or "Hindu-ness") movement arose as a reaction to the complex impact of globalization on a highly stratified and unevenly developed society. In an effort to bolster their social and cultural position in the face of social change, some caste/class fractions have refurbished and extended older right-wing Hindu nationalist and Hindu revivalist organizations. Today the movement seeks to create a new sense of national unity by uniting "all Hindus" against internal "enemies." To accomplish this, harassment, assassination, and orchestrated mob violence have become a systematic part of the current movement's neo-fascist political program, as well as a potent threat to dissident individuals, to opposition groups, to organized minorities, and to progressive politics. Unable to guarantee public order or equal protection, India's democratic state is being steadily discredited.

The Hindu right has chosen the targets of its violence – whether communities, individuals, structures or events – for their symbolic value (van der Veer 1994a; Varshney 1993: 11). On the one hand the intent is to intimidate, destabilize and drive out those – at present Indian Muslims, Christians and intellectuals – constructed as alien Others. Beatings, bombings, murders and rapes are clearly designed to be exemplary, to offer a warning to others who might resist Hindutva policies. On the other hand, the attacks are also intended to rally and inspire participants around a triumphalist Hinduism, and to convince the uncommitted that this social movement is both righteous and unstoppable. Simultaneously, the pattern of well-publicized previous attacks lends an air of menace to any rally, speech or pronouncement on the part of Hindu rightist leaders, creating fear and chaos around even the most minor event. The threat of mobs and civil disorder has recently often frightened organs of the state into paralysis or acquiescence. Today the rightist ruling party, citing the need to avoid a total breakdown in public order, often bows to the will of its fringe groups, letting them rampage unchecked.

Clearly, then, religious violence is not an age-old attribute of Indian society, despite a virtual consensus in the West that "religious conflict" in the Third World is self-explanatory and inevitable. Comaroff has derided this kind of "primordialist" approach (1996) as have Brass (1991) and Rudolph and Rudolph (1993). The fact that Indian Muslims and Hindus have coexisted peacefully, even fruitfully, for long periods of time, despite periodic outbreaks of tension, belies this essentialist view. Furthermore, as Chatterjee (1999), Hansen (1999), van der Veer (1994b), Omvedt (1993) and Fox (1990) note in varying contexts, this conflict is a product of modernity and modernization, not an atavistic remnant of the past.

It is necessary, however, to avoid an idealist trap into which some Western scholars have fallen headlong. In delineating the cultural construction of the current Hindu religious revival, some have become lost amidst the (admittedly fascinating) manipulation of religious symbolism involved in Hindu revivalists' invention of a pan-Hindu identity (see, for instance, van der Veer 1994a, 1996), downplaying the political component. Other scholars, in an excess of cultural relativism, accept at face value the Hindu right's self-definition as a benign, even apolitical, movement of nationalist religious revitalization (see, for example, Fox 1990; Spitz 1993). To treat the Hindutva movement primarily as a religious and cultural revitalization movement tends towards de facto acceptance of its terms of debate. Although as Paul Brass notes, riots are complex events with "a multiplicity of interpretations" and causes (1996: 3), ultimately "The struggle among competing groups ... to capture the meaning of a violent incident or riot ... is also a struggle over resources and policy" (Brass 1996: 5). We must, Brass suggests, examine the *uses* of violence (1996: 46). Danish scholar Thomas Blom Hansen (1999) and Indian scholar Achin Vanaik (1997) more successfully represent the complex interplay between religion, culture, class and global economics which are evident in the contemporary Hindutva movement. Many Indian intellectuals, obliged to live under the Hindutva phenomenon, have treated it in explicitly political terms as a neo-fascist movement articulating emergent class interests of various sectors of Indian society – primarily agrarian elites and urban lower-middle classes. These scholars are assuming the responsibilities of public intellectuals to take a stand, to name atrocity and political repression. As Brass says, "the selection of a form and level of explanation for riots and pogroms, a context in which to place the discourses of violence – for scholars as well as journalists and politicians – is a serious political act" (1996: 6).

The critical factor in understanding the new scope and power of Hindutva is the linkage between the movement's rise to national prominence, the diminished role of India within a global system of capitalism, and the resulting acceleration of rapid social change, social dislocation and class/caste tensions. As political scientist H.D. Forbes (1997: 142–147) notes, globalization both homogenizes cultural differences and, by bringing different groups into contact with each other, heightens the impetus to preserve and defend difference.

The global dislocations which have catapulted the Hindutva movement to power may also weaken it internally. Now that the Hindutva movement – rooted in the petty bourgeoisie, not in India's capitalist classes – has assumed control of a national economy, the Hindu right faces its greatest contradictions in trying to manage India's relationship to global capital. Ideologically opposed to the kind of modernity that Western-oriented capitalist development has brought, the Hindu right must, if it is to retain national political power, also represent, or at least avoid alienating, the bureaucratic and entrepreneurial classes most committed to that modernity (see also Hansen 1999: 224–225). In so doing, the Hindutva movement risks widening the ideological cracks already present within its own ranks, between "moderate" and "militant" wings (Jaffrelot 1996: 523–526), between ideologues and pragmatists (Muralidharan 2000; Ramakrishnan 2000b).

The first act – a farce followed by tragedy

The Ayodhya mosque destroyed

On 6 December 1992, some 300,000 right-wing Hindus, who had been gathering in the northern Indian town of Ayodhya for weeks, tore apart a massive sixteenth-century Mogul mosque. The Babri Masjid (Babur's mosque) was erected in 1528 by the Muslim ruler Babur to memorialize the consolidation of Mogul rule over North India. The mob used hands and crowbars to demolish the massive structure, reducing it to mounds of shattered brick and plaster within hours.

Startling as the action was, it was hardly unexpected. Planning in Ayodhya, widely reported, had been in high gear for months before the actual attack, while agitation to replace the mosque with a temple to Lord Rama had been underway for a decade or more (Oberoi 1995: 97). Despite advance publicity, police and army units assigned to the area melted away as the mob, whose members dubbed themselves *kar sevaks* (voluntary religious workers) swarmed towards the site. Military commanders later said they had no orders to intervene to prevent the rampage. As a result, mob organizers and their shock troops, many decked out in the saffron-colored clothing which denotes Hindu fervor and renunciation, were allowed to come and go unhindered.

The organizers of this enormous enterprise were a group of linked, conservative Hindu organizations, known variously as Hindu nationalists, Hindu revivalists, the *Sang Parivar* (organizational family) or the Hindutva combine. All these groups share an ideological dedication to the concept of Hindutva, or "Hindu-ness," a vision of India as a nation constituted around Hindu religious identity and a sense that Hinduism is embattled, in need of zealous defense against predatory alien cultures and religions. The emotional appeal of this religious nationalist discourse is partially traditional, much of it newly invented (see Kapur 1992: 46–47). The attack on the Ayodhya mosque, Hindutva organizers insist, was to "liberate" and "purify" a site usurped centuries ago by Muslim outsiders alleged to have destroyed an earlier Hindu temple on the spot. This earlier temple, Hindutva activists believe, marked the historic birthplace of the Hindu hero-god, Ram. A flurry of spurious historical, archeological and epigraphic "research" has been deployed to justify these claims of an underlying earlier temple, which are derided by serious historians and archeologists (see Mandal 1993; Thapar 1991). Scholars such as Dani insist this kind of pseudoscientific discourse is part of the Hindutva movement's larger, anti-rationalist agenda (1993: 90–92).

Within a week, organizers had installed a makeshift temple to Lord Ram atop the Ayodhya rubble, smuggled in sympathetic priests and organized a steady stream of Hindu pilgrims whose simple piety served to validate the new shrine. Meanwhile conservative Hindus all over India gloated and celebrated this striking Hindu "victory" over Islam. Government inaction was interpreted (correctly) as tacit acquiescence to a vastly effective *coup de théâtre*. As dramatic news photos of the destruction, of the new shrine and of exultant Hindutva leaders flashed around the world, the central government appeared impotent. Hindutva forces claimed total victory – both over Muslim "usurpers" and over the Congress Party which controlled the central government at the time.

The destruction of a Muslim religious site and its subsequent reconstitution as Hindu sacred space outraged Muslims not only in India but around the world, as intended. The attack also horrified large numbers of Indian Hindus. The devout were disturbed at the destruction of any shrine, even an Islamic one. The politically-minded condemned this resurgence of communalism, as religious conflict is known in India. Those committed to a democratic and secular India understood the event as a bold bid for national, rather than purely local, power on the part of a dangerous right-wing alliance.

The Bombay riots to follow

The mosque demolition moved from symbolic action to real pogroms against Muslim individuals and communities within a day. By 7 December 1992, well-organized mobs in North Indian cities began to hunt down Muslims, particularly those living in identifiable enclaves in poor or lower-middle-class areas. Starting in the town of Ayodhya itself, these terror campaigns had become extensive by January 1993, closely orchestrated and moving from town to town in a pattern which has become typical of Hindutva violence. Brass has called such patterns "institutionalized riot systems" carried out by specialists (1996: 12).

The violence was especially severe in Bombay. This metropolis is India's most modern, industrial city, heart of its most heavily industrialized region, the center of finance capital and advertising, location of the country's central stock exchange and headquarters of India's enormous movie industry. Although in other moods Bombay boasts of its cosmopolitan welcome to immigrants of all castes and religions, the city is also the stronghold of two of the most vociferous and violence-prone Hindutva groups, the Shiv Sena and the Rashtriya Swayamsevak Sangh (RSS). Both have strong followings in the city's petty bourgeoisie and in the urban working class – and consequently among city and state employees and officials. The Shiv Sena, with a thirty-year history of rabid rhetoric and violent action, also has ties to the criminal gangs for which Bombay is notorious.

For much of January, Bombay was paralyzed as mobs recruited from among the poor and from Bombay's criminal underworld surrounded, burned down and looted Muslim working-class and petty bourgeois residential areas, stores and workshops. Rumors – about imminent attacks by armed Muslims stockpiling arms in mosques, about murdered Hindus – were deliberately spread to frighten and inflame Hindus who had lived peacefully beside Muslims for years. Using what appear to have been tax or voter rolls supplied by city officials, mobs were able to pinpoint Muslims living or working in mixed areas (Gargan 1993: 1). People of all ages were hacked apart, beaten to death, blinded or set alight. Women and girls were singled out for rape and subsequent murder. Property owners arranged to have inconvenient squatter housing areas cleared through arson, while merchants had the premises of Muslim rivals burned (Sen 1993: 28). The anti-Muslim frenzy reached into affluent areas as mobs went to apartment blocks, checked name plates and attacked Muslim professionals.

Thousands died, thousands more lost their livelihoods, and an estimated 100,000 poor Muslim labor migrants fled Bombay on special trains commandeered by the railway (Gargan 1993: 1), the only state organization still functioning. Other public transport did not run, food supplies ceased coming into the city, industries shut down since their workers were either in hiding or rampaging through the streets. A delegation of major industrialists and film stars traveled to New Delhi to beg Congress Party leader and Prime Minister P.V. Narsimha Rao to send in the army to halt the destruction of their city. Rao expressed personal anguish but did nothing.

As in the original episode at Ayodhya, sluggish official response in Bombay discredited the state. It also suggests how deeply Hindutva ideology and loyalties had penetrated local bureaucratic structures and the ranks of state functionaries. The Bombay police acted slowly, if at all, as neighborhood after neighborhood went up in flames. Many of the police, loyal to the Shiv Sena or RSS, actually took part in the attacks (see Gargan 1993: 1), passing on inflammatory rumors, directing mobs to their targets, or preventing fire fighters or citizen rescue parties from reaching besieged Muslim residents. Both the state government, controlled by the right-wing BJP (Bharatiya Janata Party, part of the Hindutva coalition), and the supposedly more liberal Congress-controlled city government, initially did little to rein in the mobs or exert control over the police. The central government and the national Congress Party issued statements of shock and dismay but declined to act. Eventually, after more than a month of chaos and mounting international concern, the violence burned itself out as the central government applied pressure on local officials. The Bombay police hierarchy was reorganized (but never purged of Shiv Sena or RSS loyalists), and citizen fact-finding groups began to publicize the true magnitude of the disaster.

Other north Indian cities such as Surat and Ahmedabad also suffered rioting, arson and murder at the time. Nevertheless, there were also cities and states which remained notably calm. These exceptions highlight the social organization of the violence, and suggest ways in which determined state action could have prevented it elsewhere. Meerut, Banaras and Bhiwandi, with past histories of Hindu–Muslim conflict and sizable Muslim populations, survived unscathed because local administrators and police officials anticipated trouble and decided to prevent it. Using a whole arsenal of legal repression, a judicious mix of arbitrary arrest, curfews and coercive rumor control, combined with heavy pressure on Hindu and Muslim religious leaders to act as peacekeepers, officials prevented outbreaks. Chaturvedi and Chaturvedi (1996) describe in detail how large-scale trouble was averted in Agra, despite a high level of Hindutva provocation. Likewise, in Bihar, the state government also prevented riots. Bihar is dominated by "backward castes" (that is, castes which are low in status, and impoverished, but not "Untouchable"). The state's ruling party understood that the Hindutva political program was hostile to backward caste interests, and it declined to join the anti-Muslim movement.

Elsewhere, violence was averted by explicit anti-Hindutva organizing. In the capital of Delhi, progressives worked with neighborhood groups to forestall trouble. Door-to-door organizing in affluent South Delhi averted a planned BJP march through the neighborhood intended to culminate in attacks on Bangladeshi labor migrants. (Impoverished immigrant workers have been a perpetual Shiv Sena and Hindutva target, both as Muslims and as "illegal alien" migrants – see Weiner 1978.) Elite South Delhi disliked the prospect of bloodshed and arson on its doorstep; progressive activists mobilized this sentiment into a public outcry which frightened off Hindutva agitators.

These instances highlight the fact that communal violence is neither inevitable nor a "natural" feature of the Indian political landscape, but is a product of inaction on the part of the Indian state and passivity on the part of citizens – passivity the Hindu right tries to promote through its carefully orchestrated violent outbursts. However, the Congress Party emerged from these episodes fatally weakened and discredited. As economist Amartya Sen (1993: 29) remarked, the response from Congress was largely negative. It offered no moral or ideological leadership, undertook no education campaigns on behalf of secularism. Not surprisingly, it soon suffered a drastic loss of electoral support as some voters turned to the victorious BJP and others, disgusted at Congress, turned to small parties.

The aftermath of Ayodhya

In the wake of Ayodhya and the Bombay riots, the BJP governments in four states were temporarily suspended, five Hindutva organizations were temporarily banned, and a special court of inquiry was called to consider charges filed by the Central Bureau of Investigation. However, little in the way of concrete legal action has since emerged (Ramakrishnan 2000a: 8). Since the BJP now rules at the center it has been largely able to protect Hindutva activists from legal or political reprisals.

For several years after the events of 1992–93, reports, studies, protests, films, art shows and discussion poured forth, as India digested what had happened to it and analyzed how this new political phenomenon had been constructed. Intellectuals and artists, immune to religious arguments and outraged by the strong anti-intellectual, anti-rationalist, undemocratic tendencies in the Hindutva movement, flung themselves into the fray, writing, speaking, organizing plays, concerts and art shows in protest, in an effort to counteract the cultural hegemony the right was beginning to establish. In some cases Hindutva forces have retaliated by sending goon squads to shout down and threaten speakers, to tear up art exhibits, to prevent the screening of films, to beat up journalists and trash newspaper offices (Swami 1993: 18–21).

The extent to which Hindu nationalists were able to define the terms of debate was visible in the letter pages of India's "responsible" English-language dailies as well as in Indian immigrant newspapers in the USA. For every correspondent who decried the events in Ayodhya and Bombay, two more focused obsessively on religio-historical issues, arguing seriously over the extent to which Muslims have "wounded" Hindu religious sentiments, asking whether Muslims have gained undue privilege in India recently, wondering whether Muslims are loyal Indians or not.

An interesting aspect of this debate over the meaning of Ayodhya is the speed with which Hindutva thinking and organizing has penetrated India's transnational communities in Britain, Canada and the USA. Historian Romila Thapar reports that Indian immigrants in Britain spoke proudly of raising hundreds of thousands of pounds there for the BJP shortly after the Babri Masjid had been reduced to dust (Thapar 1993). From 1993 onwards, the BJP has sent high-ranking emissaries (a Muslim among them) to address national Indian immigrant organizations in the USA. They get a cordial reception, despite protests from more progressive Indian immigrants and student groups. The letter pages of Indian immigrant newspapers here in the USA reflect the same astonishingly solemn debate about the historic wrongs Muslims have done Hindus which rage in India. Clearly this first generation of Indian immigrants, uneasy amidst an alien culture, responds to the Hindutva messages emerging from the motherland about spiritual-religious revival, renewal of Hindu identity and national pride (Kurien 2001; Rajagopal 1993, 2000a, b). The VHP (Vishwa Hindu Parishad, a prominent Hindutva grouping) has been particularly energetic in promoting the Hindutva message outside India.

Not surprisingly, the anti-communism of Hindutva groups in India resonates particularly strongly among prosperous Indian professionals and entrepreneurs now living in the USA, who have embraced American anti-communism to supplement that inherent in Hindutva teachings. A 1993 Columbia University event, where a panel of academics offered a restrained critique of the Ayodhya incident, was disrupted by shouting and death threats from RSS cadre. A BJP speaker turned to the startled American audience and exclaimed in self-justification, "You don't *understand*! These people [the academic panelists] are all communist agitators!"

Today, directly as a result of popularity engendered by the destruction of the mosque, the BJP, parliamentary arm of the Hindutva combine, has won numerous state elections, gaining about a quarter of the popular vote nationally and the single largest block of parliamentary seats. In 1996 and again, more securely, in 1998, the BJP formed a national government leading a multiparty coalition known as the National Democratic Alliance (NDA). At present the BJP is in the midst of trying to implement many of its objectives, both symbolic and practical.

For all its public optimism, however, the BJP and the Hindutva movement face a dilemma: they cannot claim true national legitimacy without broadening public support. At present, Hindutva views are not those of India's majority. Broader support is unlikely to be forthcoming as long as Untouchables (known also as Dalits), backward castes, tribal people (also known as Adivasis) and Indian Muslims and Christians fear and distrust the BJP and its affiliates. At present, the Hindutva reaction is to extend its tactics of religion-based intimidation, hoping to scare or mobilize further middle and high castes (plus whatever Dalit or Adivasi groups can be persuaded to join) into the Hindutva fold.

When taking power in 1998, the BJP pledged itself to political "responsibility" in an effort to gain parliamentary allies. However, the Hindutva movement has not changed its central tactics. By late 1999, continuing local provocations against Muslims (see Swami 2001), had been extended into more than a hundred orchestrated attacks against Indian Christians (Menon 2000;

Panikkar 1999; Swami 1999). None have been as large-scale and dramatic as the Ayodhya–Bombay events, but priests, nuns and lay prayer-leaders have been beaten, raped and killed, sacred sites have been burned and desecrated, and a coordinated bombing campaign has demolished churches and prayer halls. In some cases these attacks may have been the work of hired assailants, sent from town to town to place bombs. In others, however, local people (often low caste) have been worked up and inflamed until they have attacked Christian neighbors (also frequently low caste). Typically, under BJP leadership, few attackers have been caught or punished. Like low-intensity conflict everywhere, these attacks keep religion, violence and disruption in the forefront of national politics without provoking widespread retaliation or political backlash.

Religion as the fault line

In the contemporary fracturing of nation states, "ethnic groups" are the most common participants in the increasingly common form of contemporary nationalist violence known as "ethnic conflict." Yet as political scientist James Kellas notes in writing about nationalism and ethnicity, "theories ... do not accurately predict the *form* which that nationalism will take" (1991: 117; emphasis added). As the Indian case shows, religion, harnessed to class and nationalist aspirations, proves fully as effective as ethnicity in mass mobilizations around new senses of identity. It also functions to justify civic disorder on moral grounds, since mob violence can be portrayed as a simple excess of religious sentiment – a form of emotion deeply respected in India.

Localized regional or linguistic identities have periodically become the basis of violent separatist agitation in India. The current civil war in the state of Kashmir is one such dispute. Nativist movements, in areas such as Bombay, have opposed in-migration (see Weiner 1978). Gupta (1995: 78), however, argues that one of the most enduring bases of division in India is culture.

In this respect religions, envisioned in India as separate communities with discrete cultural identities, are probably one of the most effective bases of mobilization precisely because religious "communities" are *not* localized. Muslim and Christian minorities are found scattered all over the country, and can thus be constructed as an ubiquitous internal enemy threatening the (Hindu) nation. Yet Muslims and Christians can simultaneously be symbols of a perceived external threat, since both Islam and Christianity link their believers to transnational influences from other societies. Furthermore, the nationalist component is already built in: Hinduism is uniquely identified with India as a nation, while Pakistan defines itself as Muslim and the West is seen as Christian. It is thus not only possible but relatively easy to turn religion into the fault line along which group and national identities can be reified, class conflicts mobilized, nationalist aspirations molded and existing state structures undermined.

As events in India show, religion, perhaps even more strongly than ethnicity, provides wellsprings of strong collective emotion and pent-up energy waiting to be tapped. Because it pervades every aspect of daily life in India, religion offers endless potential arenas for conflict. Not only ritual practices, sacred sites and national history, but language, education, dress, law, sports, music, films, uses of public space, gender and kinship relations are potentially contested domains. Furthermore, religious mobilization structures opposition to progressives and leftists, who can be condemned for their rationalist, secularist and internationalist outlooks, thus negating their anti-capitalist modernizing critique. (In practice the BJP has been eager to accommodate capitalism, despite Hindutva's anti-modernist stance.)

The protagonists in the conflict

A discredited Congress Party

Central to the current conflict is the Indian state, which was controlled by the Congress Party almost continuously from 1947 to 1996, when the BJP made its first successful foray into forming a national government.

The Indian state and the Congress Party had been closely intertwined since the colonial period when Congress put together the cross-class, multi-caste and multi-religious coalition which eventually forced an end to British domination. After Independence in 1947, the Congress Party committed itself to policies which it often called "secularism." In practice, these amounted simply to a toleration of religious pluralism and a commitment to the protection of religious minorities – a path followed by many other modernizing capitalist states. Today the Congress pluralist coalition is in tatters. Presently the parliamentary opposition party, Congress is exhausted, factionalized, corrupt, unwieldy and ineffectual. Without moral authority or a clear social agenda, it failed while in power to bring effective economic development or distributive justice to a country of vast cultural, linguistic and religious diversity and deep class/caste stratification. As the Hindutva movement grew, Congress failed to protect Muslim or Christian minorities, and lost much of their support. Consequently, in the 1970s and 1980s regional opposition parties joining highly unstable coalitions won power in many states within India's federal structure. When the Congress Party fell in 1996, many of these regional parties put aside ideological distaste for Hindutva and made haste to ally with the newly-popular BJP, propping it up when it was unable to command a parliamentary majority on its own. In some cases, small-party alliances with the BJP have allowed the reinsertion into local politics of a Brahminical vision of the social order. That vision had been delegitimized in recent years with the rise of low-caste militancy (Krishnakumar 1993).

Indian Muslims

After the collapse of the Mogul empire, British colonial domination weakened the Muslim aristocracy, strengthened the Hindu bourgeoisie and created the bases for communal mobilization in both religious communities. British imperialism used, and often fostered, Hindu–Muslim competition and tension to undermine potential class alliances (see, for example, Chakrabarty 1989). From this early twentieth-century communal competition emerged both contemporary Hindu nationalist organizations and their Muslim counterparts, such as the Muslim League (Vanaik 1990: 143). Out of this competition also arose a pattern of Hindu–Muslim communal violence, periodic outbreaks of localized rioting – often over issues of worship – which have persisted into the present.

Indian independence in 1947 was marked by bitter Hindu–Muslim clashes in which anywhere from 250,000 to 1 million people died. At the partition of colonial India into two new nations, India and Pakistan, some two-thirds of the 100 million Muslims living in undivided India opted for Pakistani citizenship (Varshney 1993: 24). Many did so unwillingly, driven out of ancestral areas by Hindu mobs. Yet many Muslims remained in India – today they number about 140 million or about 12 per cent of the Indian population, and constitute India's largest religious minority. Indian Muslims tend to be urban, poor or petty bourgeois, and tradition-minded, since much of the educated Muslim elite relocated to Pakistan. Distinguishable by dress, customs and religious practice, Indian Muslims remain an obvious and vulnerable target for social hostility. One of the recent trends which has exacerbated anti-Muslim hostility in India is the growth of a global "Islamic fundamentalism." Its impact has made many Indian Muslims more assertive and more visible.

It is important to note that Muslims in India do not control any strategic resources or any particular professions which might make them objects of Hindu envy and hatred. At most, some urban Muslim shopkeepers, artisans and small entrepreneurs may compete with Hindus at the same level, but Muslims hold no economic monopoly anywhere. In the past twenty years a small class of educated Muslim professionals has emerged, whose modern, secular outlook also antagonizes the Hindu right. As Engineer notes, the increase in dramatic anti-Muslim violence has served to isolate this group, which finds itself caught between a hostile, Hindutva-dominated society and reactionary Muslim clerics (Engineer 1991, 1992).

The Hindutva "family"

The BJP is part of a grouping of four major conservative, Hindu revivalist organizations and parties, united by shared history, common ideology and hostility to the Congress Party. The Bharatiya Janata Party (BJP), the Rashtriya Swayamsevak Sangh (RSS), the Vishwa Hindu Parishad (VHP) and the Shiv Sena party, with multiple affiliated small groups such as the Bajrang Dal, are known collectively to their opponents as the "Hindutva combine." All share a commitment to Hinduism as a central identity.

Critics lump all the Hindutva groups together as "a combine" because, despite different regional bases and organizational structures, and slightly different ideological emphases, the groups presently function as a single political entity. They are articulated through overlapping leaderships and shared funding, as well as a common political agenda. For instance the small Bajrang Dal, active in recent anti-Christian agitations, is said to be an affiliate of the RSS, but has cooperated extensively with the VHP as well and probably receives its funding from the two larger groups. There is a rough division of labor within the movement. While the BJP contests elections, the RSS specializes in organization and ideology, the VHP is a major ideological center promoting Hinduism, and the Shiv Sena emphasizes inflammatory rhetoric, provocations and the production of mobs.

The Hindutva groups' insistence on their distinctiveness and autonomy from each other is a strategy particularly useful for creating "deniability" when murder and mayhem break out. Thus the parliamentary BJP has been able to protest its innocence in any number of recent attacks on Christians – always the work of elusive, untraceable "other" groups. However Jaffrelot (1996) is one of several observers who question how long the movement can maintain its unity as the BJP struggles to maintain national and international political legitimacy in the face of extremist statements and actions from other members of the Sangh Parivar (family). For instance, by the summer of 2001, the Shiv Sena was accusing its BJP allies of corruption, and threatening to withdraw from the coalition.

Historically and ideologically, the RSS is at the core of the Hindutva grouping. Founded in 1925 to train nationalist cadres for the independence struggle (Anderson and Damle 1987), the RSS has developed great organizational and ideological sophistication over the years spent training thousands of young men of "the brotherhood." A hierarchical leadership teaches paramilitary techniques, an ascetic life style, religious purity and leadership skills. The core of RSS ideology is summarized by B.D. Graham:

> a great battle for the cultural heart of the nation, a battle in which those who believed in the corporate integrity of the Hindu community would be aligned against the forces of Islam on one side and the forces of communism on the other.
>
> (1990: 48)

Although the RSS has historically eschewed direct involvement in politics, it has often encouraged members to join other organizations; it also encourages sympathetic organizations to affiliate with it as part of the RSS "family" (Anderson and Damle 1987; Graham 1990). Hansen suggests that the RSS is now having difficulty controlling and mediating between the ideological and the pragmatically political wings of the movement it leads (1999: 225, 228–229).

For years, there has been debate about whether the RSS is fascist or simply deeply reactionary (Anderson and Damle 1987: 78–83; Chatterjee 1999: 228–230; Graham 1990: 11; Vanaik 1997: 18–22, 266–277). Certainly the historical circumstances of RSS's origin are reminiscent of German National Socialism, as is the group's preoccupation with paramilitary training, marching, uniforms, group singing of religious songs, and the creation of pure (Hindu) souls in fit (male) bodies. Indeed in the 1930s the RSS flirted with the Nazis as part of its anti-British campaign (Anderson and Damle 1987: 31). In 1938, RSS leader M.S. Golwalkar praised Hitler's annihilation of German Jews (quoted in Basu *et al.* 1993: 26–27). As Amartya Sen notes (1993: 28), the contemporary willingness of the RSS and its affiliates to use extralegal violence and genocide as habitual modes of political action reopens the question, as does the fact that the organization, intertwined with the BJP, is now increasingly intertwined with the state as well.

RSS ideology and practice also contain several contradictions. One of these is the question of whether the organization and its allies, in promoting a pan-Indian Hindu identity, simultaneously uphold Hinduism's built-in caste hierarchy and resulting social inequality, or whether the concept of an over-arching Hindu-ness makes caste differences irrelevant. Certainly RSS recruitment policies and internal relations have been caste-free at the rank-and-file level. Yet while the membership tends to be made up of a heterogeneous collection of lower-middle- and middle-class urban youth, the leadership has continued to be educated, high caste, often Brahmin. More importantly, leaders articulate a highly Brahminical form of Hinduism (Anderson and Damle 1987; Basu *et al.* 1993; Graham 1990; Jaffrelot 1996) which projects divinely ordered social and gender hierarchies. Both leadership and membership remain overwhelmingly male, despite the recent formation of a women's wing and recruitment of female leaders whose emotional appeal has been useful in stirring up crowds (see Sarkar 1991).

There is little evidence that the RSS's essentially opportunistic moves toward inclusion of women and low-caste people imply a permanently egalitarian outlook. The movement sidesteps the specifics of social inequality, except to imply that in a better, more moral (Hindu) world, caste would remain a source of identity, minus the suffering of exclusion. However, Muslims and Christians (all envisioned as low-caste converts from Hinduism) have no place in this ideal social order, unless they renounce their foreign ways, return to the Hindu fold and accept their proper (subordinate) positions. Hansen is one of several observers to note that the inability of the RSS and the Hindutva movement generally to incorporate low-caste people must eventually limit its political expansion (1999: 224). However Hindutva's current political answer to this contradiction is to expand violence-based mobilizations in an effort to draw more high- and middle-caste Hindus into the movement and to frighten low-caste people into silence.

The BJP, the only group within the Hindutva movement organized as a conventional political party, was founded in 1951 by RSS members, taking its present name in 1980 (Graham 1990). Acting as an RSS surrogate in electoral politics, the BJP continues to rely for organizational and ideological leadership on its centralized, highly-disciplined parent organization. The BJP first challenged the Congress Party after 1991 mid-term elections gave it control of four state governments, and major strength in two others. Varshney estimates that in

1991 the BJP won 20.2 per cent of the popular vote (1993: 14). Those early electoral successes paralleled Hindu–Muslim riots and attacks on progressive activists across North India (see Basu *et al.* 1993) which provided the BJP with the publicity, the popular appeal and the image of invincibility it needed to win still further elections.

The VHP sprang from the ranks of the RSS "family" in 1964, specifically to help overcome sectarian divisions within Hinduism and to encourage the "reconversion" of Indian Muslims and Christians (Anderson and Damle 1987: 133–134). As an organization it can generate a religious fervor which is more accessible than the rarefied self-discipline advocated by the RSS. The VHP has now added a youth wing to tap the frustrations of young, unemployed urban men who enjoy marching about, armed with spears (religious symbols but potential weapons), draped in saffron scarves, shouting slogans.

Much of the anti-Western ideology circulating within Hindutva circles seems to emanate from the VHP, preoccupied as it is with the sinister role of Christian and Islamic missionaries and the corrupting influences of Western culture. On the educational–intellectual front, the VHP promotes the revival of Sanskrit as a living language, and the adoption of *The Code of Manu* and the *Arthashastra* as central, guiding texts. Both are religio-legal works promoting a rigid, caste- and gender-stratified vision of the social order (Basu *et al.* 1993: 66).

The VHP, with a sophisticated use of the Internet, web sites, and video and tape cassettes, has had considerable influence in promoting Hindu orthodoxy among Indians of the diaspora (see Kumar 1993a; Rajagopal 1993, 2000a, b). According to Anderson and Damle (1987: 137), the VHP claimed forty branches in England alone. After the Ayodhya incident, its influence in Britain widened, according to Romila Thapar (1993). Today the VHP is active among Indo-Caribbeans in the USA as well as among immigrants born in India. It runs summer camps and retreats for the young, supplies inspirational literature to groups, and helps aspiring priests get scriptural training in India.

The fourth leg of the Hindutva combine is the Shiv Sena, a militant nativist party founded in Maharashtra in 1966. The group was specifically founded to agitate against South Indian labor immigration to Bombay. The group has a history of instigating bloody riots directed against non-Maharashtrian "foreigners," Muslims, low castes and trade unionists (Gupta 1982; Sen 1993; Weiner 1978). By linking itself to the Hindutva campaign in 1984, the Shiv Sena made a bid for national, as opposed to local, prominence (Omvedt 1993: 185). In 1991 the Shiv Sena held roughly one-third of the seats in the Bombay municipal corporation and four seats in the national legislature. Like the RSS, the Shiv Sena attracts a mix of poor and middle- or lower-middle-class men. Unlike the ascetic and puritanical RSS, the group also has close links with Bombay's notorious criminal underworld. Shiv Sena organization is hierarchical and paramilitary; in 1993 leader Bal Thackery told the press he admired Hitler's final solution and suggested similar action to rid India of Muslims (quoted in Sen 1993: 28).

Modernity and its discontents

Who is "the Other" and why?

If the current Hindutva mobilization, violent as it is, is a product of modernity, where does the Hindutva discourse of a victimized and endangered Hinduism come from? After all, India is officially pluralist, 85 per cent of the population is Hindu, and Hinduism permeates daily life. What has become of India's previous tolerance? And if the current "religious violence" is indeed a product of modernity, what aspects of contemporary life have created it?

Today India is increasing engaged with, and absorbed into, a global capitalist order after the failure of a decades-long attempt at a separate, non-capitalist form of development. As a result, India now plays a diminished and marginalized international role, with little political, economic or moral influence outside its own borders (Amin 1990). A steady stream of urban, highly-educated migrants leaves India each year for the West, looking for a higher standard of living and greater professional satisfaction (Lessinger 1992). At the same time, the society has experienced internal restructuring, as globalization realigns both economy and culture and strains caste/class relationships. These trends form the context for the growth of Hindutva ideology and organizing since the 1980s.

Under particular stress are the newly marginalized middle- and lower-middle-classes. Their traditional caste status is relatively high, but these people today feel increasingly anxious and threatened by globalization's structural, economic and cultural changes, by the inroads of Western-style consumption, and by a new assertiveness on the part of women and India's low-caste and tribal people. Traditional high-caste status alone no longer confers wealth or influence in a world dominated by transnational corporations, modern media and a technocratic elite. The anxiety – and the adherence to the Hindutva movement – is greatest in North India, a region which contains both some of India's most "modern" and heavily industrialized areas and some of its poorest and most socially backward districts.

As in so many other parts of the world, the Indian response to these stresses has been an invocation of tradition (some of it newly minted), a reclaiming of particular aspects of the (quasi-mythical) past. The appeal of Hindutva is in ideology and in organizations which hold the promise of moral regeneration, a sense of ready-made community, and the mechanisms to create spectacular, media-capturing, and cathartic violence. That violence, its practitioners believe, has the potential to unify a society fracturing along caste and class lines, restoring an ancient and harmonious social order in which high castes ruled, Muslims, low castes and women knew their place, intellectuals were still devout, and global influences were nil.

Demonic Muslims

Muslims have been the first and most enduring hate objects of the Hindu right because Islam and Hinduism, envisioned in India as communities of believers, have been pitted against each other at two critical historical junctures in the development of India as a nation: the establishment of the Mogul empire and the creation of an independent India. The histories of both periods are part of the current Hindutva construction of Muslims as demonic outsiders.

In the Mogul period, conquest engendered much Hindu–Muslim conflict as invading Muslims subjugated Hindu kingdoms and incorporated them into the Mogul state. These wars were often perceived by contemporaries as political, not purely religious. The period also produced a great deal of voluntary Hindu conversion to Islam. Yet Hindutva history erases the fact that Mogul India, for all its wars, also saw the flowering of syncretic aristocratic and popular cultures. Seventeenth-, eighteenth- and early nineteenth-century court culture supported art, architecture, philosophy, classical music and poetry – today thought of as prototypically Indian – which was produced by both Hindu and Muslim artists and reflected an aesthetic derived from both traditions. Today Hindutva can only accommodate the Taj Mahal by insisting that it is actually a Hindu monument. In contemporary urban Indian popular culture, Hindus visit the tombs of Muslim saints, Muslims pray in certain Hindu temples which have traditionally welcomed them, and each group attends the public festivals of the other.

From the more recent and well-remembered partition period comes the specific model for contemporary Hindu–Muslim communal violence. Psychologist Sudhir Kakar has written eloquently about this persistent wound in the Indian psyche (1996). There are still people living who remember the thousands of traumatized refugees streaming in each direction across the newly established border, as Hindus fled territory soon to belong to Pakistan, and equally terrified Muslims fled India. Each group had been driven to flight by mob violence, arson, riots, rape and murder, organized by rightists on both sides of the religious divide. The visual images of trains laden with dead or dying refugees, crossing the border after attacks by mobs of "the other" religious community, haunt the collective memories of both India and Pakistan. It is the horror and the violence of that period that the Hindutva movement seeks to invoke, both as a model for its own actions and as a justification for them.

The final source of Hindutva hatred towards Muslims has to do with the transnational character of modern Islam. Indian Muslims are today closely linked to a global Islamic movement, centered in the Middle East but manifest worldwide. Indian Muslim contact with the Middle East began under Mogul rule and has been continuous ever since. Today the transnational movements for Islamic religious renewal, plus Middle Eastern oil money, have intensified this contact. Books, cassettes and missionaries from the Middle East flow into India, emphasizing doctrinal purity and orthodoxy to counteract Indian Islam's long slippage towards Hindu patterns of worship, dress and behavior. More and more Indian Muslims are able to afford to make the Haj pilgrimage to Mecca. Many others travel as labor migrants to the Middle East. Today remittances from these migrants, plus direct donations from wealthy Middle Eastern states, fund the renovation of Indian mosques and the construction of new ones. Electronically amplified calls to prayer now ring out over neighborhoods once dominated by the sound of Hindu temple bells. Some returned Gulf migrants affect Middle Eastern-style dress and encourage their wives and daughters to veil themselves elaborately, even in poor neighborhoods where Muslim women were once content with a simple head covering. These new transnational ties, this trickle of new wealth and this new orthodoxy mean that Indian Muslims are more visible, more assertive and less assimilationist than they have been for generations. These trends become an inevitable focus for Hindutva ravings about "disloyalty" and creeping "foreign influence" permitting Indian Muslims to be construed as foreign wolves concealed within the Hindu fold.

Traitorous Christians, uppity Dalits

The historical basis for the current Hindutva demonization of Indian Christians lies also in the period of British colonialism. Western missionaries first became active in India in the nineteenth century, and left behind communities of converts, often of Dalit, low caste or Adivasi origin. For more than a century, certain Christian schools and colleges have offered both Christian and Hindu students a Western-style curriculum better than anything available in state schools or Hindu-run private schools, providing desperately poor, marginalized families some hope of mobility into the social mainstream. At the other end of the social spectrum, certain elite Christian schools and colleges turn out cadres of Hindu, Christian and Muslim graduates destined to join India's cosmopolitan ruling class (Panikkar 1999).

Today, in a cruel parody of Gandhi's anti-British "Quit India" movement, the Hindu right promotes a "Quit India" movement directed against Christian missionaries, and, covertly, against native believers. Like Indian Muslims, Indian Christians have been told they should leave India unless they agree to embrace Hinduism. The recent anti-Christian violence has paralleled a rhetorical campaign against missionaries said to be using foreign funding to carry out "forced conversions," seducing naive Adivasis or Dalits and decimating Hindu ranks. The solution, Hindutva groups insist, is missions to reconvert Christians.

It is easy to see that the current anti-Christian agitation stems not only from caste/class competition, but also from Hindutva's ideological hostility to the Westernization and modernization Indian Christians represent. Evangelical missionaries using American-style religious radio programs and bible tracts printed in the USA promote the Protestant ethic as a path to social mobility. Many Indian Catholic priests and nuns study abroad and return steeped in the activism of Latin American-style liberation theology. The most dangerous of Christianity's modernizing concepts is probably the rejection of caste. Many Indian Christians (like Muslim converts in earlier centuries) have sought to escape both the symbolic and material exclusion of caste by embracing Christianity's promised equality among believers (Panikkar 1999).

Some Dalit, tribal and low-caste groups have understood how threatening their attempts to scramble into the lower middle class are to those above them in the caste hierarchy, and see that the Hindutva emphasis on Hindu orthodoxy also implies a rejection of such meager progress. In many areas, however, the current campaign has turned local Dalits and Adivasis against local Christians by inciting envy of the benefits Christians are imagined to be getting from abroad, or from affirmative action policies (Swami 1999). Thus local people may approve, or even participate in, the attacks Hindutva operatives organize.

In June 2000, a young priest was beaten to death in the town of Mathura. In September 1998, nuns were raped in two separate incidents in Uttar Pradesh and in Madhya Pradesh states. Elsewhere, Hindu idols were forcibly installed in churches, effectively desecrating them. Prayer halls and churches were bombed or burned down (Swami 1999). After the BJP government announced plans to remove churches from the list of recognized places of worship, on the grounds that churches served wine (anathema to devout Hindus), Hindutva activists understood that the BJP government was tacitly sanctioning further attacks.

One instance of this anti-Christian campaign caught national attention in India, and caused the BJP government some international embarrassment. Amidst an upsurge of Hindutva rhetoric about forced conversions and the need to expel foreign missionaries, Australian missionary Graham Staines and his two small sons were burned to death as they slept in their van outside Manoharpur village in Orissa during the night of 23 January 1999. Staines had worked for years with Santhal tribals and with lepers. The killers were a mob of Santhals, led by an activist of the Bajrang Dal, part of the RSS "family." The episode reflects the growing Hindutva tendency to carry out attacks in isolated backwaters where it is harder for the press, or for the urban elite, to scrutinize sordid events. In this case the fact that Staines was white and had dedicated many years of his life to medical work for the poor caused an international stir, as did the children's deaths. The public forgiveness Staines' wife extended to the killers deeply touched many Indians. The government was obliged to take some action.

Staines' murderer, Dara Singh, was finally arrested a year later. His trial, begun in 2001, has moved with glacial slowness. In an interview Singh denied membership in the Bajrang Dal, the RSS and the BJP, but professed great admiration for Shiv Sena leader Bal Thackery, known for his bloodthirsty rhetoric (Banerjee 2000). Singh has a background typical of many low-level Hindutva activists. He is an unemployed factory worker and petty trader, born in small town Uttar Pradesh, who worked in Delhi before drifting to Orissa. He is also charged with the earlier murders of a Muslim trader and an Indian Christian priest elsewhere (Pattajoshi and Krishnaswamy 2000).

Blasphemous intellectuals, rebellious young – the culture wars

An important aspect of the Hindu rightist program is its ongoing attack on intellectuals and their cultural production. This is hardly surprising since Indian intellectuals – generally rationalist, secular and international in outlook – compete with Hindutva forces for many of the institutions and arenas where identity is produced: schools, the media, popular culture. Journalists have been beaten up, art exhibits trashed, paintings destroyed, lectures, concerts and drama performances broken up by "outraged" mobs. The Hindutva intention is to intimidate artists and intellectuals, to disrupt the creation of intellectual or artistic work, and to frighten off audiences by associating certain ideas with disruption, chaos and danger. Such ideas are thus effectively placed off-limits for discussion and debate, leaving a Hindutva analysis to fill the void.

A recent episode in the culture wars has caused the BJP government further international embarrassment. Feminist film director Deepa Mehta, was forced to abandon her movie *Water*, being filmed on location in Banaras. First a small but vociferous band of RSS demonstrators invaded the set and threatened the film crew, then rumors were floated about a mob of 10,000 massing to attack. A frightened state government eventually asked Mehta and her crew to leave, since it could not guarantee their safety. Because Mehta now lives in Canada, and her film crew was international, the incident drew protest from other artists around the world (Yuen-Carrucan 2000). The incident highlights the ways in which Hindutva mobs are able to intimidate local authorities into carrying out a Hindutva agenda. In this case, the local administration was particularly fearful of unrest since Hindutva activists have for years promised to make Banaras "the next Ayodhya."

For many years Hindu revivalist groups have sought to penetrate and control schools and universities (Kumar 1993b), in an effort to make sure that the young are molded to a purely Hindu identity. Much of this effort is directed at rooting out vestiges of Western thought. In the past decade the Hindutva movement has produced large numbers of school texts, then agitated to have them adopted in school systems, over the protests of parents, teachers and educational officials. This effort has gained ground as the BJP comes to control state governments and their education departments. Historian K.N. Panikkar (1999) asserts that the RSS has established some 20,000 parallel schools around India, to which the BJP national government is now trying to lend legitimacy and support. The Hindutva push into education is particularly significant in light of the special role Christian schools play.

The Hindutva curriculum emphasizes the study of Hinduism and Sanskrit (at a time when most young Indians are yearning to learn English, science and computer use). It offers revisionist history and literature courses, which glorify a mythical Hindu past while eradicating any reference to Muslims, the Islamic contribution to Indian culture, or the West. Math and science are a further arena of struggle, linked as they are to Western-style scientific rationality, upward social mobility or possible migration to the West. Math and science courses have been infiltrated by "Vedic mathematics," a form of math teaching which S.G. Dani (1993) castigates as neither Vedic nor mathematical, but simply incoherent. This kind of determined anti-rationality (with a pseudo-scientific gloss) is particularly dangerous for the public schools of a country still plagued by illiteracy. Poor children need (in addition to pencils, books, decent classrooms and more and better teachers) an education which is accessible, practical and rooted in daily reality. Clouds of saffron-tinted fantasy threaten the achievement of cultural literacy by millions of poor children. In a metaphorical sense, this too is violence.

Hindutva anxieties about gender relations, which cropped up in the uproar over Deepa Mehta's film *Water* (and her earlier *Fire*) underlie recent rightist agitation against Valentine's Day. The holiday, wholly un-Indian in origin, has been popularized by commercial interests, and has caught the fancy of young, affluent urban people able to afford cards, flowers and romantic dinners, and eager to follow modern, Western trends. What seem to have driven Hindutva activists into a frenzy of protest marches, threatening speeches, and destruction of shop displays, however, are the new social relationships such a holiday implies: gender equality, romance before marriage, and individual choice of a partner. Can the collapse of the Hindu family be far behind?

Second-rate members of the world economy

The move to economic reform

The Hindu right has been part of the Indian scene since the 1920s. However its current rise to national prominence began in the 1980s, paralleling a massive politico-economic shift in Indian society. Political economist Samir Amin (1990) describes the 1980s as a time when India abandoned its efforts at non-alignment with and disengagement from Western economic and political domination. In the 1960s India had tried, via the Non-Aligned Movement, to lead other recently decolonized countries into a separate, quasi-socialist path of development. India adopted protectionist policies and internal economic regulation which kept it partially insulated from the trajectory of global capitalism. By 1975, says Amin, that experiment was moribund and India, along with the rest of the Third World, entered "a decade of drift." (1990: 42). The next stage, Amin says, was the effort of these decolonized nations to cope with this failure and to come to terms with their peripheral position within a new international division of labor (1990: 49).

For India, this attempt to reposition itself has evoked a sense of inferiority and yearning envy *vis-à-vis* both the West and India's more economically vibrant Southeast Asian neighbors. Within India there is a profound disillusionment with social planning and a frantic scramble to catch up economically and to modernize the economy via foreign investment, export-oriented industrialization and international loans. In so doing, India has been increasingly exposed to an American-inflected global culture, reaching people through advertising, an increasingly privatized media and transnational migration. Today television, videos, CDs, books, magazines, and foreign travel all flood India with new images of Western-style consumption and behavior.

The process has involved India in an increasing polarization of internal class relations. One of the legacies of colonialism is a bifurcated class structure, in which some segments of the bourgeoisie and the elite are more highly Westernized than others, and thus have greater access to modern sectors of the economy, or to the West itself. This bifurcation is exacerbated by modernizing capitalist development. When that development fails to complete its task, society is left with vast numbers of semi-educated, under-employed young Indian men who drift, like Staines' killer Dara Singh, from rural areas to cities to small towns, looking for work and for meaning in their lives (see interview with Singh by Banerjee 2000). Hindutva powerfully attracts such young men, who go on to act as the movement's shock troops, carrying out bombings, vandalism and murders in the name of faith (and to earn a little cash).

However, many of the core supporters of the Hindutva movement are not unemployed or semi-criminal. Members of India's urban and small-town petty bourgeoisie or rural landowners also feel themselves losers in the current period of modernization with only a partial share in India's prosperity and booming consumer culture. In general they now find themselves without the capital, the technical expertise, the education or the skill in English to join the new, technocratic or entrepreneurial urban bourgeoisie. They are now increasingly irrelevant in local and national politics, both bewildered and shamed by many aspects of India's Western-style consumer culture. They resent the apparent new privileges of women and of caste and religious minorities. For this culturally conservative section of Indian society, Hinduism (and religion generally) remains a central concern, giving meaning and shape to daily life. Western ideas, secularism and rationality provoke deep suspicion and unease.

In its current phase of economic liberalization, India now assiduously courts foreign investment of a kind formerly held at arms' length. For instance, the once-expelled Coca-Cola Corporation has been welcomed back with open arms (Lessinger 1992) while Kentucky Fried Chicken and McDonalds (anathema to religious Hindu vegetarians but beloved by young moderns) have been allowed to establish franchises. Externally, the government was pushed toward these "reforms" by pressure from Western investors, anxious for access to India's cheap labor and its huge, untapped consumer market. However parallel pressure also came from a new, more Western-oriented Indian capitalist class, begging to be unleashed so it could compete (it dreamed) on equal terms with foreign capital. Simultaneously, Indian politicians and planners became uncomfortably aware that a tide of rising consumer expectations posed an internal political threat. When affluent Indian tourists to Singapore and Malaysia return with amazing tales of clean, safe streets, full employment and abundant, reasonably-priced electronic goods for sale, Indian planners squirm at the implied comparison.

In pursuit of this "economic reform" path, India began to reverse longstanding state policies which subsidized industry, agriculture, education, medical care and food distribution; maintained tight national control over certain key industries, banking, currency exchange and imports, and avoided international debt. Fiscal reform since 1991 has led the country to seek International Monetary Fund loans as well as foreign aid from North America, Europe and Japan. Predictably, international lenders have demanded deficit reduction. As the Indian government has hastened to comply, formerly state-owned industries are being sold to private investors; industry and banking are being deregulated;

social spending for food distribution, farm subsidies, medical care, education and public transportation is vanishing. There is less and less public money available to maintain urban infrastructure. Road networks, bus systems, electric power, water and sewage, and public health systems, along with such amenities as libraries, parks and museums, are visibly decaying. Despite its nationalist rhetoric, the BJP, once in power, became as deeply involved in these processes as its predecessor, the Congress Party.

The class impact

With debt service come balance of payment crises and inflation (Dehejia 1993). India has not yet had to endure as much austerity shock treatment as some third-world debtor nations, but some of the population is now visibly worse off as a result. As the government has abandoned support for certain industries such as textiles, and promoted foreign imports, male industrial employment has declined and women's employment, often in the informal sector, has grown. Cuts in agricultural subsidies for fertilizers and electric pump irrigation further burden sharecroppers and small farmers, and increase the cost of food. Even optimists note that income and employment are growing more slowly than the government had hoped. Although the percentage of Indians living in absolute poverty has been almost halved since 1960, the absolute numbers of poor remain about the same (Dehejia 1993: 83). At the same time there are now several private airlines criss-crossing the country, cell phones are prevalent and new hotels in Bombay advertise themselves as "environment friendly." Pessimists note that India is still characterized by high levels of unemployment, under-employment and desperate poverty (Bagchi 1991: 202–207). The employment situation directly affects out-migration on the part of both technically trained professionals (who go to the West) and working-class people (who go to the Middle East or, illegally, to the West).

For those who remain in India, the cumulative effect of these economic changes is to make life, particularly in urban areas, far more difficult than it was even two decades ago. The growing urban middle class is embarked, as Dubey (1992) remarks, on a consuming binge. There is a good deal of trickle-down prosperity, so that lower-middle-class families may have a TV, and a bus driver can buy his wife a battered second-hand kitchen blender for preparing *masaala* (spice paste), yet most urban dwellers except the very rich experience daily scarcities. Even for those who have jobs, there is not enough housing, no water, gridlocked traffic, power blackouts, choking air pollution, public transportation too crowded to board, insufficient medical care. It is little wonder that so many people, both bourgeois and working-class, are susceptible to Hindutva ideology which on the one hand promises moral regeneration and a new social order, and on the other hand identifies an internal enemy allegedly sucking up the benefits and privileges of education, government affirmative action programs, and international ties. The real target of much Hindutva rhetoric and action is the Western-oriented model of modernization itself.

The sons and daughters of the professional middle class now eschew public sector jobs or the professions in favor of entrepreneurship, where the quick money is. If they cannot run advertising agencies, manufacture scooters, assemble personal computers, or build tourist hotels, they can become distributors of foreign-made cell phones or proprietors of Internet cafés and fitness centers. What is involved in this modernizing shift is not only new forms of employment and consumption, but also an abandonment of certain nationalist ideals prevalent among the post-Independence generation. The pride an older generation took in public service, in an indigenous life style, in being Indian, is gone, replaced by a passion for what is new, expensive and Western, and a haunting sense that one would be better off in the West.

For those without access to this brave new world of wealth, consumption and transnational taste, there is a sense of exclusion which feeds the Hindutva attack on both the Congress Party and on rationalist, secular ideologies. At the same time consumerism, advertising and the growth of mass culture have eroded traditional culture, with the support, stability and sense of community it offered. Into the breach steps the Hindutva movement to give new meaning to life with its male-bonded brotherhoods, prayer meetings, marches, songs, speeches and flags, special symbols and clothing, excitement and pageantry, spurious history and a promise of reclaimed national glory.

Caste mobilization

At the very time when segments of India's bourgeoisie are feeling squeezed from above, their dominance is also being challenged from below. Since the 1970s there have been gradually more powerful mobilizations of "backward" (economically disadvantaged low- to middle-rank) castes and of Dalits. Even Muslims, with their privileged access to labor migration to the Middle East, are asserting themselves and are no longer as poor as they once were. These disadvantaged groups, which found rhetorical support but little practical help in the Congress Party, are now beginning to form independent parties and to seek bases in state governments such as Bihar's.

In 1990, lower caste access to upward social mobility via public sector employment was greatly enhanced when the government implemented the Mandal Commission ruling that extended India's system of reservations, a form of affirmative action in jobs and education. Whereas reservations once applied only to Dalits and Adivasis (tribal peoples), reservations now must be extended to cover many other backward castes as well. Suddenly a much wider range of caste groups had guaranteed access, via reserved quotas, to lifetime government jobs – and this at a moment when economic restructuring has shrunk the amount of public sector employment available. High castes have been both frightened and outraged at this loss of economic access. Extensive protests against the Mandal Commission ruling throughout north India were often spearheaded by Hindutva groups. Thus the Hindutva rhetoric of "national unity" can be partly understood as an attack on social policies which single out some social groups for assistance or protection.

Conclusion

Over the last two decades, India has been caught up in a whirlwind of far-reaching social and economic changes as it finds a new role in the global system. The growth of the Hindutva movement, with its bigotry and brutality, is one of these changes. For some, globalization offers new prosperity, new forms of consumption, new forms of identity, incorporating aspects of Western culture and undermining older caste hierarchies and older orthodoxies. For Indian Muslims, Indian Christians, and some other marginal groups, globalization offers access to transnational religious currents and the hope of social mobility via education or migrant employment.

Significant segments of India's Hindu population, however, simply feel themselves whipsawed by social change. Caste superiority is less relevant to social dominance than it once was. For people whose class standing – now more critical than ever – has been eroded through poverty, rural origins or lack of education, the new modernity offers little hope and a great deal to fear. The previous generation's powerful sense of post-colonial national identity and optimism has been eroded as a weak state has allowed global capitalism to relegate India to the role of bit player on the world stage.

In these circumstances, it is possible to understand why so many Indians have sought solace in the embrace of a neo-fascist Hindu nationalism and thrilled to the violence it provokes. A sense of national weakness, a sense of cultural loss, a sense of class victimization – all translate into electoral support for Hindutva and a following for its ideologies. These promise a sense of belonging, renewal and national empowerment in a pan-Hindu India purged of the divisions caused by religion, caste and secularism.

The most striking aspect of Hindutva at present is the movement's calculated use of violence. The various attacks and provocations against Muslims, Christians and intellectuals, despite statements from perpetrators, are not spontaneous outbreaks of "traditional" religious sentiment, but carefully orchestrated moves against chosen symbolic targets – mosques, churches, missionaries, film crews, school texts or Western-style holidays. Religion, interwoven as it is with daily life, becomes the language, the vehicle and the emotional fuel for political mobilization, but not its root cause. As a marker of cultural difference, however, it serves to mobilize the majority against those whose minority status makes them vulnerable, and who can simultaneously be castigated as subversive, anti-Indian agents of the outside world.

In general, Hindutva violence is intended to paralyze the existing state apparatus by creating chaos, terror and breakdown of community, until particular localities are ungovernable – a serious threat in a country with an enormous, impoverished population and a poorly funded, rather fragile state mechanism. Violence itself is therefore a powerful recruiting tool. Meanwhile, dissenting voices, particularly those of intellectuals, artists or Christians, who offer alternative models of social change, can be silenced. It is the Hindutva use of violence to impose its will, to create hegemonic ideas and to undermine existing democratic structures, which has led opponents to dub the movement a fascist one.

What one can hope – and what recent developments seem to confirm – is that the internal contradictions of the Hindutva combine may eventually weaken it, although not before the movement has instigated further spasms of violence intended to regain a popular following. Buried within the movement's pan-Hindu rhetoric of social reform is a conservative class agenda which seeks to reassert a traditional gender- and caste-based social hierarchy and to undo social changes of the past decades. Women, currently being mobilized by the BJP on the basis of their traditional religiosity, would be sent back to the kitchen. Low castes would return to their divinely-ordained positions of deference and service. Muslims and Christians would be bodily expelled from India or killed off. Regional separatist movements would be brutally put down. Troublesome intellectuals would be silenced. Education, in the hands of religious leaders, would return to a study of the "basics": Sanskrit, Hinduism, a contemplation of India's glorious past, untainted by mongrelizing foreign influences.

This political/cultural program is doomed to failure simply because it is so out of harmony with what large numbers of Indians want right now. A modernizing bourgeoisie – growing in size – wants access to science, technology, stock markets, English-language education, transnational linkages and a global consumer culture. Although not deeply committed to "secularism," this bourgeoisie would prefer to operate within a meritocracy, overlooking all differences except those of class. Such a bourgeoisie actually values a stable state apparatus as a shield against mob violence, since social chaos derails their modernizing capitalist agenda.

This modernity of outlook is not wholly confined to India's urban, technocratic elite. Some of India's poor and marginal now aspire to their small portion of prosperity and social mobility through education, affirmative action and the formation of new political parties. Because religious minorities, Adivasis, Dalits and other backward castes are heavily represented in this newly aware sector, a state committed to religious and cultural pluralism is an important bulwark in protecting their gains.

Meanwhile the current trajectory of social change will continue as long as India remains enmeshed in a global capitalism. Although the social stresses produced by this change have initially fed Hindutva support, they are also likely to undermine Hindutva strength, to sow division in its ranks or to force the movement itself to change direction in the long run. In the short run, events demonstrate that localities and groups which resist Hindutva terror tactics – through counter-organizing, negative publicity and ridicule – have often been able to out-maneuver the right. What is missing, at the moment, is a well-organized opposition at the political party level. Until that can emerge, the distant thunder of civil war, audible in the Indian background since the 1930s, will rumble a little closer.

References

Amin, Samir (1990) *Maldevelopment, Anatomy of A Global Failure*, trans. Michael Wolfers. London: Zed Books.

Anderson, Walter K. and Shridhar Damle (1987) *The Brotherhood in Saffron, the Rashtriya Swayamsevak Sangh and Hindu Revivalism*. Boulder: Westview Press.

Bagchi, Amiya Kumar (1991) "Predatory Commercialization and Communalism." In Sarvepalli Gopal (ed.), *Anatomy of a Confrontation, Ayodhya and the Rise of Communal Politics in India*. Delhi: Penguin, pp. 193–218. (Also London: Zed Books, 1993.)

Banerjee, Ruben (2000) "'I Have No Regrets': interview with Dara Singh." *India Today* 22 May, pp. 26–27.

Basu, Tapan, Pradip Datta, Sumit Sarkar, Tanika Sarkar and Sambuddha Sen (1993) *Khaki Shorts and Saffron Flags, A Critique of the Hindu Right*, Tracts for the Times 1. New Delhi: Orient Longman.

Brass, Paul (1991) *Ethnicity and Nationalism, Theory and Comparison*. New Delhi: Sage.

—— (1996) "Introduction: Discourses of Ethnicity, Communalism and Violence." In Paul Brass (ed.), *Riots and Pogroms*. New York: New York University Press, pp. 1–55.

Chakrabarty, Dipesh (1989) *Rethinking Working-Class History, Bengal 1890–1940*. Princeton: Princeton University Press.

Chatterjee, Partha (1999) "Secularism and Toleration." In *The Partha Chatterjee Omnibus*. New Delhi: Oxford University Press, pp. 228–262.

Chaturvedi, Jayati and Gyaneshwar Chaturvedi (1996) "Dharma Yugh: Communal Violence and Riots and Public Space in Ayodhya and Agra City, 1990 and 1992." In Paul Brass (ed.), *Riots and Pogroms*. New York: New York University Press, pp.177–200.

Comaroff, John L. (1996) "Ethnicity, Nationalism and the Politics of Difference in an Age of Revolution." In E. Wilmsen and P. McAllister (eds), *The Politics of Difference: Ethnic Premises in a World of Power*. Chicago: University of Chicago Press.

Dani, S.G. (1993) "Myths and Reality: On 'Vedic mathematics.'" *Frontline* 22 October, pp. 90–92.

Dehejia, Jay (1993) "Economic Reforms: Birth of an 'Asian Tiger.'" In Philip Oldenburg (ed.), *India Briefing 1993*. Boulder: Westview Press, pp. 75–102.

Dubey, Suman (1992) "The Middle Class." In Leonard Gordon and Philip Oldenburg (eds), *India Briefing, 1992*. Boulder: Westview Press.

Engineer, Asghar Ali (ed.) (1992) "Introduction." In Ali Asghar Engineer (ed.), *Politics of Confrontation, the Babri Masjid-Ramjanmabhoomi Controversy Runs Riot*. Delhi: Ajanta Publications, pp. i–xxiii.

—— (1991) "Hindu–Muslim Relations Before and After 1947." In Sarvepalli Gopal (ed.), *Anatomy of A Confrontation*. Delhi: Penguin, pp. 179–192. (Also London: Zed Books, 1993.)

Forbes, H.D. (1997) *Ethnic Conflict, Commerce, Culture and the Contact Hypothesis*. New Haven: Yale University Press.

Fox, Richard (1990) "Hindu Nationalism in the Making, or the Rise of the Hindian." In Richard Fox (ed.), *Nationalist Ideologies and the Production of National Cultures*, American Ethnological Society Monograph Series No. 2. Washington, DC: American Ethnological Society, pp. 63–80.

Gargan, Edward (1993) "Trust Is Torn: Police Role in Bombay Riots." *New York Times* 31 January, p. 1.

Graham, B.D. (1990) *Hindu Nationalism and Indian Politics: the Origins and Development of the Bharatiya Jana Sangh*. Cambridge: Cambridge University Press.

Gupta, Dipankar (1982) *Nativism in a Metropolis: the Shiv Sena in Bombay*. Delhi: Manohar Publishers.

—— (1995) "Ethnicity, Religion and National Politics in India." In Berch Berberoglu (ed.), *The National Question: Nationalism, Ethnic Conflict and Self-Determination in the 20th Century*. Philadelphia: Temple University Press, pp. 77–94.

Hansen, Thomas Blom (1999) *The Saffron Wave, Democracy and Hindu Nationalism in Modern India*. Princeton: Princeton University Press.

Jaffrelot, Christophe (1996) *The Hindu Nationalist Movement in India*. New York: Columbia University Press.

Kakar, Sudhir (1996) *The Colors of Violence: Cultural Identities, Religion, and Conflict*. Chicago: University of Chicago Press.

Kapur, Anuradha (1992) "Militant Images of a Tranquil God." In Asghar Ali Engineer (ed.), *Politics of Confrontation, The Babri Masjid-Ramjanmabhoomi Controversy Runs Riot*. Delhi: Ajanta Publications.

Kellas, James (1991) *The Politics of Nationalism and Ethnicity*. New York: St. Martin's Press.

Krishnakumar, Asha (1993) "Path of Provocation, in the name of religion in Madras." *Frontline* 22 October, pp. 119–120.

Kumar, Krishna (1993a) "Behind the VHP of America, Responding to the Challenge." *Frontline* 10 September, pp. 10–12.

—— (1993b) "Hindu Revivalism and Education in North-Central India." In Martin Marty and R. Scott Appleby (eds), *Fundamentalisms and Society*, The Fundamentalism Project, volume 2. Chicago: University of Chicago Press, pp. 536–557.

Kurien, Prema (2001) "Religion, Ethnicity and Poltics: Hindu and Muslim Indian immigrants in the United States." *Ethnic and Racial Studies* 24 (2): 263–293.

Lessinger, Johanna (1992) "Nonresident Indian Investment and India's Drive for Industrial Modernization." In Frances Rothstein and Michael Blim (eds), *Anthropology and the Global Factory*. New York: Bergin and Garvey, pp. 62–84.

Mandal, D. (1993) *Ayodhya, Archaeology After Demolition*, Tracts for the Times 5. New Delhi: Orient Longman.

Menon, Parvathi (2000) "An Assault on Christians." *Frontline* 7 July, pp. 21–23.

Muralidharan, Sukumar (2000) "Raising the Stakes." *Frontline* 7 July, pp. 4–6.

Oberoi, Harjot (1995) "Mapping Indic Fundamentalisms Through Nationalism and Modernity." In Martin Marty and R. Scott Appleby (eds), *Fundamentalisms Comprehended*, The Fundamentalism Project, volume 5. Chicago: University of Chicago Press, pp. 96–114.

Omvedt, Gail (1993) *Reinventing Revolution: New Social Movements and the Socialist Tradition in India*. Armonk, NY: M.E. Sharpe.

Panikkar, K.N. (1999) "Towards a Hindu Nation." *Frontline* 30 January–12 February. http://www.frontlineonline.com

Pattajoshi, Lalit and Chetan Krishnaswamy (2000) "Erasing a Stain." *The Week* 13 February. http://www.the-week.com/20feb

Rajagopal, Arvind (1993) "An Unholy Nexus, Expatriate Anxiety and Hindu Extremism." *Frontline* 10 September, pp. 12–14.

—— (2000a) "Hindutva Movements in the West: Resurgent Hinduism and the Politics of Diaspora." *Racial and Ethnic Studies* 23(3): 407–416.

—— (2000b) "Hindu Nationalism in the U.S.: changing configurations of political practice." *Racial and Ethnic Studies* 23(3): 467–496.

Ramakrishnan, Venkitesh (2000a) "The Post-demolition Trial." *Frontline* 7 January, p. 8.

—— (2000b) "Back to Ayodhya." *Frontline* 7 January, pp. 9–10, 12–13.

Rudolph, Susanne H. and Rudolph, Lloyd I. (1993) "Modern Hate." *The New Republic* 22 March, pp. 24–28.

Sarkar, Tanika (1991) "The Woman as Communal Subject: Rastrasevika Samiti and Ram Janmabhoomi Movement." *Economic and Political Weekly* 26: 2057–2062.

Sen, Amartya (1993) "The Threats to Secular India." *New York Review of Books* 8 April, pp. 26–32.
Spitz, Douglas (1993) "Cultural Pluralism, Revivalism, and Modernity in South Asia: The Rashtriya Swayamsevak Sang." In Crawford Young (ed.), *The Rising Tide of Cultural Pluralism*. Madison: University of Wisconsin Press, pp. 242–267.
Swami, Praveen (1993) "Beyond Slogans, the Mukt Naad Success." *Frontline* 10 September, pp. 12–14.
—— (1999) "A Catalogue of Crimes." *Frontline* 30 January–12 February, p. 12.
—— (2001) "Fundamentalist designs in Punjab." *Frontline* 18(3), 3–16 February. http//www.frontlineonline.com
Thapar, Romila (1993) Lecture given at Southern Asian Institute, Columbia University, March 1993.
—— (1991) "A Historical Perspective on the Story of Rama." In Sarvepalli Gopal (ed.), *Anatomy of A Confrontation*. Delhi: Penguin, pp. 141–163. (Also London: Zed Books, 1993.)
Vanaik, Achin (1990) *The Painful Transition: Bourgeois Democracy in India*. London: Verso Books.
—— (1997) *The Furies of Indian Communalism: Religion, Modernity and Secularization*. London: Verso Books.
van der Veer, Peter (1994a) *Religious Nationalism, Hindus and Muslims in India*. Berkeley: University of California Press.
—— (1994b) "Hindu Nationalism and the Discourse of Modernity: The Vishva Hindu Parishad." In Martin Marty and R. Scott Appleby (eds), *Accounting for Fundamentalisms*, The Fundamentalism Project, volume 4. Chicago: University of Chicago Press, pp. 653–658.
—— (1996) "Riots and Rituals: The Construction of Violence and Public Space in Hindu Nationalism." In Paul Brass (ed.), *Riots and Pogroms*. New York, NY: New York University Press, pp. 114–153.
Varshney, Ashutosh (1993) "Battling the Past, Forging a Future? Ayodhya and Beyond." In Philip Oldenburg (ed.), *India Briefing, 1993*. Boulder: Westview Press, pp. 9–42.
Weiner, Myron (1978) *Sons of the Soil, Migration and Ethnic Conflict in India*. Princeton: Princeton University Press.
Yuen-Carrucan, Jasmine (2000) "The Politics of Deepa Mehta's *Water*." *Bright Lights Film Journal* 28 (April). http://www.brightlightsfilm.com

8 The specter of superfluity

Genesis of schism in the dismantling of Yugoslavia

Bette Denich

Introduction

In the spring of 2001, a rebellion by ethnic Albanians in Macedonia closed the circle of violence that had begun nearly ten years earlier in Slovenia and subsequently spread through each of the six republics that had composed the former Yugoslavia.[1] Except for Slovenia, which emerged with minimal damage, the five other republics have been left with severe disabilities, with two of them partially or wholly under the control of international "peacekeeping" forces and threatened with continued violence. Because it was in the "heart of Europe," the brutality of Yugoslavia's breakup particularly shocked public opinion in Europe and North America. Yet, ironically, the horrors of "ethnic cleansing" were committed on behalf of statehood theories that originated in Europe and are quintessentially European.[2] Furthermore, the Yugoslavia that disintegrated into civil wars was no longer a backward Balkan hinterland, but had substantially modernized since World War II. Nor had it been isolated from the West, since the Yugoslav socialist regime was independent of the Soviet bloc and for decades the country had been open to worldwide travel, trade and media.

At issue among the leaderships of Yugoslavia's component republics was the ultimate question of Yugoslavia's statehood: how it should be reconstituted, or whether it should continue to exist at all. Intellectuals and political leaders intensely debated those questions for several years prior to the disintegration of the state. Although but a small portion of the citizens of most countries, including Yugoslavia, were concerned explicitly with constitutional law, it was the entry of the public into marches and rallies, and then into voting booths, that placed power in the hands of leaders espousing nationalist ideologies and programs that divided the peoples of Yugoslavia against each other. The fact that a revolution had overturned the social order within recent memory, during World War II, was a reminder that it was possible for an elite to lose control over the state and for others to lose their previous channels of access. In that case, the reformulation of statehood would be of vital interest to everyone seeking to assert, maintain or re-establish claims to the rights and privileges that define access to the vital resources under the aegis of state control.

Yugoslavia's collapse occurred within the kind of brief time frame that political scientist David Apter (1987: 304) has called a "disjunctive moment," when "[s]pectators, citizens, participants, are forced to take sides, to line up on one side or another ... according to some social fault line. Events of confrontation take on metaphorical ... significance." Yugoslavia's fault lines were ethnic and the metaphors appeared in the recasting of political issues into the imagery of conflicting nationalist theories of statehood. Current events recalled the past, linking history, myth, folklore, literature, language – all the distinguishing markers of national ideology.[3] But what prompted some of Yugoslavia's citizens to secede from it, even in the expectation that it would not be accomplished without violence?

Considering the past history of ethnic violence in the Balkans, it is tempting to explain the present in terms of the influence of the past and to assume that "age-old" animosities were the cause of both secession and violence. This explanation has been used to justify ethnic separation and has been widely accepted by outsiders who did not know Yugoslavia before its violent breakup attracted worldwide attention. By then, historic ethnic grievances had been revived, so that it appeared credible that they had inevitably led to the breakup of Yugoslavia. Therefore, it is important to examine the period that preceded the actual breakup of Yugoslavia and to trace the emergence of the interethnic polarization and mutual animosities that preceded the armed conflict, which occurred first in Slovenia. This examination will show that the disintegration of Yugoslavia was precipitated by the opening of a cleavage between two ethnic populations, Serbs and Slovenes, which *lacked* any previous history of animosity or conflict. On the contrary, there was even a tradition of friendship between Serbs and Slovenes. Lacking a common border, and not living in substantial numbers in each other's home republics, there had been no previous occasion on which they had taken opposing sides as ethnic nationalities. And yet, it was the unraveling of the Slovenian thread that precipitated the unraveling of the entire tapestry of Yugoslav ethnic nationalities, initiating the chain of violence that eventually reached all of the six republics.

Yugoslavia's disjunctive moment was marked by public discussion on the theoretical premises of statehood, drawing in average citizens who picked up their cues from television sets and newspapers, and discussed among themselves, with families, friends, and workmates. Thereby, constitutional philosophy entered popular culture, affecting how people viewed their own prospects in the face of imminent change. These discussions drew upon the cultural knowledge available to Yugoslavs, consisting of two European intellectual traditions. First, the Marxian tradition, as applied in Yugoslavia, designated the working class as the special bearers of the state, and granted a political monopoly to the Communist Party. The complex fabric of political, economic and social institutions was subordinated to that party, while any political organizations outside that framework were illegal. Secondly, the tradition of ethnic nation-statehood (originating in the German philosophical concept of *Volk*) designates the territory of a state as "belonging" to its dominant ethnic population, relegating all others residing there to the secondary status of "minorities." Neither of these traditions considers individual citizens as inherently equal, regardless of ancestry or affiliation, and since they presume that one category of citizens will be privileged, the key question is: which category will be privileged? Because the Yugoslav republics, with the exception of Slovenia, did not coincide with ethnic boundaries, using ethnicity as the principle of statehood would result in ethnic inequalities between the "privileged" ethnic nation and the minorities within "its" state. Yet, it was widely understood that if mono-ethnic Slovenia were to secede it would undermine the balance that kept Yugoslavia unified as a federation, and open the door to revivals of hostility among those ethnic populations that did have histories of violence.

What conditions led to such a disjunction? Apter warned of a "specter of superfluous[4] man" that threatens the stability of modern states:

> Marginalization ... is a condition resulting from prolonged functional superfluousness. Marginals are people who not only do not contribute to the social product, they consume more than they produce. ... In turn, if deindustrialization produces endemic marginalization, then the state is set for violence, the search for disjunctive moments, for a world turned upside down.
>
> (Apter 1987: 316)

This essay will show how, as the Yugoslav economic system was perceived as marginal to the global economy, and even to Europe, the state became vulnerable to the radical redefinitions that were to tear it apart along ethnic lines. While economic oppositions are but one dimension of the symbolic and emotional complexity involved with ethnic nationalism, that is the domain which most acutely links individual survival with the sense of collective destiny that depends on how statehood is defined. The disjunction did not result directly from economic factors, but in how they were interpreted and presented to the public by nationalist elites, communicating through mass media. Gregory Bateson's (1972) concept of "schismogenesis" will elucidate how separate, incompatible images were communicated to the publics in different regions of the country with regard to their economic positions within Yugoslavia.[5] While others have written comprehensive narrative accounts of the actual events (see Cohen 1993; Silber and Little 1997), my task here is to describe the framework of how the incompatible public perceptions of events precipitated the schism.

During the summer of 1987, I returned to Yugoslavia after an absence of fifteen years. Outwardly, I found the society I had first come to know during the late 1960s, where citizens in all the republics, and of all ethnicities, were still managing their lives within the idiosyncratic framework of Yugoslavia's version of socialism. The government and political organizations were constantly issuing optimistic assessments, balancing the International Monetary Fund's demands for austerity and "long-term stabilization" with reassurances about the soundness of "self-managing" socialism. In 1987, I found people accustomed to the "crisis" that had already lasted since the beginning of the decade and they tutored me about the situation. But I did not find people openly doubting the durability of their political order. Instead, they were absorbed in coping ingeniously with circumstances that were ever changing, still confident of mastering whatever challenges their unpredictable social order would throw at them.

At the summer's end, however, I witnessed, via television, a political "scandal" that can now be seen as the start of the disjunction, in that it shook the confidence of ordinary citizens in the economic viability of the Yugoslav system and opened the door to their questioning the continuation of Yugoslavia as a multi-ethnic state. Subsequently, I spent much of 1988–90 in Yugoslavia as a witness to what was obviously history in the making. The country was full of "talk," and I became, in effect, an ethnographer of public opinion as the same thoughts and concepts circulated between political and intellectual elites and in the conversations I overheard, and participated in, wherever people gathered. In the analysis to follow, I describe the emergence of what became the dominant viewpoints among ethnic populations during that time period and characterize them according to the ethnic categories defined in that system of power. Dissenting viewpoints were suppressed, but always present.

"Self-management" in crisis

In contrast to the Soviet bloc, Yugoslavia's socialism was not based on deprivation, and Yugoslavs enjoyed Western-style personal freedoms in the non-political spheres of life. The combination of rapid industrialization and urbanization during the post-World War II years and ingenious coping mechanisms enabled large numbers of people with comparatively low wage levels to attain impressively high living standards, with comfortable housing and the accoutrements of consumerism that emulated European and North American lifestyles. Thus, Yugoslavia's unique "self-managing socialism" had long seemed to be immune from the ills that affected its neighbors and appeared to have fulfilled its promise to provide a "better life" for one of pre-World War II Europe's poorest, least developed countries. As Yugoslavia's brand of socialism developed endogenously, rather than being imposed from without, the sources for the vulnerability of the state must be sought within Yugoslavia's own institutions, in the nature of its own economic crisis that spanned the entire decade of the 1980s.

As a result of the "oil crisis" of the 1970s, Yugoslavia was among the developing countries enjoying the sudden largesse of Western banks, extending credit to Third World and East European countries.[6] In Yugoslavia, the oil crisis coincided serendipitously with major constitutional reforms that restructured Yugoslav socialism along the lines of "self-management" institutions featuring a "consensual economy" ("*dogovorna privreda*").[7] The 1974 constitution also reconstituted the Yugoslav state, dispersing its major powers among six republics and two "autonomous provinces" (nominally located within Serbia).[8] As citizens and as employees, people found themselves reorganized into an alphabet soup of acronyms, designating bureaucratic entities. Considering that the previous reformulations of Titoism had led to rising living standards and toward social liberalization, the citizenry adapted stoically to yet another set of reforms. As the 1970s proceeded into a boom of construction projects, with concomitant flows of income into local areas and personal incomes, the utopian-bureaucratic visions depicted in the 1974 constitution seemed validated. However, a closer look into the apparent prosperity of those years reveals that, by the late 1970s, 85 per cent of investments depended on foreign loans (Ramet 1985: 8) and Yugoslavia's illusion of continuous economic expansion was exposed at the start of the 1980s, when it appeared on the long list of Third World and East European debtor countries, from whom repayment was demanded by international banking institutions.

By 1981, the widespread inability of debtor countries to make payments, the so-called "Third World debt crisis," threatened the stability of the international financial system. To enable banks to recover their investments, the International Monetary Fund took the lead in arranging "stabilization plans" whereby Yugoslavia, owing some $20 million, was among the countries that agreed to refinance their loan payments by increasing their exports while reducing domestic spending. In practice, the decline of purchasing power was linked with inflation, which hovered at around 40 per cent between 1980 and 1983 (Ramet 1985: 8), and then began an ascent that increased exponentially in the late 1980s, to peak at the astonishing "hyperinflationary" annual rate of 10,000 percent by the end of 1989 (Sekelj 1993: 257). At the start of 1990, the inflation was broken by the "shock therapy" administered by Prime Minister Ante Markovic,[9] but not before political polarizations had already undermined the future of Yugoslavia as a state.[10]

Intellectual critiques began to unmask the pretensions of "self-managing socialism" and openly characterized the leadership as an entrenched "politocracy," concerned only with protecting its access to positions of power and privilege while mismanaging the economy with investments that combined pork barrel with patronage (cf. Goati 1989; Sekelj 1993). It was bad enough that the country was deeply in debt. Worse was the realization that much of the money had been squandered by party leaders at the republic level, who used powers, granted by the decentralized 1974 constitution, to pour resources into their own regions, disregarding rational criteria. Citizens in each republic prospered while these projects were under construction, but afterward found themselves saddled with unprofitable "white elephants." Many industries ran at a deficit, supporting their employees at the expense of industries that were viable and efficient.

In sum, the "generosity" of international banks during the 1970s coincided with Yugoslav constitutional reforms that decentralized power from the federal government into the republics. Development loans placed money into the hands of republic leaders who declined to coordinate with each other, and sponsored projects without regard for their economic viability. In effect, these leaders were already acting as though their republics were independent countries while incurring debts for development projects that would never produce the income necessary to repay the loans.

Although Yugoslavia spent its final decade in an economic crisis, its people showed little outward appearance of distress. The consumer economy continued to prosper while ineffective reform plans and inflation accelerated into hyperinflation. During the previous decades, people had acquired skills, education, modern appliances, fashionable clothing, and the other basic elements of the Western way of life that they viewed on their TV screens, as well as enjoying entertainment, vacations, and travel abroad. When the 1980s crisis threatened to undermine it all, people rediscovered skills from the peasant life they had once left behind, and reinvigorated their kinship ties, rituals, and non-market ways of exchanging and redistributing goods. As the crisis deepened and the inflation rate climbed, people channeled their anxiety into increasingly sophisticated financial maneuvers designed both to hedge the spiraling prices and to take advantage of them. Credit cards and bank accounts with credit lines were the key to buying now and paying later with devalued dinars. Shopping trips to foreign consumer meccas as far away as Hong Kong and Singapore enabled travelers to import merchandise on which they could make a profit, even after paying customs duties. Private small-scale entrepreneurship, permitted under Yugoslav socialism, proliferated in a diversity of commercial ventures, with boutiques, bars and coffee shops representing the visible surface.

The global connection: development and debt

In 1987, I also found people aware of how the global economy affected them. Since the 1960s, Yugoslavs had traveled in large numbers to Western European countries as "guest workers" and then, during the 1970s and 1980s, engineering and construction firms from Yugoslavia carried out many major projects in the Middle East and North Africa. These opportunities added an international dimension to the experience and outlook of people throughout Yugoslavia, whose neighbors and family members went forth on these foreign ventures and returned, driving new cars with foreign license plates, and bringing hard currency to invest at home. The international opportunities were double-edged, however, as working abroad compensated for the inability of the Yugoslav economy to provide the employment for all who strove toward the living standards of the West. Working in more advanced countries emphasized the continuing lag "at home," while working in the so-called Third World provided a view in the other direction, even more peripheral to the First World image.

In 1987, there was still a saving grace: with all its faults, the Yugoslav system made it possible to maneuver between capitalism and socialism, enjoying some of the benefits of each, without paying the full price, as expressed in the phrase that was constantly interjected into conversations of comparison with Western standards: "But nowhere can you live so well and work so little as in Yugoslavia," pronounced in a tone of conspiratorial satisfaction. As long as their options seemed viable, people were willing to cut the system a lot of slack and count their blessings. People peppered their social conversation with tales about anomalies at their workplaces, developing a picture of the everyday reality that contrasted with the official portrayal of self-managing socialism that the media reported. The key to success was being able to function within the framework of the official structure while simultaneously recognizing and manipulating the "informal" structure of personal relationships that were the real avenue to power, position, and material benefits.

People were looking, from the bottom up, at a patronage system, of which they could directly perceive the managerial structure into which they came into immediate contact. That is where they witnessed everyday peculiarities, which they experienced as contrary to economic efficiency and rationality. At the heart of these anomalies was the issue of competence. Supervisors who went through the proper channels in attempting to dismiss employees on the grounds of incompetence or flagrant absenteeism would find those employees "protected" by the same connections that had gotten them the job in the first place. In everyday conversation among less sophisticated employees, these connections were perceived in personal terms, usually kinship, so that the industrial workplace resembled a village, in which personal ties had priority over the impersonal criteria of professional expertise and job performance. Inasmuch as people had a sound understanding of the relationship between the profitability of their workplaces and their own incomes, the tolerance of poor performance on behalf of personal ties was constantly irritating to those who took pride in their own competence and aspired to get ahead.

At the same time that I was hearing conversations over kitchen tables in which people were analyzing their own experiences, intellectuals were producing sophisticated "top-down" critiques of the system. As an outside observer, I collected both kinds of interpretation, and found that they meshed.

Systemic ills of Yugoslav socialism

The Yugoslav state responded to the 1980s economic contraction in a "paternalistic" manner (cf. Verdery 1993) resembling that of its Soviet bloc neighbors, in that socialist enterprises avoided dismissing employees, attempting to keep their workforces intact despite declining production.

At the local level, people understood that their own enterprises were run by the patronage appointees of Communist politicians. They also observed the prevalence of inefficiency, incompetence, and low productivity. In contrast, the small-scale private sector[11] provided expansive opportunities for a vigorous "informal economy."[12] As the crisis of the 1980s deepened, families ingeniously combined income sources from whatever skills and assets they had available. During Yugoslavia's decades of rapid development, peasants had become massively urbanized in order to pursue the benefits of *"moderni"* life.[13] Now that process was partially reversed, as the same families reactivated their claims to inherited land, where they could raise their own vegetables and even sell crops to supplement their incomes.

At the least, public sector employees could regard their jobs as a security base from which to cleverly add other forms of income. A more intractable problem consisted in the lack of workforce expansion, particularly the inability of the socialist economy to absorb the younger generation. Unemployment statistics climbed, while new graduates typically stayed at home, "waiting at the employment bureau" for indefinite periods that often stretched into years. While supported by their parents, growing numbers of young people were rendered "superfluous" to the socialist economy. Increasingly, they resorted to emigration, to small private enterprises, to activities of dubious legality or outright crime, and to combinations thereof. Private economic endeavors gained respectability under the new term *biznes*. As the young ceased to believe that the Titoist system would provide for them, they more actively sought alternatives.[14]

As the state of crisis became endemic, people at all social levels engaged in critiques of their own local circumstances, connecting what they knew personally and by word of mouth. However, public representations kept on reiterating the basic soundness of the Titoist system while explaining yet another round of adjustments and reforms. The duality between private and public knowledge enabled institutions at all levels to function in the face of a widening gap between the collaborative performances required for the "self-management" institutions and the realities that were common knowledge. Just as the stability of Yugoslavia's economic institutions depended upon "collaboration" between workers and managers within individual industries, the stability of the political system relied on public images that maintained the division between private knowledge and public opinion.

From private knowledge to public scandal

The pretenses on all sides were abruptly breached in late August 1987, when television and print media revealed news of a financial scandal of proportions previously unimagined. A falling-out between political factions in Bosnia-Herzegovina led to the public exposure of the financial practices of the large, well-known Agrokomerc agricultural conglomerate in northwestern Bosnia. Under its director, Fikret Abdic,[15] this enterprise had transformed the previously impoverished Bihac region into a food production and processing industrial center. Now the media revealed that Abdic had financed Agrokomerc's expansion through a tissue of unsecured promissory notes, implicating Yugoslavia's major banking institutions with debts amounting to hundreds of millions of dollars. As television news brought the same revelations throughout the country, the hidden "backstage" (see Goffman 1959) of Titoism was suddenly exposed. As people experienced a shock of recognition, they could no longer separate their knowledge about dubious local practices from knowledge that questioned the viability of the entire financial and industrial system.

Quickly, people began to speak of the scandal as Yugoslavia's "Agrogate." In the USA, the shock of Watergate led to a reaffirmation of constitutional legitimacy, as the countervailing branches of government publicly enacted their constitutionally-defined roles. But "Agrogate" was to have the opposite effect, lifting the "taboos"[16] from public criticism of the constitutional order. Rather than confining debate to the economic sphere, circles of intellectuals, journalists and politicians in the capitals of the three dominant republics (Serbia, Croatia and Slovenia) were already covertly considering options in terms of differing regional and ethno-national perspectives. Thus, questions about Yugoslavia's economic viability were transferred into the political sphere, into an increasingly public debate about the basis upon which Yugoslavia had been and should be constituted as a state and even whether it should continue to exist.

In retrospect, August 1987 appears as a final moment of calm, when the elements of approaching turmoil were becoming visible, but did not yet appear threatening to the established order. A review of popular print media for that month[17] includes the following featured items: a debate over proposed amendments to the constitution of Serbia; protest demonstrations by Serbian inhabitants of the Albanian-dominated Kosovo province; the publication of an open letter from a Slovenian intellectual that questioned the continuation of the "brotherhood and unity" upon which socialist Yugoslavia had been founded; and the increase of the inflation rate to 300 per cent annually. Each of these reports reflected an aspect of the malaise that had become endemic, but without any sense that problems could not be solved by yet another round of adjustments by Party leaders maneuvering within the existing framework. However, the sensational revelations about the Agrokomerc scandal moved questions about the system to a different plane. The opposing views of Yugoslavia's future that had been germinating privately among intellectuals in the major capitals more and more openly entered the public arenas.

The 1980s debt crisis had already revealed that Yugoslavia's success in emulating West European lifestyles could not be credited to its own productivity, but to dependence on foreign debt. The Agrokomerc scandal demonstrated the extent to which the system was permeated with debt, raising doubts about the capability of the economy to meet increasingly stringent global standards. It is in this light that Apter's concept of "superfluity" may be extended to characterize an entire economy that existed in negative balance to the world economic institutions. Growing awareness of this relationship, among both elites and the public at large, constituted an imminent threat, drastically undermining attachment to the existing system. The moment of disjunction was timed by the realities of economic unviability; the form, however, was determined by those who chose the ideological basis for dismantling the state of Yugoslavia, in favor of ethnic nations "imagined" (cf. Anderson 1983) in terms of conflicting territorial claims. Those who saw themselves being rendered marginal, with whole industries on the verge of collapse, instead of upholding the social order, were growing ready to abandon it for the promise of a different kind of state, defined according to ethnic privilege. However, those who were not members of the dominant population of a particular republic saw instead the threat of further marginalization.

Nationalism and schismatic communication

Within a month of the Agrokomerc revelations, Yugoslav politics entered a new phase when Slobodan Milošević led an upstart faction to take control of the Communist League of Serbia. Considering that Milošević would quickly gain worldwide notoriety as the initiator of aggressive Serbian nationalism, it is important to emphasize that Milošević presented himself as an economic and political reformer,[18] as well as the defender of the Serbian inhabitants of the Kosovo province, dominated by ethnic Albanians. Milošević linked the grievances of the Kosovo Serbs with demands for constitutional reform, provoking open confrontations with the leaderships of the other republics, particularly those of Slovenia and Croatia. The following summer, nationalist leaders in both Slovenia and Serbia[19] mobilized public participation in mass demonstrations. Wishing to remain in power, Communist politicians appropriated nationalist programs and rhetoric antithetical to the socialist concept of Yugoslavia.

In the fall of 1988, I rented an apartment in downtown Belgrade from Stevan K., whose situation could be taken as an embodiment of the failure of Titoism. At that point he was so financially desperate that he was eager to use his apartment as an income source although it left him temporarily homeless and dependent on the hospitality of friends. Stevan was a draftsman, employed by a major engineering firm, and he had prospered during the earlier 1980s by working on foreign construction projects that his firm contracted in the Middle East. He was glad to earn the hard currency, which he had saved and used to purchase appliances for his apartment, as well as to construct a "weekend" country house. However, the lack of investment in Yugoslavia meant that his firm was dependent on foreign projects. Rather than dismissing employees, Yugoslav firms retained employees, but at nominal salaries that were insufficient to live on and constantly losing value due to inflation. The firm was negotiating to build a mammoth hydroelectric project in Iraq, and Stevan was hoping to get a job there. In the meantime, he needed the cash that my rent provided.

The fall of 1988 coincided with the spread of mass rallies throughout Serbia in support of Milošević, and Stevan K. was among the many people who explained to me Milošević's appeal, in more or less the same words. These narratives emphasized that, unlike the other party leaders, Milosevic was not primarily a politician, but had pursued a career "in the economy" as a manager, most recently of a major bank. Therefore, he understood what was wrong with the economy and was in a position to fix it. Unlike other party officials, Milošević did not live in a luxurious apartment or own a private vacation house, but resided, with his wife and two children, in a "modest two-room apartment" in an ordinary Belgrade neighborhood several trolley stops beyond the downtown area. His mission was to reform the political system, get the economy moving again, and return to private life as a manager. In Stevan's eyes, Milošević was not motivated by personal ambition, but wanted to replace self-serving corruption with economic rationality. Although this image was almost entirely false, people throughout Serbia believed it and viewed Milošević as one of their own, a man who understood their needs and frustrations and who would set things right for them.

In a media innovation of the late 1980s, meetings of the federal and republic central committees were televised, and what had been bureaucratic abstractions took on the faces of the top officials of each republic. In televised central committee sessions, the public watched the officials in a new way, arguing against each other while appealing to their own home audiences. It was an electrifying change, considering that the Communist leaders had not previously felt any need to appeal to constituents. The conflict between Albanian and Serbian interests in Kosovo served as the dramatic focus of acrimonious central committee sessions in which the viewing public began, for the first time, to support the leaders representing their own republics and/or ethnic identities as they read into the Kosovo situation underlying issues that involved their own vital interests. People in different republics, with differing ethnic affiliations, began to perceive the same information in ways that were separate and mutually exclusive.

The trick for the republic leaderships was to get their own populations to support them. Milošević did it by posing as an "anti-bureaucratic" reformer; the Croatian and, particularly, the Slovenian party leaders portrayed Milošević himself as the threat, while edging toward secession. That was the way for them to retain power in their republics, which would become independent countries instead of republics of Yugoslavia.

No longer confined to the sphere of discussion, opposing visions for Yugoslavia's future (or non-future) were expressed in an escalating spiral of public confrontations over a variety of issues. Concurrently, the inflation rate also spiraled upward, from the 300 percent annual rate reported in August 1987 toward the eventual peak of 10,000 percent in December 1990. The media vividly reported on extreme and dire circumstances faced by enterprises, local communities and families. In the wake of the Agrokomerc scandal, the media also turned toward divulging previously unpublishable revelations about the inner workings of the Titoist system. Insofar as both the Serbian and Slovenian leaderships were counterpoising themselves to the existing constitutional system, they had no interest in suppressing news that would discredit that system. On the contrary, both had an interest in actively undermining public confidence in the existing arrangements. However, they had contrary interpretations of the causes for Yugoslavia's ills, as well as of the desired outcomes.

Schismatic perceptions of blame

As people had to cope on a daily basis with the effects of the economic crisis, they were susceptible to explanations that emanated via mass media, from the political and intellectual leaders of their republics. Separate, mutually exclusive perceptions led rapidly to a schism along regional and ethnic lines. Views emanating from the northwestern republics of Slovenia and Croatia, on one side, were counterpoised to those from the eastern and southern republics of Serbia and Montenegro, on the other. (The remaining two republics – Bosnia-Herzegovina and Macedonia – were relegated to the sidelines from that point until Yugoslavia broke apart, when those republics suffered the consequences of the schism which their leaders had attempted to avert.)

(1) Slovenes and Croats complained about development policies that channeled funds to the least developed regions, which they saw as brakes on their own advancement.[20] Thereby, the federal and Serbian capital, Belgrade, was identified as the source of Communist inefficiency, draining off the profits of the most prosperous regions to subsidize the low productivity of the least developed.[21] Increasingly, the Slovenian and Croatian publics viewed the rest of the country as a drag on their prosperity.

(2) In Serbia and Montenegro, the onus for Yugoslavian economic decline was placed upon the Communist leadership structure, which had entrenched so-called "chair warmers" (*"foteljaši"*) in all managerial positions through a tissue of patronage that rewarded loyalty (*"podobnost"*), while discouraging competence (*"sposobnost"*). Serbian politicians and media identified the leaders of the "northwestern republics" as responsible for this structure, to the detriment of the rest of Yugoslavia. Serbs and Montenegrins rallied behind the "anti-bureaucratic revolution," calling for the removal of the leadership as the remedy for economic failure.

Each interpretation defines a separate basis for opposition, in one case between regions, in the other, between the political "ins" and "outs" throughout Yugoslavia. Structural logic would permit two possible axes for schism within a system, defining divisions along either horizontal or vertical lines. The "anti-bureaucratic revolution" construed a vertical, hierarchical division between entrenched Communist political-managerial elites and the rest of society, while the secessionist visions of the northwest republics divided the country according to horizontal segments separating region from region. The lack of convergence between these separate images of societal division meant that there were no grounds for cross dialogue. The public communication of these formulations via party-controlled media in different regions of the country served as an opening wedge in the division of public opinion, particularly along the axis that counterposed a Slovenian-Croatian view against a Serbian-Montenegrin view.

In Slovenia and Croatia, the northwest/southeast opposition gave voice to a dense cultural and historical nexus of tradition and prejudice, and fanned resentment toward the ties that bound the "Western," "modern" and "European" republics to a country that was predominantly "eastern," "primitive," and "Balkan" (even "Byzantine") (cf. Bakić-Hayden and Hayden 1992). Such attitudes took on a sudden urgency in view of West European integration, particularly as the date was set at 1992 for the drawing of boundaries for the coming European Union. The Slovenian slogan "Europe Now!" (*"Evropa Zdaj!"*), revealed the Slovenes' attitude that Yugoslavia was not already in Europe, and that it was their last chance to "enter" Europe or be left behind, marginalized, with the rest of the Balkans and the less-developed world.

In Serbia and Montenegro, the media blamed instead the incompetence, patronage, and petty corruption that permeated the self-management of workplaces and local governments throughout Yugoslavia. The so-called "anti-bureaucratic revolution" presented Milošević as the leader of a reform movement that would replace the old guard – including the leaderships of the other republics – with a younger generation of technically competent and incorruptible managers who would restore the Yugoslav economy and its workforce to a viable position in the global economy.

Each of these interpretations had a corresponding counter-argument. In Serbia, media presentations emphasized the quasi-colonial arrangements whereby Slovenia imported raw materials from less-developed regions of Yugoslavia, which also served as the primary market for Slovenian manufactured products, while closing its markets to manufactured goods from Serbia. Serbs who had purchased Slovenian appliances in preference to products from Serbia reacted indignantly to the revelation that products from Serbia were actually excluded from the Slovenian market. Just as some customers in Serbia were willing to pay higher prices for Slovenian products, they reasoned, shouldn't residents of Slovenia have the choice of buying lower-priced products manufactured in Serbia?

On the other hand, Slovenes viewed Miloševic not as a reformer, but as an authoritarian who threatened to re-centralize the same single-party political structure that had failed, and which would subject them to a Yugoslavia in which Serbian interests would have more influence than their own. Both counter-arguments were valid, but neither was communicated to the other side by media that were committed to presenting a one-sided picture. The resulting systematically distorted communication[22] blocked the possibility of corrective cross-discussion. TV and print media in each republic presented only what they saw as the minus side on a balance sheet of inter-republic relations that actually had plusses and minuses on all sides.

From 1988 onward, open confrontations interwove economic conflicts with contentious issues that evoked ethnic oppositions and solidarities attached to history, culture and symbols with highly emotional associations. In the split images that led to schism in Yugoslavia, each side consistently presented itself as the victim of the Other, according to separate, conflicting definitions of the situation. Thereby, neither side responded to the Other's concerns, but only to its own projections of the Other. Along the lines of the communication pattern that Bateson (1972) named "schismogenesis," each reacted to the Other as a threat to its own interests, while its reactions reinforced the behavior that was perceived as threatening. In Bateson's cybernetic terminology, mutually "positive feedbacks" *exponentially* increased the split between opposing images, leading at an accelerating rate toward polarization and schism.

In the foreground of dissension was the province of Kosovo, which ethnic Albanians claimed as their national territory, in opposition to the ethnic Serbian minority there. The larger importance of Kosovo was the focus it provided for opposing visions of Yugoslavia, as articulated by Serbs, on one side, and Slovenes, on the other. While Serbs throughout Yugoslavia sympathized one-sidedly with their co-ethnics in Kosovo, Slovenes interpreted the situation there through the lens of their own experience, and took the Albanian side. In February 1989, the Serbian public was shocked when leading Slovene intellectuals and politicians met to express, one after the other, public support for

Albanian demands, and to denounce the Serbian side. While Milošević and other Serbian nationalists continued to use the Kosovo issue to incite Serbian nationalism, schismatic perceptions of the same issues simultaneously fueled the cause of Slovenian secession.

In November 1989, after a group of Albanians from Kosovo held a rally in Slovenia's capital, Serbs responded by organizing a pilgrimage to bring the "truth" about Kosovo to the Slovenian public. Milošević supporters scheduled special trains and buses to transport what promised to be multitudes of Serbs to stage the very sort of rally they had already held throughout Serbia, and which had antagonized and even frightened Slovenes viewing the TV coverage of those spectacles.

Rather than attempting to conciliate, Slovenian and Serbian leaders responded to each other's action with a stronger counter-action. First, the Slovenian government announced the closing of its border on the appointed day to travelers from Serbia, an assertion of the sovereignty they had recently declared in an amendment to their constitution. The Serbs canceled their "truth rally" and stayed home. However, the Serbian government declared a boycott of all economic relationships with Slovenia, and favorite Slovenian products disappeared from the grocery shelves and specialty shops in Serbia. Slovenia was sacrificing one of the largest markets for its products, yet neither side softened its stance. Slovenes prepared to do without their customers in Serbia, while Serbs changed their brand names. What started as a symbolic "invasion" by Serbs was swiftly transformed into a border closing that permanently severed the economic ties between the two republics. It was the opening wedge of Slovenia's secession.

From schismatic perception to civil war

Alternative nationalist ideologies could be resurrected from the past, both by those who had been excluded under Titoism and by those opportunistically wishing to retain elite positions. But the transformation of political conflict into civil war involved a vast dimension of social reality, beyond the confines of the institutions regularly associated with states and their political realms. It is necessary to bring another dimension into this analysis, to explain the transformation of debates among political elites into popular revitalization movements and military violence. Bourdieu suggests a conceptual bridge across the great divide between elite political discourse and populations at large, from which mass movements and armies are mobilized in the name of particular causes.

> The capacity ... of making public ... that which, not yet having attained objective and collective existence, remained in a state of individual or serial existence – *people's disquiet, anxiety, expectation, worry* – represents a formidable social power, that of bringing into existence groups by establishing ... the explicit consensus of the whole group.
>
> (Bourdieu 1991: 236; emphasis added)

Accordingly, as the economic crisis grew into a crisis of legitimacy for the state, there was a new interest in alternative statehood ideologies that could be resurrected from the past. Playing upon the disquiet and anxiety that had become endemic among Yugoslavia's disparate peoples, prominent intellectuals attached current economic grievances and discourses of blame to the ethnic nationalist ideologies that had been suppressed since World War II, but which now crept into the media of the various republics.

During the late 1980s, rival nationalist platforms were debated with increasing openness, but the Communist League still retained its monopoly over all public institutions in all republics. That situation changed abruptly after the general collapse of East European communism in the fall of 1989. For the first time, non- and anti-communist organizations appeared in public, and after the Communist League abruptly disbanded in January 1990, explicitly nationalist ethnic parties came to the fore with strength surprising to the Communists themselves. When the first multi-party election campaigns were held in Slovenia and Croatia during the spring of 1990, contenders (based on their previous political culture) expected the winning party to claim, as its "spoils" of victory, the resources and privileges controlled by Communist political machines. Since these entailed the most basic resources of personal survival, particularly jobs and housing, the question of how the state would be constituted, and in whose name, directly involved the well-being of every household. If their state was to be redefined, average citizens needed to redefine their way of accessing it and had reason to fear being "left out in the cold" in the prospective power allocation along ethnic lines. Those who had previously used personal ties to maneuver within the Communist system therefore looked for personal ties that would attach them to the new nationalist parties. The bonds of kinship and friendship – which had always been primary – were decoupled from the multiethnic socialist structures and re-attached to the new politics of ethnic identity. In the regions of mixed ethnicity in Croatia, and later in Bosnia-Herzegovina, neighbors, schoolmates, workmates, lifelong friends, and even members of intermarried families abruptly parted ways to join the campaign rallies of their own ethnic parties.

In Slovenia and Croatia, new parties called openly for secession from Yugoslavia, putting on the table the ethnic boundary disputes that were to prove so lethal. As militant nationalist parties dominated the election campaigns of 1990 in all republics, citizens who had not previously questioned the survival of Yugoslavia began to align themselves ethnically, eventually voting for parties espousing their "national" cause. It is necessary to emphasize that substantial portions of the electorates in all republics and from all ethnic backgrounds supported parties that were explicitly anti-nationalist, but were outvoted in the critical elections of 1990.

The new nationalist parties represented a continuum of viewpoints and leaders, ranging from renamed sections of the Communist League to another brand of leaders, who revived the ideologies of the defeated World War II nationalists, particularly the Croatian Ustashas and the Serbian Chetniks. Rather than limiting their criticism to the years under socialism, these extremist parties revived the "greater" Serbia/Croatia programs of territorial expansion and interpretations of history that reciprocally projected collective memories of grievances upon each other. Memories of ethnic victimization during World War II served as a template to justify calls for revenge that had been suppressed by the Yugoslav state. A panoply of previously banned flags, songs, insignia and uniforms provided a made-to-order "anti-hero" image, massively attracting the same young people who had found themselves "superfluous" during the years of economic crisis. The nationalist parties offered them a chance to overturn hierarchies and promised to open paths of opportunity for those who had been excluded, especially during the previous decade. During 1990, nationalist extremism spread like a new fashion among the young, who publicly flaunted its forbidden symbols. The first outbreaks of violence took the form of riots between the fan clubs of the major soccer teams of Serbia and Croatia. By then, the fan clubs were already a recruiting ground for nationalist parties and, soon afterward, many of the same young men who had sung nationalist songs at soccer games eagerly joined the paramilitary units sponsored by nationalist parties.[23]

The election of nationalist parties to government resulted in the rewriting of constitutions in the republics to emphasize the privileged status of the dominant ethnic "nation," while relegating others to the lesser status of "minorities." Finding oneself in a minority position led immediately to negative consequences, justifying the fears of exclusion that had already motivated people to support their own ethnic leaders. In both Croatia and Bosnia-Herzegovina, an initial non-violent form of ethnic "cleansing" was committed when the victorious nationalist parties on all sides provided employment for their supporters in territory they controlled by dismissing workers of the "wrong" ethnicity from their jobs.[24] Winning parties used their legislative majorities in the same manner that the Communists had used their monopoly, disregarding the opposition parties representing other ethnic populations. For example, one Serbian official in Bosnia was quoted as explaining, after the Muslim party had won the local elections, "In the 1990–92 period, nothing proposed by Serbs could pass in the town council" (Cohen 1994: 8).

The simultaneous secessions of Slovenia and Croatia, in June 1991, initiated the dismantling of the Yugoslav state. The swift transition from the constrained forums of political argumentation to warfare took the form of young men in battle camouflages, attacking the opponents defined by their respective nationalist movements. For Slovenes, that was the Yugoslav People's Army, representing the republics that still remained in Yugoslavia. But in Croatia, as later in Bosnia-Herzegovina, the territorial ambitions of ethnic statehood meant that the military forces on all sides attacked each other and brutally routed each other's co-ethnics from territories each claimed for their own national states.[25]

The remarks of a former Bosnian Serb camp guard (who later testified about atrocities against Muslims) provided some insight into the outlook of the members of armed units that committed the acts for which the new term "ethnic cleansing" was coined: "Economic stagnation fueled the rise of the nationalist parties because so many people of 25 had never had a job. The Muslim nationalists and the Serbs offered these people 100 marks and could do what they liked with them. You could feel the war coming." The conflict also attracted young fighters from both Serbia and Croatia to the sides of their co-ethnics in Bosnia and Herzegovina. The former camp guard described the influx of "gangsters and criminals from Serbia, and others who saw a chance to make money. With a mass of unemployed people under 25, you can do what you like. These people were longing for action and a chance to loot Muslims" (Cohen 1994: 8).

Concluding comment

Yugoslavia's "disjunctive moment" was contingent upon two global historical occurrences: (1) the 1973 "oil crisis" and the subsequent transfusion of capital to developing countries, followed by the 1980's "debt crisis"; and (2) the collapse of East European communism in the fall of 1989, combined with the formation of the European Union, scheduled for 1992. These external parameters emphasized the marginality of Yugoslavia to both the global economy and the political institutions of Europe. As the public at large followed dramatic events over television and print media, the anomalies of their own experiences were revealed to be a societal condition, opening the door to ethnic nationalist challenges to the socialist system that was perceived as failing. Redefining each republic as an ethnic national state meant establishing new categories of privilege for some, while threatening others with exclusion and marginalization.

Yugoslavs at all social levels perceived the state as the source of all significant power and large-scale economic resources. Although Yugoslav socialism permitted a substantial private sector, consisting of small family farms and businesses, the major avenues for economic and social success were located in socialist industries and institutions. In its diversified and ubiquitous manifestations, the public sector was controlled by leaderships attached at various levels to the Communist party structure, which maintained its monopoly over the state by controlling all the legal, political and economic institutions. Party-run organizations allocated such basic necessities as employment and housing. Therefore, the state was far from an abstraction in the practical lives of most people, but was embodied in specific human beings to whom they had personal access through networks of kinship, friendship and patronage. The fact that a revolution had overturned the social order within recent memory, during World War II, was a constant reminder that it was possible for an elite to lose control over the state and for others to lose their previous channels of access. However, that was an exciting prospect for those who had been "superfluous" to the Communist order but who saw the opportunity to benefit from a new allocation of power along ethnic lines. Rather than learning from the previous history to avoid repeating the ethnic horrors that had occurred as recently as World War II, the leaders of ethnic national movements instead directed them over exactly the same ideological terrain.

As Benedict Anderson (1983) has located the formation of nation-states within the context of "imaginings" that have specific social boundaries within particular time frames, it would follow that the dismantling of a state would also occur within the same kinds of communicative spaces, in which public information media are the key to reformulations of perception and identity. This interpretation has demonstrated how – even between ethnic populations having no previous history of violence – a schismatic pattern of communication led rapidly to mutual antagonisms, incited and encouraged by leaders who understood violence as their instrument for gaining power.

Acknowledgements

This chapter is based on field research in Yugoslavia between 1987 and 1990, supported by grants from the Wenner-Gren Foundation for Anthropological Research and the International Research Exchanges Board (IREX). Analysis and writing were supported, in part, by a postdoctoral fellowship from the Social Science Research Council and the American Council of Learned Societies, and by a research contract with the National Council for Soviet and East European Research. I am very grateful to each of these institutions and to all the individuals who have participated in supporting this work.

Notes

1 The republics (from West to East) were: Slovenia, Croatia, Bosnia-Herzegovina, Serbia, Montenegro, and Macedonia. Except for Bosnia-Herzegovina, each was named for its dominant ethnic "nation," but all except Slovenia included large populations not of the dominant ethnicity. In addition to the six republics, the 1974 constitution granted equivalent status to the two "autonomous provinces" within Serbia (Vojvodina and Kosovo). The anomalies involved with the autonomous provinces became a major point of contention in the inter-republic conflicts that emerged in 1988.
2 Works on the philosophical traditions of European nation-statehood include Dumont 1986; Greenfeld 1992; Hobsbawm 1990. There is copious literature on nationalism among the peoples of Yugoslavia: for comprehensive presentations from opposing viewpoints, see Banac 1984; Djilas 1991.
3 For an interpretation of the conjunction between nationalist ideologies, historical memory, and the incitement of interethnic violence in Croatia, see Denich 1994a.
4 Rubenstein invokes the term "superfluous" in a more demographically-oriented global view. It is noteworthy that Rubenstein traces the concept to Hegel, in his observations about the dialectical relationship between increasing productive efficiency and superfluous labor, and the destabilizing potential of the ensuing "rabble of paupers" (Rubenstein 1983: 4).
5 See Denich 2000 for a discussion of schismogenesis in the re-emergence of ethnic identities in Yugoslavia.
6 According to economist Laura D'Andrea Tyson:

> After 1973–74, the oil-exporting countries began to provide substantial savings to be recycled by the commercial banks. ... Most of the newly industrializing countries (NICs) and most of the East European countries took advantage of the improved credit-market conditions by building up their international indebtedness.
>
> (Tyson 1986: 65)

7 According to Shoup:

> the adoption of the self-management system in Yugoslavia between 1971 and 1975 was nothing less than a cultural revolution, imposing a vast bureaucratic structure of self-management boards, interest communities and the like on Yugoslav society. ... [T]he republics were given broad powers in the 1974 constitution, laying the groundwork for today's regionally fragmented economy and administration.
>
> (Shoup 1989: 131)

8 For differing views of the Yugoslav political structure after the 1974 constitution, see Burg 1983; Golubović 1988; Ramet 1984; Rusinow 1988; Zimmerman 1987.
9 These policies comprised a "shock therapy" package of reforms, under IMF encouragement and the advice of Harvard economist Jeffrey Sacks, subsequently acclaimed as an architect of market innovations in Poland and Russia.
10 Sources on the 1980s economic crisis include: Horvat 1984; Martin and Tyson 1985; Nikolić 1989; Pjanić 1987; Shoup 1989; Tanasić 1988; Tyson 1986; Woodward 1995.
11 It is important to emphasize that Yugoslavia's private sector included most of its agriculture, as well as a substantial portion of crafts, restaurants, and guesthouses. The size of these enterprises was strictly curtailed by limits on hectares of land and number of employees. The nature of private enterprises was also limited to those in which proprietors were directly producing services or products. Over time, restrictions were gradually liberalized, but the basic public/private distinction remained through the end of Titoism.
12 For a comprehensive discussion of these practices throughout Eastern Europe, see Sampson 1986. Wedel (1986, 1992) presents an analogous view of Poland during and after Communism. Milić (1991) analyzes family networks as the basis of informal relations in Serbia. For a journalistic account of "survival" under communism, including Yugoslavia among East European countries, see Drakulić 1991.
13 American anthropologists were particularly active in observing these processes (e.g., Denich 1974; Halpern and Halpern 1972; Hammel 1969; Simic 1972).
14 One indicator of defection from the political system is the decline of interest among young people in joining the Communist League. In 1974, 9 per cent of those surveyed throughout Yugoslavia stated that they did *not* wish to join the League; by 1986, that figure had risen to 50 per cent, where it still hovered (at 51 per cent) in 1989. Regional disparities were marked, with 92 per cent of Slovenian young people rejecting the Party member at one extreme, with Montenegro at the other end, with only 34 per cent rejection (cited from Cohen 1993: 48).
15 Abdic was tried in a show trial lasting over a year on charges of which he was eventually found not guilty. In the first post-Communist elections, he was elected to the collective presidency of Bosnia-Herzegovina, receiving the largest number of popular votes. During the civil war, although a Muslim, he broke from the Muslim-dominated government centered in Sarajevo, and declared autonomy for his small Muslim-inhabited region. Subsequently, his supporters formed their own army, which fought against the Bosnian government army.
16 The word "taboo" as in *tabu teme* (taboo themes) was used in Serbo-Croatian to denote the numerous topics that could not be publicly discussed under Titoism.
17 I reviewed the following weekly news magazines, collected during my visit during that time: *Danas* from Zagreb and *NIN*, *Ilustrovana Politika* and *Duga* from Belgrade.
18 Sekelj notes that:

> Slobodan Miloševic and his patronage group ... legitimized themselves as people of change and irreconcilable advocates of political and economic reform. At the notorious Eighth Session of the Serbian Communist League central committee

(1987) ... Milošević announced the program of economic reforms. Its substance was autonomy of enterprises, responsibility and independence of management, and therefore professional instead of political criteria in selecting it.

(Sekelj 1993: 164)

19 According to Sekelj:

> The way national communist oligarchies transformed themselves to national political elites took different forms in Serbia and Slovenia, but with the same content and outcome: national homogenization through the replacement of Bolshevik collectivism by a nationalist one [sic]. ... Under the new pattern, first Slovenian and then Serbian communist leaderships appealed to their own national public [sic] seeking support and participation in national politics, thus creating a politically active population for the first time in Yugoslavia's postwar history.
>
> (Sekelj 1993: 208–211)

20 For an analysis of the federal aid to less developed regions, see Bombelles 1991.
21 While redistribution did result in considerable development in the poorer regions, their relative position actually declined in relation to the most developed regions during the post-World War II decades (see Cohen 1993: 34–35). Poorly conceived policies contributed to this effect, particularly the funneling of investment into capital-intensive and extractive industries, rather than labor-intensive ones that would alleviate unemployment (Ramet 1985: 8). Development funds were typically squandered in industrial projects based on "political" rather than economic criteria. The lack of inter-republic coordination resulted in duplication of facilities, without regard for the eventual marketing of products.
22 Such a pattern resembles what Jurgen Habermas calls "systematically distorted communication," the opposite of "communicative rationality" in which parties strive to reach mutual understanding. For a succinct explication of Habermas's communication theory, see Pusey 1987: 69–86.
23 For an excellent summary of military and paramilitary forces in Slovenia and Croatia, see Gow 1992. This article includes a table showing the relationship between specific Croatian and Serbian parties and leaders and the armed units that they controlled. Glenny (1992) presents vivid accounts of the activities of these various forces, in addition to those fighting in Bosnia-Herzegovina.
24 Instances of ethnic job dismissals were widely reported. A convenient source is Glenny 1992: 77 (on Croatia), 152 (on Bosnia-Herzegovina).
25 I have elsewhere analyzed the rush to war from a feminist perspective (see Denich 1994b).

References

Anderson, Benedict (1983) *Imagined Communities*. London: Verso.
Apter, David (1987) *The New Mytho-logics and the Specter of Superfluous Man*. Newbury Park, CA: Sage.
Bakić-Hayden, Milica and Robert M. Hayden (1992) "Orientalist Variations on the Theme 'Balkans': Symbolic Geography in Recent Yugoslav Cultural Politics." *Slavic Review* 51: 1–15.
Banac, Ivo (1984) *The National Question in Yugoslavia*. Ithaca: Cornell University Press.
—— (1990) "Political Change and National Diversity." *Daedalus* 119: 141–161.
Bateson, Gregory (1972) "Culture Contact and Schismogenesis." In *Steps to an Ecology of Mind*. New York: Ballantine, pp. 61–72.
Bombelles, Joseph T. (1991) "Federal Aid to the Less Developed Areas of Yugoslavia." *East European Politics and Societies* 5: 439–465.

Bourdieu, Pierre (1991) "Social Space and the Genesis of Classes." In *Language and Symbolic Power*. Cambridge: Harvard University Press.
Burg, Steven L. (1983) *Conflict and Cohesion in Socialist Yugoslavia: Political Decision Making since 1966*. Princeton: Princeton University Press.
Cohen, Lenard (1993) *Broken Bonds: The Disintegration of Yugoslavia*. Boulder: Westview Press.
Cohen, Roger (1994) "Ex-Guard for Serbs Tells of 'Cleansing' of Bosnian Muslims." *New York Times* 1 August, p. 8.
Denich, Bette (1974)"Why Do Peasants Urbanize? A Yugoslav Case Study." In A.L. LaRuffa, Ruth S. Freed, Lucie W. Saunders, Edward C. Hansen and Sula Benet (eds), *City and Peasant: A Study in Socio-Cultural Dynamics*: 546–59. New York: New York Academy of Sciences.
—— (1994a) "Dismembering Yugoslavia: Nationalist Ideologies and the Symbolic Revival of Genocide." *American Ethnologist* 21: 367–390.
—— (1994b) "Of Arms, Men, and Ethnic War in Former Yugoslavia." In Constance Sutton (ed.), *Feminism, Nationalism, and Militarism*. American Anthropological Association.
—— (2000) "Unmaking Multiethnicity in Yugoslavia: Media and Metamorphosis." In Joel Halpern and David A. Kideckel (eds), *Neighbors at War: Anthropological Perspectives on Yugoslav Ethnicity, Culture, and History*. University Park: Pennsylvania State University Press.
Djilas, Aleksa (1991) *The Contested Country: Yugoslav Unity and Communist Revolution, 1919–1953*. Cambridge: Harvard University Press.
Drakulić, Slavenka (1991) *How We Survived Communism and Even Laughed*. New York: Norton.
Dumont, Louis (1986) *Essays on Individualism*. Chicago: University of Chicago Press.
Glenny, Misha (1992) *The Fall of Yugoslavia*. London: Penguin.
Goati, Vladimir (1989) "Slatki Život Privilegovanih" (The Sweet Life of the Privileged), No. 6 in series *Ko Drži Vlast u Jugoslovenskom Društvu* (Who Holds Power in Yugoslav Society). *Osmica* 7 December, p. 11.
Goffman, Erving (1959) *The Presentation of Self in Everyday Life*. Garden City: Doubleday Anchor.
Golubović, Zagorka (1988) *Kriza Identiteta Jugoslovenskog Društva* (The Identity Crisis of Yugoslav Society). Belgrade: Filip Visnjic.
Gow, James (1992) "Military–Political Affiliations in the Yugoslav Conflict." *RFE/RL Reports* 1(20): 16–25.
Greenfeld, Liah (1992) *Nationalism: Five Roads to Modernity*. Cambridge: Harvard University Press.
Halpern, Joel M. and Barbara K. Halpern (1972) *A Serbian Village in Historical Perspective*. New York: Holt, Rinehart and Winston.
Hammel, E.A. (1969) "Economic Change, Social Mobility, and Kinship in Serbia." *Southwest Journal of Anthropology* 25: 188–197.
Hobsbawm, E.J. (1990) *Nations and Nationalism Since 1780*. Cambridge: Cambridge University Press.
Horvat, Branko (1984) *Jugoslavenska Privreda 1965–1983* (the Yugoslav Economy 1965–1983). Zagreb: Cankareva Založba.
Martin, Chris and Laura D'Andrea Tyson (1985) "Can Titoism Survive Tito? Economic Problems and Policy Choices Confronting Tito's Successors." In P. Ramet (ed.), *Yugoslavia in the 1980s*. Boulder: Westview Press, pp. 184–200.
Milić, Andjelka (1991) "Socijalna Mreža Porodićnih Odnosa i Društveni Slojevi" (The Social Network of Family Relations and Social Strata). In Mihailo Popović (ed.), *Srbija*

Krajem Osamdesetih (Serbia at the End of the 1980s). Belgrade: Institute for Sociological Research.

Nikolić, Milan (1989) "Yugoslavia's Failed Perestroika." *Telos* 79: 119–128.

Pjanić, Zoran (1987) *Anatomija Krize* (Anatomy of Crisis). Belgrade: Ekonomika.

Pusey, Michael (1987) *Jurgen Habermas*. London: Tavistock.

Ramet, Pedro (1984) *Nationalism and Federalism in Yugoslavia, 1963–1983*. Bloomington: Indiana University Press.

—— (1985) "Apocalypse Culture and Social Change in Yugoslavia." In P. Ramet (ed.), *Yugoslavia in the 1980s*. Boulder: Westview Press.

Rubenstein, Richard L. (1983) *The Age of Triage*. Boston: Beacon.

Rusinow, Dennison (ed.) (1988) *Yugoslavia: A Fractured Federalism*. Washington, DC: Wilson Center Press.

Sampson, Steven (1986) "The Informal Sector in Eastern Europe." *Telos* 66: 44–65.

Scott, James C. (1990) *Domination and the Arts of Resistance: Hidden Transcripts*. New Haven: Yale University Press.

Sekelj, Laslo (1993) *Yugoslavia: The Process of Disintegration*. Boulder: Social Science Monographs (distributed by Columbia University Press).

Shoup, Paul (1989) "Crisis and Reform in Yugoslavia." *Telos* 79: 129–147.

Silber, Laura and Allan Little (1997) *Yugoslavia: Death of a Nation*. New York: Penguin.

Simic, Andrei (1972) *The Peasant Urbanites: A Study of Rural–Urban Mobility in Serbia*. New York: Seminar Press.

Tanasić, Dragan (1988) *Smišljene Besmislice* (Planned Nonsense). Belgrade: Sociological Society of Serbia.

Tyson, Laura D'Andrea (1986) "Debt Crisis and Adjustment Responses." In Ellen Comisso and Laura D. Tyson (eds), *Economic Strategy in Socialist States*. Ithaca: Cornell University Press.

Verdery, Katherine (1993) "Whither 'Nation' and 'Nationalism'?" *Daedalus* 122(3): 37–46.

Wedel, Janine (1986) *The Private Poland*. New York: Facts on File.

—— (1992) *The Unplanned Society. Poland During and After Communism*. New York: Columbia University Press.

Woodward, Susan (1995) *Balkan Tragedy: Chaos and Dissolution after the Cold War*. Washington, DC: The Brookings Institution.

Zimmerman, William (1987) *Open Borders, Nonalignment, and the Political Evolution of Yugoslavia*. Princeton: Princeton University Press.

9 From the margins to the center

The Macedonian controversy in contemporary Greece

Anastasia Karakasidou

In the last decade of the twentieth century, war, national fanaticism, civil unrest, ethnic cleansing, economic embargo, and peacekeeping troops became the icons of everyday life in the Balkans. The 1980s were a period of intense debate and political maneuvering in the disintegrating federation of Yugoslavia. While nationalist voices in the northern republics of Croatia and Slovenia demanded economic reforms and a looser administrative confederation (if not independence), those in Serbia insisted on a continuing centralized federation. It was in 1989 that Slobodan Milosevic made his famous pledge to the Serbs of Kosovo, promising to be their protector and the defender of their rights. Over the next few years, a strong discourse concerning "brothers in danger" developed in Serbia (and elsewhere in the Balkans). Open aggression and armed conflict soon followed in its wake.

In the Krajina region of Croatia, sporadic violence between Croats and Serbs erupted in 1990, and by March 1991 the conflict had escalated to widespread clashes between demonstrators, police and paramilitary groups. In June of that year, Croatia and Slovenia declared independence from Yugoslavia, and Belgrade mobilized the Yugoslav National Army. During the summer and fall of 1991, there was widespread apprehension that conflict and violence might spread to Bosnia-Herzegovina, to Kosovo, and perhaps even to Macedonia.

In September, the Yugoslav Republic of Macedonia followed the lead of Slovenia and Croatia in declaring its secession from Yugoslavia and its establishment of an independent nation-state. This action was resisted by a campaign waged on ideological, political and economic fronts. The fact that no single ethnic group was large enough to constitute an absolute majority in Macedonia led many observers to fear that this land-locked region, with a history of violent strife, was headed for trouble. A substantial ethnic Albanian population (constituting nearly one-quarter of the total population) inhabited the western and northern parts of the republic. Given this internal national demography, there was considerable local and international concern that Macedonia would become the next chapter in the most recent series of Balkan tragedies. United Nations peacekeeping forces were dispatched to Macedonia in 1992 to monitor its borders with Albania, Kosovo and Serbia. Of particular concern were the claims, emanating from Belgrade, that thousands of Serbs living in Macedonia were in danger, fearing the spread of open hostilities.

Bosnia was in flames in the spring of 1992, and sensationalist reporting of ethnic cleansing filled journalistic accounts and scholarly analyses of regional events. The 1995 Dayton Accord created a rather fragile multi-ethnic political entity in Bosnia. But smoldering animosities erupted in violent conflict a few years later in Kosovo. The NATO bombings of Serbia and Kosovo in 1999 attempted to put an end to violence in the region, but recent reporting suggests that the conflicts are far from resolved, either in Kosovo or in Macedonia.

Violence is no stranger to the Balkans. Their history has shown how defensive patriots and aggressive liberators have engaged in seemingly endless conflicts and strife since the early nineteenth century. One would be hard pressed to deny that many Europeans look upon the Balkan states as pretenders to the throne of "Europeanness," as rush upstarts who are somehow not yet qualified to bear the mantle of "civilization." The Balkans are often viewed as a "corner" of Europe, populated by "pockets" of ethno-national zealots bent on annihilating one another. But most problems in the Balkans today are inherently European problems. Much like in Africa, European diplomacy drew maps and set boundaries, carving out "national" territories and erecting artificial barriers to once largely heterogeneous patterns of interaction.

The strife that still haunts the present-day Balkans is largely a product of what we generally refer to as "nation building processes." Today, through our news and academic discussions, we are inundated with talk of "ethno-national genesis," "nationalisms," and "national ideologies." The vague way in which many of these concepts are often discussed cloaks them in a veil of mysticism. We hear frequent talk of deep-seated historical consciousness of national grievances. Serbs and Croats, Greeks and Bulgarians, Christians and Muslims, Turks and everyone: public discourse is peppered with claims about national heritage, rightful territories, and foreign oppression. But, the Cold War and the Iron Curtain may have made it easy to forget the critical importance of the Balkans as an overland route between Europe and Asia. Even in the age of air and sea freight, overland transport still constitutes the principal form of shipping. Tito's Yugoslavia was, generally speaking, an accessible country for international transit, as anyone who witnessed the long lines of trucks and tourists passing through en route to Greece can testify.

The wars in Yugoslavia have helped elevate the Macedonian issue to an emotional topic of public discussion in Greece. Until recently, Macedonia was largely a topic of conversations about art and archaeology. It was a place known for the splendor of its glorious ancient rulers, rather than being seen as the site of no less than six wars in this past century alone. But during the closing decade of the twentieth century, an international dispute rooted in nineteenth-century nation-building contests over Macedonia festered like a smoldering volcano, threatening to erupt once again. For those familiar with national developments and popular culture in Greece, the term "Macedonia" again came to lie at the forefront of an emotional and sometimes volatile debate over history, national pride and international politics. The very name, "Macedonia," became a highly contested metonym for competitive nation-building campaigns in the region, and the focal point of recurrent crisis. Macedonia became a rambunctious issue of international politics that drew millions to protest rallies in Greece and abroad, provoked confrontations between demonstrators and counter-demonstrators, and prompted heated, emotionally charged debates on issues of historical interpretation, government policy, civic responsibility, and academic freedom. Given the history of the region, many in Greece were understandably concerned.

The Socialist Republic of Macedonia was one of Yugoslavia's five republics, and traces its political existence to 1944, when it was established in the southernmost part of Yugoslavia. Following an intense but brief crisis during the Greek Civil War of 1947–49 (see below), when communist leaders in the region spoke about creating an independent Macedonian state for the Macedonian Slavs at the expense of Greece, the issue passed into relative obscurity. The idea received renewed public attention in September 1991, when the Yugoslav Republic of Macedonia voted by popular referendum to secede from Yugoslavia, and national leaders there declared the establishment of the independent "Republic of Macedonia."

Greece took strong exception to the move, describing it as threatening and destabilizing. A new nation-state on Greece's northern border had been created: a foreign country that had not only adopted the same name as Greece's northernmost region (Macedonia), but also claimed to have a national minority living in conditions of forced assimilation within that part of Greece. The material issues involved were, I believe, ones of territorial integrity and national sovereignty over a rich grain-producing area and an important intercontinental trade corridor. Ideologically, however, the conflict was expressed in the rhetoric of rightful claims to an ancestral land of Greece's national heritage. Alexander the Great, in fact, soon became the mythical national ancestor of all present-day Greeks, and former Prime Minister Konstantinos Mitsotakis declared proudly that "all Greeks ... are Macedonians."

Actually, in Greece itself, there had been a small but ongoing scholarly debate over the relative Greekness of Alexander and of the Macedonian culture of his time. In the 1990s, while some intellectuals in Greece spoke up about such issues, few could challenge the growing national dogma that emerged over Macedonia and its history, both ancient and modern. Greece has taken quite a different route than its northern socialist and communist neighbors, having been a founding member of NATO, and a recent member of the European Union. But for decades Greece remained a country rather divided between opposing political patrons and their party-based interest groups. It is a highly bureaucratized society that in the early 1990s was in the midst of a transition to full membership of the European Community. Hence, the Macedonian issue emerged as nothing short of a movement for national revitalization, providing "all Greeks" – in the words of the former Prime Minister – with a common sense of identity and solidarity.

Many Greeks, both at home and abroad, argued that the neighboring state to the north could not adopt the name "Macedonia" because Macedonia "was, is, and always will be Greek." In fact, there was a florist on Manhattan's Upper West Side handing out free bumper stickers that proudly advertised such claims. Highly indignant that Slavs would appropriate for themselves a name tied so closely to Ancient Greek history, many denied the existence of Slavic-speakers in Greek Macedonia. Greek scholars recognized the existence of such a group, but claimed that they had always had a Greek national consciousness – a consciousness of their Greek heritage and an emotional bond to the Greek nation. Such were the "national truths" that most Greeks came to hold as being self-evident.

The authorities in "Skopia" as Greeks commonly refer to the Former Yugoslav Republic of Macedonia, have since officially renounced any territorial claims against Greece. But other actions and developments across the border left most Greeks skeptical and worried. Maps and T-shirts, for example, have been printed there – albeit unofficially – depicting a "greater Macedonia" that encompasses Northern Greece and the port of Thessaloniki, Greece's second largest city and a principal port of the Balkans. There was novelty currency sold in shops, adorned with the image of the "White Tower," a prominent landmark in Thessaloniki. And the national flag adopted by the new republic depicted a red field emblazoned with the sixteen-rayed golden "Star of Vergina," an image discovered by Greek archaeologists in a tomb believed to be that of Philip II, father of Alexander the Great, at Vergina, a small town west of Thessaloniki.

The national angst created by such events prompted even a hit by Yiorgos Dalaras, a popular singer in contemporary Greece:

> 3,000 years gone
> 3,000 years forgotten
> Come! Vergina! Thessaloniki!
> Which belonged to Alexander the Great
> A dusty history
> A wounded Macedonia
> Slowly dying from mistakes
>
> Beautiful Macedonia
> Of whom all are jealous
> Even the unworthy want to acquire you
> Where are you Alexander?
> To see your lordly possession
> And to hear all the wise say
> That it is no longer yours.

On 9 February 1992, the *New York Times* reported that the USA was prepared to follow the lead of several European allies in according full diplomatic recognition to the "Former Yugoslav Republic of Macedonia" (or FYROM), a move that Greece had hitherto successfully blocked. In response, the then-newly-elected socialist government in Greece announced that it was considering closing its borders with the northern neighbor, threatening an economic blockade of the emergent nation-state.

International recognition of the FYROM was regarded as a diplomatic defeat to many Greeks, a bitter pill to swallow for citizens with a wounded national pride. The rhetoric in the debate over Macedonia came to be called the "Battle for the Name." For decades, Greeks have been taught that Macedonia is a proud and inalienable cradle of Greek civilization. Alexander the Great was Greek, we are all taught; his teacher, Aristotle, was the most renowned of the Greek philosophers. Archaeology has brought to light Greek inscriptions dating from the time and place of Alexander's rule, providing what many Greeks consider to be "conclusive evidence" of the indisputable "Greekness" of this venerable ancestor of the Greek nation. As for the Slavs who migrated down through the Balkan Peninsula in the sixth and seventh centuries, Greek national historians told us that they had been assimilated into the Greek way of life, and had effectively vanished from the southern tip of the Balkans.

Ethnographic fieldwork, however, has revealed quite different ethnoscapes in contemporary Macedonia. My research on the subject has shown how ethnic imagery was suppressed under the shadow of national ideology. In the late 1980s, and before the controversy emerged, I began ethnographic and historical research in Assiros, a rural township in Central Greek Macedonia, less than an hour by car from Thessaloniki. Initially, following the "common knowledge," I wanted to explore how a shared culture of co-existence had been constructed between local Greek families and those of refugee Greek nationals who had been "repatriated" from East Thrace and Asia Minor following the Greco-Turkish war of 1922. I sought to examine how a diverse aggregate of Greek Orthodox Christians, speaking different languages, practicing different customs, shaped by different historical circumstances, and displaying what might be characterized as different ethnic identities, have come to share a common Greek national identity over the last sixty-odd years.

In the course of my interviews and archival research, however, I discovered that the issue was considerably more complex, and that the history of the region had been significantly different from that portrayed by national historians in Greece. All evidence suggested that prior to the region's incorporation into the Greek nation-state in 1913, a diverse ethnic tapestry had characterized Ottoman Macedonia. Occupational specialization and divisions of labor, to a surprising degree, followed along ethnic lines, while patterns of social exchange, both commercial and ritual, tended to cut across those lines. In Assiros, for example, many elderly respondents recalled how the region had been populated largely by Turkish-speaking land owners, share-croppers and administrators, Slavic-speaking share-croppers and herders, Greek-speaking merchants and traders, Ladino-speaking Jewish merchants and shop-owners, Vlach-speaking pastoralists, as well as Armenians, Roma, and other groups. Virtually everyone spoke Turkish, but by the mid-eighteenth century, Greek had become the language of the market place, and of commerce and exchange: the language of the nascent bourgeoisie on its way to national liberation and independent statehood (Karakasidou 1997).

Greek influence had become dominant by the late nineteenth century – mainly because of trade, religion, education, and the presence of settlers from the Greek kingdom to the south (established in 1829). In other parts of Greek Macedonia that were not located across major trade routes (as Assiros was), the process of Hellenization did not really take hold until half a century later, and it then followed a significantly different path. In the western part of Greek Macedonia, for example, Slavic dialects are still spoken in the countryside, though rarely in the presence of native Greek-speakers. Although by the late twentieth century the vast majority of the population of Greek Macedonia – Slavic-speaking or not – have come to identify themselves nationally with the Greek state, many Slavic-speakers and descendants of Slavic-speakers continue to share a sense of a "distinctiveness" that somehow sets them apart from other Greeks. It was to this group that the Macedonian nationalism from across the border was especially appealing.

The last decade of the twentieth century, however, was characterized by an atmosphere of fervent Greek nationalism, which effectively delegitimized expressions of cultural distinctiveness (Karakasidou 1993). Nevertheless, many Slavs in Western Greek Macedonia still narrate and perform their ethnicity, some more openly than others, and some performances more subversive than others. When discussing their "difference," such people are deliberately vocal about their political loyalties to the Greek State. In a line of reasoning that might be familiar to those acquainted with "segmentary lineage organization" theory, they maintain that Greece should pay more attention to the common enemy these two groups share, namely "Turkey." That's where the danger comes from, they argue, and this should be the link, the brotherhood, the binding force between Slavs and Greeks. They evoke notions of a former shared existence under Ottoman bondage, and the memory of past "enslavement" is reinstated in an effort to minimize the subversiveness of their expressions of cultural distinctiveness. The atmosphere of intolerance that dominated academic, media and political circles in 1990s Greece led to the politicization of any notion of ethnic identity and distinctiveness that Slavs in Greek Macedonia may have possessed.

My past research has not endeared me to those Greek compatriots who preferred to believe that Macedonia has been "purely Greek" since time immemorial. While it is true that, by the close of the twentieth century, Greek Macedonia had become indisputably Greek, nevertheless, I find that questions concerning historical processes, and how this state of affairs came to pass, how ethnic identities have been transformed, how national consciousness has been inculcated, how national ideology has been constructed, and how its hegemony has been cultivated among the general population, are more intriguing issues. Over the past ten years I have come to believe that the best hope we have for defusing nationalist-inspired animosity and aggression lies in defrocking national ideologies of their tautological assumptions: to peer behind the veils of mysticism constructed around notions of "the nation" (*to ethnos*) and reveal the hidden face of nationalism. In many ways, my professional work has guided my own personal journey beyond the shadows of nationalist historiography, as I have come to question many of the categories and assumptions with which I myself, as a Greek, had been enculturated and socialized.

I can recall now, as a child in 1960s Greece, I would wait expectantly for the national holidays each year. My elementary school classmates and I would dress in blue skirts and white blouses (the colors of the Greek flag), our hair pulled back with blue and white hairbands (loose hair and bangs were prohibited). Our rituals of nationhood included a public parade, in which many of us found a certain personal thrill and pride. The best male student in the class had the privilege of carrying the national flag (*simeoforos*), while the five next-ranked students, male and female, made up an honor guard to the sides and rear of the standard bearer. It was a great distinction to be chosen as a member of this prominent delegation of *parastates*, or those next-to-the-flag, and I can still recall how we would compete fiercely for the honor.

A large wreath would be delivered to our school, and we would make a modest pilgrimage to one of many city monuments dedicated to national heroes: perhaps a dead king, a leader of the 1821 Greek War of Independence, or a prominent "fighter" from the turn-of-the-century Macedonian Struggle against the Bulgarians. After commemorating our hero or martyr, we would join other school groups, along with troops and tanks, in a grand parade along Tsimiski Street or Egnatia Steet, two major thoroughfares in downtown Thessaloniki.

Greek national flags flew from every home on such days. It was an offense, punishable by a fine, not to display the flag on national holidays. The parade avenues were quite long, and always lined with crowds of spectators, many of whom also waved Greek flags, especially the young children. Cheers, yells and applause would erupt sporadically but frequently, as bystanders acknowledged family members, relatives and friends in the procession. It was difficult not to feel moved or even elated.

On the preceding day, in school, we were invariably treated to a day of special programs. One teacher would always give a *panighirikos*, or festive speech, followed by a series of theatrical sketches produced by the students themselves. These portrayed the suffering of the Greeks under their perennial enemies, such as the Turks, or the Bulgarians, or the injustices of the German occupation, or the evils of communism (a particularly favorite theme during the military junta (1967–74) of my teenage years). Sometimes we would dress as women from Ancient Greece, or as women warriors of the 1821 War of Independence, or as peasant mothers. The point was that we were play-acting carefully scripted, heroic yet often tragic roles that conveyed the common suffering endured by members of the Greek nation at the hands of foreign oppressors.

Those children too young to act in such school productions would recite poems, and then we would all join in singing patriotic songs. There was one tune in particular, to which lyrics were subsequently added in the 1920s, shortly after Greece's borders were extended to include the southern half of the Macedonian region:

> Renowned Macedonia,
> The Country of Alexander,
> Who has expelled the Barbarians,
> And now you are free.

> You are and you will be Greek,
> The pride of Greeks,
> And we, the Greek children
> We weave you a wreath.

Some thirty years later in the 1990s, this song was still popular in Greece. In 1995, I saw soldiers marching down the streets of Florina to this tune, singing in step, on their way to lower the town flag. The scene provoked dismay in some bystanders. "This is not a marching song," objected an elderly local folklorist, who also witnessed the sight. Macedonia was once again at the forefront of popular consciousness and national concern. As the "Battle for the Name" began to heat up, the word "Macedonia" began appearing in many places, both public and private. The Ministry of Northern Greece changed its name to the Ministry of Macedonia and Thrace; radio and television stations bearing the name "Macedonia" were set up in Northern Greece; the port of Thessaloniki was renamed the Port of Macedonia, and likewise the city's airport. There is now a taxi company named "Alexander the Great," whose door decals – like the T-shirts and cigarette lighters widely available at local stores and kiosks – proclaim: "Macedonia is Greek." Even in distant Athens, as one drove away from the international side of the old airport, one was greeted by an enormous new billboard that proclaimed, in English: "Macedonia: 4,000 Years of Greek History."

In the space remaining, I would like to outline the history of Greek nation-building in Macedonia, which, as I have suggested, has been a successful project. Nevertheless, while a common national consciousness – a sense of affiliation with the Greek nation-state – is shared by most of the population regardless of ethnicity (a fact that probably distinguishes Greece from any of its Balkan neighbors), there still exist small groups of activists among the Slavo-Macedonians of Western Greek Macedonia (and a much larger group among the Muslims of Greek Thrace) who lobby for minority rights and advocate a closer affiliation with neighboring states. By highlighting material derived from observations, interviews, oral histories, scholarly studies, popular presentations in mass media, local and national government archives, as well as local and regional newspapers, I hope to explain and interpret the origins of the Macedonian Controversy in 1990s Greece, and to bring about a productive discussion that may diffuse some of the tension surrounding it.

Both Slavs and Greeks claim descent from the ancient Macedonians, who built one of the greatest empires of antiquity. It stretched, at different times, from the Balkans to the Indian subcontinent. But over the two millennia that followed, various parts of that former empire fell under the dominion of a succession of imperial state systems. Byzantine followed Roman rule, and many in Greece believe that the Byzantine Empire was a "Greek" empire, because Greek was the official language used in the empire's administration and religion. Slavic tribes migrated into the Balkans during the sixth and seventh centuries, and transformed the ethnological character of the region. At the same time,

Bulgars, a non-Slavic people from the Central Asian Steppes, intermingled with the Slavs and eventually developed a power that posed a significant challenge to Byzantium. This was symbolized in the establishment of a brief medieval Bulgarian state, the "Macedo-Bulgarian Empire" in the ninth century.[1] Over the next several hundred years, there were repeated, though unsuccessful, revolts by Bulgars, Slavs and others against Byzantine rule, but it was not until the fourteenth century that another power briefly extended its influence over Macedonia. Ottoman forces began encroaching on the Byzantine Empire, prompting the latter to shift its resources to the defense of its eastern frontier. Taking advantage of this situation, the Serbian Empire of Dusan had a short-lived reign over Macedonia. Later that century, however, the Ottomans overran most of the Balkan Peninsula, which they occupied, controlled and administered until the twentieth century.[2]

During the more than 400 years of Ottoman rule, the empire was administered through the *millet* system, which classified and organized inhabitants on the basis of religion. *Millets* were administrative and not territorial jurisdictions. While Muslims belonged to the Muslim *millet*, all Orthodox Christians belonged to the Orthodox Rum *millet*. As such, they were under the direct and indirect control, supervision and administration of the Greek Orthodox Patriarchate in Constantinople. The Patriarchate, in fact, enjoyed an extremely privileged and powerful position within the Ottoman Empire, in large part because of the wide and sweeping powers that the Sultans had granted them to collect taxes, mediate disputes, hear lawsuits, and even imprison criminals among the Christian population. An English folklorist commented on the evident power of the Greek Orthodox Church during his travels through Macedonia at the turn of the twentieth century, calling it a "national organization" with its own aristocracy of bishops (Brailsford 1906).[3]

It was this affiliation and identification with the high Orthodox Church clergy that gave rise to a Greek national identity. Notions of common national descent were constructed later, in a familiar Gellnerian manner, after the establishment of the Greek nation-state (Gellner 1983). The Orthodox *millet* administered a culturally and linguistically diverse Christian population, that covered a wide area with its differences in social, political and economic status (Vucinich 1965: 59). The basis of twentieth-century Greek scholarly definitions of nationality and ethnicity[4] developed out of administrative categories of the late Ottoman era. It is important to note that they embodied a sense of sacred religious authority, having been based largely on the concepts, categories and language of the Greek Orthodox Patriarchate.

In addition to religious hegemony, Greeks enjoyed commercial dominance throughout the Balkans and the eastern Mediterranean region, as Greek historians frequently note with evident pride. Moreover, where commercial towns existed, the early establishment of schools under the auspices of the Greek Orthodox Church soon followed. Formal education and the development of a local "literate" class in the Greek-speaking market towns of Macedonia created a cultural schism between such communities and the predominantly Slavic-speaking villages of the countryside. My historical ethnographic work on Assiros documents the strong differences that emerged between the Greek market towns of Macedonia and communities in their surrounding hinterland during the late Ottoman era. By the end of the nineteenth century, those differences were apparent in subsistence strategies, language, social organization, kinship terminology, and ritual customs. In addition, commercially important local centers of Greek language and letters controlled Christian political, judicial, and ecclesiastical hierarchies. In this manner, they monopolized the production and interpretation of the iconic and symbolic imagery that was crucial in the subsequent struggles for national emancipation.[5]

In 1870, a major event altered the face of Balkan politics. The Ottoman Porte granted the re-establishment of an autonomous Bulgarian Orthodox Church, known as the Exarchate. More than a century earlier, the Greek Ecumenical Patriarchate had used its influence with the Porte to have the Sultan abolish both the Bulgarian and the Serbian Orthodox Churches.[6] By at least 1840, however, emerging Bulgarian elites were attempting to use Slavic languages in church ceremonies, and had sought the appointment of Bulgarian priests and bishops in predominately Slavic-speaking communities.[7] The Greek Patriarchate resisted such developments, fearing they would compromise their "ecclesiastical and economic interests" (Augustinos 1977: 19). Official recognition from the Ottoman Porte gave Bulgarian elites a degree of legitimacy in their separatist struggle for ecclesiastical and secular regional autonomy.[8] With the formal re-establishment of the Exarchate, Bulgarians took control of secular and ecclesiastical institutions in Slavic-speaking communities throughout Macedonia (Perry 1988: 27). The Sultan had decreed that any village could join the Exarchate provided two-thirds of its inhabitants voted for such a move. This stipulation laid the foundations for the political, economic and ideological contest over Macedonia between Greece and Bulgaria in the late nineteenth century. The legacy of the language issue has continued well into the twentieth century, as Greek authorities periodically have been preoccupied with the suppression of the Slavic vernacular in Greek Macedonia.

Thus, by 1900, Macedonia had become embroiled in an increasingly violent territorial and religious-cum-national dispute between two young, expansionist states competing for control over the region. The early twentieth century was a period of intense nation-building activities in Macedonia, directed by Greece to the south and Bulgaria to the northeast. To a lesser extent, Serbian activities were also aimed at the hearts and minds of the Slavophones of Macedonia, while Romania was interested in helping the Vlach population to annihilate itself. Greek and Bulgarian churches were spreading across the Macedonian countryside at a feverish pace. National societies were formed in Athens and Sofia (and again less prominently in Belgrade and Bucharest) to sponsor the dispatch of priests, educators and propagandists into the perceived no-man's land of Macedonia. There was a great deal of population movement as well, with Greek settlers coming from the south and Bulgarians from the north. But the growing commercial strength of Greek-speaking notables enabled them to play an increasingly dominant role in the political life of villages and especially towns. Secular merchants enjoyed authority and influence in their local communities, based in no small way upon their close relations with the Orthodox Church. It was the latter that provided the institutional forum for political and ideological mobilization of the population for the Greek cause. Religious teachings, both in church and in schools, became the conduit through which Greek national elites to the south attempted to extend their hegemony northward, in an effort to construct a new national Greek identity for the region's Slavic speakers who remained faithful to the Patriarchate.

The Macedonian Struggle of 1904–08 marked the first open conflict between Greece and Bulgaria over Macedonia. As armed bands of partisans moved into the region, many local Slavic-speaking communities became divided. While some towns and villages expressed strong affinity for and professed allegiance to either Greece or Bulgaria, the accounts of elderly respondents suggest that many inhabitants had no particular inclination towards either national group. Nationalism, it seems, was unappealing to most. Since villages of "resisters" were often burned and the inhabitants murdered, many of these "non-aligned" communities found it expedient to declare their allegiance to whichever group of armed partisans happened along their way.

The Macedonian Struggle ended inconclusively, and a few years later the First Balkan War of 1912 saw an alliance of Bulgaria, Greece and Serbia against the ailing Ottoman Empire. While these three young Christian kingdoms drove the Ottomans from the Southern Balkan Peninsula, the buffer zone between their respective nation-states disappeared and Macedonia became the site of converging frontiers of expansionist states with nation-building agendas. A year later, the Second Balkan War of 1913 pitted Greece and Serbia in a victorious alliance against Bulgaria that redrew the common borders between those three states, much to the latter's expense. In 1913, the European-brokered Treaty of Bucharest formally partitioned the region of Macedonia between Greece (which received 51 per cent of the disputed area), Serbia (34 per cent) and Bulgaria (15 per cent). Almost immediately, each of these young nation-states begun pursuing assimilationist policies towards the inhabitants of those parts of Macedonia now under their political sovereignty.

In Greek Macedonia, a campaign of national enculturation was adopted to extend Greek national consciousness to the area's diverse cultural inhabitants, especially the Slavic-speaking population. Administrative incorporation into Greece and subsequent Greek nation-building efforts in the new northern territories did not follow a unified course of practice in all districts, and the experiences of inhabitants differed. In Greek-dominated market towns of Central Greek Macedonia such as Assiros, for example, there was little resistance to incorporation into Greece; Greek influence had already become hegemonic by the early twentieth century. Yet, in many areas of Western Greek Macedonia, where Greek influence had been less extensive, such as the area around the town of Florina (near the northwest borders with Albania and the former Yugoslavia), incorporation took on a different character. Harsh policing measures were adopted to physically remove Slavic-speakers whose non-Greek-oriented national consciousness defied eradication. Confidential documents in Greek government archives indicate that by 1925, Bulgarian influence in the Florina prefecture was growing.[9] While 38.6 per cent of the region's Christian inhabitants were described as Greek, none were monolingual in Greek.[10] On the other hand, the majority of the Christian population (59.4 per cent) were described as Bulgarians, as many as 70 per cent of whom were monolingual in Bulgarian.

These and other primary sources indicate that Greek national identity did have a presence among the inhabitants of Macedonia, from at least the turn of the twentieth century. But the hegemony of the Greek nation and its implied legitimation took much longer to take root in Western Greek Macedonia. In addition, identity and consciousness changed over time in response to material circumstances and historical developments. Elderly *Graecomani*, for example, Slavic speakers who openly identified themselves with Greece, often maintain in discussions that they did not really have an unchanging national consciousness. The tern *Graecomani* literally means one who has a mania for Greece. But even for them, identification with Greece was not a fixed sentiment.

It was during the 1920s that out-migration, displacement and deportation of Slavic-speakers took place. A voluntary exchange of populations between Greece and Bulgaria was supposed to create homogeneous nations. Those with Bulgarian consciousness living in Greek territory left for Bulgaria, and those with Greek consciousness who lived in Bulgaria left for Greece (Jelavich 1983: 136; Ladas 1932). In addition, some 500,000 refugees began arriving in Greek Macedonia from Turkey. The European-brokered Treaty of Lausanne (1923) decreed a compulsory "repatriation" of nationals between Greece and Turkey in 1923. These refugees from Asia Minor, Thrace and the Pontos area were resettled in vacant communities throughout the Macedonian countryside. This influx dramatically transformed the ethnic composition of Greek Macedonia. Moreover, nearly all of these "repatriates" had a strong Greek national consciousness, many having been forcibly evicted from what they had called home, and having suffered for their perceived Greek identities.

The Metaxas dictatorship of the late 1930s embarked on a harsh policy of forced assimilation. Slavic names were changed into Greek. Languages, songs, dances and other signifiers of ethnic culture were banned. Violators paid steep fines, were often forced to drink castor oil, and in some cases even beaten and exiled. Compulsory night schools were also set up throughout the region, in which adult men and women were taught Greek.[11] It was during the Metaxas period that the obligation to display the Greek flag in homes and shops on local and national holidays became compulsory. Some inhabitants even embarked on house-painting campaigns. Whitewashed structures were decorated with blue trim to resemble the colors of the Greek flag.[12]

When the Axis troops occupied Greece in 1941, the fate of the Slavs of Greek Macedonia was once more influenced by developments outside the realm of their own lives, and the Bulgarians were brought once again into their everyday lives. While German occupation forces were concentrated in towns and cities, their Bulgarian allies moved about the countryside, undertaking new efforts of nationalist propaganda. The occupation introduced effectively another polarizing schism to the inhabitants of the region. Some collaborated with the occupiers, others allied themselves with the Greek national forces. Yet others joined the ranks of the communist-led National Liberation Front (EAM) and the National Popular Liberation Army (ELAS). The decades of conflict, struggle and schism that had strained inter-ethnic relations in the region led to full-scale national political hostilities in the Greek Civil War (1947–49). The communists had won the support of many Slavo-Macedonians by holding out the promise of a future independent Macedonian homeland for them. Armed conflict was particularly fierce in the mountains of Greek Macedonia, where partisans on both sides of the conflict burned villages, executed suspected opponents and abducted children. After the communist defeat, many Slavs (along with Greek communists) fled to Yugoslavia and beyond, and the Greek–Yugoslav border was closed.

By the mid-twentieth century, the perceived Bulgarian threat to Greece's northern territories had diminished, owing in part to a strong NATO presence in Greece. At this point, the principal axis of conflict over Macedonia had shifted to one pitting Greece against Yugoslavia. The Socialist Republic of Macedonia, established in 1944, embodied Tito's efforts to promote an autonomous regional government to counterbalance Serbian influence in southern Yugoslavia. The event also had implications for Greece, and inaugurated a new era of competitive nation-building in the region. A new republic was created on Greece's border, with a standardized language similar to the vernaculars spoken in Greece's northwestern region. The elites of the new Macedonian republic immediately began to present themselves as a separate "nation," distinct from neighboring Serbia and Bulgaria. Much of this effort was in response to earlier Serbian attempts to label or characterize the Slavs of the region as "Southern Serbs." A national Macedonian historiography was created in this period, as intellectual elites of the new nation attempted to link (in a familiar fashion) the present-day population to the glorious legacy of historical personages, such as Alexander the Great of Macedonia, or Cyril and Methodius (who had spread Christianity to the Slavs in the ninth century). Providing the modern population with a heroic ancestry helped to legitimize the existence of an emerging Macedonian nation in the twentieth century.[13]

During this same period, the Slavs of Greek Macedonia were slowly losing their cultural and linguistic distinctiveness. The 1950s saw many of them reconciling themselves with the realities of life under Greek sovereignty. Many of their relatives, friends and co-villagers had left for countries of the Eastern Bloc. Others emigrated to Australia, Canada, or the USA. At the same time, the Greek state began peaceful, clientelistic Hellenizing efforts in the region. Even King Paul and Queen Frederika made several visits to the Florina area, where the Queen baptized many village girls with her own name and contributed to their future dowries by opening bank accounts for them in their names. The elaborate pomp and pageantry of national rituals were also played up, providing a festive stage for a rite of passage to Greek nationhood for many Slavs (Karakasidou 2000). In a few cases, entire villages in the northwest were obliged to swear language and loyalty oaths, professing their supposed Greek ancestry, avowing their allegiance to Greece, and promising never to speak Slavic again. Local elites (the *Graecomani*) also began to assume important roles as local mediating agents for the Greek state.

National enculturation efforts had a conservative tone, often stressing a love for the monarchy from the Florina area that appealed to many in the region. "We hated the Greeks," an elderly woman related to me, "but we loved the King and the Queen." In fact, when Constantine, the deposed king of Greece, returned to the country from exile for a "personal" visit in August 1993, his first stop was Florina.

The advent of free education in the 1960s saw an increase in the numbers of Slavo-Macedonians attending secondary schools and universities in Greece. While Greek education had been much resisted in the preceding decades, with many Slav parents refusing to send their children to the compulsory Greek schools, the promise of upward mobility in the 1960s changed their relations *vis-à-vis* the Greek state. The bureaucratic state now became a benevolent patron, providing an education for their children and prospects of coveted civil service jobs for themselves. Mothers consciously made decisions not to speak Slavic at home, and the language soon lost its prominence. Many of the present-day activists in Florina, who grew up during the 1950s with tales of past oppression and discrimination, cannot speak the language.

The democratization of the Greek polity after the fall of the military junta (1967–74) brought significant changes for all of the population of modern Greece in general, and for Slavo-Macedonians in particular. The borders were re-opened, and seasonal migrant laborers from the Yugoslav Republic of Macedonia helped boost the local economy. Yugoslav tourists on day-shopping trips were a common sight in downtown Florina in the 1980s. At the same time, a good number of those who left after the Civil War began returning to Greece, either to settle permanently or to visit relatives. Entry into Greece was not permitted to everyone, however, and those who refused to declare themselves to be of Greek origin were denied entry.

Many young Slavo-Macedonians, however, still found their opportunities for advancement limited, and new signs of protest and resistance had begun to emerge by the late 1980s. Political activists began to lobby, in a familiar European manner, for "human rights" and for official recognition of a Slavic-speaking ethnic minority in the region. They called for the teaching of Slavic in local schools, an end to the discrimination in employment and promotion, and the unrestricted right of return for all political refugees. The breakup of Yugoslavia accentuated these transformations, and led to a period of mounting tensions and crisis in the 1990s. Border controls tightened, human rights activists stepped up their lobbying efforts, police and security forces increased their vigilance, and demonstrators were arrested and imprisoned.

It is clear that the controversy surrounding Macedonia is far from resolved.

The protracted contest between Greece and the Former Yugoslav Republic of Macedonia to prove the supposed national identity of the ancient Macedonians is not as heated today as it was a few years ago. Greece, now at the threshold of the new century, has a new "Balkan profile." It is now heralded as a "bridge" between the "bloody" Balkans and the "civilized" European Union. Its leaders are coming to play an increasingly influential role in developing close economic and political relations between all Balkan states. Greek businessmen are deeply involved in the construction of international transport and telecommunications networks in these new states. Certainly, some nationalist rhetoric persists in Greece, but for the most part it has fallen dormant, save for a few ideologues engaged in personal crusades to prove the falsification of the history of Macedonia. The Former Yugoslav Republic of Macedonia is also abandoning the ultra-nationalist rhetoric of descent from the ancient Macedonians. They have given up their claims to the Star of Vergina as a national symbol; they have amended their constitution to indicate respect for international borders; and they have stopped talking about a Slavo-Macedonian minority living in conditions of forced assimilation in northern Greece and Bulgaria.

Until very recently, Macedonia has been heralded as a tremendous success for peace-making efforts (Ackerman 2000). Western diplomats and observers were pleased and amazed by the fact that the "spillover" effect of war did not spread to this proverbial tinderbox of the Balkans. The yearning for security, modernity and prosperity among the republic's inhabitants worked, at least for a decade after the collapse of socialist rule, against ethnonational animosities between the Slav majority and the Albanian minority. Local ethnic politicians were willing to enter into a coalition government in 1998, and the republic seemed on its way to becoming "the Switzerland" of the Balkans. But the conclusions that westerners had drawn, that "history has ended" in Macedonia and that the "art of preventative diplomacy" had worked miracles has been shattered during the past few months. The international pressures for a peaceful resolution of conflict went awry. The ethnonational conflict could not be fought on the cultural front anymore, and military confrontation began in late February 2001.

Slavo-Macedonian and Albanian nationalisms came into military confrontation. Ethnic Albanians began open warfare in villages close to the Kosovo border, and the conflict quickly spread throughout the northwestern areas of the country. Villages were evacuated, homes were burned, people were left dead, injured or homeless. Western mediators stepped up their efforts to coordinate peace talks and agreements. Eventually, on the eve of an open declaration of civil war in mid-August, ethnic Slav and Albanian politicians signed a peace accord. As I write these comments, NATO troops are arriving in Macedonia to disarm the Albanian rebels and maintain peace in the countryside. Everyone remains skeptical, however, whether such an agreement will bring an end to the animosity between the two groups. Sporadic clashes are still taking place and observers are not certain whether the promised constitutional changes will satisfy the Albanian demands for more cultural, linguistic and political representation.

Greece, in the meantime, with its new Balkan profile, is congratulating itself for its positive efforts to secure stability in "Skopia" (as they call the republic). Very rarely one hears the nationalist jargon of the last decade. The government's main concern is to support the existence of a stable and peaceful political entity next to their own politically volatile northern border. For observers, there is not much choice except to wait and see what the events of the present will add to the historical record of the Balkans. One hopes that ethno-national conflict will disappear and civil society will be built according to western models and prototypes. But one should also keep in mind that these developments reveal new types of dependencies which represent new forms of domination within the larger global regime of subjugation.

Notes

1 This empire established by Simeon the Great (893–927AD) eventually divided into two parts. The Byzantines quickly recovered the eastern part, while the western portion remained an independent Bulgar state with a flourishing ecclesiastical culture. It was eventually subjugated by the armies of Byzantine emperor Basil II ("the Bulgar-slayer" or *Voulgharoktonos*) in 1012 AD (Singleton 1976: 37–38).
2 Much of this brief historical overview is drawn from Singleton 1976.
3 Brailsford described how bishops administered the laws of marriage, divorce and inheritance, controlled schools and hospitals, amassed considerable wealth and lived in great houses. Their avarice and corruption showed little concern for the spiritual and material welfare of the population. As opposed to the bishops, Brailsford found that most local priests in the Macedonian countryside were relatively uneducated, living a lifestyle not unlike that of the peasants around them. Their ties to the ecclesiastical hierarchy, however, made these priests village leaders (Brailsford 1906: 62).
4 I would also suggest here that Greek "ethnicity" today is only conceived of within the encompassing dogma of Greek "nationality." We may play the chicken-and-the-egg game over whether Greek ethnicity was a transitional stage to Greek nationality, but in the present-day most Greeks cannot conceive of the former outside the context of the latter.
5 Other scholars working in Greece offer evidence to support this interpretation. See Angelopoulos 1973: 61; Cowan 1990; Panayiotidis 1912: 194.
6 The Bulgarian Church was eliminated in 1765, and the Serbian Orthodox Church in 1767 (Friedman 1986: 289).
7 Wilkinson also argued that the publication of A. Boue's (French) map of Macedonia in 1847 triggered "the attention of the European powers towards the idea of a possible Slavic hegemony in the Balkans." At the same time, it also stimulated Bulgarian nationalist activity towards the establishment of an independent Church (Wilkinson 1951: 37–39).
8 The so-called "Slavic-schismatics" of the Exarchate were excommunicated by the Patriarchate. It is interesting to note that for years following its excommunication, however, the Exarchate still enjoyed the patronage of the Ottoman Sultan and was permitted to maintain its administrative seat in Constantinople (Raikin 1984).
9 Historical Archives of Macedonia/General Directorate of Macedonia (HAM/GDM), File No. 90 ("Propagandas: 1924–1925"), Letter from the Prefect of Florina to the General Directorate of Macedonia in Thessaloniki, Confidential Protocol No.6, Florina, 13 January 1925, p. 4.
10 Historical Archives of Macedonia/General Directorate of Macedonia (HAM/GDM), File No. 53 ("Population Statistics of the Educational Districts of Vodena, Karatzova, and Gevgeli, 1911, 1913, 1915"), Table A: "Florina District:

Ethnological Census of the population." Put another way, there were no monolingual Greek speakers among the Florina population during the period 1911–15, right after incorporation. Of those multi-linguals that were described as Greek and could speak Greek, 52.8 per cent also spoke Bulgarian, 32.5 per cent also spoke Koutso-Vlach, and 14.7 per cent also spoke Albanian.
11 Metaxas Archive, File No. 36, "The Performed Attempt to Hellenize Western Macedonia and the Achieved Results During the Last Two Years," Confidential, by Yiorgos Papadopoulos, Elementary School Teacher, 22 July 1938, p. 6.
12 *Ibid.*, p. 4.
13 For some examples of Macedonian national historiography, see *A History of the Macedonian People* (Institute of National History 1979), and Taskovski (1976).

References

Ackerman, Alice (2000) *Making Peace Prevail: Preventing Violent Conflict in Macedonia*. Syracuse: Syracuse University Press.
Angelopoulos, Athanasios (1973) *The Foreign Propagandas in the Polyani District in the Period 1870–1912*. Thessaloniki: Institute for Balkan Studies, No. 137 (in Greek).
Augustinos, Gerasimos (1977) *Consciousness and History: Nationalist Crisis of Greek Society, 1897–1914*. Boulder: East European Monographs.
Brailsford, H.N. (1906) *Macedonia: Its Races and their Future*. New York: Arno Press/*New York Times*.
Cowan, Jane (1990) *Dance and the Body Politic in Northern Greece*. Princeton: Princeton University Press.
Friedman, Victor A. (1986) "Linguistics, Nationalism, and Literary Languages: A Balkan Perspective." In Victor Raskin and Peter Bjarkman (eds), *The Real-World Linguist: Linguistic Applications in the 1980s*. Norwood, NJ: Ablex, pp. 287–305.
Gellner, Ernest (1983) *Nations and Nationalism*. Ithaca: Cornell University Press.
Institute of National History (1978) *A History of the Macedonian People*. Skopje: Institute of National History.
Jelavich, Barabara (1983) *History of the Balkans: Twentieth Century*. Cambridge: Cambridge University Press.
Karakasidou, Anastasia, (1993) "Politicizing Culture: Negating Macedonian ethnicity in northern Greece." *Journal of Modern Greek Studies* 11(1): 1–28.
—— (1997) *Fields of Wheat, Hills of Blood: Passages to Nationhood in Greek Macedonia (1870–1990)*. Chicago: Chicago University Press.
—— (2000) "Protocol and Pageantry: Celebrating the Nation in Northern Greece." In Mark Mazower (ed.), *After the War was Over: Reconstructing the Family, Nation, and State in Greece, 1943–1960*. Princeton: Princeton University Press, pp. 221–246.
Ladas, S.P. (1932) *The Exchange of Minorities: Bulgaria, Greece, and Turkey*. New York: Macmillan.
Panayiotidis, Yeorgios (1912) "The Greek Schools of the Macedonian Literary Brotherhood of Constantinople in Tsotili," *Macedonian Almanac*, 193–197 (in Greek).
Perry, Duncan M. (1988) *The Politics of Terror: The Macedonian Liberation Movements, 1893–1903*. Durham, NC: Duke University Press.
Raikin, Spas (1984) "Nationalism and the Bulgarian Orthodox Church." In Pedro Ramet (ed.), *Religion and Nationalism in Soviet and East European Politics*. Durham, NC: Duke University Press, pp. 187–206.
Singleton, Fred (1976) *Twentieth Century Yugoslavia*. New York: Columbia University Press.

Tashkovski, Dragan (1976) *Radjanjeto na Makedonskata Nacija* [The Genesis of the Macedonian Nation]. Skopje: Nasha Kniga (in Macedonian).

Vucinich, Wayne S. (1965) *The Ottoman Empire, its Record and Legacy*. Princeton: Van Nostrand.

Wilkinson, H.R. (1951) *Maps and Politics: A Review of the Ethnographic Cartography of Macedonia*. Liverpool: University of Liverpool Press.

10 Liberia

Civil war and the "collapse" of the settler state[1]

Diana DeG. Brown

On Christmas Eve, 1989 Charles Taylor, a former member of President Samuel Doe's cabinet, launched his campaign to overthrow Doe with an attack on a remote town along Liberia's border with Cote d'Ivoire. Within six months, Taylor occupied over 90 per cent of the country, including its largely rice-growing agricultural interior, and the Liberian state had "collapsed." Taylor never succeeded in capturing the capital, Monrovia, which was held by the Doe government until Doe's assassination by the leader of a breakaway faction of Taylor's army in September 1990. Reduced to a city-state dependent on foreign assistance for food and protection, Monrovia then became the caretaker of the Liberian state through an internationally organized coalition government charged with organizing elections and implementing disarmament. "Greater Liberia," Taylor's territory in the interior, was subsequently contested by other factions and much reduced. By 1994, after nearly five years of fighting, three major factions and several smaller militia groups contended for control of the Liberian state. As internationally guided efforts to wrest a peace accord and restore political unity proceeded, the factions multiplied and realigned themselves. Elections were finally held in 1997, and the government and the territory of the Liberian state were formally reunified under Charles Taylor as its elected president. But the situation remains highly unstable and Taylor himself has become increasingly embattled. Sporadic fighting continues as rival factions mobilize against Taylor within Liberia and from outside its borders, and war refugees in neighboring countries threaten increasingly fragile border relations. Taylor fomented civil war in Sierra Leone, and the Liberian Civil War has destabilized countries bordering on Liberia, and now threatens the entire region. The role of Taylor's cross-border diamond-smuggling activities in perpetuating the fighting has been well-publicized, and at the time of writing the United Nations has unanimously resolved to impose economic sanctions against Liberia if the smuggling is not stopped.

Like many recent civil wars, the violence of this war has been directed mainly at civilian populations. In this tiny country the size of the state of Ohio, with a pre-war population of 2.5 million people, over 200,000 are now estimated to have died in the conflict, and two-thirds of the population have been displaced, with many refugees still in other West African countries. The economy lies in ruins, though Taylor and other faction leaders have made individual fortunes exploiting the country's natural resources. In the countryside agricultural production remains disrupted and in the capital, whose population has more than doubled since the war began, Liberians continue to suffer hunger and lack of services. The dangers from marauding soldiers and the constant fear of further eruptions of violence persist.

When the Liberian Civil War broke upon the quiet Liberian landscape I was living in the interior city of Gbarnga with my family, teaching and conducting research. This account, written in 1994, weaves together an analysis of the Liberian state and its "collapse" with my own experiences of the early months of the war. These provide a situated perspective on the war from the interior of the country, where news and opinions often differed from those found in the political hub of the capital. My disciplinary positioning as an anthropologist leads me to emphasize, wherever possible, ethnographic perspectives on this material. I begin by briefly situating the city of Gbarnga and my own vantage point on these events at the time just prior to the war and during its initial months. I then discuss the Liberian state and its "collapse," emphasizing both the features that contributed to the consolidation of state power for well over a century, and to its breakdown. I highlight aspects of state weakness, the development of ethnic conflicts during the Doe government, and international factors related to the world recession of the 1980s and the waning of the Cold War. My account registers the shock and disbelief felt by many Liberians and students of these events during the early 1990s, that so sustained and violent a conflict could so suddenly engulf a country long regarded as a model of a stable African democracy. Such reactions have now given way to routine citations of Liberia as one of the worst-case scenarios of state "collapse," in Africa, or anywhere in the world, and an extensive literature has built up on this topic, to which I refer briefly.

I then turn to the less explored and more ethnographic territory of local perspectives on the war during its early months among sectors of Gbarnga's population. This approach enables me to explore some of the less examined issues that lie at the heart of the literature on state collapse, concerning society's relation to the state. It also serves to counter the prevailing tendency in interpretations of the Liberian crisis to provide top-down accounts that emphasize state structures, particular regimes, or particular forms of political leadership, and say little of how local populations have experienced these events (though exceptions are found in the work of Huband (1998) and, particularly, Ellis (1995; 1999)). My exploration of local experiences of the war in Gbarnga focuses on its impact on constructions of ethnicity and the ways in which it was played out in the interior of the country in the immediate pre-war period and during the early months of the war. I present data on ethnic encounters and briefly review the historical development of ethnic distinctions in Liberia. This serves as a basis for speculating on the impact of the ethnic conflicts of the war on local populations, and for commenting on the role of ethnicity in the war.

The view from Gbarnga

Gbarnga, with a pre-war population of perhaps 20,000, is the largest city of the interior, a center of commerce, home to a large military barracks, and county seat of rural Bong County, known as the breadbasket of Liberia. Bong County is dominated by the Kpelle, the largest of the sixteen ethnic groups known in Liberia as "tribes."[2] Gbarnga was strategically located with respect to the Civil War. Some one hundred and twenty miles north of Monrovia, it is the major city along the route from the capital through Nimba County to the Cote d'Ivoire border, where the war began. It stood in a likely path of encounter between Taylor's forces, moving south through Nimba County toward Monrovia, and government troops and material moving north to meet them. After the war began we witnessed growing numbers of refugees fleeing southward from the fighting, and heard at night the sounds of government military convoys moving north. Although official government news sources continued to assure people that everything was under control, reports from the BBC, rumors, and accounts by refugees from the fighting told another story. These sources conveyed Doe's failures: the inability of his heavily armed AFL troops to contain an initial invading force of only some 150 men; the brutalities enacted on local populations by his AFL army; and spreading conflict, extensive support for Taylor, and local recruitment into his army. They portrayed towns and villages emptying in the path of the fighting. Gradually, as Taylor's forces proceeded with their own brutal depredations of the countryside and Taylor broadcast his self-aggrandizing pronouncements on the BBC,[3] many Liberians began to sense that the devastation was the result of a contest waged not in their interests, nor over political alternatives, but rather as part of an individual quest for power, what Reno has termed "warlord politics" (Reno 1998).

As the fighting neared Gbarnga, anxieties increased, and the flight of other refugee populations became a prelude to our own. People discussed their plans for flight, and in early April, following a violent military incident just outside the city, Gbarnga too began to empty out, and within three days over half the population had fled. We followed at the end of April, just before the road to Monrovia, and the airport, was closed. Soon after, as Charles Taylor consolidated his territory of Greater Liberia, Gbarnga became its capital, and the college where we had been teaching became his military training center (Tokpa 1991). These initial months of the war, from January through mid-March of 1990, a period of increasing local anxiety and uncertainty as to whether the war would continue to escalate and engulf Gbarnga, or whether Doe's military forces would be able to contain the fighting, provide the framework for my examination of local dimensions of the war.

The Liberian state

Until 1980, Liberia was viewed as exceptional in the African context: an independent state since 1847, with well over a century of continuous stable rule. Its legitimacy in the international community was confirmed by its position as a charter member of the United Nations. It was regarded as a modernizing state, and the violence that had marked its history was excused as part of the growing pains of modernization. Even Doe's violent 1980 coup was initially viewed as part of this same process by a leading analyst of Liberian political development (Liebenow 1982/83). This image unraveled over the course of the 1980s with the escalating violence of the Doe regime, and with the prolonged Civil War, Liberia moved from being the showpiece of Africa, the exception to Africa's colonial encounter, to a symbol of the continent's opposite extreme – the violence, chaos, and state disintegration whose roots are often associated with colonized states. Hindsight in the charting of Liberia's downfall draws on well-identified but less exceptional dimensions of its development: its quasi-colonial structure; its development as a patrimonial state; its increasing weakness during the 1980s; its loss of US support at the end of the Cold War, and the problematic character of the ensuing intervention of West African states in the Civil War.

The Americans of African ancestry who settled in Liberia in the 1820s, despite their hopes for reasserting their freedom and identity on African shores, created a state that in many ways closely resembled its African colonial neighbors. Liberia was never formally a colony, the American government refusing it this status, judging the enterprise to be too great a financial and diplomatic risk. It remained a US dependency under the American Colonization society until 1847, when it became an independent republic. Primarily a coastal settlement through the nineteenth century, it came under increasing pressure from European colonial neighbors to establish control over the indigenous populations of its interior. In 1905 the Liberian government undertook the military "pacification" of these populations, initiating a form of indirect rule over them that was copied directly from the Nigerian colony. As Mamdani (1996) has noted, the need of tiny foreign elites to establish control over large indigenous populations bred common structures of power throughout the African continent.[4] Liberia conformed also to Mamdani's contention that it was precisely the poorest colonial governments that generated the harshest treatment of the indigenous populations. In 1930 Liberia was the target of an international League of Nations inquiry into slavery and the forced labor of indigenous Liberians provided to plantations outside of Liberia, conditions that apparently differed little from those in its own rural interior.[5] I shall have more to say later about indirect rule, of the creation of "tribes" as a way of incorporating the indigenous population into the Liberian polity, and of their role in the Civil War. Suffice it here to say that indirect rule, and the structures of power and ethnic divisions it spawned, have had a lasting effect in structuring the relationship of indigenous populations to the Liberian state.

The new Liberian constitution was modeled on that of the USA, but from its beginnings it served as the instrument through which a tiny elite, never totaling more than some 3–5 per cent of the Liberian population, exercised power over a large indigenous majority. This elite was originally composed of settlers and their descendants, known as "Americo-Liberians," but also absorbed an almost equal number of repatriated Africans captured at sea, known as "Congoes," as well as West Indians and individuals of the indigenous Liberian population able to gain access to an education and to the attributes of Americo-Liberian culture.[6] The great majority of indigenous persons, however, while incorporated within the Liberian state through the structures of indirect rule, remained excluded from participation in the state, and continued to be isolated from the national society by differences of language, literacy, religion and other cultural practices, which were reified by a dual judicial system. "Civilized" Liberians, literate, Christian, and speaking English, the official language of Liberia, were governed through urban statutory law, while "tribal" persons, rural, non-literate, non-English-speaking (though often tri- or quatri-lingual in indigenous languages) and largely non-Christian, were governed through customary laws designated for each "tribe." Despite its mask of democratic governance, the realities of the Liberian state came closely to resemble the familiar African model of the highly centralized and authoritarian one-party state (Liebenow 1962), or "patrimonial regime" (Sawyer 1992: 6–7). Power was concentrated in the personal rule of the president, was exercised through state-controlled patronage networks, and maintained through the use of repressive force, with the only legal political party, the elite True Whig Party, serving as its supporting legislative arm.

The economy, after an initial involvement in coastal commerce, was based on the extraction of local resources, mainly rubber and mining. The Firestone rubber plantation, founded in 1926, was followed after World War II by the opening of the resources of the interior to other enclave operations, revenues from which formed the basis of the economy, and enriched government leaders able to capture profits for their personal use. A US-sponsored economic survey team investigating the impact of these economic arrangements in the early 1960s labeled their report "Growth Without Development" (Clower *et al.* 1966). Initiatives taken by the government of President Tubman (1944–71) during the post-war decades of economic prosperity, to expand economic opportunities and extend the franchise to populations of the interior, were carefully controlled through patronage and repression.[7]

But by the 1970s, the succeeding Tolbert regime (1971–80) faced the deterioration of the international markets for Liberian exports, resulting economic decline and unemployment, and growing numbers of educated, indigenous migrants to Monrovia pressing for participation in the Liberian economy and polity. A new indigenous elite, many educated in Europe and the USA and representing a broad spectrum of political views, presented electoral challenges to elite rule, urging democratic reforms and broadened political participation. However, Doe's 1980 military coup, which overthrew the Tolbert regime and brutally murdered many of its key members, preempted these democratic challenges. This coup ended over a century of Americo-Liberian-led elite rule and brought to power the first indigenous president, a non-commissioned officer from one of the smallest and most rural of the Liberian "tribal" groups, the Krahn.

Whatever prospects this event heralded for democratic change soon dissolved. After initial gestures at a broad coalition government including former government officials as well as a wide range of dissenters, Doe moved quickly to outdo the levels of personal power exercised by his predecessors. Installing his co-ethnic Krahn in key positions in government and the military, he began to target and exterminate his political opponents and members of their ethnic groups. Tolbert had greatly weakened the military; Doe further reduced its forces by installing mainly his co-ethnic Krahn, and created nine separate units of his own security services (Reno 1998: 84).

By 1989, when the Civil War began, the fleeting moment of popular participation had been suppressed, the country had moved to despotism (Sawyer 1992), and individual political differences within the Doe government had become transformed into violent ethnic conflicts. It was *within* the Doe government, within the corridors of power, within a state based not on the sharing of power but rather on its concentration in the person of the president, that the violent ethnic conflicts of the Civil War were born (see also Ellis 1995, 1999).

The 1980s had brought more financial disasters for Liberia: a continuing precipitous decline in world prices for its exports; the termination in 1988 of lavish US aid which had sustained the economy through much of the decade, and Doe's own excesses of corruption and mismanagement. By the end of the decade the country was in financial ruin, and Doe had lost such credibility as a leader and earned such hatred that challenger Charles Taylor was initially welcomed by many as the liberator who would restore the economy and the 1980 ideals of a democratic Liberian state, even though his own reputation was clouded.[8]

By the time of Taylor's move to capture the presidency, the Liberian state manifested all of the structural conditions associated by Jackson and Rosberg (1982) with African "weak states" prone to "collapse," although their discussion excluded Liberia from this category. Weak states are said to be exemplified by the concentration of power in the person of the president; the underdevelopment of institutions and infrastructure; minimal participation of the populace in the government or civil society; the presence of ethnic divisions within the population; a weak military; and a weak economy dependent on foreign exports and thus vulnerable to fluctuations in the world economy. Jackson and Rosberg argue that these conditions make states prone to collapse, with some states moving in and out of statehood, surviving only through international support, or "juridical" statehood. Boone (1998: 131) argues further that African states based on extractive economies, which require little infrastructural development, appear to be more prone to collapse than those based on peasant commodity production, which require greater state attention to the development of infrastructure.

In hindsight, the evidence shows that all of these indicators of state economic and political weakness, present since the founding of the Liberian state, had intensified in the 1970s and most dramatically under the Doe regime. By the end of the 1980s, Liberia was a prime example of a weak and collapse-prone state. But although the Liberian state had been greatly weakened through rampant corruption and bureaucratic mismanagement, it might have remained intact, at least temporarily, with Taylor replacing Doe as head of state, were it not for the shifting interests of foreign powers at the end of the Cold War and the withdrawal of crucial international support from Liberia.

The end of the Cold War

In their discussion of weak states Jackson and Rosberg (1982) argue that often they are kept from collapse only through the activities of international actors who in their own interests intervene to provide what they identify as the "juridical" dimensions of statehood. The Liberian case, with state "collapse" following upon the withdrawal of international – mainly US – support, appears to confirm this proposition. Through the period of the Cold War, American interests and intervention in Liberia acted to shore up, and even to conceal, the weakness of the Liberian state. While the early US presence in Liberia had largely been a symbolic one, the opening of the Firestone Rubber Plantation, World War II and, above all, the advent of the Cold War gave this small African outpost strategic importance. In return for rights to extract raw materials and set up strategic military installations, the USA provided increasing sums of financial aid, advisors and military support and took a greater interest in Liberian affairs. During the 1960s and 1970s, successive Liberian governments struggled to resist US domination, courting ties with Europe and the countries of the Eastern bloc. In the 1980s, the Doe regime quickly succumbed to US pressure and severed ties with its Cold War enemies. In return, between 1980 and 1988 the USA provided Liberia with over $500 million in aid, proportionally more than that given to any other African country, and it encouraged similar generosity from other international lending agencies, such as the International Monetary Fund and the World Bank (Dunn and Tarr 1988; Kimble 1990). American officials largely ignored mounting evidence of repression, human rights abuses, corruption and election fraud, and continued to champion Liberia as a democracy. President Reagan even invited Doe to the White House, and, in his inimitable style, introduced him to the press as "Chairman Moe" (Berkeley 1992: 60). Analysts consider this huge flow of US dollars and the tacit approval given to the Doe regime crucial to its survival during the economic decline of the 1980s (see Liebenow 1987: 167).

By 1988, the waning of the Cold War, together with mounting evidence of Liberia's massive government corruption, misuse of US aid, failure to repay loans, and human rights abuses led the USA, and with it other international lending agencies, to terminate all non-humanitarian aid to Liberia. With the end of the Cold War in 1989, Liberia lost its strategic and symbolic importance to the USA, and by the start of the Liberian Civil War in that same year, further US intervention in Liberian affairs had largely ceased. US economic difficulties at home and the Persian Gulf War dominated its concerns. As the Civil War escalated and the death toll mounted, Doe sought, and clearly expected, to receive help from his old ally. But the US refused to intervene, and stood by while Taylor's army destroyed the airport (a former US military base), the OMEGA strategic tracking system and the Voice of America transmitter for all of Africa (Holmes 1992), and while the death toll mounted. Declaring repugnance with Liberia's human rights abuses, the US refused further support and defined the war as a Liberian problem (US Committee for Refugees 1992: 7), a stance it has maintained. European governments, tending to view Liberia as an American problem, have contributed little, though non-governmental organizations (NGOs) have been active.

Many Liberians initially opposed US intervention in the Civil War, resisting further meddling in their affairs, but later, as the bloodshed increased, many more criticized the US for not intervening. This American inaction finally undermined the lingering sense Liberians had nourished that settler origins and the circumstances of Liberia's founding had created a "special relationship" between Liberia and the US, and with it a certain moral and financial obligation on the part of the US.

The West African nations who now intervened lacked the unity of purpose previously shown by the Western powers. Their interests were diverse, and the effect of their actions was to prolong the fighting, fragment the Liberian state, and delay its reunification. ECOWAS (Economic Community of West African States), which took charge of efforts to resolve Liberia's war, had a vital interest in ending the conflict, which threatened (and still threatens) to destabilize the entire area. But while ECOMOG (ECOWAS Monitoring Group), ECOWAS' military arm, was effective in reducing the bloodshed, ECOWAS' broader role in resolving the war was far more problematic. Its apparent collective unity of purpose masked conflicting agendas of its member states, which supported both sides in the Liberian war. An Anglophone faction[9] led by Nigeria, which was widely regarded as having hegemonic intentions in the region and whose president was a close personal friend of Doe, supported Doe. With his death, it worked to install the caretaker Interim Government of National Unity (IGNU), appointed to sponsor negotiations among the warring factions to resolve the conflict and hold new elections. ECOWAS was successful in preventing Taylor from capturing Monrovia and reunifying the country under his own leadership. ECOMOG troops might have defeated Taylor, ended the war, and kept Doe in power had it not been for strong financial and military support provided to Taylor by Francophone members of ECOWAS. Chief among Francophone supporters was Burkina Faso, and behind it Libya,[10] who provided Taylor with funds, arms, personnel, and military training, and Cote d'Ivoire, who allowed Taylor passage for military personnel and the transport of arms into Liberia. Both of these countries' support for Taylor rested to some degree on their hostility to Doe for his murder of family members.[11] Their support was crucial in helping Taylor to establish and maintain control over Greater Liberia. The Liberian state thus became a battleground for competing West African interests (Gershoni 1993b) as well as a victim of them.[12]

International aid had shaped the development of a state dependent upon this aid, and far more responsive to international interests than to those of its own indigenous populations. The termination of US financial support at the end of the Cold War came at a critical moment in Liberia's own internal economic and political crisis. With the withdrawal of US support for Liberia as a juridical state, the state itself soon "collapsed," or fragmented, aided by a far less cohesive and less juridically supportive West African regional coalition. It should be noted, as a refinement of the notion of the importance of international juridical support for state unity, that this notion appears Eurocentric, geared to take account of the powerful influences of the Cold-War West, but not necessarily appropriate to more local, African international interventions, as the case of ECOWAS intervention in Liberia indicates. With the radical reduction of Western superpower interests in Africa, new political actors have taken on a larger role in the internal politics of Liberia. These include Western peacekeepers and NGOs, Libya, whose opportunistic and destabilizing efforts in the Liberian conflict echo its longer term fueling of internal conflicts in other sub-Saharan African regions such as Chad (see Reyna, in this volume), and Nigeria, seeking economic and political dominance in West Africa.

In retrospect, this analysis of Liberian state collapse, and the model of the "weak state," whose major analytic premises it follows, both reflect a prioritizing of the state – its strength and cohesion, and its territorial integrity – as the proper unit of analysis both of political economic development and of civil conflicts. This same prioritizing is perpetuated through the use of the term "state collapse" (see Lowenkopf 1995; Zartman 1995) to highlight extreme state dysfunction or fragmentation. Since I wrote this analysis, other interpretations of Liberian state collapse have appeared (Ellis 1999; Reno 1998). Of these, by far the most original is that of William Reno, in whose analysis the state plays a very minor part. Reno's analysis largely ignores states and their boundaries to focus instead on regional and global economic networks that operate informally within and across the boundaries of weak states. These are managed by rival warlords, political leaders whose goal is to achieve personal power and economic aggrandizement not through recourse to the mechanisms of the state, but through improvised and shifting networks of personal ties. These networks operate independently of the state. They ignore state boundaries, and their leaders do not require control of the state to carry out their business, relying instead on regional and global contacts through which they market their products. This is an African version of flexible accumulation, based not on the fixed production of consumer goods but on the flexible accumulation of portable natural resources such as timber, rubber, gold and diamonds, marketed on a world scale according to shifting demands.

According to Reno's logic, the crucial variables of state collapse in Liberia emerged in the Doe period not because Doe lost control of or intentionally destroyed the infrastructure of the Liberian state, but because he was unable to gain control of the crucial informal patronage networks controlled by the former elite, what Reno terms the "shadow state," which were the real basis for state economic and political power. Clever at manipulating foreign aid,[13] Doe pursued this strategy and left the leaders of the former elite networks to pursue their own independent sources of power, which Doe was not able, and did not try, to control. It was these networks that formed the resource bases monopolized by the rival warlords that emerged with the fragmentation of state power, like an evil chrysalis emerging out of the shell of the state. The loss of these networks was the real source of Doe's defeat, and the warlords who then rose to control them have since dominated Liberian politics, and monopolized and violently contested the control of these resources. These networks do not require recourse to state resources. As Reno points out, Taylor did not have access to the state in the period between his bid for power in 1989 and his assumption of the presidency in 1997, and instead developed his resources independently of state power.

For Reno, the end of the Cold War is significant less as a moment of political realignment than as a time of economic realignment, of foreign investment and the opening of new commercial opportunities, among them the easy availability of weapons at bargain prices from the former Communist Eastern Bloc states. The significance of the end of the Cold War and the loss of US aid for Liberia, according to Reno's analysis, is that with the departure of US aid Doe lost the only resource he controlled which could challenge and curb the power of the non-state forces controlled by elite patronage networks of the previous regime, which were poised to take advantage of commercial opportunities. Without this aid, he could not hold these forces at bay. In this analysis, then, the state was important to Doe not for what it might offer in the way of control over a territory or population, let alone benefits for its citizens, but rather as a legitimate terminal for receiving international funds.

Since Reno's account was written before Taylor, the arch-warlord, had assumed the Liberian presidency, it remains to be seen what benefits accrue to a warlord presidency controlling the channels of the state. It also remains to be seen whether in the current international efforts to shut down the warlord commerce in diamonds, and with the threat of United Nations economic sanctions, the Liberian state will still be effective as a location through which to exert international pressure and control.

Ethnicity in the Civil War

I now shift focus from the analysis of national and international level events to the Civil War's impact on local populations. I explore ways in which the war dramatically, and often violently, intensified local awareness of "tribal" identities, drawing upon my experiences in Gbarnga and among students and administrators at nearby Cuttington College in the period just before the war and during its early months. I speculate about how ethnic dimensions of the war emerged out of the earlier constructions of ethnicity in Liberia.

It is important to distinguish the recent incendiary buildup and explosion of ethnic conflicts and violence of the Civil War, which began after 1980 within the Doe government and which was unleashed upon the general population, from earlier instances of what might be termed "ethnic" violence associated with the resistance of indigenous peoples to incorporation within the Liberian state during the nineteenth and early twentieth centuries. The ethnic violence of the Civil War, while it depended upon the prior formation of ethnic categories, was not the result of any long ethnic enmities. Rather, it was initiated within the Liberian state, and linked to the long history of the state's oppression and "structural violence" against the Liberian population. Ethnic categories gave shape to, but were not the cause of the conflict.

In discussing ethnicity, I distinguish two levels of its expression, both of which have their origins in the Liberian state. The first concerns the development of ethnic conflicts within the Doe government; the second involves the older and longer process of the formation of ethnic categories and identities initiated by indirect rule and formed historically through the combined agencies of the state and indigenous Liberians, which provided the foundation for the ethnic shaping of the war. Since my observations of ethnic changes in Gbarnga in the early days of the war relate directly to the sudden spread of ethnic conflicts that had originated within the Doe government, I begin with a brief discussion of these conflicts. I then discuss their impact upon the local population, and provide a brief background on the historical development of ethnicity in Liberia.

The beginnings of the intense and targeted ethnic conflicts of the 1980s that animated the Civil War can be located within the corridors of state power of the Doe government. They were not the eruption of ancient tribal enmities, as often portrayed in the popular news media. They emerged from and elaborated upon existing ethnic categories and identities that had also originated mainly within the Liberian state at the beginning of the twentieth century through the institution of indirect rule. The bitter ethnic conflict that developed within the Doe government primarily involved four "tribes": the Krahn, the Mandingo, the Gio, and the Mano. Enmities had begun with the ethnicizing of a personal rivalry between Doe, a Krahn, and Thomas Quiwonkpa, his chief of the army and a former close friend and ally in the 1980 coup, who was a Gio. Quiwonkpa left the government in 1985, after Doe had sabotaged the election of another Gio to the presidency, and attempted a coup. Following the defeat of the coup attempt and the execution of Quiwonkpa, Doe loaded the government and the army with his co-ethnic Krahn, and sent his troops to enact brutal reprisals against Gio civilians in Nimba County, an action in which over 1,500 Gios were reportedly killed. Ethnic enmities then spread to include these principals' closest allies: the Gio were supported by the Mano, with whom they shared close linguistic and cultural ties and the territory of Nimba County. The Mandingo, Islamic traders and merchants resident throughout West Africa, many of whom as foreigners and non-citizens in Liberia were politically obligated to Doe for economic favors, support and protection, were viewed as Doe supporters. These conflicts over power within the state, represented as ethnic or "tribal" enmities (see Lawyers Committee for Human Rights 1986), gave shape to the violence in the Civil War and furnished a central dynamic in its geopolitical configuration.

Charles Taylor, entering Liberia in 1989, capitalized on these ethnically framed enmities and acted to greatly intensify them. Taylor, himself an Americo-Liberian, married to a Gio, chose to enter the country from Cote d'Ivoire, whose president was his ally, through Nimba County, homeland of his affines, the Gio, who were also Doe's arch-enemies. Naming his army the NPFL (National Patriotic Front of Liberia), after the force first created by the slain Gio leader of the 1985 coup attempt, Taylor immediately gained supporters for his war against

Doe. He drew Doe's largely Krahn-led troops directly into the civilian rural farming areas of their enemies and benefited from their brutalities against these populations, gaining support and new recruits, often from the kin of victims. His recruitment of child soldiers for his army (see Brown 1993) took advantage of those most vulnerable to the framing of the conflict in ethnic terms.

In this way, the ethnic enmities that had formed at the heart of the conflict were suddenly unleashed upon the national landscape. Before the war, only those directly involved and well-informed members of national political circles had been aware of these intense, but still very localized ethnic conflicts (Lawyers Committee for Human Rights 1986; Dunn and Tarr 1988). Outside of these circles, Liberians were less aware of the dangers brewing, and little affected by them. But from its start, the war projected the ethnic identities of the groups identified as the four main protagonists as a central means of defining allies and enemies. Ethnic labels came to mark all members of these "tribes," and to publicly identify them as parties to the political positions and atrocities outlined above. Belonging to one of these groups thus produced guilt, or victimization, by association.

The contrast between the ethnic situation in pre-war Gbarnga and that found shortly after the war had begun was very vivid. In the months before the war various public markers of ethnic identity could be found, in placards identifying local stores, and the large signs adorning the facades of the different tribal courts which administered customary law in their corresponding ethnic neighborhoods. People with whom we spoke often spontaneously referred to their tribal affiliations in casual conversations. I found no reticence to discuss tribal identity, even among members of the four "tribes" identified above, nor did I observe any indications of ethnic hostilities within the population in Gbarnga, nor on the campus of Cuttington University College where I taught (see also Tokpa 1991). Nor were these observed by well-placed friends in Monrovia. "Tribal" identities and the cultural content of tribal stereotypes were readily acceptable topics of conversation, and I asked about them often and quite openly. Cuttington had a very diverse ethnic student population, with many students from rural indigenous backgrounds. Four months before the war started, the thirty students in my Introductory Anthropology course, representing, as I recall, fourteen different "tribes," discussed "tribal" differences and stereotypes enthusiastically and at great length. They all easily identified themselves, and wrote about and discussed freely what they thought significant and unique about their own and other "tribes" (student papers unfortunately lost in the war).

By the beginning of the next semester, two months after the war had started, such a discussion had become unthinkable. Ethnic identity had itself become a dangerous topic, and for members of the four groups designated above, it was life-threatening. Although the fighting was still some distance away, members of the groups in question had clearly become targets. The Mandingo, who owned and operated most of the taxis and gas stations in Gbarnga, as well as small markets, stores and stalls, were the first to leave the city. In late March, one of my former students, a young Mandingo woman who had often come to my office to discuss feminist issues I had raised in class, came to me to say goodbye, confiding that her family, together with others of the Mandingo community in Gbarnga, was fleeing the war to Guinea. Very touchingly, she asked if I could possibly arrange for her to have a copy of the anthropology textbook we had used, and I gave her mine. Shortly after this, the public relations director at Cuttington, a Gio who had been to college in Minnesota and had developed an enthusiasm for skiing, recounted to me a horrendous tale of his detainment at a checkpoint while returning to Cuttington from Easter vacation at his home in Nimba County. Despite the protection of his education and his employment at Cuttington, he barely escaped with his life, arrived back on campus terrified, and almost immediately fled the country. And there were other incidents involving members of these four targeted groups. A friend brought a Gio midwife to our house one day, asking me to provide her with some food and financial support. She was a refugee from Nimba County, who had returned from the market to find her village destroyed and her entire family murdered. One of my students came to my office late one afternoon when the campus was nearly empty to confide to me that he was a Krahn, and although he had never liked President Doe, he feared, quite realistically, that because of his tribal association with Doe he would be killed. By that time tribal identity had become a matter of life and death.

Beginning during the Doe government, Liberian travelers had been routinely stopped and checked for their documentation at government checkpoints set up along the road and manned by Doe's AFL army. Before the war there were four such checkpoints on the road between our home in Gbarnga and Monrovia. Our first knowledge of the war occurred through an encounter at the checkpoint near our home, just at the outskirts of Gbarnga. We had crossed it early in the evening of 24 December, the day the war began, to visit friends, finding everything as normal, with a handful of police guards lazily waving the traffic through. Returning at 10 p.m. the checkpoint was swarming with soldiers in full battle gear, questioning us and holding us at gunpoint to search the car for weapons. With the war, these checkpoints multiplied, and travelers were stopped and, often at gunpoint, asked to identify their "tribe," the crucial diacritics being language, initiation scarification, name, and county of residence. If thought to be Gio or Mano, they were frequently killed. We observed lines of men awaiting interrogation at these checkpoints, and saw some of them pulled out of line and led away. We were also told by observers of these events of Gio and Mano men brought to the army barracks near our home. We heard that they were shot, and heard the sound of gunshots from the barracks at night. Later the shots stopped, and we were told that in order to avoid the greater public attention generated by the sound of gunfire, they now had their throats cut. I now used my relative immunity as a foreigner to drive several Gio and Mano students across the checkpoint between Cuttington and Gbarnga, toward what we hoped would be their greater safety in the rural areas or across the border in Cote d'Ivoire, Guinea, or Sierra Leone. And I knew of many local students who also helped members of targeted groups to escape. These checkpoints, which subsequently proliferated among all factions in the war in the territories they controlled, and where "tribal" identities had to be publicly substantiated, constituted spaces of great danger (see also Ellis 1999: 116). They were also, I believe, major forces both in heightening consciousness of ethnic identities and in highlighting the ethnic dimensions of the conflict.

In fact any group or gathering point constituted a potential site for the investigation and hunting down of ethnic identities. For example, in late March, after the war had begun but before Cuttington College had been evacuated in the advancing path of the NPFL forces, government army officers entered the campus demanding a list of the student body, identified by "tribe." A brave dean of the college refused to provide such a list, and was taken away to the nearby army barracks. Within days of this episode, students had vacated the campus. When refugees fleeing the fighting to the northeast streamed into Gbarnga and a government rice distribution point was set up, few people showed up, despite their often desperate need. It turned out that identity cards were required to establish eligibility, and many people feared that the real intent was to discover the ethnic identities of the refugees, many of whom were Gio and Mano fleeing from Nimba County.

The war thus generated within the population of Gbarnga an almost instant heightening of awareness and sensitivity to ethnic identity, and to situations that might necessitate revealing it. But while it made ethnicity a dangerous topic, the danger was principally to members of the four targeted ethnic groups. Other "tribes" were not so targeted, nor did they seem as ready to apply their opinions of leaders to other members of their ethnic groups. For example, the ethnic enmities did not seem to involve the Kpelle, among whom we lived in Gbarnga. Many Kpelle were very angry at Doe for having imprisoned and apparently murdered a leading Kpelle politician and presidential hopeful, which led some to support Taylor. But many Kpelle seemed rather neutral in this early period (though I cannot speak for how this situation may have changed when Gbarnga became the capital of Taylor's Greater Liberia, see Liberty 1998). Nor did targeted ethnic hostilities seem to be present among the other households of the multi-ethnic neighborhood in which we lived, which was mainly Loma, but included members of several other ethnic groups, though I do not recall that it included members of the targeted ethnic groups. Some of the members of these households opposed Doe, while others had family members who were soldiers in Doe's army, one of whom would sometimes arrive after nightfall with truckloads of loot from villages in the war zone. The fears of our neighbors were not ethnic fears: they were fears of the war itself, as the fighting neared Gbarnga and threatened to overrun the city, and people began to flee. In other words, the ethnic enmities highlighted in the war intensified ethnic sensitivities, but they did not lead to generalized ethnic hostilities among other ethnic groups within the Gbarnga population, nor to hostility toward the four targeted "tribes."

It is important to distinguish ethnic categories and labels from ethnic identities. It is a distinction that I will also use in linking ethnic dimensions of the Civil War to processes of ethnic identity formation that predate the war. I rely here on Cohen's (1969) distinction between ethnic categories, imposed from outside upon aggregated populations possessing broad commonalities of territory, language and culture, and ethnic groups, self-identified, self-conscious groups formed by local populations engaged in contextually constructing their own identities in response to changing conditions. My students at Cuttington, in the context of a multi-ethnic student body, and in class discussions before the war, clearly identified themselves contextually as members of self-conscious ethnic groups, as did our neighbors. The early days of the Liberian Civil War in Gbarnga undoubtedly heightened the importance of such ethnic identities for many, and certainly for members of the four targeted groups. Yet it is my strong impression that much of the ethnic intensity that arose with the war was far more about the use of ethnic categories and ethnic labels, and the fear that their use aroused, and I am not sure how far it went in transforming ethnic identities. People labeled the assumed members of other "tribal" categories according to exterior signs, as occurred at the checkpoints, while individuals of the four targeted groups labeled each other and feared that others would label them. Such labeling occurred in the strategic case of enemies and in the contextual labeling at the checkpoints. Among the four targeted groups, self-labeling was crucial in order to be aware of potential danger.

But this process of labeling was loaded with problems and ambiguities. There were the fear and attendant dangers of mislabeling. Indigenous Liberians who were not Kpelle or native to Gbarnga told me they feared they would be mistaken for members of one of the targeted groups and killed. Reports from other areas of Liberia indicate instances where this happened – cases of Grebo people, speaking a language closely related to Krahn, being taken for Krahn, and of Muslim members of the Vai and Mende "tribes" living in Lofa County being killed as Mandingo (Ellis 1999: 114).

Issues of mislabeling also related back to problems with ethnic boundaries themselves. Though the use of "tribal" identities in the war made it appear that tribal boundaries were very clear, this was not the case. The elusive and problematic nature of "tribal" boundaries and identities, which I will discuss further below, has a long history in Liberia, and remained an important issue at the time of the Civil War. Ellis, for example, notes that among the Krahn, the "tribe" at the very center of the ethnic conflicts, the boundaries of inclusion are highly problematic. Ellis describes the Krahn "tribe" as made up of discrete clans, some of whom speak different though related languages, most of whom inhabit Grand Gedeh County, but some of whom live across the border in Cote d'Ivoire, who have at times acted politically as three different tribes. Moreover, on the local level, populations form their primary identities as members of lineages and villages, rather than as Krahn (Ellis 1999: 35–36). Ellis comments that for the Krahn, "tribal" identity may have meaning only in the context of national politics. But at this level the definition is also contested. Doe's protection and assistance to his co-ethnics included only certain clans among the Krahn to whom he was related, and excluded others. However supporters of Taylor who targeted Krahn as enemies might apply the label to all who lived in Grand Gedeh County, including non-Krahn who spoke related languages. My experience in Gbarnga was that all who could be labeled as Krahn by external markers and identity cards seemed in the eyes of non-Krahn to be equally Krahn. And this seemed to be true as well of the Gio, Mano, and Mandingo. In other words, although people worried about themselves being mislabeled, they did not seem to question the validity, nor the accuracy, of ethnic labels when they were being applied to others.

Ethnic labeling has also served as a pretext for targeting people with motives other than ethnic fear or hostility. Reno has suggested, for example, that Taylor emphasized Mandingo traders' role as collaborators with Doe in order to facilitate his troops' takeover of their trade in diamonds and gold (Reno 1998: 97). Ellis comments that "the search for national enemies became inseparable from the search for personal enemies" (Ellis 1999: 117), and notes instances of poor rural Gio and other rural ethnic soldiers targeting wealthier urban co-ethnics for robbery and murder at checkpoints. In these instances of the settling of scores, it appears that issues of class were more important than those of ethnicity.

The distinction between ethnic categories and ethnic identities in the Civil War is also relevant to the discussion of pre-war Liberia and to the historical development of Liberian "tribes." Self-conscious ethnic identities appear to arise primarily as an urban phenomenon and to be less developed in rural areas, where the use of ethnic categories and ethnic labels seems largely the action of politicians. The imposition of "tribal" categories upon the Liberian population dates mainly, as in colonial Africa, to the institution of indirect rule. Through this mechanism, the indigenous populations of the interior were organized into distinct, territorially based administrative units or "tribes" for purposes of political control, collecting taxes, imposing labor quotas, and settling legal disputes. These generally did not correspond to preexisting indigenous political forms (see d'Azevedo 1989; Ellis 1999: chapter 5), nor did they recognize the cultural diversity so common to many communities (see especially d'Azevedo 1989). But through this reconfiguration of indigenous institutions, with "tribal" labels and state-designated officials controlling the indigenous political institutions within them, the Liberian state crystallized and reified the complex, strategic, ad hoc and often relatively ephemeral realities of pre-conquest political entities and boundaries, and created the "tribes" officially recognized by the Liberian state. As elsewhere in the colonial world, these provided the basis both for the elaboration of individual "tribal" identities, and for the differentiation of the indigenous population.

From the ethnic categories constructed by the Liberian state, indigenous Liberians began the process of constructing "tribes" as self-conscious ethnic groups. This has been a highly creative, fluid and uneven process (d'Azevedo 1969/71; McEvoy 1977; Martin 1968; Tonkin 1992), and appears to have occurred mainly in urban areas. Settlers in the capital found the indigenous populations already to some degree urbanized and ethnically differentiated through prior contacts with the coastal trade, and drew them into the settler economy. They formed the basis of what by the 1950s were well-defined self-identified communities with distinctive ethnic identities, occupational niches, religious affiliations, voluntary associations and quasi-autonomous corporate political institutions administered directly by the Liberian state (Fraenkel 1964). These urban "tribes" provided models for later migrants arriving from the interior, and the development of ethnicity became widely recognized as an urban end product of migration (Breitborde 1980/81; Holsoe 1984/85; McEvoy 1977). During the 1970s, as economic decline replaced the boom years of the 1950s and 1960s, and unemployment in Monrovia reached over 50 per cent, such urban "tribal" connections became increasingly important. Rubber plantations, mining concessions, and interior towns and cities which drew diverse indigenous populations into wage labor systems, provided an additional locus for ethnic interactions and "tribalizing" encounters (McEvoy 1977).

Researchers during this period also depicted Liberia as engaged in a "detribalizing" process, with ethnic solidarities breaking down and giving way to class solidarities and nationalist ideologies (Dunn and Tarr 1988; Liebenow 1987; Sawyer 1992). This was heralded as evidence of political modernization and nation-building (Young 1993), in which "modern" forms of economic and political integration and new national identities would replace ethnic or "tribal" loyalties and identities, whose persistence was viewed as regressive, divisive, and dangerous to the modern nation-state.[14] But while post-war economic growth and the expansion of educational facilities and employment enabled the rise of an urban, educated middle class of "technocrats" (Hlophe 1979) of indigenous ancestry who became leaders in class-based challenges to elitist state power, this process was limited mainly to educated sectors in the capital, which formed only a small fraction of Liberia's still overwhelmingly rural population. Emphasis on the political ideals of this tiny minority produced a distorted idea of what was happening in Liberia, and made the intense ethnic conflicts that developed almost immediately afterwards within the Doe government appear as disjunctive. They were said to represent a reversal of the trends of the previous thirty years, a "retribalizing" of "detribalizing" populations. Some analysts of the Liberian case even claimed that "tribalism" had been unknown in Liberian politics and social life before the military coup of 1980 (Clapham 1989; Seyon 1987: 76), thus implying that Doe had single-handedly authored this transformation, which was referred to as the emergence of a "new tribalism" (Liebenow 1987: 302).

Yet as early as 1971 (reprinted in 1989), Warren d'Azevedo, writing of rural areas, had noted the strengthening of an "emergent tribalism," and issued a prophetic warning:

> "Tribalism," the avowed enemy of national unity, has been a product of Liberian nationalization itself, and the readiness with which native institutions and aspiring leaders adapted themselves to the new concept has implications for the course of development of the Liberian nation which have not yet been appreciated by students of the country.
>
> (d'Azevedo 1989: 102)

Rural ethnicity and politics has been little researched for the crucial period from the 1950s through to the 1970s (d'Azevedo 1989; Sawyer 1992: 3), though d'Azevedo's own work provides a notable exception. Within the "tribal" categories established under indirect rule at the beginning of the century, descending hierarchies of indigenous officials, paramount chiefs, clan chiefs, town chiefs, etc. exercised authority over the local kinship groups which controlled access to "tribal" lands and membership in the key institutions of local social life, politics and religion, the secret societies of the Poro and Sande.[15] For rural politicians, tribal categories served as the basis for internally elaborated patronage structures through which state obligations were imposed, and favors received, with the attendant possibilities of clientelism and graft. With the extension of the franchise to indigenous Liberians, patronage networks provided the electoral vehicle for the delivery of votes. The administrative reorganization of the interior into counties, which began in 1964, further strengthened the territorial basis of ethnic patronage politics in rural areas. The new county boundaries followed and reified many of the "tribal" territories constructed under indirect rule, and for the largest "tribal" groups of the interior, produced a rough approximation of county with "tribe," though as indicated above, this was not true of small "tribes" such as the Krahn. Through the 1980s, elders of "tribes" excluded from this pattern exerted continuing pressures and had some success in carving new county boundaries that would conform more closely to their "tribal" territories (Liebenow 1987: 268–269).[16] While politicians of indigenous background in the capital may have engaged in class-based political alliances and the nationalist politics of integration, they could do so only through mobilizing the electoral support of their "tribally" based constituencies in their rural county homelands (Clapham 1989: 101). They still relied for their constituencies on the mobilization of their rural ethnic patronage networks and clienteles in the interior.[17]

But beyond the interest they held for aspiring "tribal" leaders, in rural areas, it is not clear to what degree these categories promoted the internalization of ethnic identities for members of the various "tribes." D'Azevedo suggests that the political organization of the interior encouraged leaders to activate "latent and residual concepts of ethnicity" (1989: 101–102) among their followers. And ethnic identities established through migration to urban centers and other areas of wage labor were subsequently carried back into rural areas, facilitated by the "go-come" nature of Liberian migration patterns (Breitborde 1980/81). But researchers in various rural areas of Liberia have concurred that "tribal" identities have had little meaning for rural villagers who have formed and continue to form their primary identities around local ties of kinship, religion, and village membership (Carter 1970; Ellis 1999; Tonkin 1992). It appears then that in many rural areas, ethnicity may have consisted more in politicians' uses of ethnic categories in the exercise of patronage politics than in the development of self-conscious "tribal" identities.

National integration initiatives developed under the Tubman and Tolbert regimes, designed to give new appreciation to tribal culture and social norms, led to a greater valorizing of rural indigenous ties and "country" culture by the elite. But they also continued to emphasize the maintenance of linguistic and cultural differences among "tribal" groups. "Tribal" categories were reified as the basis of the national census, through the use of radio broadcasts in "tribal" languages as a means of reaching rural constituencies, and through cultural initiatives from the government Bureau of Folkways designed to stimulate ethnic pride by providing for the conservation and definition of distinctive "tribal" customs.[18] The influence of these initiatives in promoting distinctive "tribal" identities has not been examined.

Correspondingly, the state failed to develop institutions that would crosscut "tribal" divisions and foster the formation of multi-ethnic groups and alliances. And it repressed labor union activity and strikes on plantations and in mines (Mayson and Sawyer 1980; Wagner 1988), that might have fostered the formation of multi-ethnic class solidarities, and thwarted the persistent efforts of indigenous politicians to form multi-ethnic opposition political groups (Abasiattai 1987). The potential role of religious institutions in promoting such multi-ethnic alliances has remained largely unexplored.[19] Thus it is not surprising that frequent references to "tribal" identities and veiled references to fears of lingering, continuing "tribalism" lurk among the recitals of modernization and national integration in the literature of this period. The opposition politics of the 1970s saw the rise of "tribally" identified political parties, such as those of the murdered indigenous political leader Gabriel Kpolleh among the Kpelle and of Jackson Doe among the Gio. Although these tribal identities were not the basis for conflict or violence at this time, their existence, and their importance in many areas of Liberian life, cannot be questioned. Their centrality in structuring access to resources and power is particularly crucial in understanding what happened after 1980 when "tribal" differences rapidly became faultlines in the shaping of political conflict and violence. Bearing in mind that different levels of identity are called into play contextually, it appears that rural county politics provided a context for the strengthening of the rural identities that emerged so powerfully in the 1980s. The intensification of ethnic labeling that emerged in Gbarnga in the early months of the Civil War had its proximate origins in the Doe government, but more distant historical origins in the rural political structures of the Liberian state in the long-term state-imposed system of indirect rule.

The 1980 coup that brought Samuel Doe and the Liberian military to power represented the replacement of the long-entrenched, settler-dominated elite by indigenous Liberians long excluded from power. But more than that, it also replaced the urban nationalist politics dominated by the settler elite with the rural politics of indigenous ethnic clienteles, the politics of ethnic categories and ethnic labels. When Doe's initial efforts at a broad-based coalition failed, it was to his own ethnic, "tribal" clientele that he turned for support, and it was the rural "tribal" constituency of his chief enemy in the government that he targeted and brutalized. Ironically, some of his personal guards were not even Liberians, but Krahn from across the border in Cote d'Ivoire. In the last weeks of his presidency and his life, the image of this figure, holed up in the presidential mansion in Monrovia with his co-ethnic Krahn officers and acolytes while Taylor's forces try desperately to kill him, posed questions for many Liberians concerning the ultimate paradox of patronage: were these officers loyally defending Doe to the death, or were they, his former clients, now holding him hostage for their own protection, as many suggested at the time?

The "tribal" conflicts that emerged during the Doe government appear to be an extension of the ethnic clientele politics of the rural areas which Doe brought into the national political arena formerly controlled by the settler-dominated elite. This group, which should be seen as an ethnic group in its own right, though it has not been included among the lists of Liberian "tribes,"[20] had for over a century claimed to legitimately represent the Liberian nation as a whole, in a way that no indigenous "tribe" could claim. As of 1980, there was no mechanism for adjudicating political relations among tribes except through the now-deposed settler elite. When disputes and competition arose within the government, "tribal" differences were a ready means of identifying the parties, and mobilizing allies. But the war was not an ethnic or cultural conflict: it was about competition for power among people long denied power, where there were virtually no mechanisms in place for exclusion or inclusion, much less experience in the politics of democratic representation. The examination of ethnicity in the Liberian case speaks to the need for greater attention to the dynamic and dialectical relations among power, culture and violence, and for consideration not only of the ways in which preexisting cultural differences may produce conflict, but also of how conflicts may themselves produce new cultural forms (Warren 1993: 2).

Recent data on the warlord politics that emerged with the war suggest continuity with "tribal" politics in the use of ethnic labels to identify the various factions (Reno 1998: 93). But the members of these factions are diverse, and multi-ethnic, and Ellis notes that ethnic allegiance has been important "only when a local grievance, rooted in local history and land disputes, became caught up with national factional activity" (1999: 105). He further suggests, as I have argued for wartime Gbarnga, that "the mobilization of ethnic identity is more rhetoric than reality" (1999: 105). It appears that, in this respect at least, the war has not further "tribalized" the Liberian population. "Tribal" markers again appear to serve more to distinguish and label differences among the different factions than to identify the ethnic identities of their members. But the war may have acted to strengthen a national, Liberian identity. Many refugees fleeing across the borders to their kin in Cote d'Ivoire, Guinea and Sierra Leone were initially welcomed by local communities and host governments. But as the war dragged on, they became an economic drain on their hosts, and were marked as "Liberian" intruders, harassed and sent home. These experiences, which highlighted the refugees' national, Liberian identity over those of kin or "tribe," may well have acted to strengthen rural indigenous refugees' awareness of their national identities as Liberians (see Bick 1992; Brown and Bick 2001).

Conclusions

Returning to Gbarnga for a brief visit in 1998, we had many emotional reunions with friends there, and listened to their horrific experiences during the war, of flight, of atrocities witnessed, of threatened death, capture and forced servitude. None of these accounts mentioned "tribal" conflicts or referred to the "tribal" identities of their pursuers or captors. In fact, these war narratives, for all the details that they did give, showed a striking absence of any kind of references to ethnic identities. This was true as well of their accounts of their subsequent return to Gbarnga, of efforts to find employment, and of legal procedures undertaken to reoccupy houses, which had been occupied by others during the war. Even in recounting to us the people from whom they had sought personal favors to help them survive in the desperate post-war economy, these friends made no mention to us of "tribal" connections. Nor did they mention ethnic tensions, though they were very open about the climate of anxiety and fear in which they lived. The only evidence we found of ethnic competition in Gbarnga was in relation to small shops which before the war had been owned by local Kpelle and Mandingo, and during Taylor's occupation of Gbarnga had been taken over by the Mano and Gio.

Taylor, despite his use of ethnicity as a strategy of war, is not emphasizing ethnicity in his current government, with the exception of the Krahn and Mandingo, who are still targeted. Our brief encounter with Taylor's entourage on the highway during the first hour of our return trip in 1998 spoke of a raw power that recalled older patrimonial systems, and not ethnic domination. As we proceeded by taxi along the main road to Monrovia past the gutted public buildings and former homes of the affluent, with ragged families and their washing framed in apertures that had once been windows, a klaxon sounded ahead. Our taxi driver quickly pulled to the side of the road and stopped. "Taylor is coming, and everyone has to pull off the road or they will be shot," he explained nervously. A procession of open-backed trucks filled with soldiers, their guns aimed at the passing scene, sped by at high speed, with Taylor's limousine sandwiched in among them. "This happens every day. This is how Taylor travels to work and back home," he said. This incident formed our introduction to the palpable undercurrents of tension and fear we encountered among our friends and those we met, and which belied the apparently carefree bustle of the capital and the tranquility of the countryside around Gbarnga where we had lived. But upon reflection, it represented autocratic patrimonial politics – a partial reimagining of the Liberian state as it had existed before the Civil War – and the continuation of a political dramaturgy of a state based not on ethnicity but on raw power, the assertion and reassertion of "traditional" Liberian politics. Ellis notes that even before Taylor assumed the Liberian presidency, he had claimed, against the ethnic interests put forth by the other factions, to represent a national, Liberian identity, in part, because his "Americo-Liberian ancestry made it difficult for him to play the ethnic card" (1999: 104). During the pre-1980 regimes raw power had been somewhat camouflaged by the illusion of political civility, but everyone knows that Tubman and Tolbert both held it, and used it. Taylor's is a more open claim to legitimacy through the expressly public exercise of raw power.

The state continues; it has not "collapsed." It can come back to life because, as Ellis aptly comments (1999: 116), regardless of the weakness of the state apparatus, the state exists in the minds of both its citizens and the international community.

Notes

1 This article in its several incarnations has benefited immeasurably from discussions with Mario Bick, and also with Alexander Bick. Both of them shared peace and war with me in Liberia, and their ideas about its situation have influenced my thinking and been incorporated within this analysis.
2 Liebenow (1987: 35) lists the Liberian "tribes" and their proportionate representation in the Liberian population at the time of the 1974 census. They include the Kpelle (20 per cent); the Bassa (14 per cent); the Gio (8 per cent); the Kru (8 per cent); the Grebo (8 per cent); the Mano (7 per cent); the Loma (6 per cent); the Krahn (5 per cent); the Gola (4 per cent); the Mandingo (4 per cent); the Kissi (3 per cent); the Vai (3 per cent); the Gbandi (3 per cent); the Belle (0.5 per cent); the Dei (0.5 per cent); and the Mende (0.5 per cent). A further 2.9 per cent were recorded as having "no tribal affiliation." This last default category measures the non-indigenous settler population referred to as "Americo-Liberians" or "Congoes."
3 Radio provided the main source of political news: the government radio championed Doe and carried his speeches, while the BBC provided coverage of Taylor's activities and broadcast many of his news conferences and his communiques to Doe.
4 Some scholars reject the colonial analogy for Liberia (David 1991; Ellis 1999; Sawyer 1992). They have argued that the elite's initial iron hand in the indigenous interior was an unwilling one, the result of its powerlessness to resist the expansionist pressures of its colonial neighbors (Ellis 1999: 293) and its inability to wrest financial assistance from the American government or to assert their interests against those of their American Colonization Society patrons (David 1991; Sawyer 1992). Ellis also contests the applicability of the label "black colonialism" for Liberia, arguing that its elite did not maintain isolation but rather absorbed many indigenous persons and ideas (1999: 293).
5 The United Nations inquiry concerned reports of Liberian soldiers' midnight raids on indigenous villages to obtain labor for the cocoa plantations on the Spanish island of Fernando Po, for which members of the Liberian government were reportedly paid substantial sums. Such forced labor was frequently recruited as well for government projects, for foreign enterprises such as the Firestone Rubber Plantation, and sometimes clandestinely for the private plantations of the wealthy settler elite (see Liebenow 1987: 56–58).
6 This was at first accomplished through a system of apprenticeship, designed to train and educate African repatriates and indigenous youth, and to "civilize" and Christianize them. It later gave way to the fostering of rural children in urban households, a practice widespread in Liberia today (Sawyer 1992: 187–189).
7 Repression of indigenous groups extended to those who resisted pacification, traditional labor groups who resisted forms of economic exploitation (Mayson and Sawyer 1980), labor unions and strikes (Wagner 1988), and persistent efforts of indigenous peoples to form opposition political action groups in the period before the 1970s (Abasiattai 1987).
8 An Americo-Liberian, and member of Doe's initial government, Taylor was charged by Doe with the embezzlement of government funds. He subsequently fled to the USA, was jailed there pending extradition to Liberia, escaped mysteriously, traveled widely in West Africa receiving military training and recruiting soldiers and arms for his return to Liberia, and reemerged in public only in 1989, with his effort to overthrow the Doe government.
9 In addition to Nigeria, this faction also included Ghana, Sierra Leone, the Gambia, and non-aligned Francophone Guinea.

10 Rumors circulating during the early months of the war that Taylor and some of his troops had received military training and financial support from Libya, some of it through its ally, Burkina Faso, have been confirmed in later accounts of the war. (For more recent and complex analyses of the configurations in this conflict see Ellis 1999; Huband 1998.)

11 Ivorian president Houphouet-Boigny's adopted daughter Daisy had been married to Adolphus Tolbert, whom Doe murdered along with his father, the Liberian president, during the 1980 coup. Burkinabe president Campraore was married to Houphouet-Boigny's other daughter, and was thus the brother-in-law of the murdered son of President Tolbert, Adolphus Tolbert.

12 The intervention of the OAU in 1993 and its decision to send East African troops from Tanzania and Uganda to join the ECOWAS forces already in Liberia was intended to transcend and neutralize these West African conflicts.

13 Unlike Lowenkopf (1995), who portrays Doe as politically incompetent and naive, which he interprets as a significant factor in the Liberian state collapse, Reno (1998; see also Ellis 1999) reads Doe as an astute and wily politician.

14 This view was the result of a prioritizing of urban over rural research, and an uncritical acceptance of modernization theories. Research agendas of this period, which lasted into the 1970s, also showed the influence of efforts to avoid the colonialist biases associated with the use of the term "tribe" (Barth 1969; Fried 1967), which often resulted in a research focus on the many inaccuracies generated through the use of this term, rather than on the ways in which state-created conditions for the development of "tribes" contributed to producing them (see Holsoe 1967; McEvoy 1977; Tonkin 1985).

15 The societies of the Poro (for males) and Sande (for females) found among the western indigenous groups in Liberia were important in providing rites of passage into adulthood, and in providing instruction in sacred and local political leadership, and are spoken of as having had an important role in the creation of "tribal" identities (see, for example, Brenner 1993), though these were of interethnic composition in certain areas (d'Azevedo 1962).

16 The demarcation of counties in 1964 produced a close conformity of Nimba County with the Gio and Mano "tribes," while Bong County encompassed the greater part of the Kpelle "tribal" territories. The Loma are the largest of several "tribal" groups that occupy Lofa County, and are often identified with it, while Grand Gedeh County has been dominated by the Krahn "tribe," though as indicated above, it does not provide a particularly good fit with its boundaries. Continuing pressure exerted by Gola elders led to the later creation of two new, more "tribally" compatible counties, and pressures to further this pattern continued into the 1980s and were acknowledged by the framers of the new 1984 constitution (Liebenow 1987: 268–269).

17 References to the constituencies of leading politicians of the 1970s (Lawyers Committee for Human Rights 1986; Dunn and Tarr 1988; Liebenow 1987; Sawyer 1992) all suggest the mobilization of large county/"tribal" voter bases of their co-ethnics by such politicians as Gabriel Kpolleh of the Liberian Unification Party (Kpelle, Bong County); Edward Kesselly of the Unity Party (Loma/Mandingo, Lofa County); and, significantly, Jackson Doe (no relation to Samuel Doe) of the Liberian Action Party (Gio, Nimba County). During the 1980s, Jackson Doe's popularity, together with that of his Gio compatriot, Thomas Quiwonkpa, and his purported victory in the 1985 elections, sabotaged by President Doe, greatly intensified Krahn/Gio ethnic conflicts.

18 The Bureau of Folkways was directed by the Vai poet and scholar Bai T. Moore, whose activities there are discussed by Monts (1990) and Moore (1990).

19 D'Azevedo (1962) has emphasized the interethnic composition and role of the Poro in certain areas of Liberia. It is possible that other religious groups, including Muslims, Christians and independent Christian churches may also have had such a role,

although available studies tend to treat these in relation to particular "tribal" groups (Holsoe 1967; Korte 1971/72; Turner 1967).
20 The settler-dominated elite were not recognized as a "tribe," the distinction being reserved for the indigenous population. The basis of this distinction was the primary one between the "civilized" settlers and the "native" or "tribal" indigenous population, which Mamdani (1996) refers to as "institutional segregation" between the native institutions of the rural areas, preserved through indirect rule, and "civil" or "civilized" society of the national state.

References

Abasiattai, Monday B. (1987) "Resistance of the African Peoples of Liberia." *Liberia-Forum* 3/4: 53–69.
Barth, Frederik (ed.) (1969) *Ethnic Groups and Boundaries*. Boston: Little, Brown.
Berkeley, Bill (1992) "Liberia: Between Repression and Slaughter." *The Atlantic* 270(6): 52–64.
Bick, Mario (1992) "Border Incidents: Kinship and Ethnicity during the Liberian Civil War." Paper presented at the Annual Meetings of the American Anthropological Association, San Fransisco, 1–6 December.
Boone, Catherine (1998) "'Empirical Statehood' and Reconfigurations of Political Order." In Leonardo Villalon and Phillip Huxtable (eds), *The African State at a Critical Juncture Between Disintegration and Reconfiguration*. Boulder: Lynne Rienner.
Breitborde, L.B. (1980/81) "A Brief Note on the Urban Ethnic Basis of Kru Linguistic Diversity." *Liberian Studies Journal* 9(2): 83–92.
Brenner, Mary E. (1993) "The Decline of Traditional Initiation Schools in Western Liberia." Paper presented at the Annual Meetings of the American Anthropological Association, Washington, DC, 17–21 November.
Brown, Diana (1993) "'We Are Third World Children': Child Warriors in the Liberian Civil War." Paper presented at Conference on Violence in Africa, Columbia University Institute of African Studies, 2–3 April.
Brown, Diana and Bick, Mario (2001) "Female Peasants and Cosmopolitan Males: Speculations on Liberia's Geopolitical Future." Paper presented at the 33rd Annual Conference of the Liberian Studies Association, Charleston, SC, 29–31 March.
Carter, Jeanette (1970) "The Rural Loma and Monrovia: Ties with an Urban Center." *Liberian Studies Journal* 2(2): 143–151.
Clapham, Christopher (1989) "Liberia." In D. Cruise O'Brien, John Dunn and Richard Rathbone (eds), *Contemporary West African States*. Cambridge: Cambridge University Press, pp. 99–112.
Clower, Robert W., George Dalton, Mitchell Harwitz and A.A. Walters (1966) *Growth Without Development: an Economic Survey of Liberia*. Evanston: Northwestern University Press.
Cohen, Abner (1969) *Custom and Politics in Urban Africa: a Study of Hausa Migrants in Yoruba Towns*. Berkeley: University of California Press.
David, Magdalene Soniia (1991) "His, Hers, or Theirs: An Analysis of Conjugal Economic Relations among the Kpelle of Liberia." PhD dissertation, Department of Sociology, University of Wisconsin-Madison.
d'Azevedo, Warren (1962) "Some Historical Problems in the Delineation of a Central West Atlantic Region." *Annals of the New York Academy of Sciences* 96: 512–538.
—— (1969/71) "A Tribal Reaction to Nationalism," Parts 1–4. *Liberian Studies Journal* 1: 1–21; 2(1): 43–63; 2(2): 99–115; 3(1): 1–19.

—— (1989) "Tribe and Chiefdom on the Windward Coast." *Liberian Studies Journal* 14(2): 90–116. (Originally published in 1971.)

Dunn, D. Elwood and S. Byron Tarr (1988) *Liberia: A National Polity in Transition*. Metuchen, NJ: The Scarecrow Press.

Ellis, Stephen (1995) "Liberia 1989–1994: A Study of Ethnic and Spiritual Violence." *African Affairs* 94: 165–197.

—— (1999) *The Mask of Anarchy: the Destruction of Liberia and the Religious Dimension of an African Civil War*. New York: New York University Press.

Fraenkel, Merran (1964) *Tribe and Class in Monrovia*. London: Oxford University Press.

Fried, Morton (1967) *The Evolution of Political Society*. New York: Random House.

Gershoni, Yekutiel (1993a) "The First and Second Republics in Liberia: From a Single-Society State to a Single-Tribe State." Paper presented at the Conference of the Liberian Studies Association, Albany, GA, 15–17 April.

—— (1993b) "From ECOWAS to ECOMOG: The Liberian Crisis and the Struggle for Political Hegemony in West Africa." *Liberian Studies Journal* 18(3): 21–43.

Hlophe, Stephen S. (1979) *Class, Ethnicity and Politics in Liberia: A Class Analysis of Power Struggles in the Tubman and Tolbert Administrations from 1944–1975*. Washington, DC: University Press of America.

Holmes, Patricia (1992) "The Voice of America in Liberia: The End of the Road." *Liberian Studies Journal* 17(1): 79–93.

Holsoe, Svend E. (1967) "The Cassava-Leaf People: An Ethnohistorical Study of the Vai People with a Particular Emphasis on the Tewo Chiefdom." PhD dissertation, Boston University.

—— (1984/85) "Vai Occupational Continuities: Traditional to Modern." *Liberian Studies Journal* 10(2): 12–23.

Huband, Mark (1998) *The Liberian Civil War*. London and Portland, OR: Frank Cass.

Jackson, Robert H., and Carl G. Rosberg (1982) "Why Africa's Weak States Persist: The Empirical and the Juridical in Statehood." *World Politics* 35(1): 1–24.

Kimble, Frank B. (1990) "The United States–Liberia Operation Experts Project." *Liberian Studies Journal* 15(1): 1–12.

Korte, Werner (1971/72) "A Note on Independent churches in Liberia." *Liberian Studies Journal* 4(1): 81–87.

Lawyers Committee for Human Rights (1986) *Liberia: A Promise Betrayed. A Report on Human Rights*. New York: Lawyers' Committee for Human Rights.

Liberty, C.E. Zamba (1998) "Buto: A Liliputian Testament to a Struggle – the NPFL Journey to State-Power: How Charles Taylor Upset the Bowl of Rice and Took Home the Whole Hog." *Liberian Studies Journal* 23(1): 135–207.

Liebenow, J. Gus (1962) "The Republic of Liberia." In Gwendolen Carter (ed.), *African One-Party States*. Ithaca: Cornell University Press, pp. 325–394.

—— (1982/83) "Liberia: The Path to Civilian Rule." *Liberian Studies Journal* 10(1): 1–16.

—— (1987) *Liberia: The Quest for Democracy*. Bloomington: Indiana University Press.

Lowenkopf, Martin (1995) "Liberia: Putting the State Back Together." In I. William Zartman (ed.), *Collapsed States: The Disintegration and Restoration of Legitimate Authority*, Boulder: Lynne Rienner.

McEvoy, Frederick D. (1977) "Understanding Ethnic Realities among the Grebo and Kru Peoples of West Africa." *Africa* 47(1): 62–79.

Mamdani, Mahmood (1996) *Citizen and Subject: Contemporary Africa and the Legacy of Late Colonialism*. Princeton: Princeton University Press.

Martin, Jane (1968) "The Dual Legacy: Government Authority and Mission Influence among the Glebo of Eastern Liberia, 1834–1910." PhD dissertation, Department of History, Boston University.

Mayson, Dew Tuan-Wleh and Amos Sawyer (1980) "Labor in Liberia." *Review of African Political Economy* 14: 3–15.

Monts, Lester P. (ed.) (1990) "In Memory of Bai Tamia Moore (1920–1988)." Special Issue, *Liberian Studies Journal* 15(2).

Moore, Bai T. (1990) "Problems of Vai Identity in Terms of My Own Experience." *Liberian Studies Journal* 15(2): 10–13.

Reno, William J. (1998) "The Organization of Warlord Politics in Liberia." In *Warlord Politics and African States*. Boulder: Lynne Rienner.

Sawyer, Amos (1992) *The Emergence of Autocracy in Liberia: Tragedy and Challenge*. San Francisco: ICS Press.

Seyon, Patrick L.N. (1987) "Liberia's Second Republic: Superpower Geopolitics in Africa." *Liberian Studies Journal* 12(1): 56–82.

Tokpa, Henrique F. (1991) "Cuttington University College during the Liberian Civil War: An Administrator's Experience." *Liberian Studies Journal* 16(1): 79–94.

Tonkin, Elizabeth (1985) "Creating Kroomen: Ethnic Diversity, Economic Specialism and Changing Demand." In *Africa and the Sea: Proceedings of a Colloquium at the University of Aberdeen*. Aberdeen University: African Studies Group, pp. 27–47.

—— (1992) *Narrating Our Pasts: The Social Construction of Oral History*. Cambridge: Cambridge University Press.

Turner, H.W. (1967) "The Church of the Lord in Liberia." In *History of an African Independent Church: the Church of the Lord (Aladura)*. Oxford: Clarendon Press, pp. 133–157.

US Committee for Refugees (1992) *Uprooted Liberians: Casualties of a Brutal War*. Washington, DC: US Committee for Refugees.

Wagner, Barbara (1988) "Labor Unions in the Liberian State and Politics." *Liberia-Forum* 4/6: 33–44.

Warren, Kay B. (1993). "Introduction: Revealing Conflicts Across Cultures and Disciplines." In Kay B. Warren (ed.) The *Violence Within: Cultural and Political Opposition in Divided Nation*. Boulder CO: Westview Press, pp.1–24.

Young, Crawford (1993) "The Dialectics of Cultural Pluralism: Concept and Reality." In Crawford Young (ed.), *The Rising Tide of Cultural Pluralism: the Nation-State at Bay?* Madison: University of Wisconsin Press, pp. 3–35.

Zartman, I. William (1995) "Introduction: Posing the Problem of State Collapse." In I. William Zartman (ed.) *Collapsed States: The Disintegration and Restoration of Legitimate Authority*. Boulder: Lynne Rienner.

11 Angola and the fragmentation of the post-colonial African state

Helio Belik

Editor's foreword

Helio Belik died shortly after completing this paper in early 1995. The skepticism he expressed about a new peace accord, the Lusaka Protocol, was well-founded. For more than three years, Jonas Savimbi "talked peace while preparing for war." Small steps, false claims, endless negotiations, missed meetings and deadlines kept a UN-supervised process alive, but with little movement toward real peace, all the while with localized violence. Two critical issues were UNITA's continuing control over diamond mines, and the future personal position of Savimbi. In the middle of 1998, UNITA claimed it had disarmed and demilitarized, and Savimbi found his own position within UNITA challenged by a faction committed to implementation of the Lusaka accords. But in October and November, intense fighting broke out as government forces attempted to establish control of former UNITA lands, and in December, UNITA launched a full-scale offensive, with artillery bombardments of several cities, and up to ninety Ukrainian-made tanks, reportedly commanded by Ukrainian mercenaries. In 1999, an estimated 1 million people were driven from their homes by war. But by the end of that year, government forces had inflicted major defeats on UNITA, and occupied many of its strong-holds. In 2000, UNITA changed tactics away from conventional or even guerrilla warfare, to small hit-and-run raids, kidnappings, murders and bombs – what is generally called terrorism. In mid-2001, that pattern continues, but both the Luanda government and Savimbi have, once again, expressed willingness to negotiate with each other for peace (*Angolan Peace Monitor*, various issues; Swarns 2000).

Angola is a symbol of many things gone wrong. It exemplifies the debilitating effects of colonialism, especially the Portuguese administration in Africa, on post-colonial successor states, as Belik discusses. It is a sorrowful lesson in failed efforts at international peace-making, first by the USA, Russia and Portugal, who initially saw this as an easy case of post-Cold War multilateralism, then by the United Nations (Anstee 1996; MacQueen 1998). It illustrates both the strength and limitations of regional influence, as symbolically, Savimbi boycotted a summit meeting of twelve southern African heads of state, including Nelson Mandela and Robert Mugabe, while the fall of his allies Mobutu in Zaire and

Lissouba in Congo (Brazzaville) was a real blow (MacQueen 1998: 412, 417). It is a classic illustration of Reno's "shadow state" (as discussed in the case of Liberia by Brown, in this volume) and a new globalized war economy. Government officials have garnered enormous personal wealth from petroleum concessions and military spending, while leaving what minimal social services exist to a gusher of external aid. Meanwhile UNITA made an estimated US$3.7 billion in an illicit diamond trade from 1992 to 1998. Multinational firms and surreptitious transborder traders have been only too ready to make all this happen (Gamba and Cornwell 2000: 164–168; MacQueen 1998: 416; Reno 2000: 57). (See the *New York Times* 19 March 2001, advertising insert "Angola," which begins with the lead, "Blessed with untold quantities of petroleum, diamonds, and other mineral resources, Angola is counting on foreign investment and new-found political stability to foster economic recovery.")

Angola is also a classic illustration of the clash of nationalisms. Unlike Liberia, Angola's rebel movements began before independence, in areas with marked ethnic characters that then dominated those movements. The urban-oriented MPLA has stressed "the rights and obligations of citizenship," in contrast to UNITA's "'blood and soil' nationalism" (Pereira 1994: 8). Heywood (1998: 149) discusses how Savimbi has constructed UNITA's message as a "genuine Angolan nationalism, as opposed to the tainted (foreign) nationalism of the MPLA." She describes in detail how Savimbi has used deep knowledge of history and myth, themes relating to traditional leadership, witchcraft, etc., and local social and political institutions to forge an alliance with the rural Ovimbundu people. Savimbi, in other words, provides a perfect example of self-interested ethnic cultural manipulation, and Heywood argues that Western analysts' failure to appreciate the power of this is one reason they have underestimated his persistence.

Belik's insightful first-hand observations take us into the process on the other side, the attempt to create an Angolan nationalism that encompasses all its peoples in a universalistic framework. Those efforts were not entirely in vain. The 1992 elections "did not fragment along ethnic lines" (though UNITA did win handily in Ovimbundu areas), and a voter survey indicated "that Angolans are not irrevocably divided along ethnic and regional lines" (Pereira 1994: 18–19). Pereira also provides an extension of Belik's observation that "the Cold War was what kept Angola operating together as a national state." Not unlike what Brown reports in the case of Liberia, its civil war has had a similar effect. The leveling of localized rural differences by the destruction of war, the travail of living together in massive internal refugee settlements, the experience of serving in the Angolan army and the spread of the Portuguese language it uses, have all contributed to a heightened sense of "Angolidade." Despite the de facto fragmentation Belik describes, neither UNITA or MPLA leaders talk of anything but a united Angola in the future (Pereira 1994: 24, 28). Whether and how that can be achieved, is, of course, the question.

R. Brian Ferguson

Introduction

Angola is at peace now. But it is still a relative peace. For the third time in less than three years, Jonas Savimbi of UNITA (Uniao para a Independencia Total de Angola) and Angola's president, Jose Eduardo dos Santos of the MPLA (Movimento Popular para a Libertacao de Angola) have signed a peace agreement sponsored by the United Nations. Despite Jonas Savimbi's promises that UNITA will abide by the agreements of this latest accord – signed in November 1994 in Lusaka, Zambia, UN officials say that peace in Angola will depend on UNITA's ability to restrain his heavily-armed generals, while bargaining for a share of power in a new government of "national unity." Since the signing of the Lusaka agreement there has been some tension in the countryside, where UNITA and MPLA armies have still not laid down their weapons. Any peace in Angola would first require the demobilization of both armies – the UNITA, which became one of the most trained and heavily armed guerrilla groups in Africa; and the MPLA army that is now receiving training and arms from South Africa, which had formerly supported UNITA with weapons and personnel.[1]

Angola presents a curious case of a nation that since its inception has lived in a perpetual state of violence. Almost two decades of civil war, and more than twenty-five years of open anti-colonial struggle before that, have not given Angolans much opportunity to create an independent state or to constitute ideas of collective nationhood and nationality. The question arises: is Angola really a nation-state, or just a projection of inappropriate Eurocentric models? Is it possible to define Angola using ideas of the nation-state that were shaped by the nineteenth-century European models of state formation? Thus, what term would define Angola? Angola certainly does not exist in the form of a European-style nation-state. The nation is ethnically and regionally fragmented, and state power is not representative of the variety of ethnic and regional segments of the nation. Created by the Portuguese, who defined its territorial borders between 1870 and 1906, Angola faces questions about its identity as a nation and a state. When I was in Luanda in 1991, the debate about how to foster the reality of an Angolan nationality was everywhere, from TV and radio talk-shows to the newly-formed political parties.

Like many regional conflicts in Africa, the Angolan case reveals the extreme fragility of the post-colonial nation-state in Africa, which is being threatened by war, famine and political disintegration. Angola's fragmentation is already a reality operative on a variety of levels – from ideological, to territorial, to political and cultural. Although social scientists in the West predicted that the end of the Cold War would bring the end of regional conflicts and a more stable period in Africa, what happened in Angola was just the opposite: even without the support of old allies such as Cuba, South Africa, the Soviet Union and the USA – which provided weapons, personnel and financial support – Angola's rival factions continued their violent war. The question remains: why is it that the civil war in Angola has continued up to the present day, despite the withdrawal of the superpowers that used to finance its factions?

Now that a new era of relative peace is predicted in Angola, new questions arise: what was it that kept Angola together during so many years of war? Has the war itself contributed to the maintenance of the country? Is the peace sufficient to keep Angola together? The very idea of an Angolan nation, stretching from the forests of Lunda Norte to the deserts of Namibe, is still very strange to many Angolans, who see themselves as divided along regional, ethnic, racial and political lines. When the Portuguese arrived, Ngola was a small chieftainship consisting of only the coastal region where Luanda is today. The Portuguese colonial domain was established there for more than a century before they started to colonize in-land regions. When Antonio Salazar took power in Portugal, in the mid-1930s, he at once instituted new rules for Portugal's colonial administration in Africa, concerned that the British and French might take it over. However, Portugal had become a second-class colonial power, and the task of colonizing the African interior turned out to be an unreachable dream. In the 1950s, trying to attract white settlers, Salazar created the system of "colonatos" (farming communities), intended as a means of colonizing the countryside. His vision was of a Lusophone Africa that would one day connect Portugal's "Atlantic provinces" (Angola and parts of Congo) to Mozambique, in the Indian Ocean.

The state of war

If the idea of a nation-state in Angola is questionable, the state of war is not. The country has been at war since 1961, when the newly-created MPLA – a majority of whom were Umbundu – launched its guerrilla attacks against Portugal's more-than-four centuries of colonial power in the region, and its allies, South Africa and the USA.[2] The war was fueled mostly by ethnic and regional conflict, being supported by the superpowers in their geopolitical interests – the USA and the Soviet Union, which sided respectively with UNITA (because of its anti-communist message) and the MPLA (because of its socialist profile).

Three ethnically and regionally based movements were formed in the late 1950s and early 1960s: the UNITA of Jonas Savimbi, which represented the interests of the Ovimbundu of the central Highlands of Angola; the MPLA of Agostinho Neto and Jose Eduardo dos Santos, which represented the Umbundu, Kikongo and urban "mulattos" of Luanda (called the "assimilado" class during colonial times); and Holden Roberto's FNLA (Frente Nacional de Libertacao de Angola), a Bakongo-based movement from the northeastern parts of the country. Almost a year before independence, a civil war erupted between the three guerrilla factions for control over the disintegrating Portuguese colonial state. The independence celebrations for Angola, on 10 November 1975, were disrupted by gunfire on the streets of Luanda between the MPLA and the FNLA.[3]

After independence, the superpowers channeled their support in the form of weapons and military training to their factions of choice. While Cuba and South Africa brought in their troops, Zaire was keeping its armies at the borders, ready to invade Angola. International intervention was clearly at the roots of the endless civil war. In the beginning of the 1980s, there were more than 50,000 Cuban troops in Angola, and Cuba controlled much of the sugar industry.[4] Along with the USA and Soviet Union, China felt that it too should have a hand in Angola, and initially supported Holden Roberto of the FNLA.[5] The short-lived FNLA was created in 1956 and had its ethnic base among the rural aristocracy of the Congo, which comprised most of the well-educated Umbundu, Bakongo and young Tchoke males of Northern Angola. The origins of the organization lay in a succession struggle between the Bakongo aristocracy and the Portuguese colonial power that took place in 1955 with the death of Dom Pedro VII, king of the Congo.[6] With the aid of Mobuto Sese Seko, Zaire's long-time dictator, Holden Roberto's organization took shape and came to be recognized by Portugal in 1974 as one of the three movements that should mediate the dialogue between an independent Angola and the former colonial power, which hurriedly left the country.[7] In 1976, helped by the Cubans who came in with 50,000 troops, the MPLA destroyed the FNLA, and Holden Roberto went into exile in Kinshasa, Zaire's capital.

Also created in the late 1950s, the UNITA of Jonas Savimbi had its ethnic base among the Ovimbundu elite of the central Highlands, where a lucrative agriculture had developed during colonial times. Despite a difficult beginning, UNITA spread rapidly among the army of migrants of Central Angola, who fled the fight between UNITA and MPLA. Soon UNITA gained the support of South Africa and the USA, who used the organization as a barrier to the infiltration of the SWAPO guerrillas in Namibia, and to the propagation of Marxist-Leninist movements in Southern Africa. Savimbi built UNITA's capital in Huambo and, using an anti-communist language, gained the support of the incipient native bourgeoisie in Benguela and Huamo, but UNITA was always rejected by large sectors of the urban population, due to its anti-mulatto message and connections to the apartheid regime in South Africa.[8] Savimbi criticized the MPLA as a party of white, mulatto and light-skinned Africans, and emphasized that UNITA was formed as a reaction to the mulatto elite entrenched in Luanda. In his novels, the Angolan writer Souza Jamba, who had fled to Zaire during the civil war and today lives in London, wrote that the mulatto elite of Luanda wanted to place their Umbundu and Portuguese culture as the official culture of Angola.[9]

The first organization to step up the guerrilla war against the Portuguese, the MPLA was created in 1956 by a small circle of Umbundu and mulatto intellectuals – the colonial mulatto elite that had access to formal education, and also relied on the support of the Angolan petite bourgeoisie that had developed in Luanda, Malange and Benguela. Fanon and Leopold Senghor's ideas of an "African revolution" and "negritude" were very influential among this new mulatto elite, which studied in the Catholic missions, and sometimes sent its children to study in Portugal.[10] Helped by 50,000 Cuban troops plus financial support from former communist regimes in Eastern Europe, the MPLA easily grabbed control of Luanda after independence, and kept the South African army from entering the country. Savimbi's aversion to the mulatto elite provided a strong argument for the MPLA and the Angolan mestizo president, Jose Eduardo dos Santos, to accuse UNITA of racism.[11]

In Luanda's inferno

The conditions I found were deplorable when I visited Luanda in 1991, after the signing of the first MPLA/UNITA truce. Displaced from family lands, and afraid of getting killed in the crossfire, most agricultural producers stopped farming.[12] Luanda was besieged, and neither food nor durable goods could come in through the army and UNITA barriers. Food sold in the market was contaminated, as were the water supplies. Sanitation conditions were also deteriorating. Savimbi's troops had cut off water supplies several times that year, and only a few international companies (such as Elf Aquitaine) kept private reservoirs. The bay in Luanda was flooded with raw sewage, and during hot days the entire city reeked. The country had no public health system, and malaria and cholera were the most pressing problems. In August 1991, I can verify that around 2,000 cases of cholera among children were being registered every day in the municipal hospital of Luanda. The most common causes of death among children were diarrhea and pulmonary infections, besides cholera and malaria.

In 1989, the last year the government conducted a health survey (and the data is not very reliable), there were 46,723 new cases of cholera and 9,565 new cases of tuberculosis in the country.[13] AIDS was another problem of increasing concern, due to reports coming from Kinshasa that showed the severity of the situation in Zaire. There were more than 250,000 Angolan refugees in Zaire, and a great number of them were planning to return to the northern provinces from which they had fled during the worst years of the civil war. According to Dr. Maria Olivia Torres, founder of the Angolan Association for the Combat of AIDS, the government feared that these returning migrants could bring the AIDS virus into the country, and Angola did not have the structure for treating even simple diseases.

With the escalation of the civil war, Angola quickly became a nation of landless peasants, transformed into underemployed and semi-industrial urban dwellers. The population of Luanda doubled in less than ten years to 2 million, a quarter of Angola's total population of 8 million.[14] More than 75 per cent of the population lived in the "musseques," the shanty towns around the downtown area that were without light, running water, sewers, hospitals or police stations. Crime and violence were terrible problems. The town dwellers themselves took charge of capturing criminals, organizing summary trials, and applying punishments, sometimes burning the still-living suspects in a public place with the approval of the crowd, or cutting off their fingers or hands, in the case of theft.

More war: the failure of the Bicesse Accord

In twenty-one years of civil war, during which time almost one-third of the entire population died or left the country, Angola was reduced to rubble, the agricultural sector collapsed, and oil production plummeted. The country had only a little more than a year of peace – from 31 May 1991, when the Bicesse Agreement was signed in Portugal, to September 1992, when the MPLA and UNITA set up the date for the first election. Fifteen days after the first round of the elections, in which the MPLA won but with less than 51 per cent (and thus the need for a second round) a new outburst of UNITA–MPLA violence threw the country back to the worst of the civil war, with death tolls amounting to 5,000 civilians a week.[15] Despite guarantees from nearly 5,000 UN observers that the elections were fair, Savimbi rejected the results and reinitiated the war, this time from inside Luanda. Initially, UNITA advanced over one-third of the Angolan territory, seizing several important provincial capitals. UNITA's operation began to fail after a few months, due to lack of support from its former allies – the USA and South Africa – and wide international condemnation for having ruined the peace agreement.[16]

A new social map

In the early 1990s, the map of social categories was changing rapidly. Some Portuguese came back in 1991, intending to claim properties held before the revolution, and the government was willing to give them back. Some Cubans remained in the country, married Angolans and fathered children. Filipinos came to work in garbage collection, and thousands of Bulgarians and other Eastern Europeans were brought in through the close relationship between the MPLA and the former Soviet bloc.[17] Public servants, bureaucrats and workers in state-run companies were another highly visible group, with privileges and a higher standard of living.

The "Zairians" were the most puzzling among all the new social categories. They were actually Angolans returning from a long exile in Zaire. Widely discriminated against, they were easily recognizable by their French-accented Portuguese. Since returning to Angola, the Zairians have regained formerly held properties in downtown Luanda. There are buildings occupied mostly by Zairians, who are better educated and belong to a class of small merchants and entrepreneurs that flourished in Zaire in the years of exile. Today, they are looked down upon by Luanda's middle class, which claims, for example, that after the Zairians came back to Luanda, the crime rates went up and the number of car accidents and infractions almost doubled. According to Osseni Fassani, head of the Angola and Zaire section of the UN High Commission for Refugees, around 50,000 of the almost 250,000 Angolans in Zaire returned to Luanda and Benguela.[18]

Cabinda: signs of territorial fragmentation

Due to the continuing state of civil war, and growing starvation in the countryside, in 1993 the political and territorial fragmentation of Angola was becoming a reality in many aspects. Along with racial and ethnic conflicts, that between the Ovimbundu and Umbundu being the most outstanding, there were a number of other local and regional rivalries which were disintegrating the Angolan territory. For example, a significant separatist movement was taking place in Cabinda, an enclave in the Congo which is separated from the rest of the Angolan territory, and rich in oil, lumber and agricultural produce. Cabindans have seen themselves as a separate society because of their distinct ethnic composition as Trote and their geographical isolation from Luanda. The ELEC – Enclave of Cabinda's Liberation Front – a small but active guerrilla organization, has pressed strongly for more autonomy. Three major international oil companies operated in the enclave – the French Elf Aquitaine, the Dutch Shell, and the Brazilian state-run Petrobras.[19]

Angola's dual economy

Territorial fragmentation, along ethnic and racial lines, was just one of a number of ways in which Angola was disintegrating after the renewal of the civil war. Another way was through a complete separation of the civil society from the state and its institutions. There was a dual economy during the war: one of the supermarkets and imports for the government, the generals and the bureaucratic elite; and the other one made up of the black market and all sorts of barter economies in which great segments of the population were involved. Angola was in effect divided between those who had IDs (around 50,000 people) and those who did not (almost 8 million).[20] The official network of supermarkets and meat markets could not be used by the population unless they carried an official ID, which was issued only to government officials and public servants.

Created illegally in 1986, and named after a very popular Brazilian soap-opera that depicted a small town in Brazil's poverty-stricken Northeast, "Roque Santeiro" was a huge and dusty illegal market (kixima) in the sprawling outskirts of Luanda in which from 50,000 to 100,000 people sold, exchanged and traded everything from out-of-date medication to electronic goods. The Angolan national currency, the "kwanza," was nearly non-existent in the market. Instead everything had a value in beer, cigarettes and imported whisky. Beer had become the real currency in all the economic transactions. Women walking barefoot in the roads, carrying full cases of bottled beer on their heads, has become an outstanding image of Angola. Business at "Roque Santeiro" depended greatly upon two factors: the availability of beer in the market, and the latest shipments that had arrived in the ports of Luanda and Lobito. At least half of everything unloaded in the port of Luanda was smuggled out to "Roque Santeiro" and other parallel markets of Luanda. I saw government officials helping in this smuggling, and participating in sales of identification cards that permitted access to the official network of supermarkets.

In search of identity: images of Angola's culture

Despite the optimistic perspectives, there is still the threat of the country breaking into an Ovimbundu republic controlled by UNITA in the central-south regions, and an Umbundu republic, with its capital in Luanda, controlled by the MPLA forces. UN officials say that the current peace may be the last opportunity to keep the country together. Angola now faces the most difficult task: in peace, defining itself, seeking to achieve some kind of balance between regional and ethnic interests, on the one hand, and the idea of nationhood and nationality, on the other. There is a symbolic battle being waged, a struggle between divergent ideas of what it means to be Angolan, and how to create a nation and define nationality and nationhood without war.

In 1991–92, with the short-lived truce, I had the opportunity to observe an emergent debate about Angola's need to define itself. In the museum of anthropology, the Kinaxixi plaza and the school books, there was a search for a national representation, and a void where it should have been. The new Angolan literature that came with independence, poetry by the nation's founder Agostinho Neto and novels by Pepetela, among others, has been particularly concerned with the national question and the problems of Angola's symbolic representation. Some of the new writers tried to "reinvent" Angola's national language of Portuguese, by adding African terms and idiomatic terms from their own ethnic backgrounds. Others turned to Angolan history and mythology, searching for unifying elements of the nationality. In Pepetela's (e.g., 1988) novels, the reader is confronted with the variety of places and cultures which flourished under Portuguese domination. Agostinho Neto, on the other hand, set the tone of the new poetry, by arousing the national pride, writing about an unknown country.[21] The new Angolan literature is sponsored by the state through the Uniao dos Escritores Angolanos (Angolan Writers' Union), under the auspices of which many new writers have published and received government stipends.

The museum, school books and Kinaxixi

The display cases of the Museum of Anthropology were similarly illustrative of this lack of a national identity and the pressing search for it. In a country so devastated by war, I was astounded to find a museum of anthropology, miraculously intact in an old colonial mansion. The Museum director Ana Maria Oliveira, an anthropologist trained in France, took me on a tour of the museum, explaining to me the financial difficulties that plague an institution such as this in a country torn by war.[22] I walked through the relatively well-kept galleries that the Portuguese had built, depicting important ethnic groups and their lives as hunters and gatherers, then their evolution as a people into agriculturalists and pastoralists, and the colonizing impact brought about by the contact with the Portuguese. This was followed by another display of vegetation, climates, and local economic activities and industries of each region. The museum served the colonial power as a representation of the power and the extent of the Portuguese domain in Angola.

Ana Maria Oliveira argued that during colonial times, the museum also served as a way to convey the Portuguese colonial ideology, by placing the "natives" as barbarians in the evolutionary line, and fixing the ethnic groups and their territories, which previously were not defined and classified this way. In each room, and in the order of the displays, there was the implication that the peoples of Angola were stateless, totally lost in a confusing combination of ethnic groups, tribes and chiefdoms. When it came to independent Angola, the museum's rooms and the display cases were empty, not simply because of a lack of money, but mainly because of the lack of a consensus on how to represent Angola. Besides some photographs of the countryside, there was a complete void of history and life.

I also examined the school books for children in grades 1–5 in the subjects of geography, history and Portuguese. What I found was inverted, yet paralleled the message of the museum. The texts, full of revolutionary rhetoric, portrayed the oppression of the Angolan people during colonial times, but on post-independence Angola there was very little. Everywhere in the history books, the lack of a more complete post-independence chapter was justified by the teacher's union (responsible for all the school material) as the consequence of centuries of oppression and the lack of independent Angolan historians to do research and write about it. The books always ended with a call "for the task of putting together the new history of Angola," and left the reader with more doubts than certainties about concepts such as nationality and ethnicity.[23]

Next I went to Kinaxixi, the most important central plaza in Luanda, and the location of most political demonstrations and electoral campaigns. In the center of the plaza, on top of a large pedestal, is a Russian tank, a symbol of the battles against South Africa, the most important of which was Cuito-Canabale, because it prevented the South African troops from controlling the entire southern tip of Angola. When I talked to people about this tank they were unsure whether it had been captured from the South Africans or if it had belonged to the Cubans stationed in Angola. Was this tank, located in the most important square of Luanda, an ambiguous representation of a chaotic history of warfare, an ironic symbol of the Angolan nation?

The government is trying to present the Angolan identity as modern and clean. It plans to show the modern face of the country through building a whole new area of Luanda, a swamp it intends to convert into an esplanade of ministries, public offices and gardens. In the middle of this new area, for the last ten years, the Ministry of Public Works has been building a monument to Agostinho Neto, the leader of Angolan liberation. The monument is a post-modern obelisk on a circular base, made entirely of concrete. Because it is built on landfill in a swamp, each time the monument's inauguration has been arranged, the structure has sunk into the ground. Some people, even within the government, point to the absurdity of the work and call it the Angolan Tower of Pisa, because the further it sinks, the more crooked it appears. Ironically, the sinking monument to a national hero is a perfect image for the Angolan quest for a national identity.

The museum, the school books, and the Neto and the Kinaxixi monuments, all reflect the absence of any positive, collective idea of Angolan nationality. The symbolism of Luanda's civic culture suggested that what defines Angolan culture is only the history of Portuguese colonial rule, the liberation movement, and the subsequent struggle against South Africa.

Angolidade

In the early 1990s, Angola was going through two processes: political opening with more democracy and dissent coming from inside the MPLA, and economic liberalization which allowed people to sell their own merchandise (food, clothes and domestic utilities) without state intervention. With the elections in 1992, many political parties emerged from the underground. By the end of 1991, there were already thirteen parties legally registered with the election committee responsible for monitoring preparations for the elections for president and a new congress. Each of these parties had a platform, at the center of which was the question of national identity and the search for the Angolan culture.[24]

"Angolidade" had become the expression heard everywhere, from the political parties, to civil associations and state-run radio stations. "Angolidade" was translated as being authentic, "genuine" to the culture. Some political parties wanted a legal definition of what was seen as Angolan and what was not included in the constitution. The authentic, real, "genuine" Angolan citizens were those who had never left the country even in the worst times of the civil war, people whose families had engaged in the struggle for independence and against colonialism, and finally, people who had endured hardship in the name of the nation and the construction of a new society.

The Catholic Church also joined the debates, claiming that the ideals of Christianity should be taken into account in defining Angolidade. Ending more than a decade of absolute silence, and taking full advantage of the celebrations for the 500-year anniversary of the evangelization of Angola, the Church announced that to be Angolan meant not participating in any African or "animistic cult," but rather accepting Christ in Angola.[25] This was a significant message because it was said even among the African population that the problem of Angola resided in the black cultural influences, such as "animism" and "paganism." Along with religion, race and ethnicity will certainly have an important role in the task of defining "authenticity" and the genuine Angolan. The assimilado class took to the liberation movement a racial idea of Angolidade, an idea which implicitly equaled the Westernized mulatto with the character of Angola.

Junuel Goncalves – a white intellectual and writer, who has written about Angolidade – has argued that the debate about Angolan nationality is taking a legal turn, because it particularly involves issues of property and ownership – with regard to the Portuguese and the Zairians who were returning to Angola. In the state-run *Jornal de Angola*, Junuel also noted that Angola is following the same path as Senegal, the Ivory Coast and Zaire in developing a distinction between the "genuine" and the "non-genuine" citizen.[26] In Senegal and the Ivory Coast, due to the constant flow of migrants, the government has determined who may own property and who has the right to retain ownership after leaving the country. In Zaire, the Mobutu regime has used nationality as a way to condemn the opposition, and to play one ethnic group against the other. He has divided the country between "citizen" and "foreigner," "genuine" and "non-genuine."

Angola as a nation-state

The quest for national identity is not just Angolan. Every newly independent African nation has faced the same problem: what face and character can be given to a multi-racial and multi-ethnic society that was put together by colonialism? While in the Western technological and post-industrial societies, the discussion is about formation of transnational economies and economic blocs, Angola and other parts of Africa are still entangled in their problems of searching for the content of their identification as nation-states. The problem of the modern African state is that it was created by colonialism, which put peoples together, defining, fixing and compartmentalizing ethnic groups in boundaries created by colonial officials.

Portuguese colonialism played ethnic groups against each other, and created racial and social distinctions based on the color of skin.[27] According to Clarence-Smith (1979), the society was divided into two strata. Those who mixed with the Portuguese, developing a "mulatto" class which had privileges that were not given to the "Africans," who worked as slaves or cheap labor – for example, Mozambican slaves that Portugal provided to the Rhodesian gold mines, or to work in the sugar plantations of southern Angola. When there were indications that a nationalist revolution was about to explode, the Portuguese hurriedly fled back to Portugal, or went to South Africa, Venezuela or Canada. Kapuscinski (1988) describes well how the Portuguese left Angola, taking with them everything they could carry. Angola was emptied out, like a store that had gone bankrupt. They took with them cars and trucks and even office supplies, such as paper. As the independence date was approaching, and UNITA, MPLA and FNLA were still fighting for control of the state, Portugal left Angola without passing the state machine to anyone, without inaugurating a new government. Concerned with reprisals, the Portuguese colonial power simply dissolved and moved out, leaving the country at war and in chaos. Angola neither had the time nor the opportunity to exist and create itself. Public offices became vacant.

Angola is an example of post-colonial societies that were unified by colonialism but now, in order to keep existing as modern national states, have to create mechanisms that are, at the same time, general (for the whole population, transcending ethnic barriers) and specific (things that differentiate a society from its neighbors). Doornbos (1990) identified six factors as contributing to the problematic character of the African post-colonial state:

1   its post-colonial status, with all the implications this has for the evolution of a civil society;

2   its a priori problematic relationship between ethnic groups and their territorial jurisdiction;
3   the specific limitations of commodity production for a world market (lack of scientific knowledge, therefore lack of advanced industries);
4   its still relatively undifferentiated yet ethnically heterogeneous social infrastructure;
5   its salient processes of centralization and consolidation of power by new ruling classes; and
6   its pervasive external context and dependency.

In the face of all these obstacles, Doornbos (1990: 181) points out that the emphasis on nation-building and national identity reflects "a genuine desire of regional elites to create a national society." African elites have equated nationality with modernity and Westernization, and sought the nation-state as the most evolved form of political organization that a society can attain. Nationalism has become a state ideology, which previously was used against colonialism, but is now used against dissenting regional, ethnically oriented, cultural and political groups. "Thus, through indirect rule and other devices the colonial state displaced and incorporated various pre-colonial formations, while today processes of incorporation by global state-like institutions are again setting definite limits and parameters to the development of state forms and functions in the post-colonial era" (Doornbos 1990: 191).

Duarte de Carvalho (1989) has noted that ethnic identity was identified by post-colonial national elites as a colonial category, whereas national identity is presented as the result of a new culture emerging from the struggle against oppression. This national ideology is seen as crucial for the maintenance of the ruling class itself, which is, in fact, ethnically and regionally based.

Once a colonial territory, Angola had become a battleground for the superpowers' geopolitical interests during the Cold-War era. Now, what role will Angola play in the new geopolitical configuration of post-Cold War, international capitalism? The fact that the war kept on going even after the end of the Cold War, and the withdrawal of the superpowers, raises questions about whether Angola can exist at peace, and have its second chance of becoming a national state?

I suggest that the Cold War was what kept Angola operating together as a national state. Because of the Cold War and not despite it, Angola has existed and avoided a complete political fragmentation. Through the support of the superpowers, which channeled great amounts of money into UNITA and MPLA, the Angolan state machine with its armies kept operating. The war also kept regional elites in power and entrenched in their cities and territories. Whether it can remain a national state in peace is a real question.

Conclusion

We also need to consider whether the nation-state is the best form of political organization for Angola, and whether a new concept of the nation-state is needed for Africa, post-colonialism and post-Cold War. Now that the tendencies to dissolution of nation-states are manifesting throughout the world, it sounds anachronistic to suggest that there are no better choices for Angola outside the nation-state form. Maybe, forms of a loose political federation among smaller states and provinces would be more advantageous. Finkel (1993) senses that the general feeling in Angola is a desire to construct the nation. She argues that Angola's dominant classes do not want a political fragmentation, which only would weaken their economic power, transforming a nation rich in oil, diamonds, lumber and fish into a quilt of small countries without any political presence in Africa.

During the Cold War period, anthropology had left political theory to political scientists. The incorporation of some of the questions emerging after the Cold War, such as the prospects of nation-states, only enlarge anthropology, making the boundaries looser between disciplines in the social sciences. Anthropology needs to look at old and new political structures and organizations as they relate to changing patterns and ideas about race, ethnicity, gender and social class formation at this stage of transnational capitalist development. Unfortunately, in human terms, Angola provides a particularly intense experiment in these new patterns.

Notes

1. With the inauguration of Nelson Mandela in 1994, South Africa's policies in the region have shifted from isolationism and financing wars in the neighboring countries to a more participatory role in African politics. Mandela cut off South Africa's support to UNITA, which has made Savimbi withdraw from war and switch to peace-making. According to recent reports from the *New York Times*, South Africa is now supporting the MPLA mostly because of Savimbi's failure to abide with the results of the 1992 elections. Mandela has also suggested that South Africa will sell weapons to other African nations, as it is already doing to the MPLA government in Angola. According to the same reports, South Africa has given some training to the MPLA army.
2. During colonial times, there was a military and political alliance between Portugal, South Africa and the former Rhodesia.
3. While people were commemorating independence on the streets of Luanda, there was a fierce war between the FNLA and the MPLA for control of the capital. In 1991, I visited a city, Barra do Dandi, around 70 km north of Luanda, where the battle that finally annihilated the FNLA took place. Barra do Dandi was in ruins, and with it, the largest sugar mills left by the Portuguese.
4. The presence of 50,000 Cubans had an impact upon the economy and the culture of Angola. Over almost ten years, the Cubans were not only in the forefront of major battles against UNITA and South African troops which penetrated through the southern border with Namibia, but were also involved in the black market of dollars and American goods. I heard from some government officials complaining that the Cubans brought down the Angolan sugar industry so that they could export sugar to Angola.
5. China had made huge investments in East Africa, and planned to expand its "socialist cooperation" with Angola and other countries of Central and Southern Africa. Snow (1988) argues that China helped in the liberation of Congo and Zaire, and that it was developing projects of railroads and dams in Mozambique in the late 1970s.

Regarding its initial support to the FNLA, it seems that China wanted to have a participation in Angola's rich resources. On the other hand, the FNLA did not have a clear ideological profile, and it became impossible for China to continue supporting it. Sometimes the FNLA was allied to Zaire, at other times it built alliances with Savimbi and the USA.

6 The Portuguese used the word "dom" before the names of their aristocracy and their kings. Dom Pedro VII was African and had been in power due to Portugal's military support. Lisbon wanted to expand its colonial domains up north, incorporating the Congo, which Portugal already had under its sphere of domination.

7 In a hurry to leave Angola, fearing some kind of revenge, Portugal did not transfer power to any new government. It just recognized the three movements (UNITA, MPLA and FNLA) as representatives of the Angolan people.

8 Heywood (1989) argues that UNITA was initially formed as a reaction to the increasing concentration of power in the hands of the MPLA and its "mulatto" elite. Although she does not talk about race, her analysis implies that Luanda and its mulatto elite were getting all the power after independence.

9 Jonas Savimbi himself has recognized that the anti-mulatto message of UNITA created problems for the organization in the cities, among the middle class. In a 1988 interview with Fred Bridgland, Savimbi was quoted as arguing that "it can sound racist, and certainly it is not what we think today. But it was very difficult for us to understand how the movement of liberation in Angola had been led by the mestizos. For us, it was not clear that the mestizo had suffered in the hands of the Portuguese as much as they claimed now. Weren't they the privileged class?"

10 In the 1960s, when most of West Africa was immersed in the struggle against colonialism, the ideas of Fanon and Senghor were an affirmation of the African life and culture. Amilcar Cabral was also a very important intellectual mentor of the African liberation against colonialism, particularly that of the Portuguese (Cabral 1973). Founder of the PAIGC, the revolutionary party that conducted Guinea-Bissau and the Cape Verdean Islands to independence even before the independence of Angola and Mozambique, Cabral had a perspective on the culture of the colonized, arguing that it was through the colonized getting to understand his culture that they would reach an independent mentality and nationality.

11 Jose Eduardo Agualusa (1990, 1993) argues that the ethnic content of Savimbi's speeches raised fears among the urban middle class, which turned to the MPLA despite the fact that the MPLA social ideology did not meet their own requirements as a middle class.

12 Angola had a profitable agriculture, particularly in the central and southern provinces, where the Portuguese had their farming colonies with coffee and sugar cane plantations. After independence, these lands were "collectivized," and the production of coffee and some fruits continued with good results. However, long years of war displaced the rural population and transformed their lands into guerrilla camps. Angola's countryside is littered with land mines, which is why we find so many people today who have had their legs amputated. There are the mines laid by the Portuguese during colonial times, and the ones laid by UNITA and the MPLA. The problem is that no one knows exactly where the mines are located. One of the first tasks after the signing of the peace accord was the conduct of "de-mining" operations.

13 Information on diseases and the state of public health was provided by Carlos Lau, health official of the Angolan government and representative of Angola in the WHO (World Health Organization), during an interview in Luanda in August 1991.

14 Data on the population was drawn from the Angolan census of 1980, which was only partially completed, because the MPLA could not get into UNITA areas. The "8 million" number was reached through a projected estimate based on the last Portuguese census in 1970.

15 Vicki Finkel (1993) described how the civil war was reinitiated at the end of 1992. There were dead bodies in the streets of downtown Luanda. After UNITA launched an attack against government positions around the airport, the MPLA decided to bomb the hotel Turismo where top UNITA officials had set up the organization's headquarters.
16 The failure of the 1991 peace accord hit the UN hard. It had set up one of its largest operations in Africa, with more than 5,000 observers and peace-keepers to monitor the peace treaty and, later, the elections. In the 1994 elections in Mozambique, the UN was a little more cautious by setting up the dates and the electoral procedures only after the government forces and the guerrillas of Renamo had laid down their weapons. But the political situation in the region was quite different compared to the climate of the 1992 elections in Angola, when the South African regime of apartheid was still channeling money and weapons to the UNITA.
17 The Soviet and Bulgarian embassies had set up a large infrastructure for their officials and their families in Luanda. In 1991, I was taken by Serguei Krittski, the Tass correspondent on assignment in Angola for two years, to visit the Soviet installations on Marechal Tito Street. Next to the embassy, there was a Russian facility with all amenities, including a high school, a cultural center where Russian newspapers and magazines were available, and a food coop, where they could find all sorts of meat and dairy products from Russia. At Serguei's apartment a parabolic dish captured images from Russian TV. He estimated that the Eastern European community in Luanda consisted of about 20,000 people.
18 Information on the issue was provided in Luanda by Osseni Fassassi, a United Nations official for Angola and Zaire.
19 In 1990, Elf Aquitaine's oil production was 160,000 barrels per day. In 1991–92, the company made investments of US$1,265 million in the development of Bloc 3, which consisted of thirteen new rigs in the ocean, in the Cabindan basin. Data on investments and production were provided by the Angolan directory board of Elf Aquitaine in Luanda, in August 1991 (Elf Aquitaine 1991).
20 Several times I saw government officials standing in front of the official supermarket reselling products purchased inside for double their purchase price. The products were then likely to be resold in the parallel markets for at least double the second-hand mark-up price. This escalation of prices was responsible for an inflation of 1,230 per cent in 1991 alone (*Publico Economia* 14 October 1991, p. 22). Because the currency no longer had value, people did not use it in their transactions.
21 Some of the best poetry of Agostinho Neto (1922–81) is found, in its English translation, in the *International Journal of Prose and Poetry* (Neto 1992).
22 The first time I went to the museum, they were trying to dry the attic where a huge collection of books about colonial Angola had become wet because of the rain that came through the roof. There, among the wet books, I found the dairies of Gilberto Freyre's brief passage to Luanda.
23 *Historia de Angola, Geografia and Literatura Angolana 1989*. Luanda: Ministry of Education and Culture.
24 See PRD 1991. This is one of a number of political statements that the newly-formed political parties released in the pre-election period in 1991–92, stating their principles of "Angolidade."
25 See, for example, *Africa Hoje* 1991, in which the Angolan Church stated its purposes in the "Angolidade" debate.
26 In 1991–92, Goncalves wrote several articles in Portuguese and Angolan publications about his perspectives on "Angolidade" (for example, Goncalves 1991a, b).
27 For more information on Portuguese colonialism in Angola, see Barnett and Harvey 1972; Buijtenhuijs 1989; Marcum 1969; Okuma 1962.

References

Africa Hoje (1991) "Cinco Seculos de Evangelizacao en Angola." *Africa Hoje* 42 (April/May).
Agualusa, Jose Eduardo (1990) "Sousa Jamba, uma estrela solitaria." *Publico* 18 December, p. 31.
Angola Peace Monitor http://www.anc.org.za.angola
—— (1993) "Tentativa de explicacao de Angola – a componente etno-cultural da guerra civil." *Politica Internacional* 1(6): 73–91.
Anstee, Dame Margaret (1996) *Orphan of the Cold War: The Inside Story of the Collapse of the Angola Peace Process, 1992–1993*. London: Macmillan.
Barnett, Donald and Roy Harvey (1966) *The Revolution in Angola*. San Francisco: Bobbs-Merrill.
Buijtenhuijs, Robert (1989) "Movements of Maturity?" *Journal of the International Institute* 59(3).
Cabral, Amilcar (1973) *Return to the Source: Selected Speeches of Amilcar Cabral*. London: Monthly Review Press.
Clarence-Smith, W.G. (1979) *Slaves, Peasants and Capitalists in Southern Angola, 1840–1926*. London: Cambridge University Press.
Doornbos, Martin (1990) "The African State in Academic Debate: Retrospect and Prospect." *Journal of Modern African Studies* 28(2): 179–198.
Duarte de Carvalho, Ruy (1989) *Ana a Manda–Os Filhos da Rede*. Lisbon: Ministerio da Educacao, Insituto de Investigacao Cientifica Tropical.
Elf Aquitaine (1991) *Report on Ten Years of Operation in Angola*. Luanda: Elf Aquitaine.
Finkel, Vicki R. (1993) "Savimbi's sour grapes." *Africa Report* 38(1): 25–28.
Gamba, Virginia and Richard Cornwell (2000) "Arms, Elites, and Resources in the Angolan Civil War." In Mats Berdal and David M. Malone (eds), *Greed and Grievance: Economic Agendas in Civil Wars*. Boulder: Lynne Rienner, pp. 157–172.
Goncalves, Junuel (1991a) "Angola na Via da Segunda Republica." *Publico* 24 November, p. 14.
—— (1991b) "'Genuinidade' e Desenvolvimento." *Jornal de Angola*, 5 June, Section 2, p. 10.
Heywood, Linda M. (1989) "UNITA and Ethnic Nationalism in Angola." *Journal of Modern African Studies* 27(1): 47–66.
—— (1998) "Towards an Understanding of Modern Political Ideology in Africa: The Case of the Ovimbundu of Angola." *Journal of Modern African Studies* 36(1): 139–167.
Kapuscinski, Ryszard (1988) *Another Day of Life – A Haunting Eyewitness Account of the Civil War in Angola*. New York: Penguin.
MacQueen, Norrie (1998) "Peacekeeping by Attrition: The United Nations in Angola." *Journal of Modern African Studies* 36(3): 399–422.
Marcum, John (1969) *The Angolan Revolution: The Anatomy of an Explosion (1950–1962)*. Cambridge: The MIT Press.
Neto, Agostinho (1992) *International Journal of Prose and Poetry* 36(1). Tulsa: Arts and Humanities Council.
Okuma, Thomas (1962) *Angola in Ferment: The Background and Prospects of Angolan Nationalism*. New York: Beacon Press.
Pepetela (1988) *Yaka*. Luanda: Uniao dos Escritores Agolanos.
Pereira, Anthony W. (1994) "The Neglected Tragedy: The Return to War in Angola, 1992–1993." *Journal of Modern African History* 32(1): 1–28.
PRD (1991) *Comunicado do PRD sobre a Problematica da Informacao no Periodo de Transicao*. Document PRD, number 21, August.

Reno, William (2000) "Shadow States and the Political Economy of Civil Wars." In Mats Berdal and David M. Malone (eds), *Greed and Grievance: Economic Agendas in Civil Wars*. Boulder: Lynne Rienner, pp. 43–68.

Snow, Philip (1988) *Star Raft, China's Encounter with Africa*. New York: George Weidenfeld & Nicolson.

Swarns, Rachel L. (2000) "Angola's Goal: Stepping Back from the Abyss." *New York Times* 24 December, A1, p. 8.

12 A Cold War story
The barbarization of Chad (1966–91)

S.P. Reyna

There are three stories being told concerning Africa these days: one *by* Africans, another *about* Africans, and a third by the evidence. Both of the first two stories are different imaginings of the same thing, the state of the besieged African state. Consider a first story. I stayed in the 1970s with the family of Hadji in N'Djamena (Chad's capital). One evening, he came home aghast. He explained that he had been walking near the president's residence. Francois Tombalbaye, then Chad's ruler, was in the midst of losing a civil war. Things were twitchy in N'Djamena, just as they were at that time a world away in Saigon, another, more famous, Cold War hot-spot. Hadji had observed an old man in robes walking and waving a knife towards the palace. This was an ambiguous gesture. The waving of a knife over the head can be a salutation in Chad, or it can be the preparation for an attack. But the old man was clearly a *gada* (a white beard). He was alone, hardly a threat. He was first machine-gunned. Then his body was blown into small bits by his executioners using hand grenades. Into "mini morceaux, mini mini morceaux, mini mini mini morceaux," Hadji kept repeating. Now consider a second story that is told by some intellectual elites of advanced capitalist states – journalists, academics, and officials. One person telling this story is Robert Kaplan (1994, 2000) and his tale is that African states, as well as lots of other states, are pretty corrupt places; debased by the resurgence of traditional ethnic violence, harbinger of a coming "anarchy."

It may seem that these two insider and outsider stories *by* and *about* Africans are the same; after all, they both feature horror. But they are really quite different. The African story is about what it is like to live through the horror. Kaplan's story is that things are horrible for Africans because they, the Africans, are pretty horrible. Students of Africa will recall that Africans in the nineteenth century were portrayed as racially inferior barbarians. Now, at the beginning of the new millennium, they are anarchically violent ones. So there was an earlier outsiders' story of Africans, which might be called the Old Barbarianism, and now Kaplan tells the story of what Paul Richards has called the "New Barbarism" (1996: xiii). Richards shows the inappropriateness of this story to Sierra Leone. The present article does the same for Chad.

It does so by examining the civil wars in Chad, which began in 1966 and continue today. The argument proceeds as follows. First, Kaplan's case for the violent anarchy of the African state is explored. Next the position of Jean Francois Bayart, a French political scientist, is examined. At first glance, Bayart's position resembles Kaplan's. He too sees Africa as approaching a "heart of darkness" (1999a: 114). But there is a difference. Bayart insists that the current African state is to be explained as the result of Africa's "historical trajectory." The remainder of the article performs two analyses. First it puts in the missing trajectory for Chad, utilizing what might be termed a *structural history of force* approach. The second analysis investigates Kaplan's story as a simulation, in Jean Baudrillard's (1983) sense of the term, whose accuracy is evaluated. Finally, the conclusion summarizes the evidence exploring the implications of the structural history of force for a Kaplan-esque simulation of the Chadian state. The conclusion tells a third, ugly story.

The new barbarism

> Kaplan's vision of the future is a bleak one ... full of ethnic conflict as the world falls away from a Cold War that at least provided a kind of stability.
> (Amazon.com 2000; John J. Miller, advertising copy for *The Coming Anarchy*)

Kaplan comes from a recent breed of American intellectuals, including Samuel Huntington and Francis Fukuyama, who have become prominent since the end of the Cold War. Such intellectuals advance their careers by interpreting the Cold War and prognosticating what comes next in terms of a US triumphalism. Kaplan is of the opinion that what is next in the poorer countries of the world is "bleak," as the above advertising copy for his recently published *The Coming Anarchy* (2000) makes clear. Violent anarchy is what is up for parts of the world such as Africa, that are not advanced capitalist states. How does this prediction of a new barbarism relate to a triumphalist view of the USA?

A "triumphalist" position is one that portrays the actions of any social group as a sequence of "jolly good" shows. There is a good deal that is triumphalist in Kaplan. This is because he proposes that not only was the USA following its own interests during the Cold War but also those of all of humanity, because it provided stability, both within and between, countries. However, the end of the Cold War has unleashed the hounds of old "cultural conflict" where the "borders" are those of "culture and tribe" (Kaplan 1994: 58), and "primitive ends" will out (1994: 70). Kaplan has an African explain the primitive to him and he implies that this African is especially knowledgeable because of his, the African's, social position. He says his "friend the Minister" told him that "Western religion is undermined by animist spirits not suitable to a moral society. ... Here spirits are used to wreak vengeance by one person against another, or one group against another" (1994: 46). The primitive involves ghastly "animist spirits," beyond the pale of morality, that "wreak vengeance." Kaplan calls those fighting with spirits "juju warriors." This sort of representation of the "primitive ends" of African conflict is an African Hobbesianism where juju warriors are involved in a war of all spirits against all, and during the Cold War the USA prevented this war from occurring. A crucial claim made by Kaplan is that the Cold War ensured stability by keeping the juju warriors at bay. It is time to consider Bayart, in order to develop an alternative explanation of why the Hadjis of this world must endure horror.

Bayart comes from a French intellectual tradition indifferent to the *grandeur* of US triumphalism. He made a name for himself in the late 1980s with *L'État en Afrique* (1989), which insisted that African officials practiced a "politics of the belly," using the privileges of public office to privately accumulate wealth. His more recent work, *The Criminalization of the State in Africa* (1999), with chapters contributed by two colleagues, broadens the attack upon the African state. Now not only do officials enrich themselves at the public's expense; but they are involved in clandestine organizations, both within government and beyond, which conduct criminal activities that often involve violence. It might seem that Bayart's position resembles Kaplan's – an increasingly violent criminalization of the state certainly seems to portend a coming anarchy. However, there is a difference between the positions, which has to do with what they believe is causing the barbarism.

Kaplan ultimately lays it at the door of the Africans themselves. Their violence is essentially rooted in primitive tribal or ethnic hatreds, and it erupts like angry boils without the soothing lotion of a *pax Americana*. Bayart provides the key to his alternative view of the causation, though in a round-about manner, when he says, "'social capital' and culture are epiphenomena or expressions of the historical trajectory" (1999a: 43). This suggests that everything is pretty much "epiphenomena" except for "historical trajectory." Further, this trajectory "is related to the manner in which Africa is inserted into the international system through economies of extraction or predation in which many of the leading operators are foreigners" (1999a: 114). So for Bayart the contemporary African anarchy is not caused by a resurgence of pre-existing "primitive" ethnic antagonisms, as is the case for Kaplan, but by a new and particular trajectory of incorporation into the global system.

However, there is an ambiguity in Bayart's text concerning just who is responsible for the barbarism. This is because he says that the "main consequence" of the African trajectory of incorporation into the global system was a "progressively greater degree of dependence." But, he also insists that "this dependence has often been created by Africans" (1999a: 43). First, Bayart announces that the "leading operators" are "foreigners," and then he pronounces that "Africans" create their own dependence. The ambiguity, of course, centers on the degree to which it is the "Africans," the "foreigners," or some combination of the two who have created the barbarism. This, then, is the topic of the present article, to explore the particular historical trajectory that created the present situation in Chad, with an eye to both explaining the barbarism and identifying its agents.

It is important to challenge Kaplan's claim that the Cold War provided stability. Actually, there really was no such thing as a Cold War: cold was hot. Let me make clear that this point is not hyperbole. The socialist bloc vigorously contested the development of capitalism between 1945 and 1990, and it is true that the Soviet Union and the USA did not engage in direct warfare during this time. This absence of direct conflict has justified talking of a Cold War. Nevertheless, for the period between 1945 and 1976 there were well over 120 wars between other countries, with there being an average of eleven and a half wars raging during any one year (Kende 1978: 227, 228). Furthermore, roughly 65 per cent of these wars involved capitalist bloc participation (Kende 1976: 134), and many either initially, or eventually, became part of confrontations between the capitalist and socialist blocs. This is why it is not hyperbolic to insist that cold was hot during the Cold War. Though I shall continue to employ it, the term "Cold War" is actually misleading.[1]

The exact magnitude of US government intervention in these hot wars is unknown. The term "intervention" does not only mean sending its troops to fight, but additionally includes providing training, money, equipment, logistics and intelligence. According to one source the US government intervened overtly in over 27 per cent of the conflicts between 1945 and 1976 (Kende 1976: 134). Another source reports that the US Pentagon, as of 1998, had provided training 110 times for the militaries of other countries since 1945 (Johnson 2000). Such information indicates that the US government has continually supplied military resources throughout the globe since 1945. A rationale behind this policy was expressed in a speech of President Kennedy that insisted, "our assistance makes possible the stationing of 3.5 million allied troops along the Communist frontier at one-tenth the cost of maintaining a comparable number of American soldiers" (cited in Kende 1978: 239). Unfortunately, Kennedy never gave this speech about the virtues of cheap violence, because he died violently in a world of violence that he was helping to build, one sunny day in Dallas.

However, the global militarization he fostered was a roaring success, and I contend that it was, and is, inimical to stability. The civil wars in Chad, which began in 1966, and which escalated throughout the 1970s, eventually became involved in Cold War confrontation. This means that the historical trajectory that Chad followed is a Cold War story. Below I suggest the rudiments of a structural history of force approach for investigating how instability and barbarism developed in this trajectory.

Structural histories of force

A structural history-of-force approach is based on an understanding of what makes history (a fuller introduction to this approach can be found in Reyna 1994a, b, 1999, forthcoming). Human populations may be represented as organizations of force, and this force produces power. Understanding how such networks are constituted, and how their constitutions change, depends upon further conceptualizing the two, related notions of force and power. Force is not power. Power is what is made – *outcomes*. Force is *abilities*, that which makes power. Power ultimately results from the exercise of force, which is the utilization of combinations of different resources that can generate different outcomes. The amount of powder in a cartridge relates to its force. The fact that the bullet when fired penetrated six inches has to do with its power. Force is not always violent. Force is *any* antecedent ability that produces subsequent outcomes, or powers. The shaming of a person that results in their being good or the courting of a person that results in their being married are both exercises of non-violent force.

Isolated individuals possess only the force of their single bodies. Social structures, on the other hand, stockpile resources that give them, relative to individuals, enormous endowments of force. Such resources include capital, people, tools, raw materials, authorities, and the knowledge of how to combine these to attain different outcomes. These forces are always structured. This means that so many people are organized in such and such a way – for example into armies or businesses – that uses so much capital, so many tools, and so much knowledge in so many ways to achieve their outcomes. Different structures of force may be distinguished in terms of the types of force resources they utilize. Armies are structures of violent force; businesses those of economic force; courts those of authoritative force. The essential point here is that it is organizations that effectively possess the force that can be exercised to cause different powers. This implies, if history is temporal orderings of what happened, and if what happened is different outcomes, that it is exercises of force in networks of organizations that generate the powers, the outcomes, that make history. Of course, such a history is a structural history, and different structural histories follow different trajectories or logics. It is time to theorize one trajectory that descends into instability.

Instability occurs where there is an inability to achieve control in fields. Organizations, such as state and non-state institutions, exercising different forces, constitute a force field. Organizations intentionally exercising force against each other to control each other are in conflict, if the actors in at least one of these institutions do not desire to be controlled. Control is attainment, following an exercise of force, of a desired outcome. Colloquially put, it is getting them to do what you want. It is the boss getting the help to do what is intended. It is the store getting its suppliers to deliver on time and in the proper amounts. Not all control is conflictual and, though control has a bad name, not all control is bad. If there is no control, things do not work especially well. Instability is the inability to achieve control following exercises of force in either conflictual or non-conflictual fields. The more times control is not achieved subsequent to the exercise of force the greater the instability.

Inability to achieve control occurs under certain distributions of forces in a field. The distribution of forces in a field refers to what groups have *how much* of *what kind* of force, and this distribution is the result of processes of concentration and dispersion. Processes where force is accumulated within a particular institution are those of concentration. Processes where the reverse occurs, and force is diffused among a number of institutions, are those of dispersion.

If in fields of force involving states, the dispersion of violent force is low, being confined to government institutions, and the concentration of force is high, being also confined to those institutions, then the resulting field of state will resemble the Weberian state. Such a state is one where the government has an effective monopoly upon violence (Weber 1958). Here there is likely to be little violent instability during conflicts. After all, in such a violent force field, the distribution of violence is such that you will get your head blown off if you oppose the government's monopoly of the means of destruction.

However, if the dispersion and the concentration of violent force are both high, then violent force is no longer confined to government institutions. It has been both dispersed and concentrated into the institutions of civil society. This makes it possible for these institutions to be downright uncivil, and to meet violent force with violent force. So long as such distributions of force persist, exercises of violent force are not likely to be decisive; that is, they are not likely to give one side control over the other side's violent force. Absence of the power to control an opponent's violent force in a field of violent stately conflict is a situation of violent instability, which, of course, is what is meant by barbarism. The most famous example of this sort of distribution of violent force was feudal Europe, where the sovereign faced an aristocracy whose combined capacity for violence often exceeded the sovereign's.

I employ the expression "*VF[c+d]*" to symbolize a distribution of force including both the dispersion and concentration of violent force, and that of "*Iv*" to symbolize violent instability. Specifically, I hypothesize that *increasing VF[c+d] produces increasing Iv*. Below I show that violent instability emerged in Chad during the Cold War. The argument is developed as follows. A history of the postcolonial Chadian state is provided in the following section. Next the possibility that this history might be simulated and represented as a tribalism or ethnic nationalism in a manner congenial to Kaplan is discussed and rejected. Then there is a demonstration of how states in competition during the Cold War instituted a trajectory leading to the dispersion and concentration of violent force that destabilized the field of violent force in Chad. Finally, the conclusion ponders certain implications of this Cold War story for Kaplan's representation of it.

A brief word is in order about Chad. It is a large country of 1,284,000 square kilometers, roughly twice the size of France, that occupies most of what is known as the central Sudan. One hundred and fifty or so tribes or ethnic groups are reported to populate Chad (Chapelle 1980). The term "tribe" is believed by a number of anthropologists to have an "ignoble history" (Barfield 1997: 475). The term "ethnic group" is only slightly more reputable. However, you can ask someone in Chadian Arabic (Chad's *lingua franca*) "*nafar shenu?*" (What is your kind?). The answer you receive to this question is likely to classify that person into one or other of the country's tribes or ethnic groups. It is in this sense that these terms are used in this article.

There has been a tendency on the part of both officials and scholars to imagine Chad as being composed of two very different parts – a north and a south. The latter region is to the south and west of the Shari River. It is an area of relatively well-watered savanna, occupying perhaps a fifth of the country, with about half of its population of approximately six million. The major ethnic groups in the south prior to colonization were stateless, non-Muslim Sara and Masa speakers.

The north is a far more arid region. The extreme north – in a rough parallelogram running from the Tibesti mountains to the Ennedi Highlands to the Wadai plateau to Lake Chad – is desert. Immediately south of the desert is a sahelian zone. Most of the ethnic groups in the north were Muslim. Camel pastoralists, called Tubu, controlled the desert. Cattle pastoralists, often Arabs, transhumed south of the Tubu. Stretching from west to east in this zone was a string of precolonial states such as Bagirmi and Wadai. The French, starting around 1900, colonized Chad. It was they who first imposed a state organization over the north and south and who dominated the two regions from their capital in what is today N'Djamena. Independence was granted in 1960.

A stately field of barbarism

Chad, thus, has been independent for roughly forty years. During this period, which roughly coincides with the Cold War, there have been five presidents: Francois Tombalbaye (1960–75), Felix Malloum (1975–79), Goukouni Oueddeni (1980–82), Hissen Habré (1982–90) and Idriss Déby (1990 to the present day). Civil war began in 1966, existed in 1991, when the Cold War ended, and continues today at the end of the year 2000.[2] Particulars of each ruler's reign until roughly the end of the Cold War are described in order to establish the existence of a distinctive praxis in the field of the Chadian state.

An election was held a year prior to Independence (1960) that was won by the *Parti Progressiste Tchadien* (PPT), whose head – Tombalbaye – had the right to become the first president of the fledgling republic. Throughout 1961–62 Tombalbaye disposed of all his southern party rivals. In 1963 he turned against the northerners. At the same time, he made the PPT the sole legal party and himself president for life. At this point many of those who would rebel against Tombalbaye fled the country.

A national liberation movement called the *Front de Libération Nationale du Tchad* (Frolinat) was formed, and initiated hostilities in 1966. This was the beginning of the civil wars. Initially Frolinat included *la Première Armée* – which operated in the east-central regions – and *la Deuxieme Armée* – which fought in the extreme north. These "armies" were rather ragtag organizations. However, their existence induced France to supply up to 3,000 troops to support Tombalbaye's *Armée Nationale Tchadienne* (ANT) between 1969 and 1971. These troops employed tactics that emphasized the use of air power for ground support, tactics that resembled those that the USA was using at the same time in Vietnam. The French won every engagement, and were gratified by the success of their 20 mm helicopter-mounted cannon, but could not eliminate Frolinat.

Qaddafi gained control of Libya in 1969 and, though initially wary of Frolinat, by 1970 he had come to see it as useful to his ends. With the support of Soviet bloc nations, especially East Germany, the First and Second Armies were trained and armed by the Libyans (Buijtenhijs 1978). When the French ceased direct military intervention in June 1971, the strengthened Frolinat forces crushed the ANT. As a result, Tombalbaye was assassinated (1975) by elements of his own security forces.

Felix Malloum, former Chief of Staff of the ANT, replaced Tombalbaye and governed as head of the *Conseil Supérieur Militaire* (CSM). The forces opposing Tombalbaye had not been defeated, and they continued to oppose Malloum. However, a split occurred in the Second Army, with its former leaders dividing it into two new forces. One part became the *Forces Armées du Nord* (FAN). Habré, a former official in the Tombalbaye regime, led this. The other part became the *Forces Armée Populaire* (FAP). Goukouni, the son of the head (*derdê*) of the Teda, and the only major leader who was not an ex-official, commanded this. The French would support Malloum. FAN and especially FAP would have Libyan assistance. During the first three years of the Malloum regime, French military support for the CSM gradually eroded. Libyan support, especially for the FAN, greatly increased. FAN troops continued to receive training from the Libyans as well as sophisticated arms such as SAM missiles and incendiary phosphorous mortars.

As a result of this situation, Malloum was routed by 1978. However, by this time Habré and Goukouni were in conflict with each other over Libya, with the latter pro- and the former anti-Qaddafi. A defeated Malloum sought to profit from this split by inviting Habré to join his government. Habré did so, infiltrated FAN into the capital, and overcame Malloum (when the French deserted him) in 1979. However, a year later, Goukouni, massively supported by the Libyans and their Soviet bloc allies, fought Habré in the streets of N'Djamena. A US military person who was a veteran of Vietnam witnessed this combat. He described the fighting as more intense than he had experienced at Hué during the Tet offensive. Habré, unable to stand against an estimated 200 Soviet T54 and T55 tanks, was driven for the first time into exile at the Novotel in the northern Camerouns.

Goukouni, then, proceeded to rule in 1980, presiding over a government known as the *Gouvernement d'Union Nationale de Transition* (GUNT). However, the FAN had not been destroyed. On the Sudan/Chad border Habré enlarged, rearmed, and retrained his forces. US support during this period seems to have been decisive. One source estimates that US$100 million in military aid was delivered to the Sudan destined for the FAN (Joffe 1986: 95). Habré was of interest to the Americans because his anti-Libyan stance was seen as a useful instrument for Reagan's anti-Qaddafi policy. A CIA-backed FAN marched largely unopposed during the dry season of 1982. The French remained neutral. GUNT was evicted from the capital in June 1982. Habré was declared President.

Just as Goukouni could not destroy the FAN, Habré did not destroy the GUNT, and it immediately plotted armed opposition, finding a willing ally in Qaddafi. By early 1984 an army was created, the *Armée de la Libération* (ANL). This was organized into two main fronts. In the north were units that ultimately were descended from Frolinat. These included the FAP, firmly under the control of Goukouni, and pro-Libyan. There was also a revived First Army, the CDR (which in late 1984 provided 60 per cent of the GUNT's manpower), the *Volcan* Army and the FAO. There was also a non-Frolinat contingent in this northern front. These were soldiers from Tombalbaye's ANT. A southern leader led them, Colonel Abdul Kadir Kamougue, who had been both a former officer in Tombalbaye's military and Goukouni's Vice-President in the exiled GUNT. Kamougue's men supplied about 25 per cent of the GUNT's manpower through the latter part of 1984.

After assuming the presidency, Habré had sent his forces into southern Chad to establish authority. The troops led by Déby were involved in atrocities that precipitated the creation of purely southern guerilla movements. These were called *codos*, an abbreviation of commandos. There were at least six of these by the middle of 1984: the *Codos Rouge, Vert, Espoir, Noir, Vert Aigle,* and *Cocotier*. Most *codo* fighters came from the defunct ANT. Though originally autonomous, the *codos* agreed in October 1984 to unite with the GUNT. Thus, by 1984, Habré faced a considerable coalition of ANL forces. This, however, was their high point.

The ANL was supported by Libya. In 1986, with very considerable assistance from the Soviets and East Germans, Libya invaded northern Chad, ostensibly in support of its allies.[3] This had a double effect. On the one hand, a number of GUNT leaders went over to Habré because he, compared to Qaddafi, was viewed as the lesser of two evils. On the other hand, the Libyan invasion brought both the French and the Americans strongly into Habré's camp. French, American and Chadian personnel campaigned together throughout 1987. When it was over a tenth of Libya's army was lost and "Fred," an American of unknown connections, was busy "turning" Libyan prisoners into a contra force.

The extent of great power involvement at this time was considerable. From 1983, when the French became firmly committed to Habré, they were estimated to have spent on the order of US$500,000 per day defending him against the ANL (James 1987: 81). During the period 1986–87, when Goukouni was defeated, the French were reported to have spent US$100 million in Chad (James 1987: 22). These were the largest French military operations since the Algerian War (Lemarchand 1984: 65). US support during the 1986–87 period was also substantial. It rushed in "$25 million worth of military aid in addition to the regular $5 million in military assistance. ... At times giant American Hercules C-130 cargo planes landed almost on a daily basis in N'Djamena, ferrying in military supplies in the form of trucks, guns, ammunition, and Redeye anti-aircraft missiles" (James 1987: 21). Habré could not have defeated the GUNT coalition without the help of his capitalist bloc friends.

However, even in victory, opposition to Habré reemerged swiftly from elements of his own administration. He had originally come to power with considerable assistance from Idriss Miskine, who had led a rebel group from the Guera. Miskine died in 1984, officially as a result of "malaria," though it was widely believed that a unit of Habré's secret service known as "the Vultures" had killed him. As a result, persons from the Guera in Habré's government became disaffected and in 1987 formed a rebel force called the *Mouvement de Salut National* (MOSNAT).

The architects of Habré's success against the Libyans had been two persons often said to be Zagawa. The first of these was Hassan Djamous, who had been the Chief of Staff in the war against Libya. The second was Idriss Déby, the army commander. Fearing that they might perish, as did Miskine, Djamous, Déby and the then Interior Minister, Itno, staged a coup in April 1989. It failed and Itno and Djamous paid with their lives. Déby fought his way to the Sudan. There, after receiving "money and military equipment" from Libya, he created a rebel force, the *Mouvement Patriotique du Salut* (MPS) (*Africa Confidential* 1990a: 8). The MPS united with MOSNAT. This force is reported to have received assistance from Togo and Burkina Faso (*Africa Confidential* 1990b: 4).

Habré, for his part, concentrated his forces aggressively in the heart of Zagawa territory in early 1990. He did this with military assistance from Zaire, Israel, Iraq, and the US (see *Africa Confidential* 1990a: 4, 1990b: 4–5). If there was not a formal US/Israeli/Iraqi alliance to aid Habré, there was certainly an "informal" working relationship. The level of US support for Habré at this time is unclear. He was described as having "close connections with the US" and as employing "former US Marines as personal bodyguards" (*Africa Confidential* 1990b: 3). Nevertheless, on 25 November there was a spectacular defeat of Habré at Iriba. A month latter Habré was on the road again – to the now familiar Novotel.

During the early 1990s, the pattern appeared to repeat itself. There were probably seven rebel movements that sought to destroy Déby's government. The most important of these was the *Conseil de Salut National pour la Paix et la Démocratie au Tchad* (CSNPDT) located in southern Chad. Moise Ketté, who was a member of Habré's notorious secret security service, headed this. The CSNPDT was described as "growing" in 1993 (*Africa Confidential* 1993: 6). A spokesman for the group, said to number 7,000, announced in September 1993, "We are prepared to die, they will have to exterminate us" (FBIS 1993: 1).

In the region near Lake Chad a *Mouvement pour la Démocratie et le Développement* (MDD) was operating. This group seems to have been created by Habré. It was described as having an "impressive range of military hardware" (*West Africa* 1992: 69). The MDD, nicknamed the *Khmer Rouge*, was largely composed of members of Habré's old secret police and his army. It was described as wealthy and as CIA-supported (*Africa Confidential* 1993: 6). As a result of the raids of groups such as the CSNPDT and the MDD there was again talk of the "fragmentation" of Chad (*Africa Confidential* 1993: 5).

Every president's rule, save for that of the current office-holder, ended in his violent overthrow. These unintended endings, at least from the vantage of the dispossessed president, were the signature of Chadian political praxis during the Cold War. They involved an alternation between disintegration, towards the end of a reign, and reintegration at the beginning of a new reign. The historical trajectory of the Chadian state is one in which the violent force of governments has lacked the ability to control rebel movements. Five times the government has had its domination unravel as taxes were not paid, officials went unpaid, roads crumbled, schools closed, and legal cases went unheard. The government had its ANT but out there in civil society there was the First Army, the Second Army, FAN, FAP, etc. Readers should understand that nobody in Chad desired this instability. This poses the question, why the field of stately barbarism?

Simulations I: tribal war

You see it on TV. In the background there is something, usually ominously smoldering. In the foreground there is a reporter, smartly done up in a bush jacket. She tells you that you are in a war zone in some unpronounceable place, but that she has managed to find chief somebody, who knows all about it, and he will tell you the score. She is pretty, and your mind wanders to thinking how plucky she is. But you snap to attention when you see the chief talk and you know – because you heard it with your very own ears – that the war is between some tribes with unpronounceable names fighting, like they always do, since time out of mind. Kaplan is right. They are engaged in tribal war.[4] It is time to talk of simulation.

Simulation, according to Baudrillard (1983), is a process where representations of reality come to replace the reality being represented. "Replace" here means that the representation seems more "real" than the real. Seen in this light, the TV report and the Kaplan book are both simulations that represent African war as the result of primitive tribal animosities. Of course, the accuracy of such representations is at issue. War may be said to be "tribal" if three conditions are satisfied. The first of these is that the immediate cause of hostilities involves disputes between existing tribes. The second condition is that these causes are "primitive," "primordial" or "traditional," with these three terms understood to mean pertaining to a tribe prior to its involvement with an expanding Euro-American capitalism. The third condition is that institutions of the tribes in conflict perform hostilities.

Belligerence is sometimes initiated in Chad as a result of confrontations between tribes. For example, in one area near Lake Chad, where in the 1970s I studied Arab herders, there was remembrance of fighting some years earlier. The opponents had been a group of Fulbe who had suddenly appeared seeking both pasture and water for their animals. They were a new group with whom there existed no agreements about joint resource use. Pasture and water were scarce as it was a time of drought. Tensions developed. The Fulbe organized raiding parties. These attacked quickly and decisively, taking Arab lives. Informants recalled the killing of a pregnant woman and the burying of a village chief up to his neck in the ground and the burning of his head. This apparently threw the Arabs off balance. They sought to organize their own kin militias, while withdrawing animals away from exposed pasture and water points. Arab withdrawal gave the Fulbe access to these resources.

By the time I arrived in the early 1970s, the Fulbe had transhumed further south, much to the relief of the Arabs who had been shocked by the severity of the attacks on them. The disputants in this fighting were segments of tribal groups. The combatants' own kin militia performed the fighting that contested access to the resources needed to maintain pastoral production, the form of production of both Arabs and Fulbe which was essential to their pastoral identities and which had existed prior to their colonization. So it seems that to simulate this fighting as tribal is not entirely inappropriate.

However, the *casus belli* of the wars described in the previous section had nothing to do with tribes. Rather, it was about the political defeat of *hautes fonctionnaires* (high officials) or would-be *hautes fonctionnaires* in contests for office in the state. Tombalbaye had overthrown Frolinat's founders. Habré rearmed FAN after 1980 because Goukouni had rejected him. Déby organized the MPS because Habré had ousted him. Furthermore, hostilities also occurred as a result of anticipated political gains in the governmental hierarchy. Habré, for example, had been a relatively low official in the Tombalbaye regime. However, he switched sides and went over to Frolinat in the early 1970s because it seems he had calculated that he could rise further as an organizer of Frolinat forces.

It should equally be noted that the civil wars did not involve tribal institutions. Neither the armies of pre-colonial states such as Bagirmi or Wadai, nor the kin-based militia of acephalous ethnicities such as the Sara were mobilized to fight the wars of high officials. Soviet bloc specialists in unconventional, low-intensity conflict trained rebel-fighting units in the case of Frolinat. Some of Habré's soldiers were probably trained by gentlemen like "Fred," that is by US specialists in unconventional war. These units, once trained, were led by ex-officials who organized them along bureaucratic lines, influenced by contemporary notions of guerilla war.[5] Certainly the soldiers of different rebel forces tended to be drawn from the ethnicities of their leaders. However, Magnant (1984: 48) emphasizes that rebel forces never uniquely constituted a single tribe. Furthermore, recruitment appears to have come as much from a specific educational and gender category as from specific tribes. Throughout Chad there are young men who have had some formal education, but who have been obliged to stop schooling prior to finishing high school. Education gives these men aspirations beyond the local community. Many, in fact, dream of becoming *fonctionnaires* (officials). Economic conditions dictate that such men become largely underemployed urban laborers or that they return to their rural kin's land, where they become ordinary *meskin* (poorfolk). To such men, joining a liberation army is a way of becoming a "somebody." Others have noted in Africa (Richards 1996) and Latin America (Mitchell 1999) the significance of young males in armies of rebellion. Rebel forces, thus, tend to be led by ex-officials who command young men that are would-be officials.

Thus the conditions needed to qualify Chad's wars as tribal are unsatisfied. Chadian presidential wars did not involve tribes fighting tribes over primordial tribal affairs. They involved officials, ex-officials, and would-be officials killing each other, and anybody who got in the way, like the old man, for control over the state. Some simulations are more imaginary than other. Simulations of Chad's instability as tribal fratricide are phantasmagoric.

Simulations II: ethnic nationalism

Sometimes Kaplan's juju warriors fight according to what might be called a logic of ethnic nationalism. Here Kaplan is following the work of Samuel Huntington in *The Clash of Civilizations* (1996). Ethnic nationalisms involve ideologies that privilege, for some primordial, cultural reason, one ethnic group's, or one block of ethnic groups', control over the state apparatus. This fires terrible conflicts as, for example, in Bosnia where Serb, Croat, and Muslim butchered each other. So why not simulate Chad's civil wars as ferocious ethnic nationalisms? (For different views concerning Chadian nationalism see Ciammaichella 1990; Magnant 1984; Michalon 1979.) Simulation of such a representation might occur as follows.

The plucky TV journalist – the cleric of postmodern simulation – returns and sets up her camera before that chief. It turns out that he is from northern Chad, and she gets him to announce that Tombalbaye is a "*kirdi kelb*". Now a *kirdi* is a non-Islamic person who in pre-colonial times could be enslaved. A *kelb* is a dog. Members of northern ethnic groups have cultivated such attitudes about their southern counterparts since far into pre-colonial times. So disdain for *kirdi* among members of northern ethnic groups seems pretty primordial. Then the TV journalist has the chief allow that the *kirdi* have no right to govern anything, what with their being dogs, so that northern ethnic groups rightfully fight to seize the government. Such an assertion brings Kaplan back into the picture, and the journalist cuts to him. He sits, back to a row of books proving him an intellectual, at his office in the New America Foundation, proclaiming that primordial ethnic animosities dog the nationalisms provoking civil wars. Perhaps true, perhaps not true: attention turns to the role of nationalist ideology in Chadian instability.[6]

An essential similarity between all Chad's presidents and most of their opponents, even as they tried to kill each other, is that they *were* nationalists. Institutions of the state as well as those of the rebels created and diffused emblems, rituals and discourse championing their image of a Chadian nation. A sense of how inventive this nationalist imagery has been can be acquired if one explores the ideological discourses of Tombalbaye. He, in a nicely tailored French suit, appealed to all Chadians in a 1961 speech, saying, "Before being Arab, Muslim, Christian or Sara, we are Chadians." He went on to promise the nation the gift of "*la vie moderne*" which would be achieved through "*développement*" (cited in Le Cornec 1963: 315). Thus, at the very beginning of Tombalbaye's rule he insisted that he would govern on the basis of a modernizing nationalism. Such nationalism was not an ethnic nationalism: the nation was not to be a particular ethnic group – Sara or Arab – but a Chadian amalgamation. Frankly, this was a nationalism designed to appeal not so much to Chadians but to the French technical advisors to his government, who probably wrote the text of his speech. Tombalbaye had to please the French because their support of his state budget was crucial to governmental operations.

By the end of the 1960s, with the rebellion making the greatest headway in northern, Islamic areas, it was clear to all that the government needed to attract Muslims. So in 1972 the president, a Baptist, made the pilgrimage to Mecca, perhaps at the instigation of Ba Abdoul Aziz, a Mauritanian who served as Tombalbaye's advisor on Islamic matters. Afterwards he exchanged his suit for the robes worn by Muslims and styled himself *el-hadj*. Thereafter his appeals for national unity had an Islamic ring to them.

However, by the late summer of 1973, Tombalbaye was concerned with creating a truly Chadian nationalism. At the end of August, the PPT was dissolved and replaced by the *Mouvement National pour la Révolution Culturelle et Sociale* (MNRCS). This new party's job was to invent tradition – lots of it, and fast. A similar movement occurring at the same time in Mobutu's Zaire inspired the MNRCS. Operating incessantly over the radio, this cultural revolution demanded a *"rétour aux sources."* Gone was the Tombalbaye of modernization. Out was *el-hadj*. In was the new Tombalbaye who spoke in terms of *"sources"*, which might seem to be getting back to primordial roots.

"Tchaditude" was the "source" to which Tombalbaye promised to return. The idea of *tchaditude* seems to have been invented by Haitian advisors. Of course, there were echoes in *tchaditude* of the *négritude* that had been important among African and Caribbean intellectuals between the 1920s and the 1950s. *Négritude* sought to celebrate universal qualities shared by all blacks. *Tchaditude* was more particularistic. It was about Chad and Tombalbaye. It was a "Chadian socialism" (see Bouquet 1982: 147). In this *tchaditude*, the president was no longer merely a president. He was *Ngarta, le Guide*. He traveled now in the presence of his *Grand Griot* (Great praise-singer) who always sang the qualities *du Guide*, such as *"Ngarta, champion des champions! Il connait tout, sans papier!"* and even in English *"Ngarta, number one!"* The griot's chants were echoed endlessly on the radio.

Tchaditide, then, appears to be the invention of Haitian advisors to Tombalbaye. It was invented towards the end of Tombalbaye's reign, roughly at the time of the butchering of the old man, when things were dicey and the modern and Islamic nationalisms had failed. Two points stand out about the preceding nationalisms. First, there is nothing ethnic, or even Chadian, in them. The nationalism of a modern Chad on the road to development was a French invention, that of *el-hadj* was possibly the invention of a Mauritanian advisor, while the "return to sources" gave to Chad a version of a *négritude* that might be said to have been a Caribbean simulation of an Africa that never existed. The principle that drove Tombalbaye's nationalism was "whatever works"; and none of it did.

His opponents are reported in some accounts to have shot him in the belly and left him to die. Of course, they did so in the name of nationalism. Frolinat, for example, which had been the key rebel organization in the struggle against Tombalbaye, stated that one of its major goals was the " unity of the Chadian nation." The nationalist ideologies that followed Tombalbaye all stressed, as he had, the entire nation not some ethnic particle. Malloum and the CSM would stress an ideology of *"Réconciliation Nationale"* that welcomed all into the *"grande famille tchadienne."* Malloum's chief opponent at the time was said to be "above all a nationalist … uncompromising in his determination to build a nation state" (Lemarchand 1984: 65). When Habré seized the government he made the day he came to power "National Liberation, Unity and Martyrs" day. To further disseminate his nationalism he created the *Union Nationale pour l'Indépendence et la Révolution* (UNIR), a party that in certain ways harked back to the MNRCS.

Déby governed in the early 1990s with a strongly nationalist ideology for the entire nation. Furthermore, in response to the urging of both France and the USA, he organized a *Conférence Nationale Souveraine*; one that sought to institute more "democratic" means of attaining his nationalist goals. Nevertheless, the two major rebel movements – Habré's MDD and Ketté's CSNPDT – attacked Déby on the grounds that his was a defective nationalism and theirs was not. There was a chameleon-like quality to Habré's nationalism. He began his political life as something of a Maoist and he initially supported the socialist bloc. At that time his nationalism expressed anti-imperialist, pro-socialist sentiments. However, when he broke from Goukouni he switched sides and came to be supported largely by the Americans. His reign, though still supported by the USA, proved to be a cruel dictatorship. However, after Déby defeated him in the early 1990s, his nationalist ideology favored the "democratization" that his American supporters preached and that he had never practiced.

Thus the major political actors on all sides consistently sought to justify their actions on the basis of some form of nationalist ideology. But this nationalism was not ethnically based. It was generally an inclusive nationalism that sought to include the entire nation. Furthermore, it was a pragmatic nationalism invented more or less as needed, usually from non-Chadian sources – be they the modernization of the French, the *el-hadjism* of the Mauritanians, the *tchaditude* of the Haitians, or the democratization of neo-liberal Americans. Such evidence, of course, is inconsistent with the view that ethnic nationalism provoked Chadian instability. It is consistent with a view that an inclusive nationalism legitimated Chadian conflict. However, I am skeptical of even this view for reasons outlined below.

The proposition that "Chadian nationalisms provoke conflict" is causal. Causal statements express the existence of spatio-temporal orderings of events and the fact that in these orderings antecedent events produce subsequent events (Miller 1987). This means that for a causal statement to be supported by evidence there must be observation of (1) spatio-temporal ordering and (2) the production of subsequents by antecedents. This would mean for the proposition under evaluation (1) that Chadian nationalism occurs first in time and that the conflicts occur subsequently and (2) that it is the nationalism that actually produces (i.e., causes) the conflicts.

Evidence bearing upon the preceding is as follows. A number of persons, such as Ibrahim Abatcha, were members of a party called the *Union Nationale Tchadienne* (UNT) in the early 1960s. This party, which has been called neo-Marxist, was in opposition to Tombalbaye's PPT. All parties save for the PPT were dissolved in 1962. This sharpened UNT strife against Tombalbaye. So the leadership of the UNT decided to draft a policy statement, written by Abatcha, that presented their position. Events moved quickly. There were anti-Tombalbaye riots in 1963 that were violently suppressed.

These made anti-Tombalbaye leaders, including most of the leaders of the UNT, flee Chad. These exiled leaders met in Nyala in the Sudan and created Frolinat on 22 June 1966. A "*programme politique*" was adopted at this time that, according to one commentator, was identical to that of the 1962 UNT policy statement (Buijtenhijs 1978: 123). This statement was the inception of Frolinat's version of Chadian nationalism.

Thus those who would be Frolinat leaders were already in conflict with Tombalbaye as far back as 1962. As a result of this, as a part of creating an organization to combat Tombalbaye violently, they also formulated a statement that would become their nationalistic justification of this combat. Thus spacio-temporal ordering appears to be the reverse of what the proposition predicts: *instead of nationalism provoking conflict, conflict produced Frolinat's nationalism.*

This spacio-temporal sequencing of conflict and ideology seems to repeat itself through the succeeding presidencies. When Tombalbaye was replaced by Malloum in 1975, Goukouni and Habré were already involved in a bloody war with Malloum's government. Consequently they devised and broadcast over their radios endless discourses that discredited Malloum and praised themselves on nationalist grounds.

Similarly, when Goukouni drove Habré from Chad in 1980, the two were in the midst of a most violent war. As a result Habré invented his own brand of anti-Goukouni ideology. The early anti-Tombalbaye discourse of Frolinat complained that Tombalbaye had sold out national sovereignty to the French. Habré, taking a page from this tactic, constructed Goukouni as a dupe of the Libyans and promised true national liberation, if he were allowed to rule.

When Déby fled for his life to the Sudan in 1989 he was in the midst of a violent confrontation with Habré. His response was to create the MPS, and then from MPS sources issued an angry discourse suggesting that Habré was a tyrant who had sold out his country to the Israelis and the Americans. Déby, of course, promised that with him good times and national autonomy were just around the corner. In Chad, then, it seems that on-going conflict causes those who are party to it to invent nationalist legitimations of it, rather than the reverse. So that simulations which represent Chad's civil wars and instabilities from 1966 until 1991 as products of nationalism, ethnic or otherwise, are inconsistent with the evidence.

Barbarians and compradors

> There was harmony among the people of Chad when I was growing up.
> (Chadian intellectual)

The person who speaks above lived through the horrors of Chad's wars. Strikingly, what he remembers is that it was not always so. There was a "harmony" prior to the barbarism. Is it time to explain how barbarism was forged out of harmony? I begin to answer this question by documenting changes in the dispersion and concentration of violence. Frolinat, in the earliest days of rebellion against Tombalbaye, had perhaps a hundred partisans who fought for the most part with lances. There were no vehicles, though some had horses and some donkeys. Tombalbaye's army initially had perhaps a thousand soldiers, armed with antiquated rifles and light machine guns. It was reported to have had only four trucks in the beginning. By the time of Habré's rule in 1986 and 1987, there were perhaps 20,000 soldiers in different liberation armies armed with everything from tanks, to missiles, to phosphorous mortars. Habré may have had up to 25,000 people in his army. At the end of the period under scrutiny, the two major rebel movements in opposition to Déby reported that they had 10,000 soldiers. Déby was supposed to have had an armed force estimated to number 50,000. In 1966 there were probably about 1,000 government and rebel soldiers. In 1991 there were well over 60,000 such soldiers. In 1966 these troops were poorly armed. In 1991 they possessed a ferocious array of the most modern weapons. In a quarter of a century the number of combatants increased sixtyfold. A first finding, then, is that there was a spectacular accumulation of the means of violence in postcolonial Chad.

The accumulation has not been associated with its concentration in the hands of the central government because of the formation of rebel military institutions that began during the early part of Tombalbaye's rule. These may be characterized as "autarkic" in the sense that they are independent of the government, which has its own institutions of violent force. This meant that violent force was dispersed across a number of autarkic and government military institutions in Chad. Thus the structural history of postcolonial Chad involved both the accumulation and dispersion of violent force.

Autarkic institutions of violence exercise their violence to compete for control over the state. The existence of such institutions means that the government institutions of violence are obliged to resist their autarkic competitors. Three necessities result. First, contests for control of the state will be violent. Second, as autarkic institutions of violence win, the state tends to disintegrate into increasing instability. Third, when autarkic institutions of violence have won, they become government institutions of violence, allowing the state to reintegrate decreasing instability. Such a structural logic has implications for the ability of the government to exhibit enduring control. Specifically, it means that autarkic institutions of violent force were able to exhibit enormous resistance to the government. Five times this resistance has been so great that the government lacked the means to control it. Thus in independent Chad dispersed fields of violent force have produced periodically bloody instability. The preceding means that the historical trajectory of the stately fields of violent force between 1966 and 1991 was one of increasing concentration and dispersion of violent force that resulted in a high level of instability. The field of the Chadian state was structured so that it could not stop fighting.

Why did this historical trajectory occur? There appears to be a major determinant of postcolonial Chadian structural history. This pertains to the supply of violent force. Cold War great powers supplied military resources throughout Africa (Foltz and Bienen 1985). In Chad, France, Libya, the USA, the Soviet Union, East Germany, Israel, Togo, Burkina Faso, the Palestinians, Nigerians, Zairois, Egyptians, and the Sudanese continually provided military resources to both liberation and government armies. However, the major suppliers of arms, training, and – at times – soldiers have been France, in aid of the ruling regime (Cox 1988); Libya, in promotion of the rebels; and the USA, in support of whoever opposed the socialist bloc.[7]

One military observer posed the question, "how can impoverished Chad afford to fight?" He responded to his question by noting, "the simple answer, of course, is that it can't. The war is being paid for by the French and the Americans" (Cox 1988: 166). The USA, it will be recalled, is reported to have spent on the order of US$100 million to rearm Habré in the early 1980s. The French then spent on the order of US$500,000 per day between 1983 and 1986 defending Habré. The Israelis, Iraqis, and Zairois have operated in many ways as surrogates of the Americans. In sum, Cold War competitors' actions to influence Chad allowed both the government and the rebels to accumulate violent force. It has been the arming of both rebels and government troops that has dispersed the accumulating violent force, and made for the instability in the fields of force. To the extent that the great powers created this instability, they were responsible for the barbarism it produced.

Chad is among the poorest, least-developed peripheries of the periphery, which poses the question, "Why the French and American interest?" There are, I believe, two answers to this question. The first is geopolitical and the second is more directly economic. Both answers ultimately bear upon the Cold War desires of French and American capitalists. A Euro-American diplomat once confided to me that Chad was a "back door" to the Middle East and southern Africa. If, for example, he went on, Libya were to "destabilize" Chad, then it would be far easier to undermine Egypt and the Sudan as well as Zaire and southern Africa. If Egypt were destabilized, Western, and especially US, control over Near Eastern oil might be in jeopardy. Similarly, if Zaire and southern Africa were removed from the Western "camp," a number of raw materials classified as being of "strategic" importance to industry might be at risk. So French and American Cold War strategists ensured better control over raw materials by holding the line in Chad.

Then there is the matter of Chad's direct value to Western industry. As one commentator notes, "The key to French interest is the south's petroleum" (*Africa Confidential* 1993: 8). It has been suspected since colonial times that Chad is rich in mineral and oil resources. Oil was discovered in commercially exploitable quantities by the early 1970s. This was in two areas: around Lake Chad, where the MDD operates; and in the south near the town of Doba, where the CSNPD is active. The southern oil reserves are considerable. Exploitation of these by a US–European consortium made up of Elf and Chevron under the leadership of Shell is supposed to begin in the near future. French and US military investments in Chad allowed them to protect the interests of Elf, Chevron and Shell, thereby helping these companies to maintain healthy profits.

It should be remembered that Henry Kissinger set much of US Cold War policy during the regimes of Presidents Nixon and Reagan. According to John Stockwell, who had been an official in the CIA during this time, Kissinger "was determined that the Soviets should not be permitted to make any move in any remote part of the world without being confronted militarily by the U.S." in the immediate years following defeat in Vietnam (Stockwell 1978: 43). The preceding quotation might be called the "Kissinger Doctrine." During those years the Soviet bloc, through its Libyan ally, militarily supplied first Frolinat and then FAN and FAP. This, given Chad's strategic location and economic potential, appears to have triggered the Kissinger Doctrine. Thus throughout the 1970s and into the 1980s both the socialists and their capitalist foes supplied violent force to both autarkic and governmental institutions of violent force.

If the Cold War competition supplied the resources for the concentration and dispersal of violent force, the stark reality of the local class structure provided the motivation to use them. Most Chadians, probably some 80 per cent, were subsistence or semi-subsistence cultivators. There were a few merchants, some employees of state-run enterprises, a very, very few manufacturers, and employees of multi-national corporations. The only occupation that permitted the accumulation of wealth was that of the *haut fonctionnaire*. The high salaries, combined with sweet political deals, enjoyed by such officials allowed them to acquire capital. This was typically funneled into local land and businesses as well as into international investments in capitalist enterprise. Thus there were really only two choices in such a class structure. One could remain a desperately poor food-producer, or one could become a bureaucrat. Given such choices, Chadians were strongly disposed to become and remain officials, even if this meant fighting for a position in the increasingly lethal autarkic and governmental institutions of violent force.

However, Chadians might be seen as military compradors in this fighting. "Compradors" were actors in older mercantile and industrial capitalisms. They were the local managers of metropolitan firms – for example, the Indians, who run Portuguese trading companies in Goa. There are, of course, still compradors in this sense – the "local hire" of the multi-nationals, middle-level managers of Elf, Shell, and the like. What crucially defines a comprador is that he or she works to satisfy the desires of advanced capitalist enterprises. The notion of a military comprador extended the notion of a comprador into political domains. A "military comprador" is a person who serves the military interests of advanced capitalist states. This means that the Chadian officials, officers and rebel leaders who accepted US and French military resources fought either in support of the Kissinger Doctrine or some other French strategy. Thus, they were a class of military compradors.

This brings us to the question posed at the beginning of the article: who were the barbarians and who were their agents? When the fighting began in 1966 there were a few hundred rebels, some horses, and the odd donkey here and there. The Chadian army was a little better off. This meant that the combatants could not fight very much when fighting began in 1966 because there were almost no fighters, nothing to fight with, and no way to get to the fight. However, by 1991 this had all changed with the enormous supply of violent force from both the capitalist and socialist blocs. The cruelest barbarian is one who sets up a fight and, then, watches it occur along the lines of his of her desire. This is what the agents of both the capitalist and socialist blocs did in Chad. They were barbarians.

What of the Chadians? The article begins with a horrific example of members of the Presidental Guard blowing an old man to bits. Bayart, it will be recalled, believes that Africans have "often created" their dependence. What was created in Chad was instability that resulted from the dispersion and concentration of violent force. Nothing could be created until it was first supplied. The USA, France and the socialist bloc did the supplying. The hand grenades that blew the old man into "*mini mini morceaux*" came from France. Chadians were compradors working to gratify the desires of the really powerful in the Cold War. So Chad's history during the Cold War was one of barbarization, its instability a Cold War story. It is time to contemplate certain implications of the present analysis.

Real juju warriors

> It would be particularly helpful for members of Congress and would-be advisors to the next president to read this disturbing and provocative work and ponder its warnings about the dangers and realities of the merging world.
> (Amazon.com 2000; Newt Gingrich on *The Coming Anarchy*)

> Fascinating. Discomforting. Bracing.
> (Amazon.com 2000; R. James Woolsey, former head of the CIA, on *The Coming Anarchy*)

> Filled with penetrating insight.
> (Amazon.com 2000; Samuel P. Huntington, advertising copy for *The Coming Anarchy*)

Recall that there are three stories being told about Africa: a first one, by Africans, of their horror; and a second one, by outsiders, of African juju warrior dreadfulness. It is time to tell a third story narrated by evidence. One piece of this evidence reveals that the second story is widely disseminated as part of a process of simulation by various advanced capitalist institutions.

First Kaplan produces his representation of Africans as juju warriors and publishes it in the *Atlantic Monthly*, a "high brow" journal circulated among the influential, and would-be influential, folk, especially in the US, in 1994. Then the same article is re-published six years later by Random House as a chapter in a book with the same name as the 1994 article. Random House is the largest English-language publisher in the world. It is part of the Bertelsmann Book Group of Bertelsmann AG, one of ten or so firms that form an oligopoly in the media industry. The right-winger Newt Gingrich tells his audience they should read *The Coming Anarchy* because "advisors" to presidents should read it. A former head of the CIA tells his readers they should read it because it is "Bracing." Samuel Huntington, guru to the center and not a few liberals, tells his readers they should read it because it is "penetrating."

This simulation process is threefold. First, Kaplan manufactures his representation of juju warrior Africans governed by spirits. Second, "wise guys," like Gingrich, the CIA boss, and Huntington, attest to its great value, so it must be true. Third, an oligopolistic institution with global reach distributes the representation to influential people in all parts of the world. So everybody knows: Africans are juju warriors. But it is a big lie.

The evidence from Chad tells another, third story. The story told by the evidence is of how Africans were supplied with violent resources and taught how to use them by agents from advanced capitalist and socialist states. Thus, Chadians were not culturally primordial barbarians. They were *made* into them. In other words, Chad's Cold War story is a tale of barbarization. This truth Kaplan and his co-simulators seek to widely *dissimulate*, and this is the third story. It is of a world of dissimulation where the real juju warriors – the Kaplans and his ilk – work for capitalistic oligopolies to blow smoke across the identity of the real barbarians. The real barbarians are powerful in capitalist enterprise and governments which fought a hot Cold War, and if this turned Chadians into those who exploded old men into "*mini mini morceaux*," so be it. Why is the third story dissimulated? To hide the horror, perhaps? We point our finger at the Nazis, satisfied that they were evil, but that we are not.

Acknowledgements

I should like to acknowledge the helpful comments of G. Schlee, Director of the Integration and Conflict Working Group, of the Max Planck Institute for Social Anthropology (Halle/Saale, Germany). Martine Guichard, Andrea Behrends and Youssouf Diallo also provided excellent advice. Additionally, I should like to acknowledge the wisdom of Raoul Tamdji who over the years has taught me an enormous amount about Chad.

Notes

1 Crockett and Friedman have both written books entitled *The Fifty Year War*, the former in 1995 and the latter in 1999. Both works treat the period 1941–91 as a period of continual US–Soviet war.
2 Discussion of the Chadian civil wars can be found in Buijtenhijs (1978), Bouquet (1982), Chapelle (1980), Boyd (1984), Joffe (1986), Kelley (1986), Lanne (1987), May (1990), Azevedo (1998) and Collins and Burr (1999).
3 The exact extent of Libyan/Soviet bloc support for Goukouni is unknown. However, it has been suggested by one source that some 14,000 Libyan troops were withdrawn from Chad on 4 November 1981 (Lemarchand 1984). These troops were conventionally armed with considerable logistical support from the Soviet bloc.
4 The interview in the text is an invention. However, during the 1970s I saw Euro-American diplomats, journalists and some intellectuals refer to Chad's civil wars as tribal conflicts. This opinion was *doxa*, in Bourdieu's sense of the term. Its "truth" was obvious and went without saying.
5 The First Army had acquired modern weapons and uniforms in the mid-1970s. It divided its zone of operations into seven *wilayas*, or military commands. There was a military council that supervised the operations of the different commands. Each *wilaya* was represented on the council by its commander and a delegate elected from its soldiers. Soldiers were given extensive training in guerilla operations, often from their own leaders, who had received such training from Middle Eastern or Soviet bloc specialists. A twenty-page manual explained to the soldiers their responsibilities and

the punishments that would be incurred if they were derelict in the execution of these. Weber would classify such a fighting force as bureaucratic.

6 Sometimes it is said that this or that liberation army is composed of Goran, Sara or Hadjerai tribesmen, as if each of these terms designate a single, discrete and fixed ethnicity. They do not. The terms Goran, Sara or Hadjerai are generic expressions applied by outsiders that classify in common different peoples with different and changing ethnic identities. The word "Goran," for example, was used by Chadian Arabs with whom I lived in the early 1970s pretty much as a pejorative to describe anyone living in the desert. Kreda, Zagawa, Teda and Daza were all lumped together as Goran. Then, as today, a Zagawa knows that s/he is not a Teda.

The particular interview in the text is invented. However, both journalists and scholars widely accounted for Chad's civil wars in terms of ethnic nationalisms.

7 The full story of Libya's involvement in Chad is untold. However, an account of it up to 1981 can be found in Neuberger 1982. A description of French/Libyan competition in Chad can be found in Somerville 1990. There are only anecdotal accounts of the US role in Chad.

References

Africa Confidential (1990a) "Chad: Operation Rezzou." *Africa Confidential* 31(9): 2–3.

—— (1990b) "Chad: Habré out, Déby in." *Africa Confidential* 31(24): 2–3.

—— (1993) "Chad: Finding Oil in Troubled Waters." *Africa Confidential* 34(4): 5–6.

Amazon.com (2000) "Editorial Reviews: The Coming Dreams" (includes reviews by John Miller, Newt Gingrich, S. Huntington and R.J. Woolsey). 20 December 2000, p. 18. http://amazon.com/exec/obidos

Azevedo, Mario (1998) *Roots of Violence: A History of War in Chad*. Amsterdam: Gordon & Breach.

Barfield, T. (1997) *Dictionary of Anthropology*. Oxford: Blackwell.

Baudrillard, Jean (1983) *Semiotext(e)*. New York: Columbia University Press.

Bayart, J.-F. (1999a) "The 'Social Capital' of the Felonious State." In J.-F. Bayart, S. Ellis and B. Hibou (eds), *The Criminalization of the African State*. Oxford: James Currey.

—— (1999b) "Conclusion." In J.-F. Bayart, S. Ellis and B. Hibou (eds), *The Criminalization of the African State*. Oxford: James Currey.

Bouquet, C. (1982) *Tchad, Genese d'un Conflit*. Paris: Harmattan.

Boyd, H. (1984) "Chad: A Civil War Without End." *Journal of African Studies* 10(4): 119–126.

Buijtenhijs, R. (1978) *Frolinat et les Révoltes Populaires du Tchad, 1965–1976*. La Haye: Mouton.

Chapelle, J. (1980) *Le Peuple Tchadien; Ses Racines, Sa Vie Quotidienne et ses Combats*. Paris: Harmattan.

Ciammaichella, G. (1990) "Ciad: conflittualita permanente e ricerca di un identita nazionale (XiX–XX sec)." *Oriente Moderno* 9(1/6): 110–135.

Collins, Robert O. and M.J. Burr (1999) *Africa's Thirty Year War: Libya, Chad and the Sudan, 1963–1993*. Boulder, CO: Westview Press.

Cox, J.T.G. (1988) "Chad: France in Africa." *Army Quarterly and Defence Journal* 118(2): 161–167.

Crockett, Richard (1995) *The Fifty Years War: The U.S. and the Soviet Union in World Politics, 1941–1991*. London: Routledge.

FBIS (1993) "Rebels Threaten to Sabotage Oil Exploration Project." Foreign Broadcast Information Service, FBIS-AFR-93-178. Springfield, VA: National Technical Information Service.

Foltz, W.J. and H.S. Bienen (1985) *Arms and the African*. New Haven: Yale University Press.
Friedman, Norman (1999) *The Fifty Year War: Conflict and Strategy in the Cold War*. Annapolis, MD: US Naval Institute.
Huntington, Samuel (1996) *The Clash of Civilizations and the Remaking of World Order*. New York: Simon and Schuster.
James, Franziska (1987) "Habre's Hour of Glory." *Africa Report* 32(5): 20–23.
Joffe, E.G.H. (1986) "The International Consequences of the Civil War in Chad." *Review of African Political Economy* 7(6): 91–104.
Johnson, Chalmers (2000) *Blowback: The Costs and Consequences of American Empire*. New York: Henry Holt.
Kaplan, Robert (1994) "The Coming Anarchy." *Atlantic Monthly* 273: 44–76.
—— (2000) *The Coming Anarchy: Shattering the Dreams of the Post Cold War*. New York: Random House.
Kelley, M.P. (1986) *A State in Disarray: Conditions of Chad's Survival*. Boulder: Westview Press.
Kende, Istvan (1976) "Thirty Years, Twenty-six Days of Peace, One Hundred and Sixteen Wars on the Post-Second World Wars." *Co-existence* 13: 126–143.
—— (1978) "Wars of Ten Years (1967–1976)." *Journal of Peace Research* 3: 227–241.
Lanne, B. (1987) "Quinze Ans d'ouvrages Politiques sur le Tchad." *Afrique Contemporaire* 144: 37–47.
Le Cornec, Jacques (1963) *Histoire politique du Tchad: 1900-1962*. Paris: Librairie générale de droit et de jurisprudence.
Lemarchand, Rene (1984) "Putting the Pieces Back Together Again." *Africa Report*. 27: 60–67.
Luckham, R. (1982) "French Militarism in Africa." *Review of African Political Economy* 24: 55–85.
Magnant, J.-P. (1984) "Peuple, Ethnies et Nation: le Cas du Tchad." *Droit et Culture* 8: 29–50.
May, R. (1990) "Internal Dimensions of Warfare in Chad." *Cambridge Anthropology* 13(2): 17–27.
Michalon, T. (1979) "Le Drame du Tchad et l'Héritage Colonial de l'Afrique: l'Echec de la Greffe Jacobine." *Le Monde Diplomatique* April.
Miller, R.W. (1987) *Fact and Method*. Princeton: Princeton University Press.
Mitchell, William (1999) "Detour onto the Shining Path: Obscuring the Social Revolution in the Andes." In S. Reyna and R. Downs (eds), *Deadly Developments: Capitalism, States and War*. New York: Gordon & Breach.
Neuberger, B. (1982) *Involvement, Invasion, and Withdrawal, Qaddafi's Libya and Chad 1969–1981*. Tel Aviv: Shiloah Center for Middle Eastern and African Studies, Tel Aviv University.
Reyna, S.P. (1999) "The Force of Two Logics: Predatory and Capital Accumulation in the Making of the Great Leviathan, 1415–1780." In S. Reyna and R. Downs (eds), *Deadly Developments: Capitalism, States and War*. New York: Gordon & Breach.
—— (1994a) "A Mode of Domination Approach to Organized Violence." In S. Reyna and R. Downs (eds), *Studying War: Anthropological Perspectives*. New York: Gordon & Breach.
—— (1994b) "Predatory Accumulation and Religious Conflict in the Early 19th Century." In S. Reyna and R. Downs (eds), *Studying War: Anthropological Perspectives*. New York: Gordon & Breach.
—— (forthcoming) "Reel History: Frank Talk About Force and Power."

Richards, Paul (1996) *Fighting for the Rain Forest: War, Youth and Resources in Sierra Leone*. Oxford: Currey.
Somerville, Keith (1990) *Foreign military Intervention in Africa*. New York: St Martins Press.
Stockwell, Robert (1978) *In Search of Enemies: A CIA Story*. New York: Norton.
Weber, M. (1958) *From Max Weber, Essays in Sociology*. New York: Oxford University Press.
West Africa (1992) *Chadian Affairs*. 3878 (Jan. 13–19): 69–70.

13 The Cold War and chaos in Somalia

A view from the ground[1]

Catherine Besteman

Over the past decade, Somalia has been at the forefront of crumbling states in Africa, Eastern Europe and the former Soviet Union, and currently may be one of the most stateless places on earth. Examining the trajectory of Somalia's disintegration is important for several reasons. Most obviously, in ethical terms, the fact that a third of a million people died in the warfare and that a million more became refugees requires an explanation of the roots of this humanitarian crisis. In political and academic terms, Somalia provides a case study representing the direction in which numerous states seemed to be moving in the early 1990s post-Cold War wave of state disintegrations and civil wars. Analyzing Somalia's political breakdown and civil war thus addresses important questions about the post-Cold War global order and the construction of states within it. The disintegration of Somalia is particularly intriguing and disturbing because the linguistic, cultural, religious and ethnic unity that seemed to characterize post-colonial Somalia offered the promise that it could quickly become the one true nation-state in Africa.[2] Instead, it became a nightmare of political and civil violence.

What caused the fracturing of Somali society? The segmentary lineage structure of Somali society described by Lewis (1961) had long accommodated inter-group hostilities without the complete breakdown of order (Adam 1992). While Somalia's recent troubles have often been characterized as the result of clan warfare, such an explanation does not clarify why clan tensions should suddenly erupt on a national scale with such brutal devastation, apparently for the first time in history. To explain the destruction of Somalia we must probe deeper to uncover the fracturing points of the Somali social order, and examine the confluence of factors that made the post-Cold War decade so volatile.

Toward this end, this chapter attempts to do two things: first, to examine the conditions which contributed to the breakdown of the Somali state, and second, to explain the form violence took. Explaining the pattern of violence requires a focus not only on the perpetrators, but also on those most victimized. In particular, the linked factors of race[3] and occupation proved critically important in the pattern of victimization. Stratification by race and occupation has rarely been included in the dominant paradigm most often used to characterize Somali society, and yet it clearly identifies those most vulnerable during the period of violence.

My analysis of the breakdown of order and the ensuing period of terror and violence emphasizes the perspective of those who became most vulnerable: the people of riverine and interriverine southern Somalia. These people, while not themselves combatants in the challenge to the state or in the following violence, experienced directly the warfare, banditry, atrocities, and resulting famine which have characterized the breakdown of Somali civil society over the past decade. In explaining the process of victimization of this particular group of people, I am attempting to demonstrate that what happened in Somalia was the outcome of tensions much more complex than a simple clan-based explanation provides.

Following an overview of internal events and international involvement leading up to the dissolution of the Somali state, I will provide a brief discussion of southern Somali social organization, pointing out internal lines of cleavage and tension. The next section identifies some of the breaking points in southern Somali society prior to 1991, clarifying the confluence of factors that contributed to the violence inflicted upon riverine and interriverine Somalis. I conclude by refocusing on the national and international arenas again, offering some speculative concluding thoughts.

Political history, colonialism and superpower involvement

The nomadic pastoralists who constitute the bulk of Somali society swept across the Horn of Africa over the last ten centuries from their point of origin in southwestern Ethiopia, pushing out other populations to achieve territorial dominance (Turton 1975). In the late nineteenth century, British colonists intent on limiting Somali expansionism joined with Italy, France and Ethiopia to subdivide the territory inhabited by Somalis among their own governments. Whereas northern Somalia was characterized by pastoralism and coastal trading ports, southern Somalia's two major rivers had supported farming communities along their banks for at least two hundred years.[4] The area between the rivers, called the interriverine region, was home to a large agropastoralist population. The major ports of the southern Somali coast, distinguished by their inhabitants of Arab descent, have been tied into the Indian Ocean trade network since the tenth century (Lewis 1988: 21–22).[5]

In the colonial division of Somali-inhabited territory, pastoralist northern Somalia was claimed by the British, and agricultural, agropastoral and pastoralist southern Somalia was divided at the Jubba River between British and Italian colonial administrations until 1925, when Britain ceded the area west of the Jubba River, dominated by pastoralists, to Italy. A British Military Administration took over southern Somalia following Italy's defeat in World War II until 1950, when southern Somalia was returned to Italy as a United Nations trusteeship. Independence in 1960 united into one nation southern Somalia, with its checkered colonial past, and northern Somalia, a British colony.

A coup in 1969 threw out the post-colonial Somali government, bringing to power the dictator and self-styled adherent to scientific socialism Siyad Barre, who remained in power until the fall of his government in 1991. Initially, Siyad depended on ties with the Soviet Union, who provided him with substantial military aid through the mid-1970s.

One of Siyad's rallying cries was the irredentist campaign to recapture land inhabited by Somalis that colonial powers had left outside of the colonially drawn borders of the Somali state. As part of this effort, Siyad attacked Ethiopia in 1977 in order to regain the Somali-dominated region of the Ogadeen, which had been retained by Ethiopia during the division of Somali-inhabited territory. The Soviets provided military assistance to Ethiopia, outraging Siyad and resulting in the severing of Somali–Soviet ties. In the aftermath of the breakdown in relations between Somalia and the Soviet Union, Cold War geopolitics caused the USA to quickly move in.

Somalia was seen as strategic because of its proximity to the Middle East and the Persian Gulf. The US government provided more funds to Somalia than to any other country in Africa except Egypt, spending hundreds of millions of dollars on military and economic support through the mid-1980s. American interest in Somalia is evidenced by the fact that in 1987, even though signs of breakdown were imminent and human rights abuses were widespread, the USA began building one of its biggest embassy compounds in the world (which included beach-front property, two swimming pools, tennis courts, and a golf course) in Mogadishu, at a cost of US$35 million. The USA was but one of Somalia's many donors – David Rawson (1994) estimates that altogether Somalia received over US$2.5 billion in aid from foreign donors between 1980 and 1989.

By the late 1980s, northerners who felt excluded from politics and state resources began protesting against the autocracy of the Siyad regime. In 1988, Siyad bombed and strafed northern towns, villages and even rural encampments in response to local uprisings against his government. By 1989, a series of reports from international human rights organizations (Africa Watch, Amnesty International) documenting the regime's massacres of rival clans, human rights abuses and torture practices finally forced the USA to sharply reduce aid to Somalia.[6] The conclusion of the Cold War undoubtedly also played an important role in this decision. During the next two years, the insurrection begun in the north spread southward, and various resistance groups (particularly the Somali National Movement (SNM) of the north and the United Somali Congress (USC) of the central area) fought to overthrow the Siyad regime. Siyad fled the country in 1991, and almost immediately one of the USC leaders, named Ali Mahdi, was prematurely proclaimed interim President by members of the USC Central Committee. Other leaders within the USC and the SNM, angered by what they saw as his preemptory power grab, refused to recognize him as President. The well-known General Aideed emerged as the most important leader from the USC contending for power. Two other contenders for control of the state also emerged in the early 1990s: Siyad's son-in-law, known as "Morgan," and Omar Jess, an Ogadeeni who managed to capture and dominate the Kismayo area in the far south.

Following Siyad's flight in 1991, the south degenerated into a war between these four men and their followers over power, and between everyone over food, water and political alliances, which seemed to shift daily. These "warlords"[7] were able to maintain their power grip through their control of large stocks of weapons, which were used to acquire food. The intensified fighting during the final period of Siyad's regime, combined with drought conditions and the earth-scorching campaign undertaken by Siyad to prevent pursuit as he fled the capital, led to the immediate displacement of farmers from their lands and undercut food production in the agriculturally important interriverine area. The warlords used their arms to cut off the food supply and to undermine the ability of the people to produce their own food in areas they wished to bring under their sphere of influence. Somalia's livestock base was decimated, as hundreds of thousands of animals were massacred or shipped to the Gulf to finance arms purchases; Somalia's farmers were forced off the land because of widespread and constant looting of farming villages. Looting of food relief by warlords became a strategy to finance the extensive patronage system on which the warlords relied. In the midst of this warfare, the north seceded along former colonial boundaries as its own independent country, Somaliland.

In 1992 the United Nations stepped in and began negotiations between warring factions, and the USA sent in troops in a highly publicized effort to secure food supplies for starving refugees. The bungled diplomacy and confused military intervention that followed – involving the withdrawal of American troops following the loss of American lives – appear only to have exacerbated local tensions, and jeopardized relief operations and attempts at international mediation.

This series of events was well-documented by the media in the early 1990s. Looking more closely at Somali social organization will allow us to delve further into some of the social, political and economic dynamics that defined Siyad's rise, fall, and the disintegration of the Somali state.

Somali social structure

As described by I.M. Lewis (1961), Somali society is characterized by a segmentary lineage system consisting of six major clan families (Isaaq, Darood, Dir, Hawiye, Digil, Rahanweyn), which in turn are divided into clans numbering 10–100,000 members each. These in turn are divided into sub-clans, sub-sub-clans, and patrilineal lineages. Lineages or groups of lineages tied together by social contracts have historically been the focus of political activity. The basis of these groups was the collective payment of *diya*, or blood compensation, for wrongs committed by any group member. Pre-colonial Somali social organization and dispute mediation was based on this combination of kinship and social contract, together with the laws of Islam (Lewis 1988: 10; Samatar 1992).

In contrast to the image of fixed clan identities balanced by a principle of egalitarianism, however, Somali society was characterized by fluidity in clan membership and important status distinctions within and between clans. The practice of *sheegad*, for example, allowed people to seek adoption by clans other than those into which they were born. Such adoptions were particularly widespread in the south, where some clan groupings contained more members by adoption than by birth. The fluidity of clan composition in the south contributed to a national distinction between southern-based and northern-based clans. Among the six major clan families on the national level, the Rahanweyn and Digil clans of interriverine southern Somalia were viewed "with a certain contempt by many of the country's nomadic pastoralists" (Helander 1996: 48–49). Their higher dependence on cultivation, practice of adopting outsiders into their clans, dialect, and the perception that they looked more "African" (Helander 1996: 48–49) contributed to the inferior position they held in wider Somali society. In the words of I.M. Lewis (1988: 14), "Traditionally these distinctions (between pastoralist northerner and agropastoralist southerner) are entrenched by the nomad's assumption of proud superiority and contempt for his southern countrymen, and the latter's corresponding resentment and isolation." This isolation was evidenced in their exclusion from participation in national politics. The Rahanweyn/Digil political party of the 1950s and 1960s, the HDMS, never saw electoral success (Helander 1996; Mukhtar 1989).

Within clans, the widespread practice of adoption and clientship in the south contributed to internal distinctions based on genealogy and racism. Southern Somalia absorbed large numbers of slaves imported from East Africa during the nineteenth century. With the rise of Zanzibar as a commercial center in the mid-nineteenth century and the availability of slaves in the Indian Ocean trade, many Somali pastoralists developed plantations along the banks of the river closest to the coast, the Shabelle. These plantations were relatively small, family-run operations, worked by imported African slaves, producing cash crops to be sold in the Indian Ocean trade (Cassanelli 1982). In addition to acquiring slaves through the seaborne trading network, up until the early twentieth century Somali pastoralists acquired slaves, through raids and warfare, from other pastoralist groups of the Horn, especially the Oromo and the Boran. I estimate that by the early 1900s, slaves constituted about a fifth of southern Somalia's population (Besteman 1999). Laws of Islam mandated that slaves were to be converted and then manumitted. Following manumission, most slaves sought affiliation with or adoption into a Somali clan, eventually settling in farming villages along the Shabelle and Jubba Rivers and in the interriverine area. By 1988, descendants of slaves in Somalia dominated the Jubba River valley and were widely represented along the Shabelle and interriverine area.

Despite the fact that most descendants of slaves became fully "Somali" through adoption, in terms of language, custom, religion and participation in the Somali clan system, some maintained their physical distinctiveness and were said to look more "African" than other Somalis (Somalis tended to emphasize an Arabic, rather than an African, ancestry). Their physical distinctiveness was captured in the term *jareer*, which means "hard, kinky hair," glossed in English by Somalis as "Bantu." *Jareer* is opposed to *bilis*, a term glossed as "noble," used to refer to lineally pure Somalis. By virtue of their physically identifiable non-Somali origins, maintained by prohibitions on intermarriage with other Somalis, ex-slaves and their descendents were clearly not lineally pure members of any clan, and were thus lumped into a low-status category in a relation of social inferiority to Somali nobles. While many, and perhaps most, *jareer* saw themselves as members of Somali clans, their status as debased minorities cross-cut clan organization.

Additionally, many Shabelle Valley residents and descendants of slaves who inhabited the lower Jubba Valley rejected membership in Somali clans, retaining a sense of ethnic distinctiveness within Somalia (while maintaining an identity as Somali citizens). The Shabelle communities were inhabited by non-Somali farmers who probably pre-dated the pastoralist Somali invasion of the Horn. These communities lived as clients to surrounding Somali pastoralist groups (Cassanelli 1982). The Jubba Valley communities were founded by the earliest fugitive slaves, who retained their language and sense of cultural distinctiveness, continuing to identify themselves as Mushunguli (Zegua) rather than Somali. In the regional and national arenas, the members of these communities shared a denigrated, racialized identity. As a group, *jareer* people never had any political voice on the national scene. Indeed, in the 1980s *jareer* people did not recognize a politicized group identity at the national level based on their ascribed race.[8]

Other dimensions of identity, in addition to genealogy and racial categorization, characterized pre-disintegration Somalia. In southern Somali villages, for example, lineage ties often took a back seat to village membership in daily affairs. While villagers in the Jubba Valley could pay *diya* as members of Somali lineages, entire villages also functioned as *diya*-paying groups, whether or not all villagers were members of the same kinship group. Decisions about resource use, inter- and intra-village affairs, and dispute mediation were often handled by village committees, rather than lineage elders (although there might be significant overlap between the two categories).

As this very abbreviated overview of Somali social structure shows, Somali identities and social relations in the interriverine south were much more complex than the segmentary lineage model might imply. While *diya*-paying groups did operate, and most southerners identified themselves as members of Somali clans, village membership and status distinctions based on genealogy and (racialized) ancestry cross-cut clan divisions and in some cases defined groups which existed outside of the clan system altogether.[9]

The breakdown of the state

During the 1970s and 1980s a number of important trends developed under the Siyad regime that cumulatively resulted in the political disintegration of the state. Siyad's socialist rhetoric emphasizing a pan-Somali unity was offset by heightened hostilities resulting from Siyad's manipulation of ties and alliances among the political elite. A growing rural/urban division and the emergence of an urban elite, based on ties to the state, fueled an increasingly predatory relationship between urban elites and rural producers. These hostilities and struggles took shape during a period of militarization and were magnified by enormous injections of foreign aid to the Somali state. After reviewing these processes, I will connect them with the emergence of warlords and the victimization of the south.

Under the rhetoric of "scientific socialism," Siyad Barre attempted to undermine clan and local authority in a number of ways, primarily in order to strengthen the authority of the state government. In a direct attack on clan allegiance, Siyad outlawed the public and private acknowledgement of the existence of clans, including the payment of *diya*. Any reference (formal or informal, verbal or written) to clan, lineage or ethnic affiliation was strictly forbidden, and offenders, if caught, could be imprisoned. The attack on "tribalism"

> culminated in demonstrations later in the year [1970] and early in 1971 when effigies representing "tribalism, corruption, nepotism and misrule" were symbolically burnt or buried in the Republic's main centres. The circumlocutary use of the term "ex" [ex-clan] tolerated by previous civilian regimes was completely outlawed, and the word comrade [*jaalle*: friend, chum] launched into general currency with offical blessing to replace the traditional, polite term of address "cousin" [*ina' adeer*], which was now considered undesirable because of its tribalistic, kinship connotations.
> (Lewis 1988: 209–210)

This political ideology of equality and homogeneity was initially welcomed by many Somalis as an alternative to the elite clan politics that had characterized the parliamentary democracy of the 1960s. However, its enforcement by the state using secret police as spies created an atmosphere of constant tension and fear, in effect driving clan politics underground. Siyad constructed pan-Somali organizations to replace clan-based allegiances, such as orientation centers staffed by uniformed state employees who were to incite revolutionary fervor in support of the regime (Lewis 1988), youth groups and women's organizations. Through a number of important laws, the state took control over critical aspects of social, political and economic life previously handled by clan or village leaders using customary law. The enactment of the Family Law Act in 1975, under which new marital and succession practices were to be managed by the state, was marked by the execution of ten religious leaders who objected to its non-Islamic basis. The Land Law of 1975 gave the state full and sole control over allocating rights to land and water throughout the country, eradicating customary tenure and the authority of local leaders.

Siyad's emphasis on a pan-Somali national consciousness that would override clan consciousness took on magnificent proportions.[10] The great literacy campaign of 1974–75 sent urban students throughout the country to teach rural Somalis their new script, as well as revolutionary ideals. The invasion of the Ogadeen by Somali forces in order to wrest this Somali-inhabited area out of the hands of Ethiopia was Siyad's greatest statement of pan-Somali unity. Many see the failure of the invasion as the beginning of Siyad's personal and political decline.

While the glorified rhetoric of pan-Somali unity was a key point of socialist ideology, all of these mechanisms were engineered to strengthen Siyad's authority and destroy the authority of clan and local leaders. Underneath these trappings of enforced socialist homogeneity and equality, however, Siyad skillfully manipulated the clan system to his own advantage. He played subtle, but hard-core, clan politics which pitted clan against clan, sub-clan against sub-clan, in order to maximize his power. Siyad's distribution of rewards and punishments was carefully calculated to ensure a network of loyal supporters spread throughout all clans.[11]

While undermining clan leaders and fanning clan hostility, Siyad increasingly surrounded himself with supporters from three clans: his own (Marehan), his mother's (Ogadeen), and his son-in-law's (Dulbahante). The prominence of these three groups in Siyad's government was reflected in "the clandestine code name 'M.O.D.' given to the regime. ... Although no one could utter the secret symbol of General Siyad's power openly, the M.O.D. basis of his rule was public knowledge and discussed and criticized in private" (Lewis 1988: 221–222). By the 1980s, many Somalis believed that the Siyad regime had a clear clan orientation.

Northern clans in particular resisted Siyad's power-building strategies and were heavily punished. The imposition of a tariff on livestock exports from northern ports, the outlawing of *qat* (a stimulant) sales, and the resettlement of Ogadeeni refugees in the north were all seen as attempts by Siyad to undermine the economic and political strength of the rival Isaaq clan-family (Cassanelli 1993). Tensions erupted into violence when Siyad ordered the bombing of Isaaq settlements in 1988.

Siyad's nationalist stance (evidenced by his socialist rhetoric, the outlawing of "tribalism," and the irredentist campaign) thus became secondary to his increasing manipulation of clan tensions and elite politics through his distribution of jobs and resources, his usurpation of control over productive activities dominated by rival clans (the overseas livestock trade, the qat trade), and his efforts to undermine local-level authority.

In this atmosphere of clan manipulation and the breakdown of clan authority, a new urban political elite emerged in the 1980s. Bureaucrats, civil servants and those well-connected to the government were positioned to channel the significant (largely foreign-supplied) resources of the state into their own pockets. As the state became a primary source of wealth and resources, competition among urban elites often played out along genealogical lines, but without the constraining rules of customary clan law (*xeer*). As Cassanelli notes (1993: 16), Siyad's "policies served only to reduce local clan authority, not clan consciousness." This urban-based-elite struggle for personal enrichment through accessing the state is what came to be known as tribalism or clannism, although it bore little, if any, resemblance to traditional clan-mediated interactions. As Samatar argues (1992: 640), "The most important lesson to be learned from the present tragedy is the recognition that Somali society has been torn apart because blood-ties without the *xeer* have been manipulated by the elite in order to gain or retain access to unearned resources."

At the opposite end of the spectrum from competitive elite politics in the urban areas was the increasing marginalization of rural agricultural people and heightened conflict over resources among rural producers. Unsustainable development of the pastoral sector, fueled first by the commercialization of the livestock economy by colonial powers, and perpetuated by international development projects which undermined the ecological balance of Somali pastoralism, led to disputes and antagonisms among pastoralists and between pastoralists and farmers over access to resources.

Furthermore, and perhaps more significantly, the rich resources of the agricultural south, increasingly recognized in the 1980s by foreign donors and the Siyad regime alike, became an object of contention by urban elites. Elites with cash to invest from family members working overseas or from plundering the coffers of the state looked to the relatively durable asset of land. The US-backed development boom of the 1980s encouraged urban elites to utilize the new land registration laws, often accompanied by the threat of armed force, to claim vast tracts of land throughout the south, dispossessing rural producers (Besteman 1994, 1996b, 1999; Menkhaus 1989, 1996; Merryman 1996).[12] The battle over agricultural resources raged between urban representatives of the state and local farmers with no authority or power in the national arena. Local smallholders were the inevitable losers.

The 1980s thus saw the growth of clan, class, and rural/urban tensions and hostilities, largely played out through struggles over the distribution of resources. After the agricultural resources of the south were defined as resources of the state, the *bilis/jareer* distinction and the historic marginalization of the Rahanweyn/Digil agropastoralist clans burst onto the national scene with new clarity and significance, and with devastating consequences.

The shift from marginalization to devastation of rural southern agricultural and agropastoral communities was a direct result of the growing militarization of the Horn during the preceding decades. Because their race and occupation had defined their inferior and marginalized position in Somali society and politics, rural southerners had not participated in the acquisition of arms; they lacked the alliances and means to obtain them. Unarmed, sedentary, and without political alliances to protect them, southern farmers became sitting ducks during the post-1991 violence, consistently raided for their foodstores, their harvests, and everything else. They also witnessed growing claims to their land made by resistance fighters, militiamen, and other outsiders. As Cassanelli (1996: 23) says,

> As the militias struggled for control of neighborhoods and districts, farmland was occupied and claimed by the "liberators" [i.e. those who fought against Siyad Barre]. The property which the state had claimed as its own, and which the rulers had exploited now became fair game for the new power brokers. Somalia's productive resources became the battleground.

The persistence of clan consciousness in the face of demolished clan authority and morality, combined with a militarized atmosphere of competition over resources, provided the arena for the emergence of "warlords." These warlords could use the language and sentiment of clan to rally allegiance along genealogical lines, but built their authority on the power of the gun. They became magnets for a generation of youth who had grown up in an era of poisoned clan relations, broken clan authority, and economic decline. The lessons of plunder taught by the urban elite of the 1980s had been well-learned. In the absence of any significant state resources after 1990, warlords and their followers turned to the agricultural resources of the south; resources which the Siyad regime had already claimed for the state through the Land Law of 1975 and the actions of state representatives.

The struggle to claim control over agricultural resources of the south continues. In the Jubba Valley, militias comprised of immigrant newcomers to the area continue to claim the right to command local resources, including labor. A significant percentage of the Jubba Valley farmers remain in refugee camps across the border in Kenya, facing a terribly uncertain future (see Menkhaus 1999; also Declich 2000). Arable land in southern Somalia will clearly continue to be an object of contention and it appears that the original landholders will continue to lack political and military strength to defend their ownership. Other objects of contention are less tangible but important in a world order based on states: the power of authority and representation in the international arena and the right to the spoils of international aid.

Conclusion

From a superficial view, Somalia appears to be a perfect case for those who argue that states on the margins in a post-Cold War world will be characterized by violence along ethnic lines, because ethnicity is potent, natural, and unavoidable. Does Somalia's trajectory mean that ethnic violence is the natural result (and inevitable future) of the conclusion of Cold War-imposed order?

Of course not. But Somalia's decade of violence does reveal some crucially important things about the world we are currently creating. First of all, Somalia's violence demonstrates just how profoundly destructive the Cold War was for many non-western countries, whose post-colonial political trajectories were shaped by First-World patronage of unpopular, abusive leaders. Just as Uvin (1998) has demonstrated for Rwanda, it is impossible to overlook the role of foreign aid to Somalia in supporting a leader who maintained power through human rights abuses and the instigation of domestic rivalries, and in paying for or encouraging the implementation of programs that reinforced racism and inequality. Political scientist Ken Menkhaus, who has worked intensively in Somalia throughout the last decade, minces no words in discussing the impact of foreign aid:

> That long episode [1960–90] of high levels of foreign aid transformed the nature of the "game" in Somali politics, and had a profound impact on the

political culture of Somali elites and, to a lesser extent, on local communities as well. Most of the prominent political and military figures in Jubbaland today are ex-government officials and civil servants; their political behavior and expectations continue to be shaped by their 1980s experience of foreign aid. It feeds inflated [and outdated] local expectations of a return of large-scale delivery of foreign aid, and, when that aid is no longer forthcoming, suspicion that aid agencies are diverting the funds meant for Somalia. ... It fuels the enduring preoccupation of Somali leaders with aid agencies rather than with their own constituencies and resources. It partially explains the exasperating tendency of Somali political leaders to value international assistance solely for the contracts, rent money, and jobs it provides [i.e., the opportunities for political patronage it gives them] rather than for the actual development or social service output it provides the community. And it has undoubtedly contributed to a local aversion to raising funds to pay for social services [such as education, health care, sanitation, potable water] which in the past were provided by international aid [sometimes via the Somali state, sometimes directly by NGOs], and which are now viewed as the "job" of international NGOs. (Menkhaus 1999, no page number available; see also Marchal 2000: 5).

These observations highlight just how difficult it will be to balance any future international assistance with the need for self-determination, social justice and political altruism. The extent to which, and the way in which, the international community should become involved in rebuilding Somali civil and political society, the country's infrastructure, and social service delivery is a question of enormous import and tremendous implications.

Second, the local experience of Cold War geopolitics also involved massive regional militarization – both in state-owned weaponry and in the widespread, but unequal, availability of arms. To a significant degree, ownership of weapons has differentiated the powerful from the powerless in post-disintegration Somalia. The need for demilitarization is quite clear, but, as Marchal (2000) notes, the process of demilitarization will have to be localized and fair.

Third, identerest sentiments are a post-Cold war reality that cannot be ignored or wished away. The impact of foreign aid in supporting a dictator and policies that produced tremendous conflict and rural impoverishment, the deleterious conduct of Somalia's leaders, and the self-serving behavior of Somalia's warlords can certainly all be blamed for the past decade of violence. But leaders, even those who maintain their power by depending on foreign aid or on weapons, do not operate in a vacuum. The importance in Somalia of clan sentiment and racism is undeniable. In a militarized context of economic insecurity and political instability, clan and race associations played a role in defining interest groups, allies, and antagonists. But clan sentiments do not motivate killing and do not define enduring interests. Ethnic violence is created, bought, nurtured and manipulated by individuals and groups with strategic agendas. The vast majority of Somalis were not combatants or involved in militia atrocities;

Somalia stands as a very clear example of how a small number of heavily armed people can terrorize and destroy civil society. Certainly clan sentiment played a role in the formation of militias along clan lines, but the larger reward for combatants – many from a generation of people with substantial fears about their economic future – was the possibility of material gain. In the riverine areas, clan sentiment was trumped by race; the clan affiliations of *jareer* farmers provided no support in the face of militia attacks intended to gain control of arable land.

The question is: what kind of identerest sentiments will come to define Somalia in the next decade? Clan associations remain very strong in some areas, but associations formed along age, gender or occupational lines are emerging in other areas. Racial categories continue to have major salience and are perhaps the least subject to transformation. Of particular note for the concerns of this chapter is the fact that in addition to the large number of "Somali Bantus" who remain in refugee camps in Kenya, tens of thousands are seeking asylum in Tanzania on the basis of ancestral ethnic identity (Francesca Declich, personal communication, November 1996; Dan Lehman, personal communication, December 2000).[13] While clan identities will undoubtedly remain an important component of identerest group formation, so will race and other dimensions of identity. To imagine that clan is the solitary basis of group formation and mobilization denies the complexity of Somali identities and overlooks other real and potential bases of political mobilization. Marchal (2000) discusses the complex ways in which clan identities interface with other group identities (based on residence, schooling, gender and Islamic associations) in the emerging business class in Somalia, Somaliland, and Puntland.

Because my research on Somalia is confined to the past, I am not the person to predict Somalia's political future. But it is clear to me that Somalia may be the most potent example that the post-colonial form of African states is not only open to change, but requires it. The form that will ultimately work for Somalia may not be one currently represented in the international community. One envisions such standard nation-state structures as a delineated territory with a centralized popularly supported government with one capital city, or a regionalized federation of geographical units with strong local leadership. The first represents the structure more familiar to the West, although it seems unlikely that such a model will successfully emerge in Somalia. Deep ethnic rivalries and profound mistrust of a centralized government are the legacy of the Siyad regime. A regionalized system offers the hope of power-sharing. The recent politicization of the Rahanweyn/Digil clan-families and the *jareer* population in the south (and the secessionist movements in the north that created Somaliland and Puntland) indicate an inclination in this direction. While a regionalized system does not mean that power will not be abused, that local or immigrant elites will not attempt to gain unwarranted access to resources or manipulate politics to their advantage, it does offer the possibility of greater accountability from leaders and greater representation. If a political solution is not forced on Somalia by an international community determined to create a new nation-state, perhaps the outcome of Somalia's bloody turmoil will be a new form of decentralized state structure, unfamiliar to the West, but attuned to the social realities of Africa. In light of recent history, however, political equity and social justice for Somalia's minorities may remain an elusive hope.

Notes

1 This chapter is based on fieldwork conducted in southern Somalia in the late 1980s and on interviews with Somali refugees and expatriates in North America in the early 1990s. Since I have not returned to Somalia and thus have no first-hand knowledge of the contemporary state of affairs, my focus here is on the period surrounding the collapse of Somalia's government in 1991. My analysis of Somalia's crisis has appeared in Besteman 1996a and 1999.
2 While Somalia may be more culturally and linguistically homogeneous than most other African states, during the 1990s this perception of ethnic homogeneity was resoundingly criticized in academic fora. Such critiques appeared in numerous presentations made at the 1993 International Congress of Somali Studies and formed the basis of a book, *The Invention of Somalia* (Ahmed 1995).
3 I am using this term very broadly to mean the identification and grouping together of people based on perceived physical characteristics and genealogies.
4 The origin and history of these riverine agriculturalists has been debated. While Jubba Valley farmers have lived in the area for only about 150 years, the Shabelle Valley may have been home to agriculturalists from before the invasion of the Horn by Somali pastoralists (see Lewis 1988; Cassanelli 1982).
5 Cassanelli's *The Shaping of Somali Society* (1982) discusses the coalescence of Somali society over several centuries.
6 It is somewhat ironic that the US government poured millions of dollars worth of arms, economic assistance and development assistance into Somalia in return for being able to maintain US military bases on Somalia's coast, the justification being that if war broke out in the Persian Gulf, a US force would be in close proximity. By the time war did break out in the Gulf, however, the seeds of destruction the USA had helped sow in Somalia by flooding the country with arms and supporting a despised and brutal dictator had blossomed, and the USA had been forced to evacuate its bases on Somalia's coast.
7 See Adam 1992 for a discussion of warlordism in Somalia.
8 In addition to status distinctions, there was also a caste-like element in Somali social organization. There were several out-caste groups that had an untouchable status as a result of supposed improprieties committed in ancient times by their ancestors. Intermarriage and other kinds of intimate interaction with other Somalis were prohibited.
9 Also outside of the Somali kinship system was the Arab-descended urban population of Mogadishu, Marka and Brava. They also suffered disproportionately during the war.
10 Cassanelli (1993) examines the emergence of a pan-Somali consciousness historically, discussing the tendency of Somali leaders to utilize this consciousness in their bids for power.
11 As Cassanelli (1993: 13) argues, "[t]hrough the 1980s, virtually every policy implemented by the Siyad government could be read as having implications for the balance of clan power in the country's economic and political life."
12 Cassanelli (1996) and Besteman (1999) identify and discuss in detail several important trends which contributed to the struggle over resources, in particular the land rush in the south.

13 Declich (2000) discusses the creation of the ethnic category of "Somali Bantu" in the refugee camps in Kenya in the early 1990s.

References

Adam, Hussein (1992) "Somalia: Militarism, Warlordism or Democracy?" *Review of African Political Economy* 54: 11–26.

Ahmed, Ali Jimale (ed.) (1995) *The Invention of Somalia*. Lawrenceville, NJ: Red Sea Press.

Besteman, Catherine (1994) "Individualisation and the Assault on Customary Tenure in Africa: Title Registration Programmes and the Case of Somalia." *Africa* 64(4): 484–515.

—— (1996a) "Violent Politics and the Politics of Violence: The Dissolution of the Somalia Nation-State." *American Ethnologist* 23(3): 579–596.

—— (1996b) "Local Land Use Strategies and Outsider Politics: Title Registration in the Middle Jubba Valley." In Catherine Besteman and Lee V. Cassanelli (eds), *The Struggle for Land in Southern Somalia: The War Behind the War*. Boulder: Westview Press, pp. 29–46.

—— (1999) *Unraveling Somalia: Race, Violence, and the Legacy of Slavery*. Philadelphia: University of Pennsylvania Press.

Cassanelli, Lee (1982) *The Shaping of Somali Society*. Philadelphia: University of Pennsylvania Press.

—— (1993) "Explaining Ethnic Conflict in Somalia." Prepared for the Woodrow Wilson Center, Washington, DC.

—— (1996) "Explaining the Somali Crisis." In Catherine Besteman and Lee V. Cassanelli (eds), *The Struggle for Land in Southern Somalia: The War Behind the War*. Boulder: Westview Press, pp. 13–28.

Declich, Francesca (2000) "Fostering Ethnic Reinvention: Gender Impact of Forced Migration on Bantu Somali Refugees in Kenya." *Cahiers d'Etudes africaines* 157(1): 25–53.

Helander, Bernhard (1996) "The Hubeer in the Land of Plenty: Land, Labor, and Vulnerability among a Southern Somali Clan." In Catherine Besteman and Lee V. Cassanelli (eds), *The Struggle for Land in Southern Somalia: The War Behind the War*. Boulder: Westview Press, pp. 47–70.

Lewis, I.M. (1961) *A Pastoral Democracy*. London: Oxford University Press.

—— (1988) *A Modern History of Somalia: Nation and State in the Horn of Africa*. Boulder: Westview Press.

Marchal, Roland (2000) "The Somali Private Sector: Its Role in Governance." Paper commissioned by UNDP for the new edition of the Human Development Report on Somalia.

Menkhaus, Kenneth (1989) "Rural Transformation and the Roots of Underdevelopment in Somalia's Lower Jubba Valley." PhD dissertation, University of South Carolina.

—— (1996) "From Feast to Famine: Land, Social Identity and the State in Somalia's Lower Jubba Valley." In Catherine Besteman and Lee V. Cassanelli (eds), *The Struggle for Land in Southern Somalia: The War Behind the War*. Boulder: Westview Press, pp. 133–154.

—— (1999) *Middle Jubba Region*. Nairobi: UNDOS, Studies on Governance.

Merryman, James (1996) "The Economy of Gedo Region and the Rise of Smallholder Irrigation." In Catherine Besteman and Lee V. Cassanelli (eds), *The Struggle for Land in Southern Somalia: The War Behind the War*. Boulder: Westview Press, pp. 73–90.

Mukhtar, Mohamed H. (1989) "The Emergence and Role of Political Parties in the Inter-river Region of Somalia from 1947 to 1960 (Independence)." *Ufahamu* 16(2): 75–95.

Rawson, David (1994) "Dealing with Disintegration: U.S. Assistance and the Somali State." In Ahmed I. Samatar (ed.), *The Somali Challenge: From Catastrophe to Renewal?*. Boulder: Lynne Reinner, pp. 147–187.

Samatar, Abdi Ismail (1992) "Destruction of State and Society in Somalia: Beyond the Tribal Convention." *Journal of Modern African Studies* 30(4): 625–641.

Turton, E.R. (1975) "Bantu, Galla, and Somali Migrations in the Horn of Africa: A Reassessment of the Juba/Tana Area." *Journal of African History* 16(4): 519–537.

Uvin, Peter (1998) *Aiding Violence: The Development Enterprise in Rwanda*. West Hartford, CT: Kumerian Press.

14 Conflicts versus contracts

Political flows and blockages in Papua New Guinea

Andrew Strathern and Pamela J. Stewart

The "weak state"

Papua New Guinea, the eastern half of the larger island of New Guinea, which lies north of Australia, gained its political independence from Australia on 16 September 1975. It was equipped with a Westminster-style parliament of more than 100 members for its roughly 3.5 million population, a Governor-General appointed by the Queen of England, and a bureaucratic and legal system derived from Australian colonial rule. Problems set in at an early stage with the style of government based on political parties, since it has been very difficult for a variety of reasons for any one party to obtain a majority of seats (see, for example, Saffu 1996). Also, each government has increasingly tended to be an uneasy coalition of factions tied together as much by the perception of forms of self-advantage as by any set of coherent policies. Papua New Guineans have proved to be adept and canny politicians, intensely interested in power games and the pursuit of short-term gains. The tremendous interest in politics in one sense holds the country together in a single absorbing pursuit; on the other hand conflicts between politicians and shifts in political alliances tend to make government policies unstable and the delivery of services to electorates patchy or non-existent.

In addition, many characteristics of the local societies have taken their toll on the operation of government. Papua New Guinea has more than 700 different language groups, and even in the Highlands where there are a few large language groups of up to 100,000 persons, each of these is split into tribes and clans that are intensely parochial and prone to conflict, as well as alliance-making, with one another and with outsiders. People are as ready to split with one another as they are to recombine. Political relations are volatile, marked alternately by violence and gift-giving in a continuous stream of negative and positive reciprocity. Groups have been prepared to oppose the state representatives and to do so forcibly on any issue where their own advantages are at stake. The idea of the state is a new, imposed construction, and carries no automatic legitimacy. Some politicians, assisted by government funds, elaborately bribe their supporters and turn elections into money games that can issue in violence between disgruntled and jealous factions. This misuse of funds drains the system of resources that might otherwise be used for public works and services. Emerging differences of social class begin to shape a new society but also produce tensions and dangers for both rich and poor (Gewertz and Errington 1999).

There is no overall narrative of the nation as an "imagined community" forged from historical struggle: such narratives belong only to lower levels of organization such as "micro-nationalist movements" or tribal or clan groups. There are widespread accusations of corruption, nepotism (the "*wantok* system"), and wastage of resources. Politicians themselves have begun openly to register fear for their lives, faced with the idea that their rivals are hiring criminals to protect themselves and attack others. The family members of some politicians reside in Australia where they are safer.

This picture of the runaway misuse of funds coupled with rising rates of gang violence has been prevalent for several years, discouraging investors and tourists from visiting the country or putting money into its enterprises. On the other hand, the country is not poor; the highland areas are rich in cash crops such as coffee and tea, and huge gold and copper mines operated by international consortia are dotted around in both highland and coastal areas. But disparities in wealth between areas have also led to instabilities, such as people holding up supplies hauled by road and forcibly taking what they think is their share of the incoming wealth. And the high value placed on land in the Highlands has meant that the large-scale alienation of land for plantations has been followed by a backlash of opposition to government acquisition of areas for the extension of government services themselves, coupled with demands for compensation and attacks on installations.

Problems of this kind have been documented earlier for the Hagen area (Strathern 1974, 1993a, b; Strathern and Stewart 1998a, 1998b; Stewart and Strathern 1998a). In this paper we seek to extend these earlier analyses in a new direction. Evidence of local "disintegration" is clear, and this is matched by the impression (shared by some Papua New Guinea citizens themselves) that at the national level Papua New Guinea is a "weak state," at risk of falling apart or failing to function properly. However, we can also see efforts being made to rectify this situation. In particular, these efforts appear to have been intensified since 1999 with the advent of a new government with Sir Mekere Morauta as Prime Minister.

The state and civil society

These efforts are being made from two main directions. First, the various Christian churches, recognizing their responsibility to society and seeing their own survival and safety as being at risk, have begun the task of moral and social reconstruction at local levels while also attempting to influence national politics. Second, state authorities are beginning to see that their role is to reassert the legitimacy of government while attempting to deal with local populations on a number of fronts, and to improve the flow of services while reducing the levels of corruption and incompetence in government.

Such efforts are connected with additional significant processes. First, the churches, while trying to offer patterns for living, also fostered a certain amount of unrest through the generation of millennial thinking and other fears in the populace, a situation not unique to New Guinea or solely derived from Christian ideology (Stewart and Strathern 1997a, 1998a, b, c, 2000a; Strathern and Stewart 1998c). Their leaders are now grasping the opportunity to envision the future not so much as marking the end of the world but as the possibility of a new era. Second, government reactions are based on the recognition that government has either lost or has never securely established legitimacy at local levels, and this is because efforts to create an ideology of the nation in secular terms have not fully succeeded as yet. In Papua New Guinea, as elsewhere in the Pacific, there have in fact been two different bases for such an ideology. One has been the ideology of "modernity," based to a good extent on the notion of the monetary economy and the purchase and consumption of commodities (Knauft 1999; Thomas 1997). The other has been the ideology of "custom," based on the notion of traditional values and ways of doing things. The two ideologies are markedly at variance with each other, despite efforts to dress up the former literally in the clothes of the latter by having, for example, advertisements for biscuits adorned by pictures of Papua New Guineans in traditional decorations and face-paint (Foster 1995). Neither ideology has prevailed. The first is a basis for individual consumerism but not for national goals and ideals. The second appeals to sentiment, nostalgia, and the hope of the cultural construction of the future from the building materials of the past, as in B. Narokobi's early vision of the Melanesian Way (Narokobi 1983; Strathern and Stewart 1999a). But traditional custom as such is ill-suited to the actual organization of contemporary society, even though aspects of it do need to be creatively channeled into social planning, and its values taken into account. It is in this impasse that leaders are using Christianity as a basis for behavior that can potentially define ideals at global, national and local levels alike.

Government officials themselves, realizing that the state cannot simply force its citizens into respecting law or agreeing to policies, have come to regard their relations with local communities in what we propose to call "social contract" terms.[1] They proffer these terms as a replacement for the "social conflict" model which local populations have themselves often adopted as their standpoint. Underlying this attempted replacement is a factor that we have identified in other papers (Strathern and Stewart 1999a, b): the problem of exchange relations. What does government owe to the people and what do the people owe in return? Answers to this question amount to "models for" the social contract which try to build in a positive way on the importance of gift relations in social contexts, setting up a legitimate alternative to the two extreme options of bribery and force.

The new social contract is not being proposed in purely secular terms. Religion is brought into play to give a sense of a morally transcendent sphere which abhors the destructive predation of criminal activities. This hybrid vision of the state, then, is the proto-solution being proposed, in an inchoate form, for

Papua New Guinea's version of the "weak state" problem. It is also being proposed as a response to what may be seen as Papua New Guinea's version of the well-known theme of "resistance to the state" (see, for example, Skalnik 1989). Resistance, of course, is a somewhat general term, covering a multitude of actions and intentions that may be peaceful or violent, passive or active (Scott 1985). Here, however, we are referring to processes that are active and potentially violent and which have a corrosive effect not just on government–citizen relations but more generally on the idea of a "civil society," founded on acceptance of notions such as the rule of law. It is in this sphere that we currently see government agents, including the police, attempting to arouse public support against criminal activities on grounds of moral revulsion as well as collective self-protection, thereby also justifying their use of forceful methods to apprehend and punish criminals.

Predation

The processes of "resistance" we are primarily referring to here are ones we call "predation." Those who commit crimes of this kind are, according to authorities, to be seen as outsiders, outlaws, marginal persons who have defined themselves as beyond and against the social codes which the state authority has established or wishes to establish. By injecting a moral tone into their condemnation of such activities state authorities make a secondary, indirect appeal to the idea of the nation, not as a vague imagined entity but as a "real" moral community, that is one in which moral norms can be successfully upheld to the benefit of the public at large.

Predation includes primarily organized gang crime, supported by education and expertise, and directed against urban assets such as banks, businesses and security firms (Strathern and Stewart 1998d). It also includes less organized rural-based activities involving violence and intimidation, as when disgruntled "landowners" (an important new legal category created by state definitions themselves) block roads, attack installations, or threaten mining and other personnel in pursuit of their aims of protest against projects and of demanding compensation for their own supposed or real loss of assets. While predation in these senses might be seen as a purely modern phenomenon, we suggest that in Papua New Guinea it carries another dimension, an underside that is comparable to the various forms of "assault sorcery" that people in the past (and today also) have imaged as threatening the boundaries of their own local social worlds (Stewart and Strathern 1997b). Assault sorcerers are traditionally seen as operating in bands or squads in quasi-military mode; lurking on the edges of villages or clan areas to waylay and kill people; magically stunning people by leaping over them and so subordinating them by embodied action; stabbing people with sago spines or hypodermic needles; removing their internal organs and stuffing their bodies with rubbish; and sending them home to die at a designated time (Stewart and Strathern 1999a). Ideas and images of this kind belong to large parts of the Highlands, and to the northern and southern coastal areas of the whole country. Today's gangs and their putatively ruthless and amoral leaders are thought of in somewhat the same way as such assault sorcerers. They are often credited with magical powers and weapons. They are seen as living in caves or hideouts away from the villages or towns. Their actions are the inverse images of those of the "heroes" who led the fighting in inter-group wars waged at local levels in the past.

Another category of action that blends in with assault sorcery and also with pre-colonial patterns of warfare is rape. Rape is a serious problem in Papua New Guinea today. In the past men practiced it as a part of inter-group warfare in the Highlands. It was a way of humiliating their opponents and claiming to be stronger than them, and it often took the form of collective action – nowadays this is referred to as gang rape. Gangs who attack houses, hospitals or schools, or who waylay females in isolated rural or urban spots also often sexually attack young girls. Rape is also practiced as a part of post-electoral violence between political factions, the contemporary version of inter-group war. Females who are humiliated, traumatized and injured in this way are sometimes reluctant to report rape to their kin for fear of complications and dangers that can arise out of demands for compensation. Significantly, narratives of rape also formed a part of traditions regarding assault sorcerers in parts of the Highlands (Stewart and Strathern 1999a), and in Hagen there is a genre of rape stories that makes up a corpus of urban tales (Strathern 1985). Rape is thus a prime symbol of contemporary cruelty and predation; but it has its long-term basis in customary images and actions as well as being a part of a contemporary malaise. Women's organizations at national and provincial levels have begun to criticize severely the lack of action to alter this situation, and the Christian churches are doing the same. Rape is one of the "human rights" issues that is beginning to gain some attention in Papua New Guinea.

Obviously such "rascals" or "predators" are not directly "resisting the state." Gangs are not directly political organizations. They do, however, directly threaten the capacity of state authorities to ensure the safety of their citizens. They also threaten the image of the nation as a body of law-abiding people. And while they are imaged as "outlaws," their more sinister side is found in the fact or the suspicion that they are also in a sense a part of the society itself. This is seen in two ways. First, criminals have community connections. Their hideouts may be in community areas. They may distribute stolen goods and money to their relatives. They may supply guns to fighters in tribal clashes or fight themselves. They are married into particular groups. Second, there is a growing feeling that gangs also gain the covert support of some politicians. They may do so by offering themselves as bodyguards, imitating the actions of security personnel. Indeed, they may themselves have been employed as guards before joining a gang and may circulate between positions. They may also act as henchmen, helping to drum up support for politicians at elections, to disrupt violently the political meetings of rivals, to break into polling booths and police stations and to tamper with ballot boxes or substitute new boxes filled with votes for their employer or patron. In both ways, therefore, the predators may in fact be serving the insiders, and therefore the insiders are also acting as predators on one another. It is this further loop in the imagery of the predator that is most threatening of all to the effort to build a picture of society based on the notion of a social contract. If the prime parties to such a contract, the people on the one hand and government personnel on the other, both have links with criminals outside of the contract itself, then the contract is subverted. It is therefore understandable that the police in Papua New Guinea have intensified their efforts to condemn criminals, and have toughened their stance towards them, for example by more readily shooting to kill in urban areas, all in an effort to dissociate themselves from any suspicion that they might be in league with criminal elements or accept pay-offs from them. They have also shifted from advising women "not to walk alone" to forthright condemnation of rape as a category of behavior in a society where both men and women would like to have the freedom to walk alone.

Because ex-policemen often take firearms with them, confiscated guns may cycle back to other criminals or be "lost," and the police can always be accused of acting in a biased way in executing their duties. They can also be accused of making mistakes by being too ready to shoot criminals rather than turning a blind eye to crimes. Relatives of persons shot, keen to claim compensation, sometimes declare that persons shot were innocent. This has happened at least twice in Mount Hagen in 1998–99. In the first instance the police chased a set of highly armed criminals who had broken into a Securimax property and followed them into a clan area adjoining the town, shooting one man in the dark. The man's relatives declared he was just a passer-by and the police promised to investigate further. In the second, a road-block was set up late at night on the Highlands Highway south of the Hagen town. A family that had been harassed at the road-block got through it and subsequently, when they got to town, complained to the police, who investigated the situation and then shot a man near to the road-block. Relatives of this man said that he was mentally retarded and was simply returning home from visiting his kin nearby, and that he was an innocent victim of police brutality. A "war of rhetoric" between villagers and police can therefore occur, denying the operation of a "social contract."

The last example points to another arena of significance: the symbol of the road as a marker of society and its problems, seen in terms of flow and blockage. Like the image of the assault sorcerer, this is a symbol that has powerful colonial and pre-colonial roots.

Highways to "development"

Papua New Guinea's rural communities were all connected in the past by intricate networks of pathways that marked the landscape as a flow of trading activities, visiting patterns, kinship networks, marriage alliances, and major enmities. These pathways might be protected by magic; they might also follow the trackways of mythical originators; they might be blocked in places at times of war; and they might harbor at their edges assault sorcerers. Wherever the colonial explorers first went they followed these pathways, relying on local knowledge, but re-marking them with the lasting imprint of the colonial presence that passed into oral traditions. Later, they ordered many of these tracks to be widened, built government stations at points along them, created new centers, and had people cut new walking tracks and make them wider and safer than before, linking communities that had formerly been enemies. In the Highlands, from the 1950s onwards, the Administration officers or Kiaps recruited an at first enthusiastic populace to build vehicular roads, eventually joining the Highlands to the northern coast and making the interior of the country open to traffic. From the 1960s onwards sections of the new Highlands Highway began to be sealed, making movement on it faster. The road and its associated bridges came to be seen as the instrument and hallmark of development. Highlands people were proud of their roles in building such roads. When the first elections for a pre-Independence House of Assembly were held in 1964, the indigenous politicians took on themselves the mantle of the Kiaps and preached the need for more roads, for iron bridges to replace wooden log ones, and for women to be relieved of communal roadwork, imposed upon them by colonial rule. Such improvements were seen as the very stuff of progress. Roads actually brought the "cargo" that was otherwise fantasized in cult and myth, even though it was not distributed freely to everyone. Roads were associated with hard work, with the white people's ways, with law and order, with safety and prosperity. They were a sign of what we are here calling a new social contract at the time.

This situation broke down some time after Independence in 1975. In the 1980s in Hagen, during warfare between the Kawelka group and others in Dei Council, the Kawelka were split in their residence between two territories and needed to travel by road between them. One clan epecially, the Kundmbo, was split in this way. A Kundmbo man was ambushed at a corner of the road near to the territory of a group allied to the Kawelka's enemies among the Minembi tribe. He was killed, signaling the fact that the road was now a source of danger rather than safety. The incident occurred in the late 1980s. It changed people's consciousness. (In fact much earlier in 1967 an accident on a road resulting in a death convulsed Dei Council, and its aftermath has deeply influenced regional politics to this day; see Strathern 1974.) Since the time of this man's death the road has become an ambivalent symbol of "modern ways," although the Kawelka and others travel extensively on it between their two territories, and are concerned at the lack of government funding for road maintenance.

Indeed, the government highways do bring new inequities as well as new opportunities for making wealth. People tend to relocate near to them and set up businesses beside them. Others wait near them to attack trucks carrying supplies to the interior and steal these. Others again directly predate on passengers in vehicles to take their money and clothes, strip them and possibly rape them or kill them (Stewart and Strathern 1999b). The Highway itself has become a venue of contemporary "assault sorcery" as well as "resistance" to the passage of goods. People in areas disadvantaged by new forms of development are most likely to attempt to redress the balance in this way. The Simbu (Chimbu)

Province, for example, is less rich than the neighboring Western Highlands. Simbu people raid trucks destined for the Western Highlands, pilfering goods. They also make road-blocks and these blocks threaten the flow of goods from the coast into the remoter parts of the Highlands. This new situation has created a regional sensitivity to problems of killings that cross provincial boundaries. The victims' kin can threaten to hold up the business of the whole Highlands region just by blocking the roads. These road-blocks affect everyone who wants to move freely. As fieldworkers in the Hagen area we ourselves often find roads are unsafe to traverse at certain times because of blocks set up to pressure those who are reluctant or slow in giving compensation payments, or simply to maraud and steal from travelers. The local people who live year round in the area express their anxieties over restrictions to free movement. In the next section we examine how in the Western Highlands in 1998, leaders made efforts to deal with this new scale of problem and to create their own symbols of a social contract.

Compensation cases

Both of the cases we discuss here involved inter-ethnic marriages or liaisons. The expansive character of marital alliance-making in the Highlands coupled with the practice of polygyny has for long brought wives of different groups together in enlarged households, making hostilities and jealousies a regular part of daily interactions. However, in post-colonial contexts inter-ethnic marriages increase further the likelihood of violence associated with such hostilities because the parties involved understand one another less well and may have quite different expectations about what is proper behavior. Also, today's contexts often involve younger people who may not know their own customary practices in any detail nor, on the other hand, be socialized into a completely new set of norms. Many women do not want their husbands to take second wives because they view this action as sinful, and therefore a woman may see the new wife as a Satanic force wedging its way between herself and her spouse – something that her Christian religion requires that she fight against (Stewart and Strathern 1998d, 2000b). The overall result is improvization, dissatisfaction, and sometimes violent conflict when people resort to force. In the two cases we discuss here, violence broke out between co-wives.

Case 1

A young woman from Chuave, a poor area in Simbu Province, was married to the son of the sister of a man from the Kurupmbo sub-clan of the Kawelka group at Kuk in Hagen. The sister's son had been accepted as a member of the Kurupmbo group, and his mother's brother was listed as his father in the electoral roll for the area (as the Kawelka put it, his "contract" is with them (Strathern and Stewart 2000a)). A young Kawelka woman, of the Membo clan, came to be married to this man. She fell into an altercation with the Chuave wife, stabbed her with a knife, then ran away. The Kurupmbo were left with an irate demand for compensation from the dead woman's kin. They were very short of resources since their whole group had been involved in a series of compensation payments for deaths in preceding years, and had recently invested great sums of money in political campaigning efforts that had failed to produce the desired ends. Their traditionally paired sub-clan, the Klammbo, brought them some money to help them and their major current political allies, the Kundmbo, shared the burden of the payment also. The Kawelka were afraid of the Chuave people, who arrived smeared in mud and charcoal and were vociferous in their demands. They spoke of them with apprehension as people of another province who would hold up the vehicles of any Hageners who tried to travel through Chuave to reach the coastal town Lae or to return from there back to Hagen. The Highway at that point winds through steep hills at an altitude up to about 7,000 feet above sea level, with houses lining the narrow road, so blocking the road is easy. It was also threatened that Kawelka women who wanted to take their foodstuff to market in Hagen town would be ambushed and raped. In discussing the payment Klammbo speakers pointed out that everyone was completely short of cash (and they were very annoyed at having to help make this payment) but that they were constrained to assist because it was for the name of the Kawelka (*Kawelka-nga-mbi*) among all the Hagen groups. By this they meant that if the Kawelka did not pay up, the Chuave people might not only block the Highway to all Hageners but might also kill, on a random basis, people from any Hagen clan. This would shame the Kawelka and would mean that they would have to pay an extra compensation to whichever group lost a person in this way on pain of warfare and expulsion from the central Hagen area. They would in fact be ruined. So they had no choice.

The Chuave people at first refused the amount offered, K6,700 and thirty-one pigs, but after leaving and returning after three days during which a few extra pigs and approximately K1,000 more were raised, they accepted it grudgingly. Christian prayers were said at the final handing-over of the goods.

In expressing the fact that they had no choice but to pay, Kawelka leaders said that if they did not and other Hageners were killed, their neighbors would combine and drive them out from their land, as they had done almost a century earlier, well before colonial times began in the 1930s (Strathern and Stewart 1998a, n.d.). The Kawelka are keenly aware that they occupy land of prime fertility near to the town and that others around them covet it. They have to keep the local "social contract" through settling their conflicts by means of compensation payments in order to hold on to their land. It is notable that they viewed the Chuave people simply as a threat, not as potential friends. Their sense of sociality was turned inwards to the Hagen area itself, and here too they were in large part afraid of the sanction of violence against them. This consciousness of present threat and the memory of old events determined their actions here far more than other considerations. The case exhibits regional realpolitik, underpinned by fear. These events took place in the first half of 1998 and the compensation was paid on 15 May. We gave K500 as our share.

Case 2

This case also belongs to 1998. We observed the compensation payment made for it on 27 June.

The son of a well-known and long-established businessman in the Angalimp part of the Hagen area was married to two women, one from Goroka to the east of Hagen, and the other Engan by descent, from the province to the west of Hagen. The Enga woman had been brought up in a re-settlement area next to the territory of the Kawelka Kurupmbo sub-clan (the same group that appears in case 1) and her father was assimilated into the Kurupmbo. She and the Goroka wife quarreled and the Goroka woman killed her, again with a knife blow.

The compensation payment organized for the event was consciously modeled on modern political and church meetings. The dead woman's kin were also related to the MP for the Hagen Central or Town electorate, Mark Mendai, himself Engan. A very large number of Engans showed up for the occasion, arriving in trucks. Police came in vehicles and warily surveyed the scene from the road. We were told that violence would not erupt as long as the payment was made, but with all the people gathered together there was a distinct air of unease which could easily have erupted into altercations. Engans were well-known for their warring propensities. The Kawelka, who had come expecting a good share of the payment because of their role in nurturing the woman as a child and helping to bring her up, complained they had never seen many of these Engans before, even at the funeral wake which had been held earlier, implying that the Engans had come only at this time to receive part of the goods.

The event was delayed for many hours, while the donors tried to ensure that they had the maximum number of pigs ready. There was a dais for speakers, loudspeaker equipment run by a generator and mounted on a truck, and much introduced vocabulary was used, deriving from government and church occasions. The chief reason seems to have been the elite political and business connections of the families involved. They made the event a basis for drawing together all the various Angalimp groups, in whose midst there are also a considerable number of Enga immigrants.

The chief speakers were church pastors, who set the tone for the whole event, and members of the province's Peace and Good Order Committee (or Trouble Committee), who had organized the actual payment. They made their speeches mostly not in the vernacular language, Melpa, but in Tok Pisin, the *lingua franca*, shared by all participants. They spoke seriously and weightily, skirting round the actual killing by calling it an "accident," and stressing the ties between all the groups in Angalimp, indeed the pre-eminent importance of the Engans themselves as well as that of the local Hageners.

When the Enga recipients entered the ceremonial ground *en masse* they cried out, yodeling, men first, the women following. The procession was preceded by a bearer, holding the Papua New Guinea flag, and a horse. The Trouble Committee leader exhorted everyone to sit down in their places. They had their own tape-recorder to document the occasion. Speakers welcomed everyone and referred to the "program" of the event, noting that the organization was novel, and was a "new law." Most striking were the speeches and prayers made by the two pastors of charismatic churches in the area, who had waited until all the pigs had been brought and tied to their stakes to await being given away along with money, the horse, a cow, and a cassowary bird. These gift items were all on display in front of the speakers' platform and served as a dividing area separating the gift-givers from the gift-receivers so as to lessen the chance of altercations leading to physical violence.

One pastor said in his prayer:

> Papa God inap long blesim dispela bung bilong yumi na Papa God inap long givim bel isi long yumi. Mi laikim yupela ologeta wanbel, rausim buai, rausim smok, yumi ologeta wanbel na pre. God inap long wokim wanpela samting long dispela taim. [Father God can bless this meeting of ours and Father God can make all of us feel at peace. I want all of you to be of one heart, to remove the betelnut juice or cigarettes from your mouths, and let all of us be at one and pray. God can make something happen at this time.]

He went on to "put the meeting in God's hands," to ask God to be its "chairman," to thank God for all the wealth items collected for the compensation, and to ask the Holy Spirit to give everyone good thoughts.

Among those who received a special word of welcome to the meeting were any lawyers present, one of whom was mentioned by name as a "permanent local lawyer"; and also any "black magic men" who were present. Both categories are worthy of comment. Lawyers are clearly depicted as being of value in today's conflicts that involve the group in entanglements with the state. They are a new kind of valuable or weapon, and their writings are like the "arrow talk," the old form of rhetoric (which was not practiced on this occasion). "Black magic men" appears to refer to ritual specialists who might be beneficial in keeping back rain from falling, which would be a bad omen (in fact rain did fall), or in keeping hostile spirits at bay. Such specialists belong particularly to the Wahgi area near to Angalimp and might have been hired by the hosts to help keep order in their part of the realm of power as a supplement to God.

The efforts of everyone were successful, since no fighting took place and the issue was settled. What was impressive was the extent of the conscious symbolism employed to keep control of the event. One dimension of control was spatial. The Trouble Committee members urged everyone to sit down, to stay put, and to listen. Another was visual: the truck, the dais, the electoral equipment were all signs of modernity and government. Most powerfully, the pastors were billed prominently as speakers, bringing God into alignment with the task of paying the compensation and keeping the peace. There was interesting symbolism of a more "intimate" kind also. The packages of money which were a part of the compensation and amounted to some K23,000 were all wrapped up in sets of K1,000, and were hung in a netbag at the dais. The netbag was a symbol of the dead woman herself, and the money represented her body

(Stewart and Strathern 1997c). As the packages were taken out and enumerated, the speaker declared that each packet was to pay for a part of her – head, neck, side, legs, and so on, at each turn adding up the cumulative total of the payment as a whole. Like other aspects of the occasion this was an innovation, but one with a distinctly customary "ring" to it, perhaps imported from a neighboring area. Special collections or "taxes" were then made. People filed past the dais to lay down small notes onto a sweater or cloth placed on the ground as the Trouble Committee members listed the names of some individuals who had helped in mediating the case and were now to be rewarded. The dead woman's mother came and sat near the dais and was given a special small sum of cash also, as was the Kawelka political leader William Pik (but the Kawelka as a whole were not given much and came home in a bad mood).

Discussion of cases

Elements of conscious "social engineering" and "invention of custom" show most clearly in the second case, in which large numbers of local dignitaries took part. One of those who attended was the Special Bodyguard of the then-Deputy Prime Minister of Papua New Guinea. He came because he was linked by marriage to the family at the center of paying the compensation. Speakers elaborately listed all persons with government or church positions who were present. The sense of order was very "officializing." Yet there were inventive customary touches also, as we have seen. There was little mention of the killing itself, and the woman who committed it was not to be seen at all. There was much talk of overall social relations between Engans and Hageners, and these concerns over-rided the more immediate and "intimate" claims of the Kawelka. We can see the event overall as part of a new creation of inter-local consciousness, dressed in the trappings of government and church.

The first event, by contrast, was part of the purely local reconstruction of the identity of the Kawelka themselves. But here too, the wider context was at work. The Kawelka saw themselves as responsible for the whole Hagen area. They thus constructed their local consciousness in regional terms, and the Highlands Highway was central here as the cause and symbol of why they must pay the compensation. The payment itself was to guarantee the flow of their relations with others and to prevent blockage of their future pathways to their own development and the maintenance of their dignity.

The home-made state: clearing the way

Our two cases show groups and sets of people essentially "making the state" out of their own ingenious inventions. They bring "government" into their own actions as a new form of "self-help." Herein lies what is probably their best hope for the future, provided democratic forms of government are not supplanted or subverted at national level, for example by a military coup. Provincial authorities are closely involved in these imaginative performances of government also, and have begun explicitly propounding elements of an exchange model between themselves and local groups.

In the Western Highlands, early in 1999, provincial authorities moved to advise local landowners that if they persisted in disrupting the operations of a large, indigenously owned plantation business, Wahgi Mek, or continued to harass a local hospital, at Kudjip, operated by the Nazarene Church, they would in turn be refused access to government services in their own areas. In other words, if they broke the social contract they would be punished. Also, the same authorities warned that they would no longer pay compensation for pieces of land used for government-based activities such as schools. They were attempting to re-set the clock on a long-standing issue (Strathern 1993c), but also to "update" people on the meaning of government itself. Their remonstrances with the landowners stemmed from two sources of exasperation with them: first, that landowners, not satisfied with their own participation in the management of plantations, were demanding that they have the power to drive out or fire company executives and managers and to threaten the families of these personnel; and second, that they had extended their attention to a mission hospital that was run efficiently and greatly supplemented the operation of the government hospital in Mount Hagen town. In other words, landowners, rather than being content to state their request to the government, had used threatening and intimidating tactics, that is, they had stepped outside of the limits of the social contract. Therefore, it seemed just to some to penalize them by withdrawing government benefits. In publicizing their actions in the media, the authorities also hoped to gain the support of the public at large.

This was not, in fact, the first time that a tactic of this kind had been tried. Earlier, in the mid-1980s, the Provincial Government of the day had issued an edict that when wounded men who had been involved in tribal fighting were brought to the town hospital for treatment, they should be denied this unless the high price of K60 was paid as a fee (whereas ordinary treatment was highly subsidized). It is not hard to understand why the edict caused resentment and perhaps also ethical qualms among the hospital staff. Men "involved" in tribal fighting need not be the aggressors. They may be the objects of ambush or unexpected attack, and so they are arguably victims of violence. Why would their situation, then, be any different from persons attacked by criminals in town? Among those brought to the hospital were, in fact, the men of a single collective "men's house group," from among the Kawelka Membo clan, who were indeed attacked in this way. It is quite different if the government withholds services from those who have behaved violently in pursuit of their aims, even if pursued otherwise some of these aims can be considered reasonable. The definition of violence itself is therefore at stake, and David Riches' remarks on this issue in general are very pertinent: violence is both inherently contestable in terms of its legitimacy, and remarkably effective at the practical level (Riches 1988: 11, 25). Rephrasing this slightly, we can say that debates about the "social contract" in Papua New Guinea have as one of their foci the issue of where to draw a line between legitimate "protest" or "resistance" and illegitimate "violence" in relation to the state. In criticizing those whose narrow interests disrupt the wider welfare of a political unit such as a Province, the provincial authorities were attempting to assert a moral hegemony on behalf of the people at large, thus giving themselves a mandate to deal harshly in the civil realm with those they saw as standing outside of civil society. They were particularly annoyed with the landowners in this context because their actions had not only been personally disruptive, but also had involved yet again the blocking of a part of the Highlands Highway. Rather than waiting for the national government to enact further legislation or simply relying on the use of force to round up suspects, the authorities decided to use a rhetoric of morality. This appeal to morality is clearly related to the messages of the churches and to their growing importance and significance in public affairs at large.[2] Ten years ago, in the mid- to late 1980s, the Dei Council area was convulsed by a bitterly fought and destructive war between the Kawelka and their enemies, the Minembi. It was in the context of this war that Kopakl, of Kawelka Kundmbo clan, was killed in a road-block in 1989. After his death, and the death of others in the same event, his clansmen held a funeral for him at the Kuk ceremonial ground, recounting the narrative of the *rot bolok* (road-block). Later, provincial government officials and local Trouble Committee members, along with senior policemen, came and announced that they would try to get all the parties involved in the war to come to Hagen and sign a treaty of peace. One of the Local Government Councillors asked (in Tok Pisin):

> Yupela i tokim ol pipol long wokim agreement long ai bilong yupela na yupela i gat wanem kain paua, yupela i gat wanem kain paua long pusim ol pipol o yupela i tokim ol pipol long wokim dispela sain o wokim agreement na sainim nem bilong ol? [You told the people to make an agreement in your presence. What kind of power did you have to push them into doing this, what kind of power? You told the people to sign this agreement, to sign their names.]

The speaker was pointing out that the authorities had arranged a formal peace agreement, but he was questioning both their legitimacy in doing so and the likely effectiveness of the agreement. He went on to say that it was he and his fellow Committee members who had actually stopped the wider fighting and who had set up a Christian cross near to the border between the fighting groups in order to mark their peace-making.

This was one of the earlier speeches in which a local leader pointed out the significance of using religious symbols to help solve political problems. It is a tactic that became much more widespread in the late 1990s. Its spread is correlated with the fact that there are now many more trained indigenous pastors at work in the rural areas, and they are beginning to form an important cadre of new-style leaders. The Christian cross can be used like a traditional taboo mark, to ban fighters from moving along pathways to make stealthy attacks on enemies. The cross, standing at the edge of a rural road built in colonial times that linked the enemy groups' territories and was intended to create friendship between them, is a kind of legitimate "road block," barring further violence between the groups, and encouraging peaceful movement. It is intended to clear the way to future peace and stands as a home-made marker of a social contract to respect that aim.

The metaphor we have used here, of flow and blockage, is one that has sources in pre-colonial images as well as in the contemporary experience of a society that depends on roads as its means of rural development. In Hagen, one traditional magical spell refers to two wild spirits who stand at the concourse of major rivers and keep them free from mud and rubbish so that the water can continue to flow and be clean. The spell, used in curing, reflects the idea of a cosmos that depends on flow (see also Goldman and Ballard 1998). Politicians in their speeches also call on images of flow, saying that "when it rains, the big river carries along with it all kinds of sticks and leaves, debris from higher places." Here they mark themselves as leaders who, like rivers that carry sticks, must carry the people's concerns with them and wash away their troubles. The idea of proper flow is also connected with notions of literacy, the Bible, and the creation of a heritage for the future (Strathern and Stewart 2000c). One of our culturally expert informants in the field, Ru-Kundil, discussing with us a project in which we would reissue his autobiography (Strathern 1993d) in an expanded form with more Kawelka history in it, declared that it would be "like the Bible," preserving stories of the past as messages for the future. Such an idea is connected with the mystique and power attached to the act of writing itself, which is seen as a kind of design, a way of making a pathway, a road. Indeed the expression that Hageners applied to the act of writing, *mon rui*, contains the noun *mon* which also means road. Keeping the roads open, and writing a narrative for the people, are seen as comparable acts of flow.

Conflict versus contract

It is evident from the above that the creation of social order is a difficult and hazardous task in Papua New Guinea today. While local groups have often been in conflict with state authorities, we have given some evidence that they are both "localizing the state" and appropriating religious symbols in order to develop a new "social contract" model between themselves that brings them more into line with state policies. These processes are threatened by the forces of predation from the margins and by the blockages of the flows of goods and services resulting from such predations; and most seriously by the involuted presence of predation within the political system itself. We have invoked the idea of the road as a symbol of either flow or blockage because this is an idea that the people themselves use, imaging their problems in spatial terms. It is not yet clear where the balance of forces will lie in the future: whether conflict or contract will prevail. Major problems that Papua New Guinea's national government continues to face in this context include the difficulties of creating a sense of national identity that can prevail over local and regional concerns; of controlling and redirecting the activities of criminal gangs joined mostly by unemployed urban or rural youths; and of halting corruption and incompetence sufficiently to achieve a better flow of services to the country as a whole. In 1999–2000 the current government appeared to be grappling seriously with these problems.

Notes

1 Jean-Jacques Rousseau developed this term in Western political discourse, in his *Du Contrat Social* (1762), arguing that a genuine social contract should be based on the voluntary agreement by individuals to give up their personal autonomy in return for their collective political liberty. This liberty is expressed in the general will to further the public interest, even if this conflicts with personal interests. Concepts of democracy and justice are clearly important components of how to make such a notion as the social contract "work." Rousseau also refers to civil society as being based on a "pledge," an idea that is similar to the earlier idea of John Locke that government is based on "trust" (Locke, *Two Treatises of Government*, vol. 2, 1690). A complicating factor in the Papua New Guinea situation is whether local ideas of personhood are compatible with these philosophical notions, and also whether these local ideas are changing, and how. This is a topic which is beyond the scope of this chapter, but it is relevant because one of the notions at stake is the conception of the individual as a choice-making agent in society. We have discussed this last issue in Strathern and Stewart 2000b, where we develop the concept of the relational-individual. In the present paper we are interested to discern the emergence of traces, at least, of an idea of social contract in political discourse and practice in Papua New Guinea today.

2 A further, and striking, example is shown in a poster printed by the Catholic Commission for Justice, Peace and Development based in the capital, Port Moresby, for the 1997 national elections. This poster reads:

1997 National Election

Vote ☒

1 My vote is precious.
2 My vote marks my life.
3 This life of mine comes from God, I am made in his image.
4 Power and freedom of decision-making originates from this life God gives me.
5 I must vote with a free and informed conscience.
6 Anybody who bribes or threatens me will disregard my right to elect someone of my choice.
7 I must not accept or let myself be influenced by bribery.
8 If I do accept bribery, I may contribute to bad government. Bad government will not provide security for me and my family.
9 I may also contribute to the downfall of my people, home, province, and country.
10 I promise to use the power God has given me to elect good leaders who can provide a good and caring government for Papua New Guinea.

The ideology proposed here makes a remarkable link between religion and political values and morality, as these bear on the individual via the notion of conscience. The poster also points out the possible unfavorable practical consequences of adopting the way of bribery, consequences that can react on the individual voter. This is the social contract sacralized and brought into alignment with enlightened self-interest. The side and bottom of the poster are adorned with traditional-looking masked faces in green, yellow, and red, to give the words a customary-seeming "edge." It is unclear how much effect the poster had in the Highlands.

References

Foster, Robert (1995) "Print advertisements and nation making in metropolitan Papua New Guinea." In Robert Foster (ed.), *Nation Making: Emergent Identities in Postcolonial Melanesia*. Ann Arbor: University of Michigan Press.

Gewertz, Deborah and Frederick Errington (1999) *Emerging Class in Papua New Guinea: The Telling of Difference*. Cambridge: Cambridge University Press.

Goldman, L.R. and C. Ballard (eds) (1998) *Fluid Ontologies: Myth, Ritual, and Philosophy in the Highlands of Papua New Guinea*. Westport: Bergin and Garvey.

Knauft, Bruce (1999) *From Primitive to Postcolonial in Melanesia and Anthropology*. Ann Arbor: University of Michigan Press.

Narokobi, Bernard (1983) *The Melanesian Way*, revised edition. Boroko: Institute of Papua New Guinea Studies.

Riches, David (1988) "The phenomenon of violence." In D. Riches (ed.), *The Anthropology of Violence*. Oxford: Basil Blackwell, pp. 1–27.

Saffu, Yaw (ed.) (1996) *The 1992 Papua New Guinea Election: Change and Continuity in Electoral Politics*, Political and Social Change Monograph No. 23. Canberra: ANU.

Scott, James (1985) *Weapons of the Weak: Everyday Forms of Peasant Resistance*. New Haven: Yale University Press.

Skalnik, Peter (ed.) (1989) *Outwitting the State*. New Brunswick: Transaction.

Stewart, Pamela J. and Andrew J. Strathern (eds) (1997a) *Millennial Markers*. Townsville, Australia: James Cook University, Centre for Pacific Studies.

—— (1997b) "Sorcery and Sickness: Spatial and Temporal Movements in Papua New Guinea and Australia." JCU, Centre for Pacific Studies Discussion Papers Series No. 1. School of Anthropology and Archaeology, James Cook University, pp. 1–27.

—— (1997c) "Netbags Revisited: Cultural Narratives from Papua New Guinea." *Pacific Studies* 20(2): 1–30.

—— (1998a) "Money, Politics, and Persons in Papua New Guinea." *Social Analysis* 42(2): 132–149.

—— (1998b) "Life at the End: Voices and Visions from Mt. Hagen, Papua New Guinea." *Zeitschrift für Missionswissenschaft und Religionswissenschaft* 82(4): 227–244.

—— (1998c) "End Times Prophesies from Mt. Hagen, Papua New Guinea: 1995–1997." *Journal of Millennial Studies* 1(1). Electronic journal, Center for Millennial Studies, http://www.mille.org/publications/journal.html

—— (1998d) "The Great Exchange: Moka with God." *Okari Research Group Prepublication Working Paper* 8: 1–19. Paper presented at the 1999 ASAO meeting in Hilo, Hawai'i.

—— (1999a) "'Feasting on my enemy': Images of Violence and Change in the New Guinea Highlands." *Ethnohistory* 46(4): 645–669.

—— (1999b) "Death on the Move: Landscape and Violence on the Highlands Highway, Papua New Guinea." *Anthropology and Humanism* 24(1): 20–31.

—— (eds) (2000a) "Millennial Countdown in New Guinea." *Ethnohistory* 47(1), special issue.

—— (2000b) "Fragmented Selfhood: Contradiction, Anomaly and Violence in Female Life-Histories." In Pamela J. Stewart and Andrew J. Strathern (eds), *Identity Work:*

Constructing Pacific Lives. ASAO (Association for Social Anthropology in Oceania) Monograph Series No. 18. Pittsburgh: University of Pittsburgh Press, pp. 44–57.

Strathern, Andrew J. (1974) "When dispute procedures fail." In A.L. Epstein (ed.), *Contention and Dispute*. Canberra: Australian National University Press.

Strathern, Andrew J. (1985) "Rape in Hagen." In S. Toft (ed.), *Domestic Violence in Papua New Guinea*. Port Moresby: Law Reform Comm. Monograph No. 3, pp. 135–140.

—— (1993a) *Voices of Conflict*. Pittsburgh: Ethnology Monographs No. 14.

—— (1993b) "Violence and Political Change in Papua New Guinea." *Pacific Studies* 16(4): 41–60.

—— (1993c) "Compensation: What does it Mean?" *Taim Lain: A Journal of Contemporary Melanesian Studies* 1(1): 57–63.

—— (1993d) *Ru-Kundil. Biography of a Western Highlander*, trans. A.J. Strathern. Port Moresby: National Research Institute.

Strathern, Andrew J. and Pamela J. Stewart (eds) (1998a) *Kuk Heritage: Issues and Debates in Papua New Guinea*. Pittsburgh: The National Museum of PNG and the JCU-Centre for Pacific Studies and the Okari Research Group, Department of Anthropology, University of Pittsburgh.

—— (1998b) "Shifting Places, Contested Spaces: Land and Identity Politics in the Pacific." *Australian Journal of Anthropology*. 9:(2): 209–224.

—— (1998c) *A Death to Pay for: Individual Voices*. Distributed by Pennsylvania State University Media Service. Pittsburgh: Department of Anthropology, University of Pittsburgh.

—— (1998d) "Seeking Personhood: Anthropological Accounts and Local Concepts in Mount Hagen, Papua New Guinea." *Oceania* 68(3): 170–188.

—— (1999a) "Global, National, Local: Sliding Scales, Constant Themes." In *Globalization and National Identities*, edited and translated by Joao Barroso into Portuguese. San Paulo, Brazil: Atlas Publishers.

—— (1999b) "Mi les long yupela usim flag bilong mi: Symbols, Identity, and Desire in Papua New Guinea." *Pacific Studies* 22(4).

—— (2000a) "Creating Difference: A Contemporary Affiliation Drama in the Highlands of New Guinea." *Journal of the Royal Anthropological Institute* 6(1): 1–15.

—— (2000b) *Arrow Talk: Transaction, Transition, and Contradiction in New Guinea Highlands History*. Kent, OH: Kent State University Press.

—— (2000c) *Stories, Strength, and Self-Narration*. Adelaide, Australia: Crawford House.

—— (n.d.) "Hagen Settlement Histories: Dispersals and Consolidations." In Pamela Swadling, Jack Golson and John Muke (eds), *Nine Thousand Years of Gardening: Kuk and the Archaeology of Agriculture in Papua New Guinea*. Adelaide, Australia: Crawford House.

Thomas, Nicholas (1997) "Nation's endings: from citizenship to shopping?" In Ton Otto and N. Thomas (eds), *Narratives of Nation in the South Pacific*, pp. 211–220. Amsterdam: Harwood Academic.

Index

Abasiattai, Monday B. 235
Abatcha, Ibrahim 275
Abdic, Fikret 184
Abdullah, Ibrahim 26
Abrams, Philip 9
accumulation 61, 62
Acharya, Amitav 5, 7, 18
Adam, Hussein 285
Adivasis 165, 166, 171, 173
Afghanistan 8
Africa 5, 6, 7, 12–13, 99; *see also* individual countries
agrarian reform, Peru 10, 122, 123–5, 131–2, 134, 135
agricultural communities, Somalia 288, 293, 294 agriculture, India 170
Agrokomerc scandal 184–5
aid 6, 29, 169, 287, 294–5; military 268, 269, 270, 277, 278, 287, 288
Aideed, General 287
AIDS 248
Aklaev, Airat 1, 24, 41, 72
Albanians 24, 177, 189, 190, 199, 213
Alexander the Great 201, 203
Ali Mahdi Muhammad 287
Allen, Tim 104
alliance-making: among firms 91; Papua New Guinea 300, 307
Alonso, Ana Maria 18
'Americo-Liberians' 220, 221
Amin, Samir 163, 168
Anderson, Benedict 8, 14, 129, 185, 193
Anderson, Mary B. 6
Anderson, Walter K. 160, 161, 162
Angola 3, 5, 13, 17, 25, 93, 243–56
Angolan Writers' Union 251
Angolidade 253–4
Anstee, Dame Margaret 243
anti-communism 156

Appadurai, Arjun 7, 29, 105
Apter, David 178, 179
Aretxaga, Begoña 103, 105
Arguedas, José, María 117
Arias, Arturo 105, 106
Armée de la Libération (ANL), Chad 268, 269
Armée Nationale Tchadienne (ANT) 267, 268, 269
armies, standing 62
arms control 5
arms supply 5, 103, 141, 226, 268, 269, 270, 277, 278, 287, 288
assault sorcery 303–4
Augustinos, Gerasimos 208
Ausenda, Giorgio 18
autocracy 64
Ayodhya mosque incident 149, 151–3, 155–6
Ayoob, Mohammed 3, 4, 5, 8, 10, 19, 39

Bagchi, Amiya Kumar 170
Bailey, F.G. 11, 119
Bajrang Dal 159, 160
Bakic-Hayden, Milica 188
Balkan Wars (1912 and 1913) 209
Ballard, C. 314
Ballentine, Karen 18
Banerjee, Ruben 166, 169
banks 84, 90, 91
Barfield, Thomas 24, 266
Barre, Siyad 13, 18, 25, 286–7, 288, 290–2
Barth, Fredrik 100
Basu, Tapan 161, 162
Bateson, Gregory 179, 189
Baudrillard, Jean 262, 271
Bautista Quispe Antitupa, Juan 126, 131
Bayart, Jean François 262, 263, 279–80
Beck, Aaron T. 110
Belik, Helio 3, 17, 93, 243, 244, 245–56

Bell-Fialkoff, Andrew 19, 20, 23
Berdal, Mats 6, 10
Berkeley, Bill 223
Besteman, Catherine 3, 13, 86, 285–97
Bicesse Accord (1991) 248–9
Bick, Mario 236
Bienen, H.S. 277
Bihar 154
BJP (Bharatiya Janata Party) 6, 154, 155, 156–7, 158, 159, 160, 161–2, 166, 167, 173
Black, Jeremy 21
Blick, Jeffery 4
Blitt, Jessica 41
'blowback' 8
Boas, Franz 101
Bombay 153–5
Boone, Catherine 222
Bosnia-Herzegovina 184, 187, 191, 192, 200, 272
Boswell, Terry 4
boundaries, state 9–10, 42
Bouquet, C. 274
Bourdieu, Pierre 190
Boutros-Ghali, Boutros 7
Bowen, John R. 22
Brailsford, H.N. 207
Brass, Paul 150–1, 153
Brazil 99
Breitborde, L.B. 233, 234
Britain, colonialism 158–9, 165, 286
Brown, Diana DeG. 3, 7, 11, 12, 217–38
Brown, Michael E. 2, 3, 6, 15, 18, 19, 41
Brubaker, Roger 5, 22, 29
Buijtenhijs, R. 267, 275
Bulgaria 208, 209, 210, 210–11
Bulgarian Orthodox Church (Exarchate) 208
Bulgarians 249
Burkina Faso 224, 270, 277
Burt, Jo-Marie 125
Burundi 32
Buzan, Barry 9, 10, 15, 42
Byman, Daniel 1, 5
Byzantine Empire 206–7

Cabinda 249–50
Cabral, Amilcar 257 n.10
Canfield, Robert L. 27
capital: transnationalization of 7, 64–5; *see also* globalization
capitalism 62, 66, 90, 120, 151, 163
Carmack, Robert 2, 102

Carnegie Commission on Preventing DeadlyViolence 28, 41
Carneiro, Robert 9
Carter, Jeanette 234
Cassenelli, Lee 289, 290, 292, 293
caste *see* class/classes
Catholic Church 108; Angola 253
Central Intelligence Agency (CIA) 141, 142, 268, 270
Chad 3, 5, 7, 13, 17, 25, 77, 225, 261–81
Chakrabarty, Dipesh 159
Chapelle, J. 266
Chase-Dunn, Christopher 4
Chatterjee, Partha 150, 160
Chaturvedi, Jayati and Gyaneshwar Chaturvedi 154
Chechnya 4
Chetnicks, Serbian 191
Chevron oil 278
Chiapas 106, 108
China 247, 256–7 n.5
Christians/Christianity: India 150, 156–7, 157, 158, 165–6, 172, 173; Macedonia 210; Papua New Guinea 301, 302, 313, 314
Ciammaichella, G. 273
Cillier, Paul 27
citizenship 66
civil society 63
clan organization 19, 26; Papua New Guinea 300; Somalia 288–90, 291, 292, 294, 295, 296
Clapham, Christopher 233, 234
Clarence-Smith, W.G. 254
class rule, state as instrument of 61
class/classes 14, 26, 61–2, 105; Chad 279; India 149, 151, 163, 168–9, 170, 171, 172, 173; Liberia 232, 233; Papua New Guinea 301
Clower, Robert W. 221
coercion 89
Cohen, Abner 230
Cohen, Lenard 179
Cohen, Roger 192, 193
Cohen, Ronald 18
Cojti Cuxil, Demetrio 108
Cold War 5, 85, 200, 223, 255, 262–4, 266, 279, 280, 287, 294; end of 1, 4, 5, 29, 64, 85, 90, 223–6, 262 Collier, George 106
colonialism 71, 99, 104; Angola 243, 246, 254; India 158–9, 165; Somalia 286
Comaroff, Jean 15, 119–20
Comaroff, John L. 9, 14, 15, 19, 65, 150

communications 65; global 7
communism: anti- 156; collapse of 4–5, 193
Communist League 185, 191, 195 n.14
Communist Party, former Yugoslavia 178, 193
Communist Party, Peru *see* Sendero Luminoso
competition, over resources 72–3
complex systems, states as 69–71
computer revolution 65
Congo, Republic of the 32, 244
'Congoes' 220
Congress Party, India 12, 16, 154, 155, 158
Conseil de Salut National pour la Paix et la Démocratie au Tchad (CSNPDT) 270, 275, 278
Conseil Supérieur Militaire (CSM), Chad 268, 274
Constantine, king of Greece 212
Cooper, Neil 5
Cornwell, Richard 244
Corradi, Juan E. 102
corruption: Liberia 222, 223; Papua New Guinea 300–1; Peru 141–2
Cote d'Ivoire (Ivory Coast) 224, 253–4
Cox, J.T.G. 277, 278
crime, Papua New Guinea 303–5
Croatia 29, 184, 186, 187, 191, 192, 199
Croats 188
Crossette, Barbara 5
Cuba 246, 247
Cubans 249
cultural difference 22, 25, 30, 40, 72, 73
cultural hybridity 105
cultural resistance 102–3
culture 18–21, 63, 96, 120; local 20–1, 30, 108
custom, Papua New Guinea 302
Cutler, Claire 90

Dalaras, Yiorgos 202
Dalits 165–6, 171, 173
Damle, Shridhar 160, 161, 162
Dani, S.G. 167
Das, Veena 2, 103
David, Steven R. 10, 28, 42
Dayton Accord (1995) 200
d'Azevedo, Warren 232, 233, 234
de Waal, Alex 6, 31, 32, 34, 35
debt, international 73, 181, 193
Déby, Idriss 267, 270, 272, 274–5, 277
decentralization policy 78–9

Declich, Francesca 294, 296
decompression effect 5
Defoe, Daniel 63
Dehejia, Jay 170
Delhi 154–5
Demjaha, Agon 40
democracy 18, 90
Denich, Bette 3, 73, 88, 177–94
Denoeux, Guilain 72
development, discourse of 96
diamonds 225, 226
diasporas 7
disintegration, tendencies toward 69–71, 73–9
Dixon, William 4
Djamous, Hassan 269–70
Doe, Jackson 235
Doe, Samuel 217, 219, 220, 221–2, 223, 224, 225–6, 227, 231, 233, 235–6
Doornbos, Martin 254–5
Downs, R.E. 2
drug trade 6–7, 122–3, 139–40, 141
Dubey, Suman 170
Duffield, Mark 7
Dunn, D. Elwood 223, 228, 233
Durate de Carvalho, Ruy 255

East Germany 277
ECOMOG (ECOWAS Monitoring Group) 7, 224
economy 73; Angola 250; former Yugoslavia 179, 180–4, 185, 187–9; global 6–7, 29, 90, 168; India 168–70; informal 183; Liberia 221, 222; Peru 122; *see also* globalization
ECOWAS (Economic Community of West African States) 224, 225
education 63; Greece 207, 212; India 167, 173; Peru 127, 129–31
Egypt 277, 278
ELEC (Enclave of Cabinda's Liberation Front) 250
Elf Aquitaine 250, 278
elites 14–15, 26, 92
Ellis, Stephen 218, 222, 225, 230, 231, 232, 234, 236, 237
employment: India 170, 171; *see also* unemployment
Engels, Friedrich 61, 62
Engineer, Asghar Ali 159
enlightenment tradition 97
Enloe, Cynthia 15, 21, 24, 26, 27
Entessar, Nader 72

Eriksen, Thomas Hylland 14, 18, 19, 22
Errington, Frederick 301
Escobar, Arturo 104
Estrade, Bernard 6
Ethiopia 286, 287, 291
ethnic cleansing 24, 177, 192
ethnicity 18–21, 30, 65–7, 85, 88, 97–101, 105, 110, 120–1; former Yugoslavia 178–9; Liberia 218, 222, 226–36, 237; Peru 135–9; Somalia 289–90, 296
ethnogenesis 72
European Union 91, 93, 188, 193, 201
Evans, Peter B. 8

Falk, Richard A. 42, 102
Family Law Act (1975), Somalia 291
Fanon, F. 247
FARC 141
Fascism 98
Fassani, Osseni 249
Feldman, Allen 2, 21
Ferguson, James 104, 105
Ferguson, R. Brian 1–43, 71, 74, 89, 103, 108–9, 243–4
Ferguson, Yale 3, 5, 8, 9, 10, 15, 23, 39, 41, 83–94, 98
Fernandez, Eduardo 2
Filipinos 249
financial markets 90
Finkel, Vicki R. 256
Firestone rubber plantation 221, 223
firms: networks and alliances 91; transnational 84, 91
Fisher, William 7
FNLA 246, 247
Foltz, W.J. 277
Forbes, H.D. 151
force, structural histories of 264–6
Force Armées du Nord (FAN), Chad 268, 272, 279
Forces Armée Populaire (FAP), Chad 268, 279
Foster, Mary LeCron 38
Foster, Robert 302
Fox, Richard 102, 150
Fraenkel, Merran 233
fragmentation 84, 91
France 98; and Chad 267, 269, 277, 278; and Rwanda 32; and Somalia 286
Frederika, queen of Greece 211
French Revolution 66
Fried, Morton 9, 19
Friedman, Edward 71
Friedman, Thomas 90

Frolinat *(Front de Libération Nationale du Tchad)* 267, 268, 272, 274, 275, 276, 279
Fujimori, Alberto 118, 139, 141, 142
Fukui, Katsuyoshi 2, 11, 20
Fukuyama, Francis 1, 23, 85, 262

Gagnon, V.P., Jr. 29
Gallais, J. 73
Gamba, Virginia 244
Ganguly, Sumit 8, 41
Gantzel, Klaus Jurgen 1, 22
García, Alan 137
Gargan, Edward 153, 154
Geertz, Clifford 15, 16, 19, 65
Gellner, Ernest 14, 88, 207
gender/gender relations 26, 168, 173
Germany 98
Germany, East 277
Gershoni, Yekutiel 224
Gewertz, Deborah 301
Gibbon, Edward 68, 70
Giddens, Anthony 8, 9
Gingrich, Newt 280
Gio 227, 232
globalization 6–7, 9, 84, 90, 100, 104; India and impact of 149, 151, 163, 172
Goati, Vladimir 181
Goffman, Erving 184
Goldman, L.R. 314
Golwalkar, M.S. 161
Goncalves, Junuel 253
Gonzales, José, E. 140
Gonzalez, Nancie 18
Gottlieb, Gidon 18, 42
Goukouni Oueddeni 267, 268, 269, 272, 276
Gourevitch, Philip 31, 37
Gouvernement d'Union Nationale de Transition (GUNT), Chad 268, 269
government 9, 10–11, 30; *see also* local governance
Graham, B.D. 160, 161
Greece: and Macedonia 3, 5, 6, 12, 17, 24, 199–214; national identity 17, 207; nationalism 204, 210, 213; occupation by Axis troops 210–11
Greek Civil War (1947–49) 201, 211
Greek Orthodox Church 207
Greenhouse, Carol 103
Guatemala 72, 99, 106, 107–9, 138
Guidieri, Remo 16
Gupta, Akhil 105
Gupta, Dipankar 157, 162

Index

Gurr, Ted Tobert 1, 19, 22
Guzmán Reynoso, Abimael 121, 133, 136, 141

Haas, Jonathan 2, 9, 19
Habré, Hissen 267, 268, 269–70, 272, 274, 275, 276–7
Habyarimana, President 32, 33, 34
Hall, Rodney Bruce 85
Hall, Thomas 4, 19
Halpern, Joel M. 2, 29
Hamburg, David A. 19, 28
Hamitic hypothesis 34–5
Hansen, Thomas Blom 150, 151, 160, 161
Harris, Marvin 9
Hartung, William D. 5
Harvey, Neil 106
Hayden, Robert M. 188
Hechter, Michael 14, 15
Hegel, G.W.F. 62
Heine, Heinrich 62
Helander, Bernhard 289
Held, David 90
Herbst, Jeffrey 4, 5, 6, 10, 26, 42
Hernández Castillo, R. Aida 105
Heywood, Linda M. 17, 244
Hill, Jonathan 20
Hindus/Hindutva movement 3, 5, 12, 16, 23–4, 72, 149–73
Hintjens, Helen M. 31, 32, 33, 35, 37
Hinton, Alexander Laban 21
history, end of 85
Hlophe, Stephen S. 233
Hobsbawm, E.J. 8, 13
Hoebel, E. Adamson 9
holism, anthropological 40–1
Holmes, Patricia 223
Holsoe, Svend E. 233
Holsti, K.J. 1, 8, 10, 42
Homer-Dixon, Thomas 31, 32, 41
Hopmann, P. Terrence 40
Horowitz, Donald 16, 20, 21, 22, 29, 102
Huband, Mark 218
Hudson, Robert 27
Huntington, Samuel P. 22, 39, 103, 110, 262, 272, 280
Hurtado, Edgar 127
Hussein, Saddam 87
Hutu 31–8, 89
Huxtable, Phillip A. 2

identerest concept 28, 30–1, 40
identity 23–9, 30, 88–9; collective 20, 21, 30; ethnic 16, 18–21, 65–7; *see also* national identity
Ignatieff, Michael 29
imagined community 15
India 3, 5, 6, 8, 12, 16, 23–4, 99, 149–73; agriculture 170; class/classes 149, 151, 163, 168–9, 170, 171, 172, 173; colonialism 158–9, 165; economy 168–70; education 167, 173; employment 170, 171; foreign aid and investment 169; gender relations 168, 173; Mogul 164; partition period 164; response to modernity 163–71
indigenous populations 97, 98–9, 100–1
Indonesia 6
intellectuals, Indian 150, 151, 166–8
interests 27, 30, 92
International Monetary Fund (IMF) 6, 7, 122, 181, 223
international relations (IR) theory 83, 85
Iraq 270, 278
Isbell, Billie Jean 137–8
Islam 72, 159, 164–5; *see also* Muslims
Israel 77, 270, 277, 278
Italy 93, 286
Ivory Coast (Cote d'Ivoire) 224, 253–4

Jackson, Jean 39, 102
Jackson, Robert 87, 222, 223
Jaffrelot, Christophe 149, 151, 160, 161
Jakubowska, Longina 80 n.1
Jamba, Souza 247
James, F. 269
Jelavich, Barbara 210
Jenkins, C. 8
Joffe, E.G.H. 268
Johnson, Chalmers 264
Jonge Oudraat, Chantal de 18, 41

Kahl, Colin 28
Kakar, Sudhir 164
Kaldor, Mary 1, 7, 10, 18, 42
Kamougue, Abdul Kadir 269
Kapferer, Bruce 2, 15, 21
Kaplan, Robert D. 1, 19, 39, 74, 103, 110, 261–2, 263, 272, 273, 280
Kapur, Anuradha 152
Kapuscinski, Ryszard 254
Karakasidou, Anastasia 3, 24, 199–214
Kashmir 8, 157
Kaufman, Stuart 29
Kaufmann, Chaim 2, 29, 39
Kearney, Michael 105

Kellas, James 157
Kende, Istvan 264
Kennedy, John F. 264
Ketté, Moise 270, 275
Kideckel, David A. 2, 29
Kimble, Frank B. 223
Kissinger, Henry 278
Kleinman, Arthur 2
Knauft, Bruce 302
Konaré, Alpah Oumar 78, 79
Kosovo 7, 42, 185, 186, 187, 189–90, 199, 200
Kotkin, Joel 65
Kpolleh, Gabriel 235
Krahn 221, 222, 227, 231–2
Krasner, Stephen D. 85
Krishnakumar, Asha 158
Krishnaswamy, Chetan 166
Kumar, Krishna 162, 167
Kurds 84, 85
Kurien, Prema 156
Kuwait 87

labor, transnationalization of 7, 65, 66–7
Ladas, S.P. 210
Laitin, David D. 5, 22, 29
Lake, David 28, 29
Lan, David 2
Land Law (1975), Somalia 291, 294
Langhorne, Richard 6, 7
language 27
Larana, Enrique 20
Latin America 98–9, 103; *see also* Guatemala; Mexico; Peru
Lawyers Committee for Human Rights 227, 228
Le Cornec, Jacques 273
Lebanon 75, 77
LeBaron, Alan 72
Lehmann, Dan 296
Lemarchand, Rene 31, 274
Lessinger, Johanna 2–3, 5, 12, 15, 149–73
Lewis, I.M. 285, 286, 288, 289, 291, 292
Li, Darryl 104
liberalism 64
Liberia 3, 5, 6, 7, 12, 24–5, 217–38; class solidarities 232, 233; economy 221, 222; ethnicity/tribal identities 218, 222, 226–36, 237; indirect rule 220, 232; nationalism 17, 233; patronage system 234, 235; secret societies 234, 239 n.15; and US 12, 220, 223–4, 226

Libya 7; and Chad 77, 225, 267, 268, 269, 277, 278, 279; and Liberia 224, 225
Licklider, Roy 22
Liebenow, J. Gus 220, 221, 223, 233, 234
Linke, Uli 20
Lissouba, Pascal 244
literature, Angolan 251
Little, Allan 179
local governance, Peru 125–8
localization 84
Lock, Margaret 2
Locke, John 315 n.1
Longman, Timothy 31, 33
Loomis, Don G. 1
low-intensity conflict 74–5
Lowenkopf, Martin 225
loyalty 86, 88–9
Lusaka accords 243, 245

McAdam, Doug 102
McClurg Mueller, Carol 20
McCommon, Carollyn 19
Macedo-Bulgarian Empire 207
Macedonia 3, 5, 6, 12, 17, 24, 177, 187, 199–214
Macedonian Struggle (1904–08) 209
McEvoy, Frederick D. 232, 233
McIntosh, Susan Keech and Roderick J. McIntosh 73
McNulty, Mel 31, 32, 33, 37
MacQueen, Norrie 243, 244
Magnant, J.-P. 272, 273
Mahmood, Cynthia Keppley 15, 21, 29
Mali 73, 78–9
Malkki, Liisa 106
Malloum, Felix 267, 268, 274, 276
Malone, David M. 6, 10
Mamdani, Mahmood 31, 32, 34, 35, 36, 104, 220
Mandal Commission 171
Mandal, D. 152
Mandela, Nelson 243
Mandingo 227, 228, 232
Mann, Michael 8, 62
Mano 227, 232
Mansbach, Richard W. 10, 83
Marchal, Roland 295
marginalization 179
Mariátegui, José, Carlos 121
Markakis, John 2, 11, 20
markets, regulation of 91
Markovic, Ante 181
marriage, inter-ethnic 307

324 Index

Marshall, Monty G. 1
Martin, Jane 232
Martin, JoAnn 2, 20, 103
Marx, Anthony W. 71, 123
Marx, Karl 61, 62
Marxism 98
mathematics, Vedic 167
Mayan culture 76–7, 107–9, 138
Maybury-Lewis, David 3–4, 15, 22, 39, 96–101, 133
Mayson, Dew Tuan-Wleh 235
media: opposition movements use of 104; representations of conflicts 104
Mehta, Deepa 167, 168
Menkhaus, Kenneth 293, 294–5
Menon, Parvathi 156
Mercado, Roger 135
Merryman, James 293
mestizos 2, 23, 117, 143 n.3
Metaxas, John 210
Mexico 99, 106–7
Michalon, T. 273
Migdal, Joel S. 10
militarization 64
military aid 268, 269, 270, 277, 278, 287, 288
military aid and supply 5, 103, 141, 226, 268, 269, 270, 277, 278, 287, 288
Miller, R.W. 275
millet system 207
Milosovic, Slobodan 17, 185–6, 187, 188, 189, 190, 199
Miskine, Idriss 269
Mitchell, William 272
Mitsotakis, Konstantinos 201
Mobutu Sese Seko 243, 247, 254
modernity/modernization 15–16, 18, 30, 71, 72, 96, 98, 100; Indian responses 163–71; Papua New Guinea 302
Moeller, Susan 104
Mogul empire 164
Montejo, Victor 109
Montenegro 187, 188–9
Montesinos, Vladimiro 141–2
Morales Bermúdez, Francisco 135 134
Morauta, Sir Mekere 301
Morgan, Lewis Henry 9
Morris, Aldon D. 20
Motyl, Alexander J. 5, 41
Mouvement de Salut National (MOSNAT), Chad 269, 270
Mouvement National pour la Révolution Culturelle et Sociale (MNRCS), Chad 274
Mouvement Patriotique du Salut (MPS), Chad 270, 272, 276
Mouvement pour la Démocratie et le Développement (MDD), Chad 270, 275, 278
MPLA 25, 244, 245, 246, 247–8, 249, 251, 255
MRTA 140
Mugabe, Robert 243
Mukhtar, Mohammed H. 289
Muralidharan, Sukumar 151
Muslim League 159
Muslims 207, 273; Indian 3, 150, 151–5, 156, 157, 158–9, 163–5, 171, 172, 173

NAFTA (North American Free Trade Agreement) 91, 107
Nagel, Joanne 4
Nagengast, Carole 2, 10
ñakaqs 137–8
Namibia 247
Narokobi, B. 302
Nash, June C. 104, 107
nation 84, 85, 88, 97
nation-state 3, 15, 62–7, 85, 98, 103, 193–4; Angola as 254–6
National Democratic Alliance (NDA), India 156
national identity 14–15; Angola 245, 250–5
National Liberation Front (EAM), Greece 211
National Patriotic Front of Liberia (NPFL) 227
National Popular Liberation Army (ELAS), Greece 211
nationalism 14–18, 30, 84, 85, 102–10; Angola 17, 244; Chad 17, 272–6; former Yugoslavia 177, 185–7, 191–2; Greece 204, 210, 213; India *see* Hindus/Hindutva movement; Liberia 17, 233; Peru 16; reactive 71–2
nationality 88; Angolan 253–4
NATO 7, 91, 200, 201, 211, 213
Nazism 98, 160–1
Neto, Agostinho 246, 251
new social movement theory 20
Newman, Edward 7
Nietzsche, Friedrich 63
Nigeria 7, 224, 225, 277
non-governmental organizations (NGOs) 6, 7, 91, 224
Nordstrom, Carolyn 2, 20, 103
Nyang'oro, Julius E. 6

Oberoi, Harjot 152
O'Connor, James R. 64
Ogadeen 287, 291
oil 250, 278
oil crisis 180, 193
Oliveira, Ana Maria 251–2
Omaar, Rakiya 6
Omar Jess 287
Omvedt, Gail 150, 162
Ong, Aihwa 103, 105
opportunism 102, 103, 106
Organization of African States (OAS) 32
Organization of African Unity (OAU) 93
Ortiz, Victor 105
Ortner, Sherry 20
Otterbein, Keith 2
Ottoman Empire 24, 207, 209
Ottoman Porte 208

Pakistan 8, 157, 159, 164
Palestinians 277
Panfichi, Aldo 125
Panikkar, K.N. 157, 165, 167
Papua New Guinea 3, 13, 18, 25–6, 300–15
Parti Progressiste Tchadien (PPT) 267, 273–4, 275
patronage systems: former Yugoslavia 183; Liberia 234, 235
Pattajoshi, Lalit 166
Paul, king of Greece 211
Peasant Confederation of Peru (CCP) 132
peer polities 76
Peluso, Nancy Lee 10
Pepetela 251
Percival, Valerie 31, 32
Pereira, Anthony W. 244
Perry, Duncan M. 208
Peru 2–3, 5, 6, 7, 11–12, 23, 26, 89, 99, 117–43; agrarian reform 10, 122, 123–5, 131–2, 134, 135; corruption 141–2; drug trafficking 122–3, 139–40, 141; economy 122; education 127, 129–31; ethnicity as weapon 135–9; local governance 125–8; *ñakaqs* 137–8; nationalism 16; regional intermediaries 128–35
Petrobas 250
Pitt, David 38
polarization 29, 30
polities 83–4; peer 76
polygamy, Papua New Guinea 307
Poro 234, 239 n.15, 19

Portugal 243, 246, 254
Portuguese 249
Posen, Barry R. 28, 29
Poulantzas, Nicos 62, 64
poverty, India 170
power vacuums 75–6, 79
Prakash, Gyan 110
predation 303–5
Premdas, Ralph R. 7, 18
Price, Barbara 76
Prunier, Gerard 31, 32, 36, 37
public-private sector distinction 90
Puerto Rico 42

Qaddafi, Muammar al- 267, 268
Quaratiello, Elizabeth 106
Quechua peasants 2, 23, 124–41 *passim*
Quiwonkpa, Thomas 227

Radcliffe-Brown, A.R. 9
Rajagopal, Arvind 156, 162
Ramakrishnan, Venkitesh 151, 155
Ramet, Pedro 181
Rao, P.V. Narsimha 154
rape, Papua New Guinea 304, 305
Rashtriya Swayamsevak Sangh (RSS) 153, 159, 160–1, 167
Rawson, David 287
reactive processes 71–2, 79
Reagan, Ronald 223
realism 10, 38–9, 84
regional developments 7–8, 103
Rejali, Darius M. 21
religion 7, 15, 23–4, 27; and the Ottoman Empire 207; Papua New Guinea 301, 302, 313, 314; *see also* Catholic Church; Christians/Christianity; Hindus/Hindutva movement; Islam
Renfrew, Colin 76
Reno, William J. 6, 7, 11, 219, 222, 225, 226, 232, 236, 244
resistance 106; cultural 102–3; Papua New Guinea 303–5, 306, 312–13
Reyna, Stephen 2, 3, 11, 25, 261–81
Rich, Paul B. 2, 10, 11
Richards, Paul 2, 7, 261, 272
Riches, David 2, 312
Riedinger, Jeffery 132–3
Robben, Antonius 2, 29, 38
Roberto, Holden 246, 247
Roman Empire 68, 70, 75–6
Romania 208
Roosevelt, Theodore 96

'Roque Santeiro' 250
Rosaldo, Renato 105
Rosberg, Carl G. 222, 223
Roseberry, William 123–4
Rosenau, James 91
Rossel, Jakob 14
Rothchild, Donald 28, 29
Rousseau, Jean-Jacques 97, 315 n.1
rubber 221, 225, 233
Rubenstein, Robert 38
Rubenstein, Steven 10
Rubin, Barnett R. 4, 8
Rudensky, Nikolai 24, 72
Rudolph, Susanne H. and Lloyd I. Rudolph 150
Ruggie, John Gerard 9
Rummel, Rudolph J. 10, 18
Russett, Bruce 18
Russia 8, 243
Rwanda 22, 31–8, 89, 104
Rwanda Patriotic Front (RPF) 31–2, 34

Saffu, Yaw 300
Salazar, Antonio 246
Samatar, Abdi Ismail 288
Sande 234, 239 n.15
Santos, Jose Eduardo dos 245, 246, 248
Sapiro, Virginia 15
Sarkar, Tanika 161
Saudi Arabia 8
Savimbi, Jonas 17, 243, 244, 245, 246, 247–8, 249
Sawyer, Amos 221, 222, 233, 235
Schirmer, J. 104
'schismogenesis' 179, 189
Schmidt, Sabine 4
Schnabel, Albrecht 7
Schoeberlein-Engel, John 72
Scholte, Jan Aart 90
schools, India 167
Schraeder, Peter J. 7
Scott, James 102, 303
Seaton, Jean 104
secular government, India 3, 12, 158
security, regional arrangements 7
security dilemma, creation of 28–9, 30
Segell, Glen 7
Sekelj, Laslo 181, 195–6n. 18
Seligmann, Linda 2, 5, 10, 89, 117–43
Sen, Amartya 153, 155, 161, 162
Sendero Luminoso (Shining Path) 2, 5, 16, 23, 26, 89, 118, 121–3, 126–41 *passim*
Senegal 253–4

Senghor, Leopold 247
Serbia 184, 185, 186, 187, 188–9, 190, 192, 199, 200, 208, 211
Serbian Orthodox Church 208
Serbs 24, 178, 189, 190, 199, 200
Seyon, Patrick L.N. 233
shadow state 11, 41, 225, 244
Shaw, R. Paul 23
Shaw, Timothy M. 6
Shearer, David 6
Shell 250, 278
Shining Path *see* Sendero Luminoso
Shiv Sena 153, 154, 159, 160, 162
Shock, Kurt 8
Shoup, Paul 195 n.7
Sierra Leone 7, 217
Silber, Laura 179
Simons, Anna 2, 29
simulation 271–6
SINAMOS 126, 131–2
Singh, Dara 166, 169
SIPRI 1
Skalnik, Peter 303
Skocpol, Theda 9
slaves, Somalia 289
Slovenes 178, 188, 189
Slovenia 177, 178, 179, 185, 186, 187, 189, 190, 191, 199
Sluka, Jeffrey A. 2, 10, 38, 103
Smith, Anthony D. 14, 15, 16, 18, 19, 88
Smith, Michael 133
Snyder, Jack 4, 18
social contract, Papua New Guinea 302–3, 307–15
social divisions 26; *see also* clan organization; class/classes; tribes/tribalism
socialism, former Yugoslavia 179, 180–4, 193
Sollenberg, Margareta 1
Somali National Movement (SNM) 287
Somalia 3, 5, 6, 13, 18, 22, 25, 77, 86, 285–97
Somaliland 288
sorcery, assault 303–4
South Africa 246, 247, 252
Southall, Aidan 4, 6, 8, 19
sovereignty 87, 103; limitations of 89–91; state as basis of 4
Soviet Union *see* USSR
Spitz, Douglas 71, 150
Sponsel, Leslie E. 41
Spruyt, Hendrik 85
Stack, John F., Jr. 16, 19
Staines, Graham 166

Stalinism 98
Starn, Orin 38, 102, 136, 138–9, 141
the state 8–14; bounded character of 9–10, 42; shadow 11, 41, 225, 244; weak 222, 225, 300–3; *see also* nation-state
Stephen, Lynn 107
Stern, Paul C. 14, 65
Stewart, Pamela 3, 300–15
Stiglmayer, Alexandra 21
Stockwell, John 278
Strange, Susan 86
Strathern, Andrew 3, 13, 120, 300–15
Suarez Orozco, Marcelo M. 2, 29, 38
Sudan 277, 278
SUTEP 130
Swami, Praveen 155, 156, 157, 166
SWAPO 247
Swarns, Rachel L. 243
Syria 77

Tainter, Joseph 3, 9, 12, 68–80
Tajikistan 4
Talbot, Strobe 7
Tambiah, Stanley 2, 15, 16, 19, 21, 26, 106
Tanzania 32
Tarr, S. Byron 223, 228, 233
Taussig, Michael 2, 21
taxation 64
Taylor, Charles 217, 219, 222, 223, 224, 226, 227–8, 231, 232, 237
Taylor, Christopher C. 31, 33, 34, 35, 36
Taylor, Diana 2
Taylor, Peter J. 10
technological progress 65
Thackery, Bal 162
Thakur, Ramesh 7
Thapar, Romila 152, 155–6, 162
Thomas, Nicholas 302
Thomson, Janice E. 85
Tilly, Charles 8, 10, 62, 85
Toennies, Ferdinand 63
Togo 270, 277
Tokpa, Henrique F. 219, 228
Tolbert, President 221, 222, 237
Toledo, Alejandro 142–3
Tombalbaye, François 17, 267, 268, 272, 273–4, 276
Tonkin, Elizabeth 232, 234
trade, international 6–7, 29, 64; militarization of 6
tradition, Papua New Guinea 302
transnational firms 84, 91

Treaty of Bucharest (1913) 209
Treaty of Lausanne (1923) 210
tribes/tribalism 19, 96–7, 99, 100; Chad 271–2; Liberia 221, 226–36; Papua New Guinea 300
Tubman, William 221, 237
Turkey 204, 210
Turner, Paul 38
Turner, Victor 20
Turton, David 2, 19, 20, 31
Turton, E.R. 286
Tutsi 31–8, 89
Tyson, Laura D'Andrea 194 n.6

Uganda 5, 31, 32
unemployment: former Yugoslavia 183–4; India 170
Union Nationale pour l'Indépendence et la Révolution (UNIR), Chad 274
Union Nationale Tchadienne (UNT) 275
UNITA 17, 25, 243, 244, 245, 246, 247, 248, 249, 250–1, 255
United Nations (UN) 4, 7, 91, 93, 97, 217, 243, 288
United Somali Congress (USC) 287
United States 5, 67, 262–3, 264; and Angola 5, 243, 246, 247; anti-drug trafficking policies 122–3, 139–40; and Chad 5, 262–3, 268, 269, 270, 277, 278; and Liberia 12, 220, 223–4, 226; and Somalia 5, 287, 288
Universal Declaration of Human Rights 97
universities, India 167
URNG rebel coalition 107
Ury, William 7, 40
USSR 264; and Angola 5, 246, 247; break up of 4–5, 8, 85; and Chad 5, 277, 279; and Somalia 5, 287
Ustashas, Croatian 191
Uvin, Peter 294

Vail, Leroy 19, 20
Van der Dennen, Johan M.G. 2
Van Creveld, Martin 1, 14, 39, 74
Van den Berghe, Pierre L. 2, 10, 15
van der Veer, Peter 150
Vanaik, Achin 151, 159, 160
Van Evera, Stephen 1, 3, 5, 14
Vandergeest, Peter 10
Varshney, Ashutosh 159, 161–2
Velasco Alvarado, Juan 123, 129–30, 131–2, 133–4, 135

Verdery, Katherine 183
Villalon, Leonardo A. 2, 11, 15, 43
Vincent, Joan 19
Vishwa Hindu Parishad (VHP) 159, 160, 162
Volcan Army 268
Vucinich, Wayne S. 207

Wachtel, Nathan 138
Wagner, Barbara 235
Wallensteen, Peter 1
Wallerstein, Immanuel 62
Warren, Kay 2, 4, 20, 26, 38, 40, 72, 102–10, 120, 122, 138, 236
Weber, M. 266
Weiner, Myron 154, 157, 162
Weiner, Tim 8
Weinstein, Jeremy M. 32
welfare apparatus, dismantling of 64, 65
Wendt, Alexander 43
White, Douglas R. 4
Whitehead, Neil L. 4, 20, 21, 42, 71
Whorton, Brad 4
Williams, Brackette F. 19
Wolf, Eric 3, 8, 42, 61–7, 120
women: Peru 26; and rape in Papua New Guinea 304, 305; *see also* gender/gender relations
women's movements 26
Wong, Yuwa 23
Woolsey, R. James 280
World Bank 223

Year of Inigenous People 97
Young, C. 2, 14, 19, 102, 135, 233
Yuen-Carrucan, Jasmine 167
Yugoslavia, former 3, 5, 6, 12, 16–17, 24, 73, 88, 177–94, 199; Agrokomerc scandal 184–5; economy 179–84, 185, 187–9; employment 183–4; ethnicity 178; nationalism 177, 185–7, 191–2; patronage system 183; self-managing socialism 179, 180–4, 193; statehood 177, 178–9
Zaire 32, 243, 246–7, 248, 253, 254, 270, 277, 278
Zairians 249
Zapatistas 104, 106–7, 109
Zartman, I. William 10, 39, 225